the CROCHET BOOK

the CROCHET BOOK

CONTENTS

INTRODUCTION

This book is suitable for all crocheters – beginners with no previous experience, and those with more advanced skills. If you have never held a crochet hook before, but want to learn, this book will take you through all the basic crochet stitches to enable you to make beautiful items, both small and large. If you already know how to crochet, you will find a wonderful collection of unique and attractive, good-value patterns to try out.

The Crochet Book guides you through the basic techniques and stitches – presented clearly and simply with step-by-step photographs – covering the relevant abbreviations and symbols on the way. Beginners can work through the comprehensive and easy-to-follow techniques section in the first part of the book, stopping along the way to try out a mini project to practise the stitch they have just learned. More experienced crocheters can dip into

this section to refresh their skills. The mini projects include items ranging from a simple chain stitch bracelet (pp.32–33) to a stylish intarsia cushion (pp.118–119).

Once you are confident with all the crochet stitches, you can launch into the projects chapter and begin to make crocheted items as diverse as a traditional granny blanket (pp.148–149), a tiny flower pin cushion (pp.186–187), and a child's summer tunic dress (pp.246–249). With more than 80 projects to choose from, there is something for everyone: from blankets and cushions, to hats and scarves; gloves, socks, and slippers; items for the home; garments and bags; plus a range of adorable toys to make. *The Crochet Book* will enable you to make your own unique, bespoke crocheted pieces for yourself, your home, and your family and friends.

CROCHET KNOW-HOW

Each project shows the yarn and stitch tension used (if relevant), but the main yarn recommendation is a generic one to enable you to make an item in a yarn that is easily available to you. For example, the simple beaded necklace on pp.30–31 is made with DMC Petra Crochet Cotton Perle No. 3 yarn, but you could use any yarn that you have for this, as long as you ensure that the thread you are using will fit through the holes of the beads. Similarly, for the chunky rug on pp.170–171, we have used an acrylic yarn for its hard-wearing properties, but you could use another super-chunky-weight yarn with a synthetic content to get a similar effect; just bear in mind that the size might be slightly different, depending on the yarn weight.

A NOTE ABOUT YARN AND HOOKS

It is also important to consider the fact that for some projects – for example, the filigree bookmarks (see pp.182–183) and the jungle finger puppets (pp.286–289) – you will only need a certain proportion of the ball of yarn recommended for each colour, and you will have yarn left over. However, look on this as an opportunity to make more of the same, or use it for a new project.

When making items such as garments, or other projects for which tension is important, it is always advisable to crochet a tension swatch first in the yarn you intend to use. If your tension swatch is smaller than that recommended, you may need to use a larger hook; if it is larger, use a smaller hook. With many projects, the tension is not a vital element – for example, the coasters on pp.58–59 and the cat basket on pp.180–181, do not need to be an exact size.

Make sure that you calculate the amount of yarn needed for a project by metreage/yardage, as the amount needed may vary and different weights of yarn have different metreage/yardage lengths. Check your hook size, too. As you become more experienced as a crocheter, so you will become accustomed to which hook sizes are appropriate for the different types of yarn.

A NOTE ABOUT CROCHETED TOYS

When making crocheted toys for babies or very young children, it is always safest either to embroider the eyes onto the toy or to use special safety eyes. Never use buttons on a toy that is for a baby or very young child, as there is a risk of choking if the buttons become detached. If you are using safety eyes on toys, always make sure that they comply with current safety regulations.

EXTEND YOUR SKILLS

As well as a comprehensive guide to basic stitches and techniques, *The Crochet Book* provides an extensive gallery of stitch textures, crocheted edgings, openwork, and colourwork, as well as a guide to making granny squares and stunning flowers, all with patterns. Use these to build on your basic stitch skills, before embarking on more adventurous and impressive crochet patterns, and you will find yourself equipped to create any project in the book.

SIZE CHART

Women's sizes	To fit bust (approx)
S (small)	80cm (32in)
M (medium)	91cm (36in)
L (large)	102cm (40in)

Slipper/sock sizes	Sole length (approx)
Babies 3–6 months	10–11cm (4–4½in)
Children 2–7 years	11–15cm (4¼–6in)
Women 3–7 (US 5–9)	22–26cm (8¾–10¼in)
Men 9–11 (US 10–12)	27.5–29.5cm (10¾–11½in)

TOOLS

YARNS

There are many types of yarns, allowing crocheters to enjoy a variety of sensory experiences as they express themselves through the medium. Yarns can be made of many different fibres and have a range of textures, as shown here.

FIBRES

Yarns, like fabrics, are made from fibres. A fibre may be the hair from an animal, artificial (synthetics), or derived from a plant. The fibres are processed and spun to make a yarn. A yarn may be made from a single type of fibre, such as wool, or mixed with other fibres to enhance its attributes (for example, to affect its durability or softness). Different blends are also created for aesthetic reasons, such as mixing soft, luxurious cashmere with a rougher wool. As a result, all yarns have different properties, so it is important to choose an appropriate blend for the project in hand.

▶ **Merino wool**
This is wool derived from the merino sheep, which is said to provide one of the softest wools of any sheep breed. The bouncy, smooth-surfaced fibre is just as warm as a more wiry, coarse wool. Merino is a fantastic choice for wearing against the skin, and is often treated to make it suitable for machine-washing. Merino wool is good for soft scarves, armwarmers, and children's garments.

▶ **Wool**
The hair, or fleece, of a variety of breeds of sheep, such as the Shetland Moorit or Bluefaced Leicester, is made into pure wool yarns or blended with other fibres. It is very warm and hard-wearing, and great for winter wear such as jackets, cardigans, hats, and gloves. Some wool is rough, but softens with wear and washing. Wool sold as "organic" contains a high proportion of lanolin, making a strong, waterproof yarn.

◀ **Cotton crochet threads**
Traditionally, crochet was worked in cotton threads that were suitable for lace. Today, cotton threads are still used for lace edgings and filet crochet (see pp.88–93 and pp.107–110).

◀ **Fine-weight cotton yarns**
This thicker yarn is a good weight for garments and accessories and will show the texture of stitch patterns clearly.

▶ **Acrylic**

Acrylic fibres are produced from ethylene, which is derived from oil, and they are very cheap to manufacture. Acrylic yarn feels slightly rougher than other synthetics, and often comes in very bright and luminous shades, which are hard to create with natural fibres. Robust and resistant to moths, acrylic yarn is ideal for toys, novelty items, and budget projects. The yarn tends to accumulate static electricity.

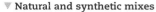

▼ **Natural and synthetic mixes**

Synthetic fibres are often blended with natural fibres to bring structure, strength, and washability; also to alter their appearance, such as to add a sheen. They help bind other yarns, such as mohair and wool, together and prevent shedding; they also prevent animal fibres from shrinking. The strength of such blends makes them perfect for socks or gloves.

◀ **Fabric**

A great way to be both thrifty and eco-friendly is to use fabric strips to crochet with, see how to make the yarn yourself on p.131. The hook size will depend on how thick the strips are. To save time, you can also buy various fabric jersey yarns, upcycled from fashion industry offcuts.

◀ **Alpaca**

This fibre has a luxurious feel and is one of the warmest natural fibres you can crochet with. Even a fine, 4-ply garment provides sufficient insulation in bitterly cold weather. The alpaca is related to the llama. Alpaca yarn is perfect for hats and socks, and cosy blankets. You will also find baby alpaca yarn available, which is softer still.

▼ **String**

Ideal for crocheting practical household items, such as bowls and boxes, string is available in a range of colours and weights. Experiment with relatively small hooks, such as 5mm (UK6/USH-8), to create a very stiff fabric capable of holding its shape. Coat finished household items with diluted PVA glue to waterproof them and make future cleaning easy: just wipe with a damp cloth.

Bamboo ▶

Bamboo fibres used in yarns are produced by crushing the stems to produce a linen-like fibre or by chemically processing the pulped plants, in which case it's termed "bamboo viscose". The fibre has a sheen and handle that resembles silk, and it crochets best when blended with other fibres. Bamboo improves the breathability and elasticity of pure cotton and is ideal for washcloths, summer-weight garments, and shawls.

BUYING YARN

Yarns are packaged for sale in specific quantities or "put-ups". The most common ones for crochet are balls, hanks, and skeins, which usually come in quantities of 25g, 50g, or 100g.

▲ Hank
A twisted ring of yarn, also called a skein, which needs to be wound into a ball before it can be used. You can do this by hand or by using a ball-winder. This gives you the opportunity to check that there are no knots or faults in the yarn as you wind it. Some yarns available as hanks consist of soft, delicate fibres, and these are unsuitable for use in certain industrial ball-winding machines.

▲ Ball
The stock in a yarn store may include balls. These are ready to use: just pull the yarn from the centre to start crocheting.

◀ Skein
A skein of yarn is ready to use without any special preparation. Keep the label in place as you work to ensure that the skein doesn't unravel totally.

◀ Cone
This is often too heavy to carry around in a project bag and the yarn is best wound into balls before you start crocheting.

YARN WEIGHTS

The yarn "weight" refers to its thickness. Some yarns are spun by manufacturers to fall into what are considered as "standard" yarn weights, such as US sport and worsted and UK double-knitting (DK) and aran. These standard weights have long histories and will probably be around for some time to come. However, even within these "standard" weights there is slight variation in thickness, and textured novelty yarns are not easy to categorize by thickness alone.

When defining yarn weight, visual yarn thickness is only one indicator of a yarn-weight category. A yarn can look thicker than another yarn purely because of its loft, the air between the fibres, and the springiness of the strands. By pulling a strand of yarn between your hands, you can see how much loft it has by how much the thickness diminishes when the yarn is stretched.

The ply of a yarn is also not an indication of yarn thickness. Plies are the number of strands twisted together around each other in the opposite direction to which they were spun to form a strong, balanced yarn (the most common yarn plies used in crochet are 3-ply and 4-ply). A yarn with four plies can be very thick or very thin depending on the thickness of each individual ply.

STANDARD YARN-WEIGHT SYSTEM

YARN-WEIGHT SYMBOL AND CATEGORY NAMES	CROCHET TENSION RANGES IN DC TO 10CM (4IN)	RECOMMENDED HOOK IN METRIC SIZE RANGE	RECOMMENDED HOOK IN US SIZE RANGE
Lace **0**	32–42*** trebles	1.6–2.25mm	6 steel, 7 steel, 8 steel, B-1
Superfine **1**	21–32sts	2.25–3.5mm	B-1 to E-4
Fine **2**	16–20sts	3.5–4.5mm	E-4 to 7
Light **3**	12–17sts	4.5–5.5mm	7 to I-9
Medium **4**	11–14sts	5.5–6.5mm	I-9 to K-10½
Bulky **5**	8–11sts	6.5–9mm	K-10½ to M-13
Super bulky **6**	5–9sts	9mm and larger	M-13 and larger

Guidelines only
The above reflect the most commonly used tensions and hook sizes for specific yarn categories. The categories of yarn, tension ranges, and recommended hook sizes have been devised by the Craft Yarn Council of America (YarnStandards.com). *** Ultra-fine lace-weight yarns are difficult to put into tension ranges; always follow the tension given in your pattern for these yarns.

YARN LABELS

Everything you need to know about a yarn is on its label. It will include symbols that tell you how to crochet with it and how to clean it. Here is just a selection of the most common symbols. Always keep the labels: they are vital for identifying the yarn if you run short and need more. New yarn needs to have the same dye lot number as the original purchase in order to avoid a slight difference in colour in the finished item.

▲ Ballband
A yarn label is also known as a ballband. It features information on the yarn's weight and thickness, as well as washing guidelines. Tie a short length of the yarn onto the ballband and keep this with your records for future reference.

Symbols
Yarn manufacturers may use a system of symbols to give details of a yarn. These include descriptions of suitable hooks and the required tension.

Yarn weight and thickness

Recommended crochet hook size

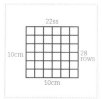

Tension over a 10cm (4in) test square

SHADE/ COLOUR **520**	DYE LOT NUMBER **313**	**50g** NETT AT STANDARD CONDITION IN ACCORDANCE WITH BS984	**100% WOOL**
Shade/colour number	Dye lot number	Weight of ball or skein	Fibre content

Machine-wash cold

Machine-wash cold, gentle cycle

Hand-wash cold

Hand-wash warm

Do not bleach

Dry-cleanable in any solvent

Dry-cleanable in certain solvents

Do not dry-clean

Do not tumble-dry

Do not iron

Iron on a low heat

Iron on a medium heat

CHOOSING YARN COLOURS

When embarking on a new crochet project, the choice of colour is a very important decision. Even a simple design gains impact from good colour choices. The colour wheel is a useful tool, which will introduce you to colour theory.

The colour wheel: The three primary colours, red, yellow, and blue form the basis of a colour wheel. When two primary colours are combined, they create "secondaries". Red and yellow make orange, yellow and blue make green, and blue and red make purple. Intermediate colours called "tertiaries" occur when a secondary is mixed with the nearest primary.

Complementary colours: Colours that lie opposite one another on the wheel, such as red and green, or yellow and violet, are called "complementaries". They provide contrasts that accent design elements and make both colours stand out. Don't forget black and white, the ultimate opposites.

Hue, shade, tone, and tint: Each segment shows the hue, shade, tone, and tint of a colour. A hue is the pure, bright colour; a shade is the colour mixed with black; a tone is the colour mixed with grey; and a tint is the colour mixed with white (pastels). The use of colour can affect the appearance of a project dramatically.

Monochromatic designs: These use different versions of the same colour. So a project based on greens will not stray into the red section of the colour wheel, but might have shades and tints of yellow and blue mixed in, which can then become "harmonious" combinations of colours that are next to each other on the colour wheel. These "adjacent" colours can also be combined to great effect, as long as there are differences in value between them.

Colour temperature: Colour has a visual "temperature", with some colours being perceived as "warm" and others as "cool". Many people tend to think of blue and its adjacent colours as being cool, while the reds and yellows are warm, but in fact there are warmer and cooler versions of all the primaries; think, for example, of a warm, azure blue and a cold, icy blue. Colour temperature is an important element in whether a colour recedes or advances – that is, in whether it stands out from or blends in with the background and surrounding colours.

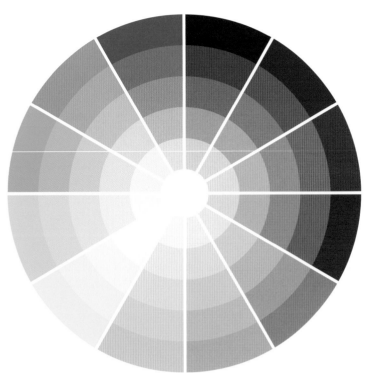

Black and white

You won't see black and white on the colour wheel as they are not classified as colours. Black is an absence of all colour and white is a combination of all colours in the spectrum. In yarns this is the opposite; black will have been heavily dyed and bright white yarn will have been bleached of all colour. Bear in mind that when using black, your work will be more difficult to see, but also that complex textures will not be seen to best effect in the final garment. White, however, guarantees that every stitch and detail will be clear.

Warm shades

The warm end of the colour spectrum consists mainly of red and yellow tones; browns, oranges, and purple are part of this group. Use these colours to bring richness and depth. A blend of warm shades can be a very flattering mixture to use, depending on your colouring: hold the yarn against your face to see what suits you.

Cool shades

Blue, green, and violet are at the cool end of the spectrum, and these can be very effective when used together. Cool colours are generally darker in tone than warm ones. If used with warm shades, their impact is lessened: if you need to balance a warm mixture in a project, you will need a higher proportion of cool than warm colours to do it.

Pastels

These very pale, often cool variations of deeper, darker colours are very popular for babies' and small children's garments; consequently, a variety of suitable synthetic yarns and blends is available in these colours. Pastels also feature strongly in spring/summer crochet patterns for adults: look for ice-cream colours in lightweight yarns, and enjoy using a delicate colour palette.

Brights

Vivid and fluorescent shades are fun to use in a project, and often make particularly eye-catching accessories or colour motifs. A great way to liven up a colourwork project that consists of muted shades is to add a bright edging or set of buttons. This burst of colour can change the project's overall impact completely.

Seasonal mixtures

Nature can be a great source of inspiration. Think about sunsets, autumn leaves, frosted winter berries, or vibrant spring flowers. Keep a record of these in a sketchbook or in photographs, and notice the proportion of each colour in view. Most good yarn stockists change their range of colours according to the season: in spring for example, more pastels and brights will be available.

HOOKS

Crochet is probably one of the most economical needlework crafts, as it requires very little equipment. Aside from yarn, you will need a crochet hook of appropriate size to the project, a blunt needle for darning in ends, and some scissors. In addition, there are some other essential pieces that you to add to your crochet kit (see pp.20–21).

CROCHET HOOKS

If you are a beginner, start learning to crochet with a good-quality standard metal crochet hook. Once you know how to work the basic stitches with a lightweight wool yarn and a 4mm or 4.5mm (US size G-6 or 7) hook, branch out and try some other types of hooks in order to find the one that suits you best.

> STANDARD METAL HOOK

▶ **Parts of a crochet hook**
The hook lip grabs the yarn to form the loops and the shank determines the size of the loop. The crochet handle gives weight to the tool and provides a good grip.

Throat

Handle | Thumb rest | Shank | Hook lip

Hook tip

> ALTERNATIVE HOOK HANDLES

▶ **More comfortable handles**
If you find the standard crochet hook uncomfortable to hold, investigate other designs of hooks. The wooden hook's curved handle (top) prevents any discomfort. An ergonomically shaped handle (bottom) fits a knife grip for the most comfortable hooking action.

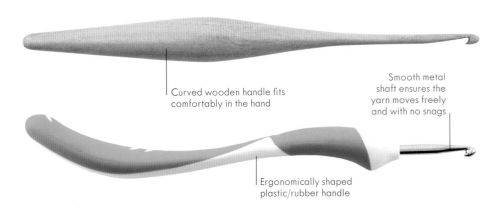

Curved wooden handle fits comfortably in the hand

Smooth metal shaft ensures the yarn moves freely and with no snags

Ergonomically shaped plastic/rubber handle

> HOOK SIZES

Crochet hooks are manufactured in the various sizes (diameters) listed in the hook conversion chart on the opposite page. The millimetre sizes are the diameter of the hook shank, which determines the size of the crochet stitches.

Although the middle range of hook sizes – from 2mm (US size B-1) to 9mm (US size M-13) – is the most commonly used, the finer and thicker hooks are also very popular for lace crochet and jumbo crochet. See p.14 for which hook size to use with the different yarn weights.

HOOK TYPES

Point protector

▲ Lace hook
Because lace crochet hooks are so fine, ranging from 0.6mm (US size 14 steel) to 1.75mm (US size 5 steel), they are always manufactured in metal. Keep them with their metal point protectors in place to avoid accidents.

▲ Wooden hook
Hardwood and bamboo hooks are lighter in weight than metal hooks. They also provide a good grip to prevent your fingers from slipping when crocheting.

▲ Metal hook
Some ranges of aluminium hooks are available in bright colours – a different colour for each size, which is handy for picking up the right size at a glance.

▲ Jumbo hooks
The largest crochet hook sizes – from a 10mm (US size N-15) to a 20mm (US size S) – are made in plastic. They are used for making thick crochet fabric very quickly.

▲ Broomstick
A broomstick is a thick stick used in conjunction with a regular hook to create the lace loops in broomstick crochet. It is best to use an oversized knitting needle such as this one.

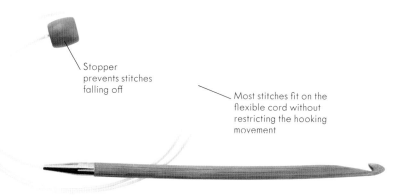

Stopper prevents stitches falling off

Most stitches fit on the flexible cord without restricting the hooking movement

▲ Tunisian hook
A Tunisian hook is longer than a regular hook, as you have to fit on many stitches. The hook can be straight and double-ended or have a flexible cord with a stopper on the end, like this one, which can be easier to work with.

CONVERSION CHART

This chart gives the conversions between the various hook-size systems. Where there are no exact conversions possible, use the nearest equivalent.

EU METRIC	US SIZES	OLD UK
0.6mm	14 steel	N/A
0.75mm	12 steel	N/A
1mm	11 steel	N/A
1.25mm	7 steel	N/A
1.5mm	6 steel	N/A
1.75mm	5 steel	N/A
2mm	N/A	14
2.25mm	B-1	N/A
2.5mm	N/A	12
2.75mm	C-2	N/A
3mm	N/A	10
3.25mm	D-3	N/A
3.5mm	E-4	9
3.75mm	F-5	N/A
4mm	G-6	8
4.5mm	7	7
5mm	H-8	6
5.5mm	I-9	5
6mm	J-10	4
6.5mm	K-10½	3
7mm	N/A	2
8mm	L-11	N/A
9mm	M-13	N/A
10mm	N-15	N/A
12mm	P	N/A
15mm	Q (16mm)	N/A
20mm	S (19mm)	N/A

OTHER EQUIPMENT

In addition to a crochet hook, a blunt-ended yarn needle for darning in yarn ends, and some scissors or snips, there are other items that can make crocheting easier or quicker, including pins, a tape measure, stitch markers, tension gauge, and a pompom maker; you may also like to crochet a craft wrap to keep hooks neat and tidy (see pp.122–125 for the pattern).

THE ESSENTIALS

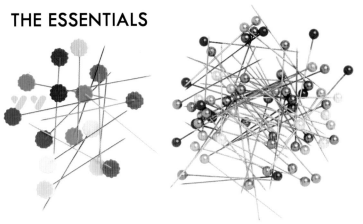

▲ **Pins**
Use pins with glass heads or large heads (such as knitting pins) for seams and blocking (see p.68).

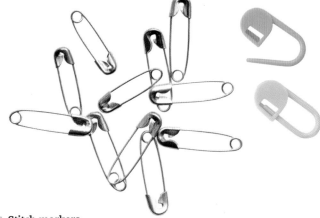

▲ **Stitch markers**
Small safety pins and stitch markers can be hooked onto the crochet to mark a specific row or a specific stitch in the row, or to mark the right side of your crochet.

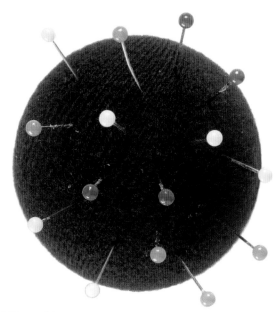

▲ **Pin cushion**
A useful item to store pins in when working.

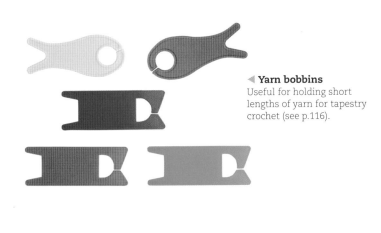

◀ **Yarn bobbins**
Useful for holding short lengths of yarn for tapestry crochet (see p.116).

▲ **Blunt-ended yarn needles**
Use these for sewing seams and darning in yarn ends (make sure the eye of the needle is big enough for your chosen yarn).

Blocking wire and pins ▷
These are used to block crochet after handwashing or before steam blocking. Thread the wires along the edge of the fabric as if sewing a long running stitch. Measure and shape the fabric to the correct dimensions before pinning the wires down and leaving to dry.

▲ Snips
These are precise, small, and work quickly, so are often more convenient than scissors.

▲ Scissors
Keep a sharp pair of scissors on hand for cutting yarn and trimming off yarn ends.

▲ Row counter
These are useful for keeping track of where you are in your crochet. String it on a length of yarn and hang it around your neck.

▲ Tape measure
Keep a tape measure on hand for checking your tension and measuring your crochet.

Sock blocker ▷
This is the best way to block finished socks to a neat shape. Handwash the sock and pull gently to shape on the blocker. As it dries, it will take on the shape of the blocker. Sock blockers are available in a range of sizes.

▽ Hook and tension gauge
A hook gauge allows you to discover what size an unmarked hook is. This hook gauge doubles up as a tension measure in a handy size.

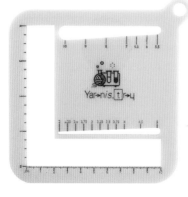

▲ Folding pompom maker
These little devices hinge open to allow you to wind the yarn quickly and evenly. Then, a metal prong holds it all together while you cut the pompom. They come in a range of sizes and colours.

TECHNIQUES

BASIC STITCHES

Learning to crochet can take a bit of time because there are several basic stitches to master. But there is no need to learn all the stitches at once. With only chain stitches and double crochet at your disposal, you can make attractive striped blankets and cushion covers in luscious yarns.

GETTING STARTED

Before making your first loop, the slip knot (see opposite), get to know the hook and how to hold it. First, review the detailed explanation of the parts of the hook on p.18. Then try out the various hook- and yarn-holding techniques (below), when learning how to make chain stitches. If you ever learned crochet as a child, you will automatically hold the hook the way you originally learned to, and you should stick to this whether it is the pencil or knife position.

❯ HOLDING THE HOOK

Pencil position: To hold the hook in this position, grip it as you would a pencil. If the hook has a shaped thumb rest, position this above your thumb and under your forefinger. The centre of your thumb will be about 5cm (2in) from the tip of the hook if the hook has a thumb rest, and this is where you should also hold a hook without a thumb rest.

Left-handed crocheters hold the hook in the exact mirror image of right-handed crocheters

Knife position: To hold a crochet hook in this position, grip it as you would when using a table knife to cut food. As for the pencil position, if the hook has a thumb rest, settle your thumb and forefinger in this shaped section with the centre of your thumb about 5cm (2in) from the hook tip. Grip a hook without a thumb rest the same distance from the tip.

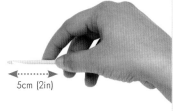

Left-handed crocheters hold the hook in the exact mirror image of right-handed crocheters

❯ HOLDING THE YARN

In order to control the flow of the yarn to your hook, you need to lace it around the fingers of your free hand (called your yarn hand).

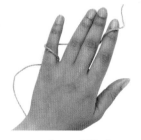

Left-handed crocheters thread the yarn through their right hand

Method one: Start by winding the yarn around your little finger, then pass it under your two middle fingers and over your forefinger. With this method the forefinger is used to position the yarn.

Both the techniques shown here are only suggestions, so feel free to develop your own.

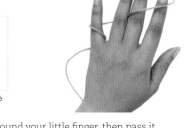

Left-handed crocheters thread the yarn through their right hand

Method two: Wrap the yarn around your little finger, then pass it behind the next finger and over the top of the middle finger and forefinger. This method allows you to position the yarn with either the forefinger or middle finger, whichever is more comfortable and gives you more control (see Tensioning your yarn, opposite).

❯ MAKING A SLIP KNOT

1 To make the first loop (called the slip knot) on your hook, begin by crossing the yarn coming from the ball over the yarn end (called the yarn tail) to form a circle of yarn.

2 Insert the tip of the hook through the circle of yarn. Then use the hook to grab the ball end of the yarn and pull the yarn through the circle.

3 This forms a loop on the hook and a loose, open knot below the loop.

4 Pull both ends of the yarn firmly to tighten the knot and the loop around the shank of the hook.

5 Make sure the completed slip knot is tight enough on the hook so that it won't fall off, but not so tight that you can barely slide it along the hook's shank. The yarn tail on the slip knot should be at least 10cm (4in) long so it can be darned in later.

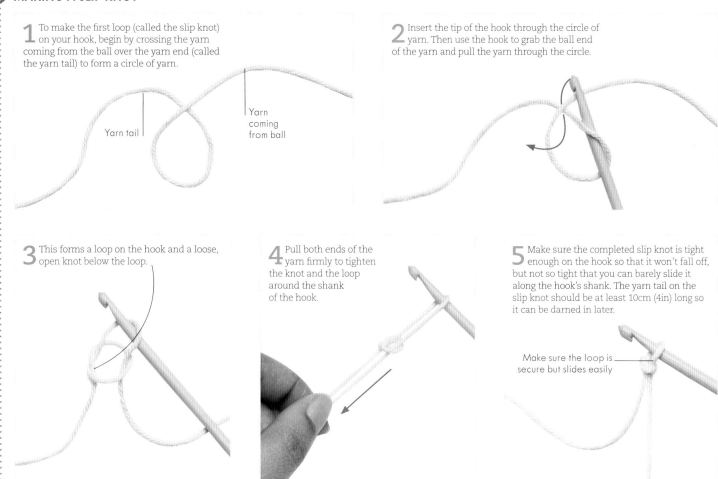

Yarn tail

Yarn coming from ball

Make sure the loop is secure but slides easily

❯ TENSIONING YOUR YARN

1 With your slip knot on your hook, try out some yarn-holding techniques. Wrap the yarn around your little finger and then lace it through your other fingers as desired, but so that it ends up over the tip of your forefinger (or your forefinger and middle finger).

2 As you crochet, grip the yarn tightly with your little finger and ring finger and release it gently as you form the loops. Use either your forefinger or your middle finger to position the yarn, and hold the base of the crochet close to the hook to keep it in place as the hook is drawn through the loops.

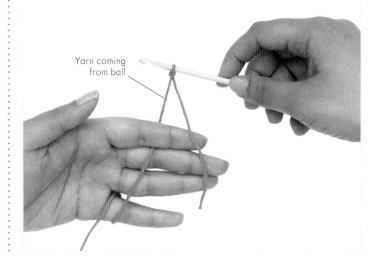

Yarn coming from ball

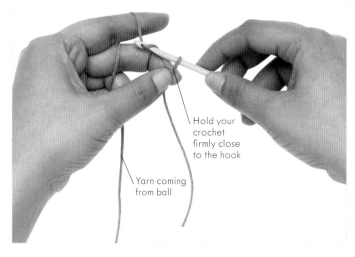

Hold your crochet firmly close to the hook

Yarn coming from ball

TECHNIQUES

CHAIN STITCHES (Abbreviation = ch)

Chain stitches are the first crochet stitches you need to learn because they form the base for all other stitches – called a foundation chain – and for turning chains (see p.66). They are used in combination with other basic stitches to create a vast array of crochet stitch patterns, both densely textured stitches and lacy ones. Practise chain stitches until you are comfortable holding a hook and releasing and tensioning yarn.

❯ MAKING A FOUNDATION CHAIN

1 Start with a slip knot on your hook (see p.25). Wrap the yarn around the hook; this action is called "yarn round hook" (abbreviated yrh) in crochet patterns. When working a yrh, move your hook under the yarn at the same time as you move the yarn slightly forwards.

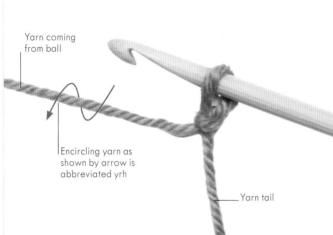

Yarn coming from ball

Encircling yarn as shown by arrow is abbreviated yrh

Yarn tail

2 With the yarn gripped in the lip of the hook, draw a loop of yarn through the loop on the hook. (Hold the base of the slip knot with the free fingers of your yarn hand as you draw the loop through.)

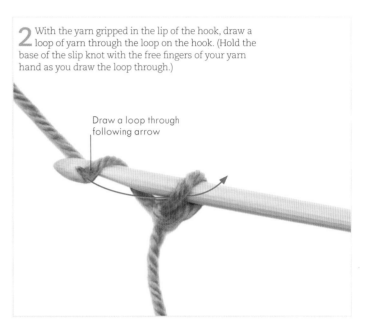

Draw a loop through following arrow

3 This completes the first chain.

One chain made

4 Yrh and draw a loop through the loop on the hook for each new stitch. Continue making chains in the same way until you have the number specified in your crochet pattern.

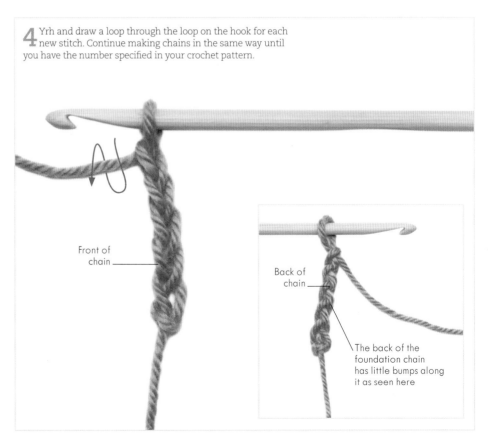

Front of chain

Back of chain

The back of the foundation chain has little bumps along it as seen here

> **COUNTING CHAIN STITCHES**

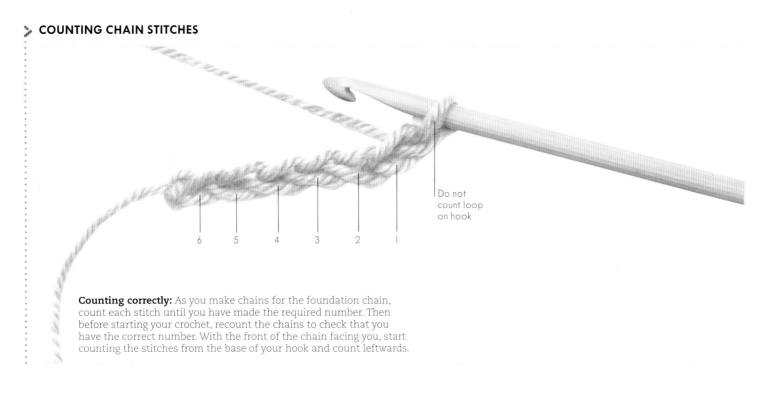

Do not
count loop
on hook

6   5   4   3   2   1

Counting correctly: As you make chains for the foundation chain,
count each stitch until you have made the required number. Then
before starting your crochet, recount the chains to check that you
have the correct number. With the front of the chain facing you, start
counting the stitches from the base of your hook and count leftwards.

FASTENING OFF CHAINS AND SLIP STITCHES

Stopping your crochet when it is complete is called fastening off. As there is only one loop on your hook,
the process is extremely simple. Here is a visual aid for how to fasten off a length of chains or a row of
slip stitches. The principle is the same for all stitches in crochet.

> **FASTENING OFF A LENGTH OF CHAINS**

1 Remove the loop from
the hook. Pull out the
loop to enlarge it so that it
does not start to unravel.

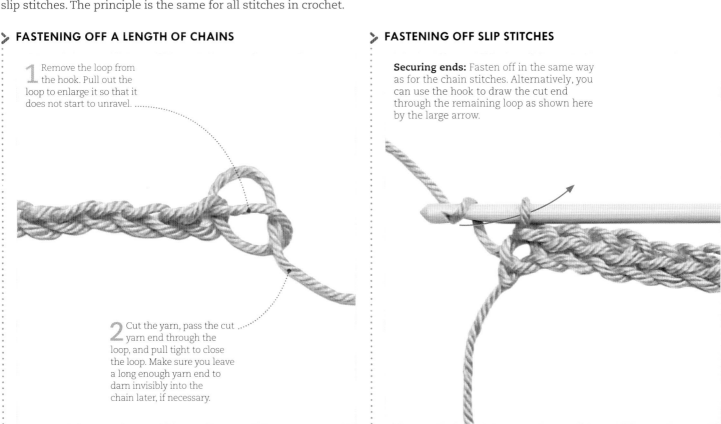

2 Cut the yarn, pass the cut
yarn end through the
loop, and pull tight to close
the loop. Make sure you leave
a long enough yarn end to
darn invisibly into the
chain later, if necessary.

> **FASTENING OFF SLIP STITCHES**

Securing ends: Fasten off in the same way
as for the chain stitches. Alternatively, you
can use the hook to draw the cut end
through the remaining loop as shown here
by the large arrow.

SLIP STITCH (Abbreviation = ss)

Slip stitches are the shortest of all the crochet stitches. Although they can be worked in rows, the resulting fabric is so dense that it is only really suitable for bag handles. However, slip stitches appear very frequently in crochet instructions – to join on new yarn (see p.39), to work invisibly along the top of a row to move to a new position (see p.53), and to join rounds in circular crochet – making them one of the most useful stitches of all.

❯ WORKING SLIP STITCH AS A FABRIC

1 Make a foundation chain of the required length. To begin the first stitch, insert the hook through the second chain from the hook, passing the hook under only one strand of the chain. Then wrap the yarn around the hook (yrh).

2 Holding the base of the chain firmly with the fingers of your left hand and tensioning the yarn (see p.25), draw a loop back through the chain and through the loop on the hook as shown by the large arrow.

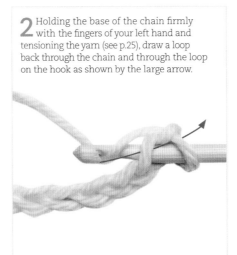

3 Continue across the foundation chain, working a slip stitch into each chain in the same way. Always work slip stitches fairly loosely for whatever purpose you are using them.

4 After the last stitch of the row has been completed, and if you want to work another row, turn your crochet to position the yarn at the right edge of the piece of crochet ready to begin the second row.

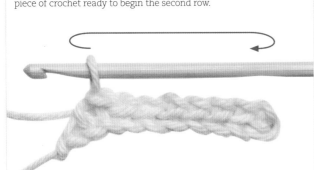

5 To begin a second row of slip stitches, make one chain stitch. This chain is called the turning chain. For the second and following rows of slip stitch, work each stitch into the back loop only of the top of the stitches below. (It is not essential for a beginner to practise working slip stitch in rows as it is rarely used this way.)

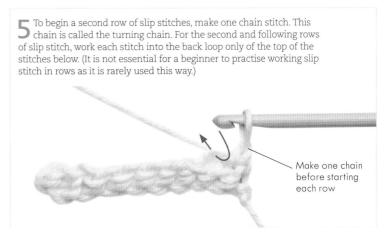

Make one chain before starting each row

❯ USING SLIP STITCHES TO FORM A FOUNDATION RING

Making a ring: Slip stitches are also used to form the foundation rings for circular crochet (see p.98). Make the required number of chains for the ring, then insert the hook through the first chain made, wrap the yarn around the hook, and draw a loop through the chain and the loop on the hook to close the ring.

▶ **These motifs are formed** by first making a foundation ring. The technique, explained left, only requires basic crochet stitches. To practise making them, see pp.102–105 for a selection of vibrant granny squares (also known as Afghan squares) and flowers.

BEADED NECKLACE

Level of difficulty

The most basic of stitches is used to stunning effect with this necklace, which uses just chains and beads. This stylish piece of jewellery includes a series of long chains, but you can reduce the number of stitches to shorten its length.

TECHNIQUES USED Making a foundation chain **p.26**, Fastening off chains and slip stitches **p.27**

SIZE
Approx 48cm (19in) long

YARN
DMC Petra No. 3 – 100g/280m/306yds
(100% cotton; you can use any yarn
for this project – it only uses a very
small amount so it's perfect for using
up scraps)

x 1

HOOKS
2mm hook
1.5mm beading hook, or size needed to fit
through your beads

NOTIONS
Yarn needle
Selection of beads (make sure the thread
can fit through the holes of the beads
you have chosen)

TENSION
Exact tension is not essential

> PATTERN
Note: To thread the beads onto the chain,
you need to ensure that the beading hook
can pass through the holes in the beads,
so don't choose any beads with tiny holes.

Make a chain of the desired length to your
first bead placement.
Pull up the loop on the hook to make it
larger and remove the hook from the loop.
Place a bead onto the shaft of the beading
hook, then insert the hook into the
elongated loop.
Pull the loop through the bead and work
1 ch to secure it, pulling on the yarn to
make sure that the yarn is tight around
the bead.
Repeat these actions at intervals to place
all the beads desired.
Work a length of chain after the last bead
has been placed, and join this with a ss
to the first chain made on the necklace to
form a ring and complete the necklace.
Fasten off yarn, weave in ends.

1 Make around 14 even chain stitches and then
slide a bead up close to the hook.

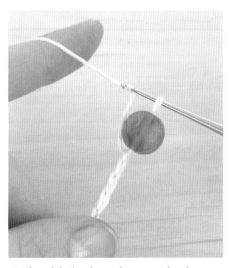

2 Thread the bead onto the yarn and make
a chain stitch tightly around the bead to
secure it in position on the necklace.

CHUNKY BRACELET

Create a bracelet with a simple charm. Work the chain to a length that fits comfortably around your wrist once for a short bracelet, or multiply this by as many times as you want for a longer, thicker-looking bracelet.

TECHNIQUES USED Making a foundation chain **p.26**, Fastening off chains and slip stitches **p.27**

SIZE

Approx 60cm (23½in) long

YARN

Sirdar Snuggly Baby Bamboo DK –
50g/95m/104yds (80% bamboo and 20% wool; you can use any small amounts of DK yarn for this project, or try different weights – the chain will simply get thicker or thinner depending on the weight of the yarn)

x 1

HOOK

3.5mm hook

NOTIONS

Yarn needle
Approx 1cm (½in) button or bead
    for fastening

TENSION

Exact tension is not essential

⟩ PATTERN

Note: Increasing the number of strands of yarn you hold together to crochet with will vary the bracelet's thickness.

With a single strand of yarn, make a chain to your desired length, plus 5 ch. Ss into fifth ch from hook. Fasten off yarn, weave in ends.

2-STRAND VARIATION

With two strands of yarn, make a chain to your desired length, plus 4 ch. Ss into fourth ch from hook. Fasten off yarn, weave in ends.

3-STRAND VARIATION

With three strands of yarn, make a chain to your desired length, plus 3 ch. Ss into third ch from hook. Fasten off yarn, weave in ends.

FINISHING

Sew a bead or button to the opposite end from the loop fastening.

1 When the chain is the desired length, make a loop by working an extra five chains and then make a slip stitch into the fifth chain from the hook.

2 Attach a bead or button securely to the opposite end from the loop using the same yarn, and then weave in loose ends.

TECHNIQUES

DOUBLE CROCHET (Abbreviation = dc)

Double crochet is the easiest crochet stitch to learn and one crocheters use most frequently, either on its own or in combination with other stitches. Take your time learning and practising the stitch because once you become proficient, the taller stitches will be much easier to master. Double crochet forms a dense fabric that is suitable for many types of garments and accessories. It is also the stitch used for toys and containers because it can be worked very tightly to form a stiff, firm textile that has excellent rigidity, prevents toy stuffing from showing through the stitches, and holds up well.

Working in rows: When double crochet is worked back and forth in rows, it looks identical on both sides. Worked in the round it looks different on the right and wrong sides, which you can see on p.98.

1 Make a foundation chain of the required length (see p.26). Insert the hook through the second stitch from the hook and wrap the yarn around the hook (yrh) following the large arrow. (You can insert the hook under one or two strands of the chain, but working under just one loop as shown here is easiest.)

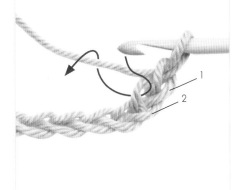

2 Holding the base of the chain firmly with your left hand and tensioning the yarn (see p.25), draw a loop back through the chain as shown by the large arrow.

3 There are now two loops on the hook. Next, yrh as shown by the large arrow.

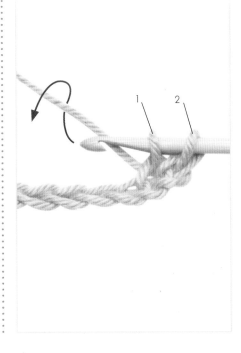

4 Draw a loop through both loops on the hook in one smooth action. As you use the yarn, allow it to flow through the fingers of your left hand while still tensioning it softly.

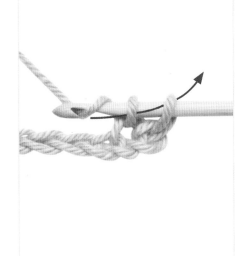

5 This completes the first double crochet. The missed chain at the beginning of this first row does NOT count as a stitch on its own (in other words, it is not counted when you count how many stitches are in the row and it is not worked into in the next row).

Top of first completed double crochet

Missed chain at beginning of foundation row

6 Continue across the foundation chain, working one double crochet into each chain in the same way.

7 At the end of the row, turn your crochet to position the yarn at the right edge of the piece of crochet, ready to begin the second row.

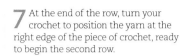
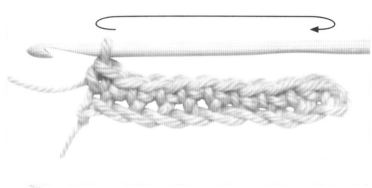

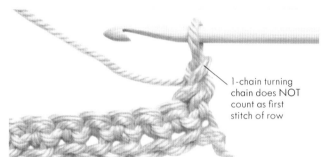

1-chain turning chain does NOT count as first stitch of row

8 To begin the second row, make one chain stitch. This chain is called the turning chain, and it brings the work up to the height of the double crochet stitches that will follow.

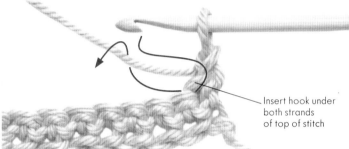

Insert hook under both strands of top of stitch

9 Work the first double crochet into the top of the first stitch in the row below. Be sure to insert the hook under both legs of the "V" of the stitch. Work a double crochet into the top of each of the remaining double crochets in the row below.

11 When you have completed your crochet, cut the yarn leaving a long loose end – at least 10cm (4in) long. Remove the hook from the remaining loop, pass the yarn end through the loop, and pull tight to close it. Fastening off like this is applicable for all crochet stitches.

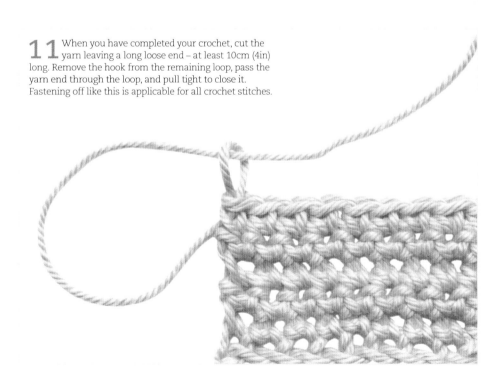

10 At the end of the row, work the last stitch into the top of the last double crochet of the row below. Work following rows as for the second row.

STRIPED WASHCLOTHS

Level of difficulty ✱✱✱

These reusable washcloths are easy to make and kind to the planet, since you simply freshen them up in the washing machine. Constructed in double crochet, with various stripe patterns, they are an ideal practice project for beginners.

TECHNIQUES USED Making a foundation chain **p.26**, Slip stitch **p.28**, Double crochet **p.34**, Simple stripes **p.39**

SIZE
20cm (8in) square

YARN
DMC Natura Cotton – 50g/155m/169yds
(100% combed cotton; any 4-ply
non-mercerized cotton would be
an acceptable alternative)

A x 1   **B** x 1   **C** x 1

HOOK
3mm hook

NOTIONS
Yarn needle

TENSION
17 dc x 20 rows per 10cm (4in) square

PATTERN

Note: When changing colours, always
add the new colour on the last step
of the last stitch of the previous row
(see p.39 for instructions).

IVORY AND GERANIUM WASHCLOTH
With yarn A, work 35 ch.
Row 1: 1 dc in second ch from hook, *dc
into next st, rep from * to end, turn. (34 dc)
Row 2: 1 ch, *dc into next st, rep from * to
end, turn.
Continue to work in dc until piece
measures 12cm (4¾in), changing to B on
last yrh of last row.

Next row right side (RS): With B, 1 ch, *dc
into next st, rep from * to end, turn.
Next row wrong side (WS): 1 ch, *dc into
next st, rep from * to end, change to A
on last yrh, turn.
Work two rows with A. Repeat stripe
sequence twice more (three stripes
worked in B).
Finish with two rows of dc with A.
Fasten off yarn. Weave in ends.

Edging
With yarn B and RS facing, rejoin yarn to
any point along the edge of the washcloth
with a ss, work a row of dc evenly around
the entire edge of the washcloth, placing
3 dc into each corner stitch to turn the
corners. When you are back at the first
stitch, ss into first stitch to join round
and fasten off yarn.
Weave in all ends.

IVORY AND TURQUOISE WASHCLOTH
Work as for first washcloth until piece
measures 7cm (2¾in), change to C on last
yrh of final dc.
Work four rows with C, change to A.
Work four rows with A, change to C.
Work four rows with C, change to A.
Continue working dc with A for 7cm (2¾in).
Fasten off yarn. Work the edging in the
same way as for the first washcloth.

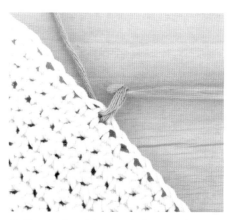

1 To make the edging, attach the new colour
to the top edge of the washcloth with the right
side facing, and double crochet into each stitch
all the way to the corner.

2 Work three double crochet into the corner
stitch to turn, and continue to double crochet
all the way up the row end edge of the washcloth,
making three double crochets at each corner. Join
to first stitch of edging with a slip stitch.

TECHNIQUES

HALF TREBLE CROCHET (Abbreviation = htr)

After double crochet, half treble crochet comes next in order of stitch heights (see p.66). It is firm like double crochet and fairly dense, but produces a slightly softer texture, which makes it ideal for warm baby garments. The texture is also more interesting than double crochet, but not too lacy. It's not advisable to move on to learning how to work half trebles until you can make double crochet stitches with confidence.

Working in rows: Half treble crochet worked in rows, as here, looks the same on both sides, making it a totally reversible fabric, just like all basic stitches worked in rows.

1 Make a foundation chain of the required length (see p.26). To begin the first stitch, wrap the yarn around the hook (yrh).

2 Insert the hook through the third chain from the hook, yrh again (as shown by the large arrow), and draw a loop back through the chain.

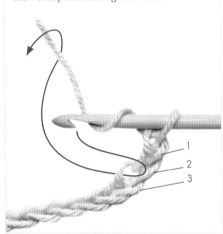

3 There are now three loops on the hook.

4 Yrh and draw a loop through all three loops on the hook as shown by the large arrow. (This motion becomes more fluid with practice.)

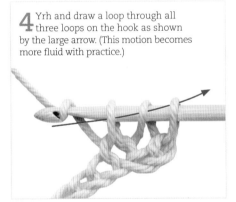

5 This completes the first half treble.

Completed half treble crochet

Two missed chains at beginning of row

6 Work one half treble crochet into each chain in the same way. Remember to start each half treble by wrapping the yarn around the hook before inserting it through the chain.

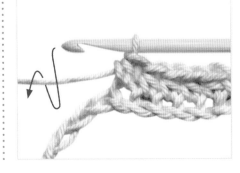

7 After working a half treble crochet into the last chain, turn the work to position the yarn at the right edge of the piece of crochet ready to begin the second row.

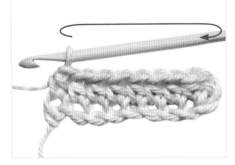

8 Begin the second row by making two chains. This turning chain brings the work up to the height of the half trebles that follow.

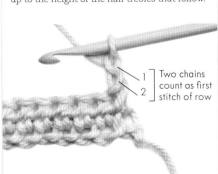

Two chains count as first stitch of row

9 Yrh and work the first half treble into the top of the second stitch in the row below.

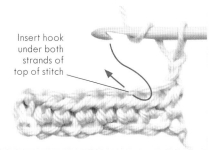

Insert hook under both strands of top of stitch

10 Work a half treble into each of the remaining half treble crochets in the row below. Work the following rows as for the second row.

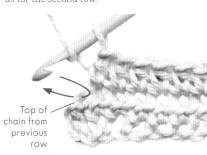

Top of chain from previous row

11 When the crochet is complete, cut the yarn. Remove the hook from the remaining loop, pass the yarn end through the loop, and pull tight to close the loop and fasten off securely.

Leave an end at least 10cm (4in) long, so it can be darned in later

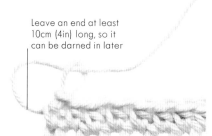

JOINING ON NEW YARN

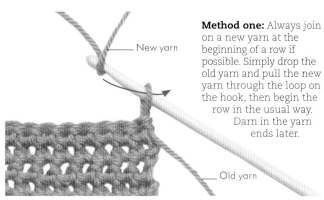

New yarn

Old yarn

Method one: Always join on a new yarn at the beginning of a row if possible. Simply drop the old yarn and pull the new yarn through the loop on the hook, then begin the row in the usual way. Darn in the yarn ends later.

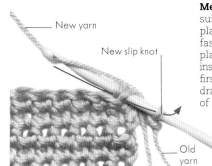

New yarn

New slip knot

Old yarn

Method two: This method is suitable for both stripes and plain crochet fabrics. First, fasten off the old yarn. Then place a slip knot on the hook, insert the hook through the first stitch of the row and draw a loop through the top of the stitch and the loop on the hook.

SIMPLE STRIPES

Stripes worked in basic stitches have more potential for creativity than most crocheters realize. The only techniques you need to learn are how and when to change colours to start a new stripe, and how to carry the yarns up the side edge of the crochet.

CHANGING COLOURS

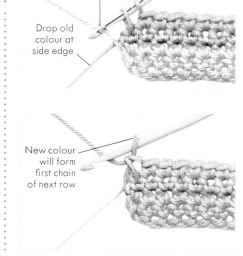

Work the last yrh of row with next stripe colour

Drop old colour at side edge

1 When working stripes in any stitch, always change to the next colour on the last yrh of the last row before the next stripe colour is started.

New colour will form first chain of next row

2 Drawing through the last yrh of the row completes the last stitch. The new colour is now on the hook ready to start the next stripe on the next row; this is so that the first turning chain in the next stripe is in the correct colour.

CARRYING COLOURS UP SIDE EDGE

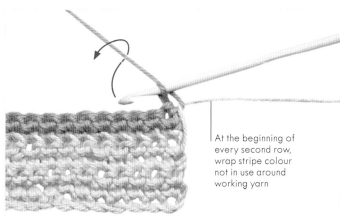

At the beginning of every second row, wrap stripe colour not in use around working yarn

Wrapping yarn: If a colour is not needed for more than two rows, wrap it around the other colour to secure it. If it is not needed for more than eight rows, cut it off and rejoin it later.

SELF-FRINGING SCARF

This long and cosy scarf is made in simple half treble stitch. Beginners will love how quickly this works up, and the colour changes in each row add interest for more experienced crocheters.

TECHNIQUES USED *Making a foundation chain* **p.26**, *Half treble crochet* **p.38**, *Simple stripes* **p.39**

SIZE
14 x 180cm (5½ x 71in)

YARN
Rowan Creative Focus Worsted – 100g/ 200m/220yds (75% wool and 25% alpaca; you can use any aran weight 100% wool or wool/alpaca blend to achieve a similar effect)

A x 1   **B** x 1

HOOK
4.5mm hook

NOTIONS
Yarn needle

TENSION
11sts x 10 rows per 10cm (4in)

PATTERN

Note: Change yarn at the end of each row, leave a 15cm (6in) long tail when joining and cutting yarn to make the fringe.

With yarn A, work 182 ch, turn.
Row 1: 1 htr into third ch from hook, *1 htr into next ch, rep from * to end, fasten off A. (180sts)
Row 2: With yarn B, 2 ch, *1 htr into each st, rep from * to end, 2 ch, fasten off B, leaving a long tail for fringe.
Continue to work a further 10 rows as row 2, changing colours at the end of each row, alternating A and B.
Row 13: With A, 2 ch, *1 htr into each st, rep from * to end, turn (do not cut yarn).
Row 14: 1 ch, 1 ss into top of each htr to end, fasten off A.

MAKING THE FRINGING
Knot long tails in pairs at both ends of scarf; add extra fringing if required (see p.71). Trim to desired length.

This scarf pattern cleverly uses tassels that are an integral part of the whole piece. They are made by leaving a long yarn tail each time you change colour at the end of a row, and knotting them together in pairs.

GLASSES CASE

Safeguard your glasses and sunglasses in this stylish drawstring case. The half treble fabric of the case offers soft but certain protection against scratches and damage.

TECHNIQUES USED Chain stitch **p.26**, Half treble crochet **p.38**, Simple stripes **p.39**

SIZE
10cm x 19cm (4in x 7½in)

YARN
Stylecraft Bellissima DK – 100g/268m/ 293yds (100% acrylic; you can use any synthetic DK yarn for a similar look)

A x 1   **B** x 1   **C** x 1

HOOK
3.5mm hook

NOTIONS
Tapestry needle
4 x 10mm (½in) wooden beads

TENSION
17sts and 12 rows to 10cm (4in) square

PATTERN

Note: The case is worked in rows and gathered at the top with a chain stitch cord.

With yarn A, work 38 ch in main colour. Begin working in rows.
Row 1: Work 1 htr in second ch from hook (2 ch counts as a st), work 1 htr in each ch to end, turn. (37sts)
Row 2: 2 ch, (2 ch counts as a st), work 1 htr in each st to end, turn. (37sts)
Rows 3–12: Rep row 2.
Change to yarn B.
Rows 13–16: Rep row 2.
Change to yarn C.
Rows 17–24: Rep row 2.
Fasten off, weave in ends.

TIES (MAKE 2)
Using yarn B, work 40 ch. Fasten off leaving a short yarn tail.

FINISHING
Fold the crochet in half lengthwise. With wrong sides together and with coordinating yarn, sew the base and side seam together. Turn right side out. Using a tapestry needle, weave in a chain stitch tie on either side of the case on row 21. Using a tapestry needle, thread a wooden bead onto each end of the chain stitch tie and fasten with a knot.

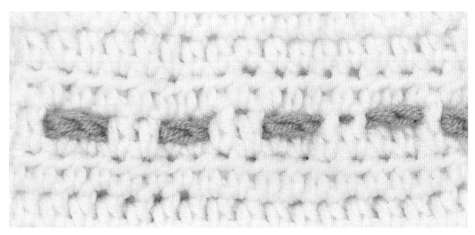

Contrast cord The chain stitch cord is woven through each side of the case to create a smooth but secure closing device to keep the glasses safely inside.

TREBLE CROCHET (Abbreviation = tr)

Treble crochet produces a more open and softer crochet fabric than the denser double and half treble crochet. Because treble crochet is a tall stitch, the fabric grows quickly as you proceed, which makes it the most popular of all crochet stitches for projects that work up quickly.

Working in rows: As you work treble crochet in rows, you will see that it looks identical on the front and the back.

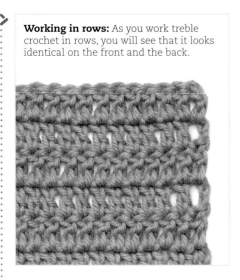

1 Make as many chains as required (see p.26). To begin the first stitch, wrap the yarn around the hook (yrh).

Make foundation chain of any length to practise trebles

2 Insert the hook through the fourth chain from the hook, yrh again (as shown by the large arrow), and draw a loop back through the chain.

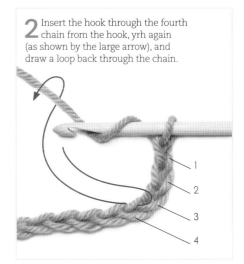

3 There are now three loops on the hook.

4 Yrh and draw a loop through the first two loops on the hook.

5 There are now two loops left on the hook. Yrh and draw a loop through the remaining two loops.

6 This completes the first treble. In treble crochet, the three missed chains at the beginning of the chain count as the first stitch of the foundation row.

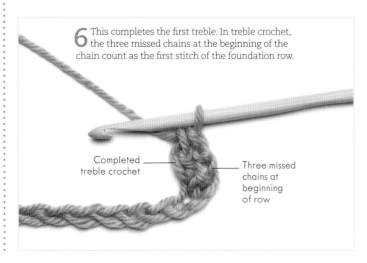

Completed treble crochet

Three missed chains at beginning of row

7 Work one treble crochet into each chain in the same way. Remember to start each stitch with a yrh before inserting the hook through the chain.

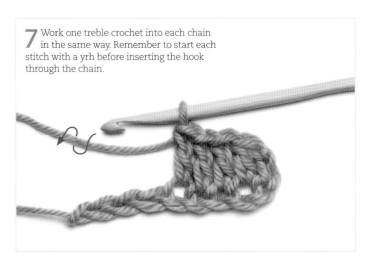

8 After the last stitch of the row has been completed, turn the work to position the yarn at the right edge of the piece of crochet ready to begin the second row.

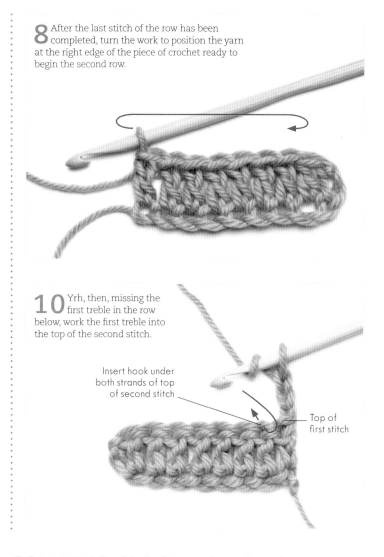

9 To begin the second row of treble crochet, make three chain stitches. This brings the work up to the height of these tall stitches.

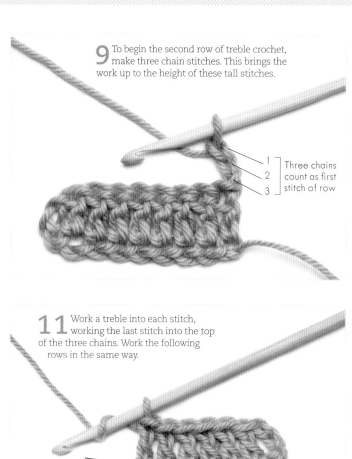

1
2
3 } Three chains count as first stitch of row

10 Yrh, then, missing the first treble in the row below, work the first treble into the top of the second stitch.

Insert hook under both strands of top of second stitch

Top of first stitch

11 Work a treble into each stitch, working the last stitch into the top of the three chains. Work the following rows in the same way.

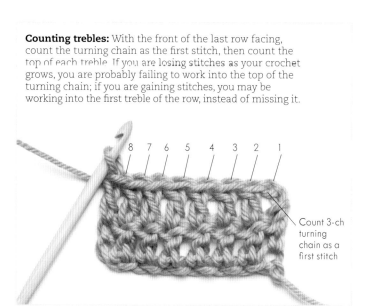

COUNTING CROCHET STITCHES

Counting double crochet stitches: With the front of the last row facing, count the top of each stitch. If you are losing stitches as your crochet grows, then you are probably failing to work into the last stitch in the row below; if you are gaining stitches, you may have worked twice into the same stitch.

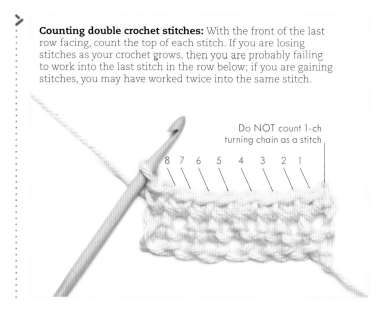

Do NOT count 1-ch turning chain as a stitch

8 7 6 5 4 3 2 1

Counting trebles: With the front of the last row facing, count the turning chain as the first stitch, then count the top of each treble. If you are losing stitches as your crochet grows, you are probably failing to work into the top of the turning chain; if you are gaining stitches, you may be working into the first treble of the row, instead of missing it.

8 7 6 5 4 3 2 1

Count 3-ch turning chain as a first stitch

TEXTURED CUSHION

Using a stylish yarn in a modern colourway, this simple but effective treble stitch cushion adds a touch of style to any room and can easily be completed by a beginner with minimal sewing skills.

TECHNIQUES USED Making a foundation chain **p.26**, Treble crochet **p.44**, Blocking and seams **p.68**

SIZE
40cm (16in) square

YARN
Erika Knight Vintage Wool – 50g/
 87m/95yds (100% wool; any
 "homespun", wool-rich yarn will
 work for this project)

x 1

HOOK
5mm hook

NOTIONS
Yarn needle
40cm (16in) square cushion pad and cover
Sewing needle and matching thread

TENSION
9 tr per 10cm (4in)

PATTERN
Work 40 ch.
Row 1: 1 tr into fourth ch from hook,
1 tr in each st to end, turn. (36sts)
Row 2: 3 ch, 1 tr in each tr to end, turn.
Repeat row 2 until work measures
40cm (16in).
Fasten off yarn, weave in ends.
Block the crocheted square carefully to
40cm (16in) square. Then sew it on to the
front of the cushion pad with a sewing
needle and the same yarn, using running or
over stitch. Finally, insert the cushion pad.

With the same yarn, sew the square on to the front of the cushion using running stitch or over stitch. Keep the stitches as close to the edge of the square as possible, so that they are invisible.

The striking texture of this cushion is created by the height of the treble stitches. Refer to pp.44–45 for more information on treble crochet.

DOUBLE TREBLE CROCHET (Abbreviation = dtr)

Worked in a very similar way to treble crochet, double treble crochet stitches are approximately one chain length taller because the stitch is begun by wrapping the yarn around the hook twice instead of only once (see p.67). Double trebles are often used in lace crochet (see pp.111–113), in crochet motifs (see pp.100–105), and in other fine cotton crochet patterns that require an open-textured result.

Double treble stitch Producing a double-sided fabric, either side can be used as the right side. This stitch worked in rows grows quickly because the stitches are taller but not that much slower to work.

1 Make a foundation chain, then wrap the yarn twice around the hook (yrh) and insert the hook through the fifth chain from the hook.

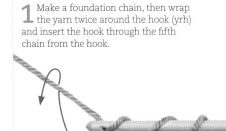

2 Yrh and draw a loop through the chain. There are now four loops on the hook. Yrh and draw a loop through the first two loops on the hook.

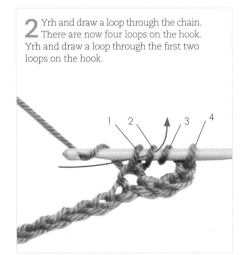

3 There are now three loops remaining. Yrh and draw a loop through the next two loops on the hook.

4 There are two loops remaining. Yrh and draw a loop through these final two loops.

5 This completes the first double treble. As for all tall crochet stitches, the missed chain stitches at the beginning of the foundation chain count as the first stitch of the foundation row.

Completed double treble crochet

Four missed chains at beginning count as first stitch of row

6 Work one double treble into each chain in the same way. Then turn the crochet and begin the second row with a four-chain turning chain.

7 Miss the top of the first double treble in the row below and work the first double treble into the top of the second stitch.

Top of first stitch

8 Work a double treble into each of the remaining double trebles in the row below. Work the last stitch of the row into the top of the four chains. Work following rows as for the second row.

TRIPLE TREBLE CROCHET (Abbreviation = trtr)

Stitches taller than double trebles are all worked in the same way as double trebles, except that the yarn is wrapped around the hook more times before the stitch is begun and they require taller turning chains. Once you have practised triple trebles and can work these easily, you will also be able to work quadruple and quintuple trebles without much effort. Triple treble stitch is a useful addition to your crochet repertoire.

Triple treble stitch This stitch worked in rows looks the same on both sides of the fabric. Notice how airy the crochet texture becomes as the basic stitches get taller.

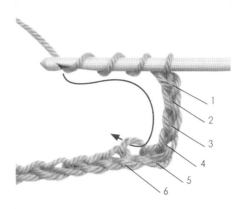

1 Wrap the yarn three times around the hook and insert the hook through the sixth stitch from the hook.

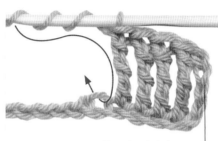

2 Work the loops off the hook two at a time as for double trebles. Remember to wrap the yarn three times around the hook before starting each stitch. Start following rows with five chains.

Five missed chains count as first stitch of row

QUADRUPLE TREBLE CROCHET (Abbreviation = qtr)

This stitch works in the same way as triple treble, except that the yarn is wound round the hook four times, and the hook is then inserted into the seventh stitch from the hook. The loops are then worked off two at a time, and following rows start with six chains.

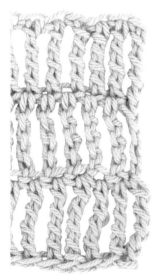

Quadruple treble crochet This stitch is noticeably taller than triple treble and also looks the same on both sides.

1 Once you know how to work the triple treble stitch, you can begin to see how each following stitch is worked. So, as a double treble wraps the yarn round the hook twice, so a triple treble wraps the yarn around three times. Therefore, a quadruple treble means you wrap the yarn around four times, and so on.

2 You work the loops off the hook in the same way as the double and triple treble, in pairs, until there is only the working loop left. Now you know the pattern, you can create a stitch as tall as you like.

STITCH HEIGHTS

Each of the next stitches gets taller progressively and is worked by wrapping the yarn around the hook once more than the previous stitch, before inserting the hook. See p.66 for a diagram with basic stitch symbols.

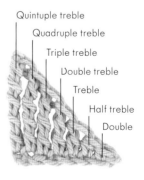

Quintuple treble
Quadruple treble
Triple treble
Double treble
Treble
Half treble
Double

SHAPING CROCHET

To progress from making simple squares and rectangles, a crocheter needs to know how to increase and decrease the number of stitches in the row to make shaped pieces of crocheted fabric. The most commonly used simple shaping techniques are illustrated in detail below.

❯ DOUBLE CROCHET INCREASES

Paired increases: Increases on garment pieces are most frequently worked as "paired increases" – an increase of one stitch at the beginning of the row and one at the end.

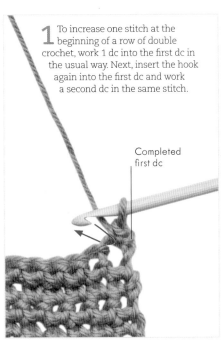

1 To increase one stitch at the beginning of a row of double crochet, work 1 dc into the first dc in the usual way. Next, insert the hook again into the first dc and work a second dc in the same stitch.

Completed first dc

2 This completes the increase. Continue across the row, working 1 dc into each dc in the usual way.

2 dc worked into same stitch

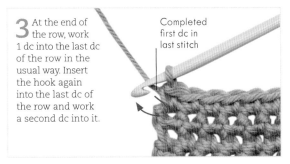

3 At the end of the row, work 1 dc into the last dc of the row in the usual way. Insert the hook again into the last dc of the row and work a second dc into it.

Completed first dc in last stitch

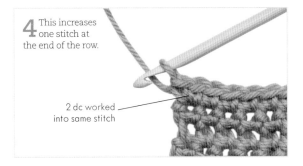

4 This increases one stitch at the end of the row.

2 dc worked into same stitch

❯ TREBLE CROCHET INCREASES

End of row: Increases on garment pieces made using treble crochet are worked using the same techniques as for double crochet. Again, these increases are most frequently worked as "paired increases" – one stitch is increased at each end of the row.

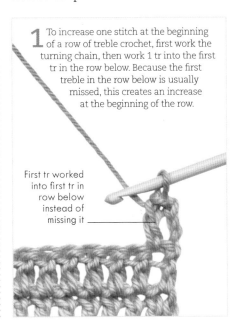

1 To increase one stitch at the beginning of a row of treble crochet, first work the turning chain, then work 1 tr into the first tr in the row below. Because the first treble in the row below is usually missed, this creates an increase at the beginning of the row.

First tr worked into first tr in row below instead of missing it

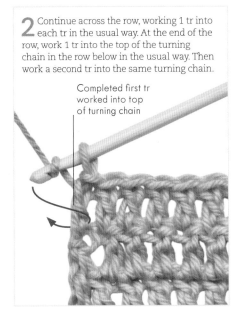

2 Continue across the row, working 1 tr into each tr in the usual way. At the end of the row, work 1 tr into the top of the turning chain in the row below in the usual way. Then work a second tr into the same turning chain.

Completed first tr worked into top of turning chain

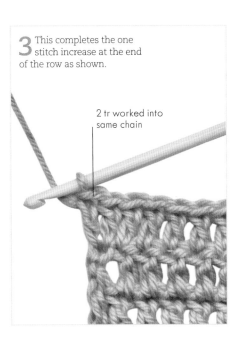

3 This completes the one stitch increase at the end of the row as shown.

2 tr worked into same chain

STEP INCREASE AT BEGINNING OF ROW

1 Increases are also frequently worked in crochet so that they form little steps at the edge. As an example, to add a three-stitch step increase at the beginning of a row of double crochet, begin by making four chains as shown here. (Always make one chain more than the number of extra double crochets required.)

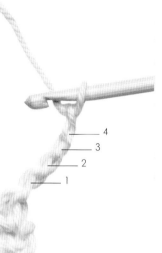

2 Work the first dc into the second chain from the hook. Then work 1 dc into each of the remaining two chains. This creates a 3-dc increase at the beginning of the row.

3 Continue the row in the usual way, working 1 dc into each dc in the row below. Any number of stitches can be added in this way and the same technique can be used for taller stitches.

Completed 3-dc increase

1-ch turning chain

STEP INCREASE AT END OF ROW

1 Before starting the row with the step increase at the end, remove the hook from the loop at the beginning of the row. Then, using a short length of matching yarn, place a slip knot on a spare hook and draw this loop through the last stitch in the row.

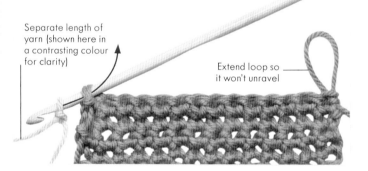

Separate length of yarn (shown here in a contrasting colour for clarity)

Extend loop so it won't unravel

2 There is now one loop on the hook – this forms the first extra chain at the end of the row. Continue making chains until you have made as many as the required number of extra stitches.

3 So for a three-stitch step increase, make a total of three chains. Then fasten off.

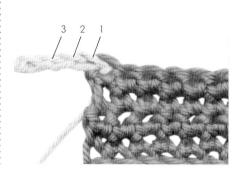

4 Return to the beginning of the row, slip the loop back onto the hook and tighten it, then work to the end of the row in the usual way until you reach the added chains.

5 Work 1 dc into each of the three added chains. This creates a 3-dc increase. Any number of stitches can be added in this way and the same technique can be used for taller stitches.

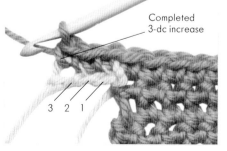

Completed 3-dc increase

DOUBLE CROCHET DECREASES (Abbreviation = dc2tog)

Paired decreases: Decreases on garment pieces, like increases, are most frequently worked as "paired decreases" – a decrease of one stitch at the beginning of the row and another at the end.

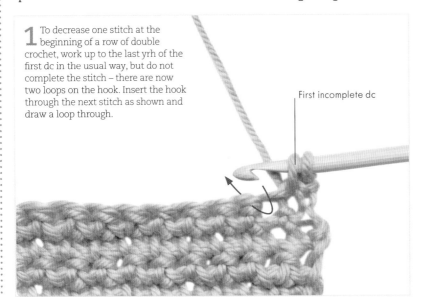

1 To decrease one stitch at the beginning of a row of double crochet, work up to the last yrh of the first dc in the usual way, but do not complete the stitch – there are now two loops on the hook. Insert the hook through the next stitch as shown and draw a loop through.

First incomplete dc

2 There are now three loops on the hook. Wrap the yarn around the hook and draw a loop through all three loops at once as shown.

Second incomplete dc

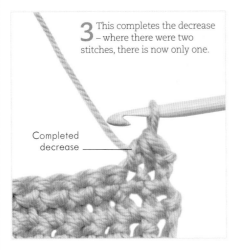

3 This completes the decrease – where there were two stitches, there is now only one.

Completed decrease

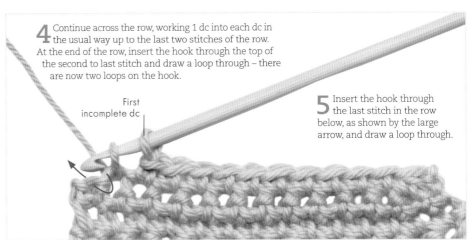

4 Continue across the row, working 1 dc into each dc in the usual way up to the last two stitches of the row. At the end of the row, insert the hook through the top of the second to last stitch and draw a loop through – there are now two loops on the hook.

First incomplete dc

5 Insert the hook through the last stitch in the row below, as shown by the large arrow, and draw a loop through.

6 There are now three loops on the hook. Wrap the yarn around the hook and draw a loop through all three loops at once as shown.

Second incomplete dc

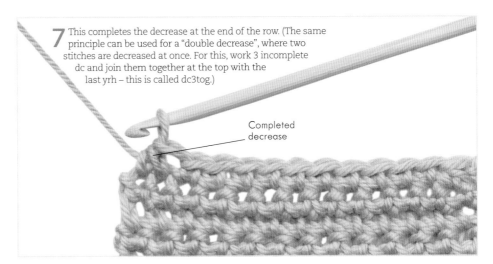

7 This completes the decrease at the end of the row. (The same principle can be used for a "double decrease", where two stitches are decreased at once. For this, work 3 incomplete dc and join them together at the top with the last yrh – this is called dc3tog.)

Completed decrease

❯ TREBLE CROCHET DECREASES (Abbreviation = tr2tog)

1 To decrease one stitch at the beginning of a row of treble crochet, first work the turning chain. Miss the first tr and work 1 tr in each of the next 2 tr, but only up to the last yrh of each stitch. Draw a loop through all three loops at once as shown.

2 This completes the decrease – where there were two stitches, there is now only one.

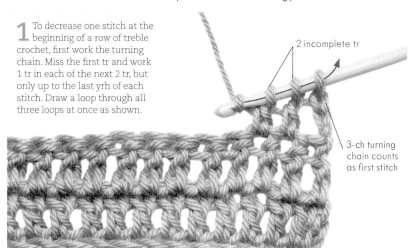

2 incomplete tr

3-ch turning chain counts as first stitch

Completed decrease

3 Continue across the row in the usual way up to the last tr in the row below. Now work a tr into the last tr but only up to the last yrh. Wrap the yarn around the hook and insert the hook into the top of the turning chain in the row below as shown.

4 Work the tr in the top of the chain up to the last yrh of the stitch. There are now three loops on the hook. Wrap the yarn around the hook and draw a loop through all three loops at once as shown.

5 This completes the decrease at the end of the row. (The same principle can be used for a "double decrease", where two stitches are decreased at once. For this, work 3 incomplete tr and join them together at the top with the last yrh – this is called tr3tog.)

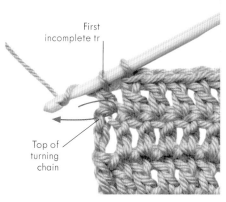

First incomplete tr

Top of turning chain

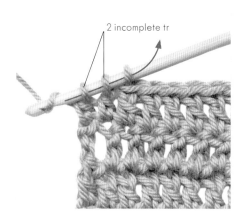

2 incomplete tr

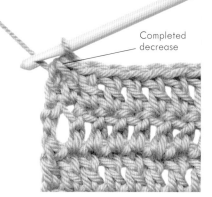

Completed decrease

❯ STEP DECREASES

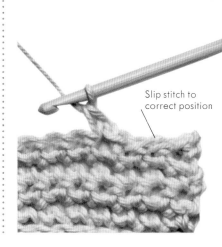

Slip stitch to correct position

At beginning of row Decreases, like increases, can also be worked so that they form little steps at the edge. As an example, to decrease three stitches at the beginning of a row of double crochet, work one chain and then one slip stitch into each of the first 4 dc. Next, work one chain, then work the first dc in the same place where the last slip stitch was worked. Continue along the row in the usual way.

At end of row For a three-stitch step decrease at the end of the row, simply work up to the last three stitches at the end of the row and turn, leaving the last three stitches unworked. This technique can be used for all crochet stitches.

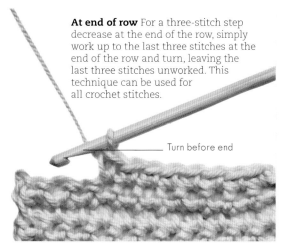

Turn before end

PARTY BUNTING

Making triangles is great for practising double crochet increases. Begin with a small number of stitches, then increase at each end until you have the desired triangle shape. Bunting is a super project to utilize the resulting shapes.

TECHNIQUES USED Double crochet **p.34**, Double crochet increases **p.50**, Double crochet edging **p.86**

SIZE
Approx 14 x 14cm (5½ x 5½in) at the widest and longest points. Using 16 evenly spaced triangles, the bunting measures approx 3.5m (138in) long

YARN
Patons 100% Cotton DK – 100g/210m/230yds (100% cotton; you can use any DK weight yarn to create the same effect, but you can use different weights to create differently sized triangles)

A x 1   **B** x 1   **C** x 1   **D** x 1

HOOK
4mm hook

NOTIONS
Yarn needle

TENSION
Exact tension is not essential

❯ PATTERN
Make six triangles in yarn A and five triangles each of B and C. Work 2 ch.
Row 1: 1 dc into second ch from hook
Row 2: 1 ch, 3 dc into next dc. (3sts)
Row 3: 1 ch, dc in each dc to end.
Row 4: 1 ch, 2 dc in first dc, dc to last dc, 2 dc in last dc. (5sts)
Rep last 2 rows until you have 25 sts.
Work straight on these 25sts for six rows, do not turn, but work two further stitches into the last dc, then work evenly in dc

down the edge of the point, work 3 dc into the point of the triangle, work up other side of the point evenly in dc, join to the top row of dc with a ss.
Fasten off yarn, weave in ends.

FINISHING
With yarn D, work a chain of 35cm (13¾in) long, then work evenly in dc along the top of one yarn A triangle, then work 10 ch and work in dc along a yarn B triangle; now work 10 ch and then work in dc along a yarn C triangle. Continue in this way, joining the triangles in this colour pattern, and finish with a red triangle.
Work a ch of 36cm (14in) long, turn. Miss 10 ch, dc into next ch, then into each ch to first triangle.
Work along the triangles and chains in dc to final 6 ch, work 5 ch, miss next 5 ch, then work 1 dc into last ch.
Fasten off yarn, weave in ends.

Using a neutral yarn, such as white, for the double crochet chain helps to emphasize the colourful triangles and makes for a neat and attractive finish.

1 Crochet a length of chain stitches, 35cm (13¾in) long. Starting at one corner of a triangle, insert the hook through the first stitch to work the first double crochet.

2 Work a row of double crochet stitches along the top of the first triangle. Work 10 more chains before attaching the next triangle with double crochet stitches.

WORKING IN THE ROUND

Making a simple circle is a good example for how other flat motif shapes are started and then worked round and round from the centre. The circle is also used in conjunction with the crochet tube to make containers (see p.164 and 166) or the parts of toys, so it is well worth practising.

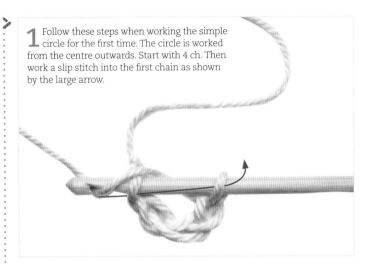

1 Follow these steps when working the simple circle for the first time. The circle is worked from the centre outwards. Start with 4 ch. Then work a slip stitch into the first chain as shown by the large arrow.

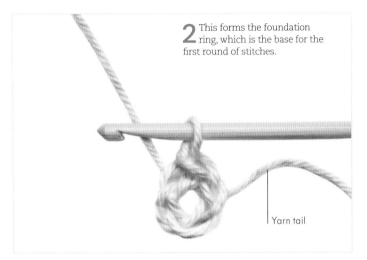

2 This forms the foundation ring, which is the base for the first round of stitches.

Yarn tail

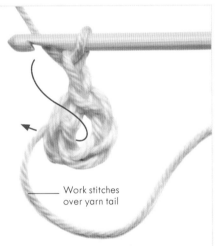

3 For a double crochet circle, start the first round with one chain. Then lay the yarn end around the top of the chain and start working the double crochet stitches of the first round through the centre of the ring and around the yarn tail.

Work stitches over yarn tail

4 When all eight double crochet stitches of the first round are complete, mark the last stitch of the round with a stitch marker as shown. Then pull the yarn tail to close the centre hole and clip it off close to the crochet.

Clip off yarn tail

Safety pin stitch marker

5 Work 2 dc into each dc in the second round as explained in the pattern, working the last 2 dc into the top of the marked stitch in the last round. Then count your stitches to make sure there are sixteen in total. Continue the pattern until the circle is the required size.

Move marker to last stitch at end of every round

TIPS FOR MOTIFS

The principle for starting any motif shape and working it in rounds is the same as for the simple circle, and many simple crochet flowers are also worked using these techniques (see pp.104–105). If you find it awkward to fit all the stitches of the first round into a tiny foundation ring (see opposite), try the simple adjustable ring below. Two other useful tips are the techniques for starting new colours and for joining motifs together (see below).

❯ MAKING A SIMPLE ADJUSTABLE RING

1 Making the simple adjustable ring is a quick way to start working a flat shape in the round, and it allows you to make the centre hole as tight or as open as desired. Start as if you are making a slip knot (see p.25), by forming a circle of yarn and drawing the yarn through the centre of it.

2 Leave the circle of yarn open. Then, to start a round of double crochet stitches, make one chain.

3 Work the first round of double crochet stitches, working them into the ring and over the yarn tail as shown by the large arrow.

4 When all the required stitches are worked into the ring, pull the yarn tail gently to close the ring. Then continue as explained in the pattern instructions.

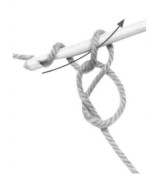
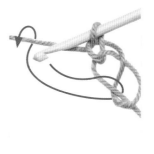
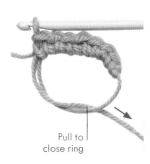

Pull to
close ring

❯ JOINING ON A NEW COLOUR

When starting a new colour at the beginning of a motif round, you can either change to the new colour with the last yrh of the previous round, or fasten off the old colour and join on a new colour with a slip stitch.

1 Joining on the new colour with a slip stitch makes a firm attachment. Make a slip knot with the new colour and remove it from the hook. Then insert the hook at the specified position and draw the slip knot through.

2 Start the new round with the specified number of chains, drawing the first chain through the slip knot. Work the stitches of the round over both yarn tails (the new colour and the old colour), so that there aren't many ends to darn in later. Alternatively, to educe bulk, start the new colour in a different place and weave in one tail at a time.

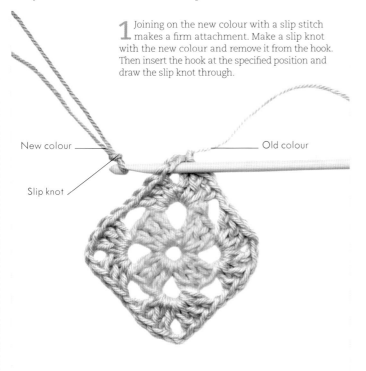

New colour

Old colour

Slip knot

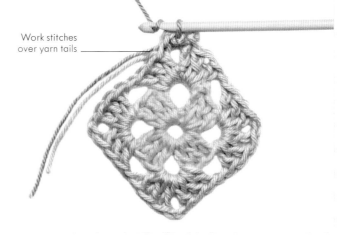

Work stitches
over yarn tails

COASTER SET

Level of difficulty ✱✱✱

Cotton is lightweight and a good insulator, which makes these coasters ideal table protectors. Work each coaster in rounds of simple trebles, working the stitches into the chain spaces from the previous round.

TECHNIQUES USED Double crochet **p.34** Treble crochet **p.44**, Working in the round **p.56**, Joining on a new colour **p.57**, Working into a chain space **p.75**

SIZE
Approx 11cm (4¼in) in diameter

YARN
Rowan Handknit Cotton – 50g/85m/93yds (100% cotton; any DK weight non-mercerized cotton would be a good substitute for this project)

A x 1   **B** x 1   **C** x 1   **D** x 1   **E** x 1

HOOK
3.75mm hook

NOTIONS
Yarn needle

TENSION
Exact tension is not essential

PATTERN
Note: This pattern uses two shades in any combination of A, B, C, D for the main part, with the trim crocheted in E.

With yarn A, work 4 ch, ss in first chain to form a ring.
Round 1: 3 ch, 1 tr, *1 ch, 2 tr, rep from * four times, (6 tr pairs made). Join with a ss into top of 3 ch. Fasten off A.
Round 2: Join B into any ch sp, 3 ch, 1 tr, 1 ch, 2 tr in same ch sp, *1 ch, 2 tr, 1 ch, 2 tr in next ch sp, rep from * 4 times join with a ss into top of 3 ch. Fasten off B. (6 tr pairs and 12-ch sp)
Round 3: Join A into any ch sp, 3 ch, 2 tr into same ch sp, *1 ch, 3 tr into next ch sp, rep from * to end, join with a ss into top of 3 ch. Fasten off A. (12 3-tr and 12-ch sp)
Round 4: Join B into any ch sp, work as for round 3. Fasten off B. (12 3-tr and 12-ch sp)
Round 5: Join E into any ch sp, 1 ch, * work 1 dc into top of each tr, 1 dc in ch sp, repeat from * to end, join with a ss into top of first ch. Fasten off yarn.
Repeat the pattern using shades C, D, and E, plus A, C, and E to make more coasters.

FINISHING
Weave in all ends and press according to the ballband instructions to ensure the coaster lies flat.

1 To join on a new colour, insert the hook into a chain space, wrap the yarn round the hook and pull it through to the right side of the coaster.

2 Then make a chain to secure the new yarn in place. Work two further chains to complete the first three chains, then continue with the pattern as usual.

3 For the edging, join the new colour in the same way as the other colours. Work one double crochet into each treble and chain space around. Join with a slip stitch.

TECHNIQUES

POT HOLDER

Level of difficulty

This pot holder will make a stylish addition to any kitchen. The scalloped trim adds a challenge, but you can make an easier version without it. Use washable yarn so you can pop it in the washing machine every so often.

TECHNIQUES USED Using slip stitch to form a foundation ring **p.28**, Treble crochet **p.44**, Treble crochet increases **p.50**, Working in the round **p.56**

SIZE
Striped: 20cm (8in) in diameter
Scalloped: 22cm (8¾in) in diameter

YARN
Debbie Bliss Cotton DK – 50g/84m/91yds (100% cotton; any DK weight non-mercerized cotton will suit this project)

A x 1   B x 1   C x 1   D x 1

HOOK
4mm hook

NOTIONS
Yarn needle

TENSION
Rounds 1–3 measure 8cm (3in)

PATTERN (MAKE 2)
With yarn C, work 4 ch, join with a ss to form a ring.
Round 1 right side (RS): 3 ch (counts as first tr), 11 tr into ring, 1 ss in third of first 3 ch, fasten off C. (12sts)
Round 2 (RS): Join A into top of any tr, 3 ch, 1 tr in same place as join, 2 tr in each tr to end of round, 1 ss in top of first 3 ch, fasten off A. (24sts)
Continue working in rounds as follows, always with RS facing:
Round 3: Join B into top of any tr, 3 ch, 1 tr in same place as join, *1 tr in next tr, 2 tr in each of next 2 tr, rep from * to last 2 tr, 1 tr in next tr, 2 tr in last tr, 1 ss in third of first 3 ch, fasten off B. (40sts)
Round 4: Join D into top of any tr, 3 ch, 1 tr in same place as join, *1 tr in each of next 3 tr, 2 tr in next tr, rep from * to last 3 tr, 1 tr in each of last 3 tr, ss in top of first 3 ch, fasten off D. (50sts)
Round 5: Join A into top of any tr, 3 ch, 1 tr in same place as join, *1 tr in each of next 4 tr, 2 tr in next tr, rep from * to last 4 tr, 1 tr in each of last 4 tr, 1 ss in top of first 3 ch, fasten off A. (60sts)

Round 6: Join B into top of any tr, 3 ch, 1 tr in same place as join, *1 tr in each of next 5 tr, 2 tr in next tr, rep from * to last 5 tr, 1 tr in each of last 5 tr, ss in top of first 3 ch, fasten off B. (70sts)
Round 7: Join D into top of any tr, 3 ch, 1 tr in same place as join, *1 tr in each of next 6 tr, 2 tr in next tr, rep from * to last 6 tr, 1 tr in each of last tr, ss in top of first 3 ch, fasten off D. (80sts)

FINISHING
Weave in all ends and, with wrong sides facing, rejoin C into top of any treble (working through both pieces), 1 dc in each tr to end of round. (80 dc) Do not fasten off. Make hanging loop as follows: 12 ch, miss 6 dc, ss in next dc. Fasten off C. Weave in loose ends.

SCALLOP INSTRUCTIONS
Do not turn work, *miss next dc, 5 tr in next dc, miss 1 dc, 1 ss in next dc, rep from * to end, finishing with a ss. Make hanging loop as follows: 12 ch, miss next 5 tr, ss into next st. Fasten off yarn, weave in ends.

CIRCULAR CUSHION

The perfect project to practise working in the round, this cushion uses the simplest of stitches, a double crochet, and uses basic increasing to work flat circles. The circles are joined with a slip stitch crochet join.

TECHNIQUES USED Using slip stitch to form a foundation ring **p.28**, Double crochet increases **p.50**, Working in the round **p.56**, Slip stitch seam **p.70**

SIZE
Approx 35cm (13¾in) in diameter

YARN
Sirdar Simply Recycled Aran – 50g/
93m/102yds (51% recycled cotton and
49% acrylic; you can use any aran
weight yarn for this project, or a
differing weight yarn to create a
larger or smaller cushion cover)

x 4

HOOK
5mm hook

NOTIONS
Stitch marker
Yarn needle
35cm (13¾in) round cushion pad

TENSION
Exact tension is not essential

PATTERN (MAKE 2)
Note: This cushion is worked in spirals. Do not join rounds, but place a marker at the first stitch of the round, moving it each round to mark the beginning of the round.

Work 2 ch and 6 dc into second ch from hook, join round with a ss to first st.
Round 1: 1 ch, work 2 dc in each st around, do not join round, place marker. (12sts)
Round 2: *2 dc in next st, 1 dc in next st; rep from * to end. (18sts)
Round 3: *2 dc in next st, dc in next 2sts; rep from * to end. (24sts)
Round 4: *2 dc in next st, dc in next 3sts; rep from * to end. (30sts)
Round 5: *2 dc in next st, dc in next 4sts; rep from * to end. (36sts)
Round 6: *2 dc in next st, dc in next 5sts; rep from * to end. (42sts)
Continue in this way, working one extra st between increases for each round until you have worked 23 rounds and have 144sts. If you want a larger cushion, you can continue increasing in this way until the desired size is achieved.
Join round with a ss.
Fasten off yarn, weave in ends.

FINISHING
Block pieces lightly. Arrange with wrong sides together, attach yarn to both pieces along edge, inserting the hook into a whole stitch of each circular piece. Work a slip stitch join around edge, trapping cushion pad in between when you have worked approximately halfway around the circumference.

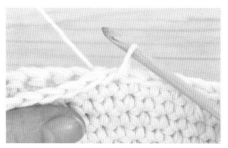

1 To make up the cushion, place the circles with wrong sides together and attach the yarn to the front piece with a slip stitch.

2 Insert the hook through both loops of the next stitch of front piece and through both loops of the corresponding stitch on back. Yarn round the hook and pull through both stitches and loop on hook to make a slip stitch.

3 When you are about halfway, stuff the cushion pad into the middle of the two rounds and continue slip stitching through both sides, joining the last stitch to the first with a slip stitch.

FOLLOWING A CROCHET PATTERN

Followed step by step and slowly, crochet patterns are not as difficult to understand as they appear. The guides here, for a simple accessory and a garment, give many tips for how to approach your first crochet patterns. This section also includes other techniques needed for working from a crochet pattern – finishings such as edgings and button loops, blocking and seams, and darning in yarn.

SIMPLE ACCESSORY PATTERNS

A beginner should choose an easy accessory pattern for a first crochet project. A striped cushion cover is given here as an example. Follow the numbered tips of the guide to familiarize yourself with the parts of a simple pattern.

The skill level required for the crochet is given at the beginning of most patterns. When starting out, work several easy patterns before progressing to the intermediate level.

Check the size of the finished item. If it is a simple square like this cushion, you can easily adjust the size by adding or subtracting stitches and rows.

Try to use the yarn specified. But if you are unable to obtain this yarn, choose a substitute yarn.

Make a tension swatch before starting to crochet and change the hook size if necessary (see opposite).

Instructions for working a piece of crocheted fabric always start with how many chains to make for the foundation chain and which yarn or hook size to use. If there is only one hook size and one yarn, these may be absent here.

Consult the abbreviations list with your pattern for the meanings of abbreviations (see p.81).

The back of a cushion cover is sometimes exactly the same as the front or it may have a fabric back. In this example, the stripes are reversed on the back for a more versatile cover.

After all the crocheted pieces are completed, follow the Finishing (or Making Up) section of the pattern.

STRIPED CUSHION COVER

Skill level
Easy

Size of finished cushion
40.5 x 40.5cm (16 x 16in)

Materials
7 x 25g/⅞oz (110m/120yds) balls of branded Scottish Tweed 4-ply in Thatch 00018 **(A)** 4 x 25g/⅞oz (110m/120yds) balls of branded Scottish Tweed 4-ply in Skye 00009 **(B)** 3.5mm (US size E-4) crochet hook Cushion pad to fit finished cover.

Tension
22 sts and 24 rows to 10cm (4in) over double crochet using 3.5mm (US size E-4) hook or size necessary to achieve correct tension. To save time, check tension.

Front
With 3.5mm (US size E-4) hook and yarn A, make 89 ch.
Row 1 1 dc in second ch from hook, 1 dc in each of rem ch, turn. (88sts)
Row 2 1 ch (does not count as a st), 1 dc in each dc to end, turn.
Rep row 2 throughout to form dc fabric.
Always changing to new colour with last yrh of last dc of previous row, work in stripes as follows: 26 rows more in A, 8 rows B, (8 rows A, 8 rows B) twice, 28 rows A. Fasten off.

Back
Work as for Front, but use B for A, and A for B.

Finishing
Darn in loose ends.
Block and press lightly on wrong side, following instructions on yarn label.
With WS facing, sew three sides of back and front together. Turn right-side out, insert cushion pad, and sew remaining seam.

Always purchase the same total amount in metres/yards of a substitute yarn; NOT the same amount in weight.

Select different colours, if desired, to suit your décor; the colours specified are just suggestions.

Alter the hook size if you cannot achieve the correct tension with the specified size (see left).

Extra items needed for your project are usually listed under Materials, Notions, or Extras.

Work in the specified stitch pattern, for the specified number of rows or cm/in.

Colours for stripes are always changed at the end of the previous row before the colour change so the first turning chain of the new stripe is in the correct colour (see p.39).

Fastening off completes the crochet piece.

See p.70 for how to darn in loose ends.

Make sure you look at the yarn label instructions before attempting to press any piece of crochet. The label may say that the yarn cannot be pressed or it can be pressed only with a cool iron. (See p.68 for blocking tips.)

See pp.68–70 for seaming options. Take time with seams on crochet, and when working your very first seams, get an experienced crocheter to help you.

GARMENT PATTERNS

Garment instructions usually start with the Skill Level, followed by the Sizes, Materials, Tension, and finally the Instructions. Most important for successfully making a garment – or other fitted items such as hats, mittens, gloves, and socks – is choosing the right size and making a tension swatch.

❯ CHOOSING A GARMENT SIZE

Sizing advice: Crochet garment sizes are usually listed as specific bust/chest sizes or in generic terms as Small, Medium, Large. (Children's sweater sizes are given in ages and chest sizes.) The best advice is not to stick strictly to choosing your preferred size by this criteria. Decide instead how you want the garment to fit you – how close-fitting or loose-fitting it should be. If you are planning to crochet a sweater, find one in your wardrobe that is comfortable and flattering and has a fabric weight and shape similar to the garment you are going to crochet. Smooth out the sweater and measure the width. Find the same, or closest, width to this on the sweater diagram of your crochet pattern – this is the size for you.

Make a photocopy of your pattern and circle or highlight all the figures that apply to your size throughout the pattern, starting with the number of balls of yarn to purchase, followed by the number of chains in the foundation chain for the sweater back, the length to the armhole, and so on. The figure for the smallest size is given first and all the figures for the larger sizes follow in parentheses. Where there is only one figure given in the instructions – be it a measurement, the number of rows, or the number of stitches – this figure applies to all sizes. Before starting your crochet, always check your tension (see below).

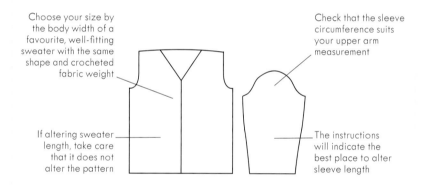

Choose your size by the body width of a favourite, well-fitting sweater with the same shape and crocheted fabric weight

If altering sweater length, take care that it does not alter the pattern

Check that the sleeve circumference suits your upper arm measurement

The instructions will indicate the best place to alter sleeve length

❯ TIPS

Choose a skill level that suits your crochet experience. If in doubt or if you haven't crocheted for many years, stick to an Easy or Beginner's level until you are confident that you can go to the next level.

White is a good colour to use for your first crocheted sweater because the stitches are so easy to see clearly. But if you do choose white yarn, be sure to wash your hands every time you start crocheting; and when you stop, put away the yarn and sweater in a bag to keep it from becoming soiled.

Avoid black or other very dark yarn for a first crocheted sweater as the stitches are very difficult to distinguish, even for an accomplished crocheter.

Purchase yarn balls that have the same dye lot number (see p.15).

Have a set of hook sizes at hand if you are starting to crochet sweaters. When checking tension (see below), you may need other hook sizes in order to achieve the correct tension.

Always make the pieces in the order given in the instructions, whether you are crocheting a garment, accessory, or toy. On a garment, the back is usually crocheted first, followed by the front (or fronts, if it is a cardigan or jacket), and lastly the sleeves. Pockets that are integrated into the fronts are crocheted before the fronts and those applied as patches are worked last.

Beginners should take care when modifying patterns as sizing/shaping and stitch patterns are often worked out in detail by the pattern designer and may turn out very differently if altered. However, beginners should not be afraid to try modifying a pattern to suit their preferences, as it can always be pulled back if it does not work as planned.

MEASURING TENSION

It is essential to check your tension (stitch size) before beginning a crochet pattern if the final size of the piece matters. Not everyone crochets stitches with exactly the same tightness or looseness, so you may well need to use a different hook size to achieve the stitch size required by your pattern.

❯ **1** Using the specified hook, crochet a swatch about 13cm (5in) square. Mark 10cm (4in) across the centre with pins and count the number of stitches between the pins.

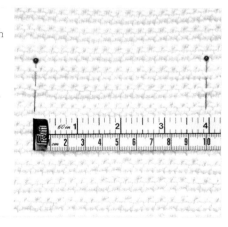

2 Count the number of rows to 10cm (4in) in the same way. If you have fewer stitches and rows than you should, try again with a smaller hook size; if you have more, change to a larger hook size. Use the hook size that best matches the correct tension. (Matching the stitch width is much more important than matching the row height.)

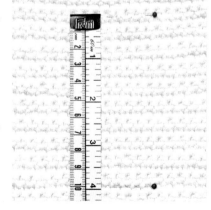

TECHNIQUES

BASIC STITCHES IN SYMBOLS AND ABBREVIATIONS

Crochet row instructions can be written out with abbreviations or using symbols for the stitches. There is a more detailed explanation for reading stitch pattern instructions on p.80, but directions for the basic stitches are given in this section in both symbols and abbreviations. This provides an introduction to crochet instructions and a quick reference for how to work crochet fabrics with basic stitches. Please note that left-handed crocheters will need to work the diagram backwards. (There are basic instructions for left-handed crocheters on how to hold the hook and yarn on p.24.)

⟩ STITCH HEIGHTS

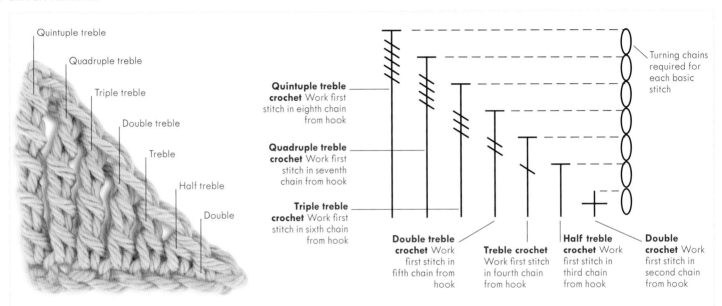

Quintuple treble

Quadruple treble

Triple treble

Double treble

Treble

Half treble

Double

Quintuple treble crochet Work first stitch in eighth chain from hook

Quadruple treble crochet Work first stitch in seventh chain from hook

Triple treble crochet Work first stitch in sixth chain from hook

Double treble crochet Work first stitch in fifth chain from hook

Treble crochet Work first stitch in fourth chain from hook

Half treble crochet Work first stitch in third chain from hook

Double crochet Work first stitch in second chain from hook

Turning chains required for each basic stitch

Stitch symbols: The diagram, above right, shows all the basic stitches in symbols and illustrates approximately how tall the stitches are when standing side by side. A double crochet is roughly one chain tall, a half treble crochet two chains tall, a treble crochet three chains tall, and so on. (The picture, above left, shows what each stitch actually looks like.) These heights determine the number of turning chains you need to work at the beginning of each row for each of the basic stitches. The diagonal bars are useful as they indicate how many times you need to wrap the yarn around the hook before working the stitch. Also provided here is a reference for which chain to work into when working the first stitch into the foundation chain.

⟩ DOUBLE CROCHET INSTRUCTIONS

Double symbol: Crochet symbol instructions, especially for the basic stitches, are very easy to understand. Roughly imitating the size and shape of the stitch, the symbols are read from the bottom of the diagram upwards. To get used to very simple crochet instructions, try working double crochet following the written directions and the symbol diagram at the same time (see p.81 for abbreviations list), then try this with the other basic stitches as well.

Double crochet in abbreviations
Make any number of ch.
Row 1 1 dc in second ch from hook, 1 dc in each of rem ch to end, turn.
Row 2 1 ch (does NOT count as a st), 1 dc in each dc to end, turn.
Rep row 2 to form dc fabric.

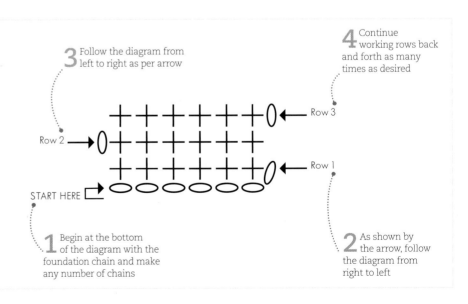

3 Follow the diagram from left to right as per arrow

4 Continue working rows back and forth as many times as desired

Row 2 →

Row 3

Row 1

START HERE

1 Begin at the bottom of the diagram with the foundation chain and make any number of chains

2 As shown by the arrow, follow the diagram from right to left

HALF TREBLE CROCHET INSTRUCTIONS

Half treble symbol: The symbol for half treble is a vertical line with a horizontal bar at the top, and it is about twice as tall as the double crochet symbol, just like the stitch is in reality. Read the written instructions for this basic stitch (below) and look at the chart at the same time. The direction of each arrow indicates whether to read the chart from left to right or right to left.

Half treble crochet in abbreviations
Make any number of ch.
Row 1 1 htr in third ch from hook, 1 htr in each of rem ch to end, turn.
Row 2 2 ch (counts as first st), miss first htr in row below, *1 htr in next htr; rep from * to end, then work 1 htr in top of 2 ch at end, turn.
Rep row 2 to form htr fabric.

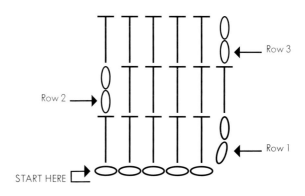

TREBLE CROCHET INSTRUCTIONS

Treble symbol: The treble symbol has a short diagonal line across its "waist". The diagram shows clearly how the 3-ch turning chain counts as the first stitch of each row.

Treble crochet in abbreviations
Make any number of ch.
Row 1 1 tr in fourth ch from hook, 1 tr in each of rem ch to end, turn.
Row 2 3 ch (counts as first tr), miss first tr in row below, *1 tr in next tr; rep from * to end, then work 1 tr in top of 3 ch at end, turn.
Rep row 2 to form tr fabric.

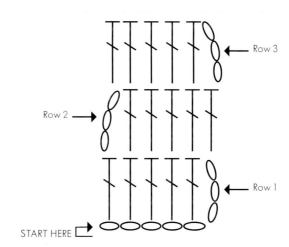

DOUBLE TREBLE CROCHET INSTRUCTIONS

Double treble symbol: Two short diagonal lines cross the "waist" of the double treble symbol, echoing the two diagonal yarn strands on the stitch itself.

Double treble crochet in abbreviations
Make any number of ch.
Row 1 1 dtr in fifth ch from hook, 1 dtr in each of rem ch to end, turn.
Row 2 4 ch (counts as first dtr), miss first dtr in row below, *1 dtr in next dtr; rep from * to end, then work 1 dtr in top of 4 ch at end, turn.
Rep row 2 to form dtr fabric.

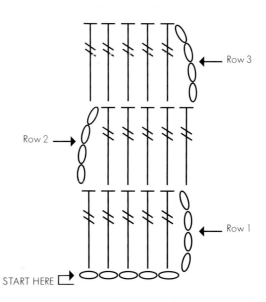

BLOCKING AND SEAMS

Always sew the seams on a garment or accessory using a blunt-ended needle and a matching yarn (a contrasting yarn is used here just to show the seam techniques more clearly); work them in the order given in the crochet pattern. But before sewing any seams, block your crochet pieces carefully. Press the finished seams very lightly with a cool iron on the wrong side after completion.

WET BLOCKING

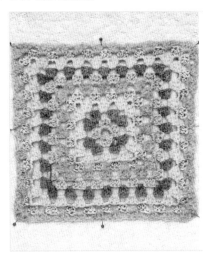

Using water: If your yarn will allow it, wet blocking is the best way to even out crochet. Wet the pieces in a sink full of lukewarm water. Then squeeze out the water and roll the crochet in a towel to remove excess dampness. Smooth the crochet into shape right-side down on layers of dry towels covered with a sheet, pinning at intervals. Add as many pins as is necessary to refine the shape. Do not move the crochet until it is completely dry.

STEAM BLOCKING

Using steam: For a speedier process, you may prefer steam blocking (if your yarn label allows it). First, pin the crochet right-side down into the correct shape. Then steam the crochet gently using a clean damp cloth, but barely touching the cloth with the iron. Never rest the weight of an iron on your crochet or it will flatten the texture. Leave the steamed piece to dry completely before unpinning it.

BACKSTITCH SEAM

Backstitch produces durable seams and is frequently recommended in crochet patterns for garments, accessories, and toys.

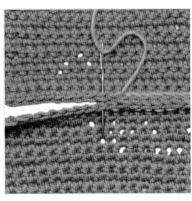

1 Align the crochet pieces with right sides together and secure the yarn with two or three overcast stitches in the same place. Then, inserting the needle close to the edge, work the seam taking one stitch forwards and one stitch back.

2 On the backwards stitch, be sure to insert the needle through the same place as the end of the last stitch. At the end of the seam, secure the yarn in the same way as at the beginning of the seam.

OVERCAST STITCH SEAM (ALSO CALLED WHIP STITCH)

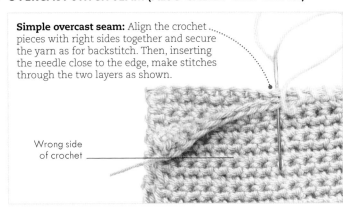

Simple overcast seam: Align the crochet pieces with right sides together and secure the yarn as for backstitch. Then, inserting the needle close to the edge, make stitches through the two layers as shown.

Wrong side of crochet

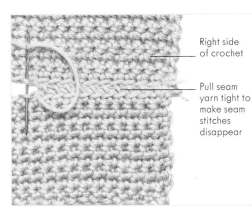

Right side of crochet

Pull seam yarn tight to make seam stitches disappear

Flat overcast seam: For a flat seam along the tops of stitches, lay the pieces right-side up and edge-to-edge. Work as for the simple overcast seam, but insert the needle through only the back loops of the stitches.

EDGE-TO-EDGE SEAM (ALSO CALLED MATTRESS STITCH)

This method creates a neat, flat seam line. It can be used, as here, on treble crochet as well as on all other types of crochet fabrics.

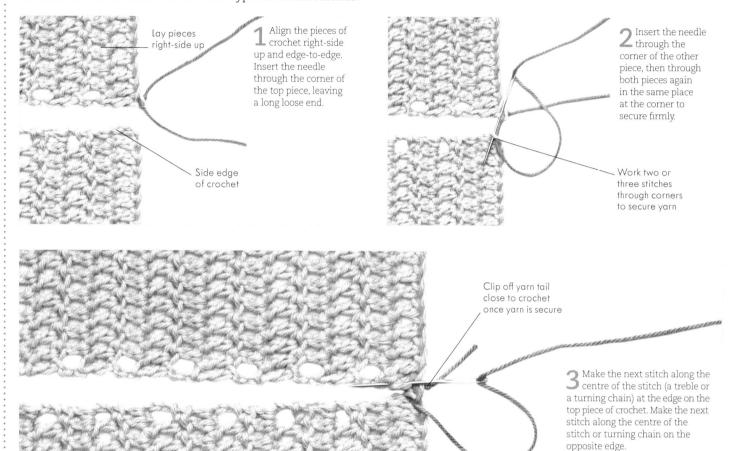

Lay pieces right-side up

Side edge of crochet

1 Align the pieces of crochet right-side up and edge-to-edge. Insert the needle through the corner of the top piece, leaving a long loose end.

2 Insert the needle through the corner of the other piece, then through both pieces again in the same place at the corner to secure firmly.

Work two or three stitches through corners to secure yarn

Clip off yarn tail close to crochet once yarn is secure

3 Make the next stitch along the centre of the stitch (a treble or a turning chain) at the edge on the top piece of crochet. Make the next stitch along the centre of the stitch or turning chain on the opposite edge.

4 Make the next pair of stitches in the same way, working a stitch along one stitch or turning chain on the top piece, then, on the opposite piece.

5 Continue along the seam, taking a stitch in each side alternately. Take shorter stitches on each piece if the yarn used for the pieces is bulky.

6 After every few stitches, pull the yarn tight so that the seam yarn disappears and is not visible on the right side of the crochet.

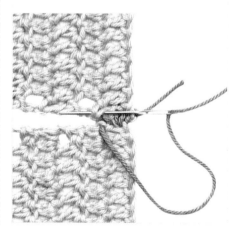 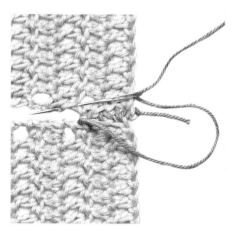 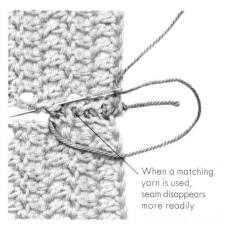

When a matching yarn is used, seam disappears more readily

DARNING IN YARN

Darning in along top row: Using a blunt-ended yarn needle, darn the yarn end through the centre of the base of six to eight stitches in the last row. Clip off the remaining end close to the fabric.

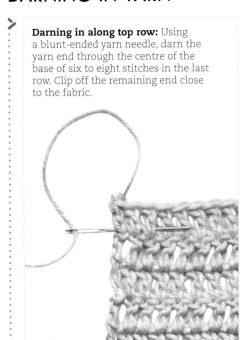

Darning in along first row: Using a blunt-ended yarn needle, darn the yarn end through the centre of the base of six to eight stitches in the first row. Clip off the remaining end close to the fabric.

Darning in along top: You can also weave the yarn in and out of the top of the crochet. This provides a slightly more secure finishing and is good for slippery yarns.

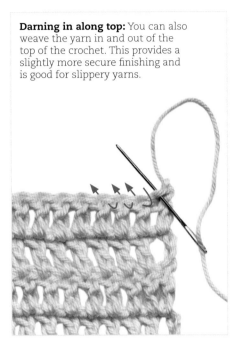

SLIP STITCH SEAM

1 Instead of using a yarn needle to join the seam, you can use a crochet hook to work a quicker seam. Although seams can be worked with double crochet, slip stitch seams are less bulky. Start by placing a slip knot on the hook.

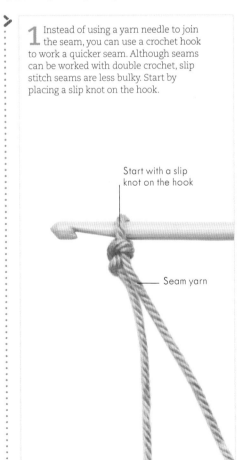

Start with a slip knot on the hook

Seam yarn

2 Align the two layers of crochet with the right sides together. Then, with the slip knot on the hook, insert the hook through the two layers at the starting end of the seam, wrap the yarn around the hook, and draw a loop through the two layers and the loop on the hook.

3 Continue in this way and fasten off at the end. When working the seam along the tops of stitches (as here), insert the hook through the back loops of the stitches only. Along row-end edges, work through the layers one stitch in from the edge.

HANDMADE YARN EMBELLISHMENTS

Yarn embellishments for crochet are easy to make, but be sure to take your time so that they look absolutely perfect. Fringe is often used to edge throws, blankets, rugs, and scarves; tassels are ideal for the corners of a cushion cover or the top of a hat. Instructions for making fringe and tassels are given here, but you could also add pompoms – handmade or ready-made – to hats, garments, and many different types of accessories.

❯ MAKING A FRINGE

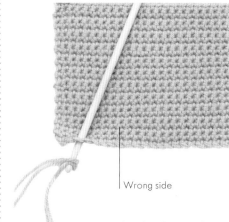

Wrong side

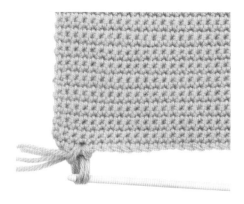

Right side

1 Cut two lengths of yarn, twice the length of the finished fringe, plus at least 2.5cm (1in) extra for the knots. Align the two strands and fold them in half. With the wrong side of the fabric facing, insert a crochet hook from front to back, 5mm (¼in) from the edge. Draw the loop through.

2 Using the crochet hook, pull the ends of the strands through the loop on the hook. Tighten the loop to secure the fringe. Measure your fringe after making this first fringe knot to ensure that it is long enough, and adjust the length of the strands if necessary.

3 Add fringe knots along the edge of the fabric, spacing them evenly apart. For a plumper fringe, use more than two strands at a time. If you have trouble pulling the fringe through the fabric, experiment using a smaller or larger hook. After completing the fringe, trim it slightly to straighten the ends if necessary.

❯ MAKING A TASSEL

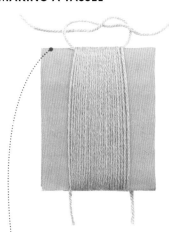

1 Cut a piece of cardboard 8cm (3in) wide and twice as long as the desired length for the finished tassel. Fold the cardboard in half widthways with the fold at the top. Wrap yarn round and round the cardboard lengthways to form a plump tassel. Using a blunt-ended needle, pass a length of yarn under the yarn strands at the top and tie tightly.

2 Insert the tip of a pair of scissors between the two layers of cardboard at the lower end of the tassel. Cut through the strands.

3 Wrap one of the long strands at the top several times around the tassel, about 2cm (¾in) from the top. Thread this strand onto a blunt-ended needle, and pass it through the centre of the tassel and out at the top next to the other strand. Use the long strands to attach the tassel to your crochet.

❯ POMPOMS

1 Draw two 8cm (3¼in) diameter circles on firm card. Draw another 2.5cm (1in) diameter circle in the centre. The diameter of the outer circle minus that of the inner will be the approximate size of the pompom. A smaller centre circle makes a denser pompom. Cut out the circles and the centres so they look like doughnuts.

2 Cut a few 1m (1yd) lengths of yarn and wind together into a small ball. Put the circles together. Hold the yarn ends at the edge of the circle, and insert the ball into centre, winding yarn through the circles. Continue winding.

3 When the first ball runs out make another. If the centre becomes too tight, thread as many strands of yarn as possible onto a large-eyed needle, and use this to complete the winding. Next, insert the point of scissors into the outside of the circle and cut through the wraps.

4 Slide a long, doubled strand of yarn between the circles, wrap and knot it tightly around the core.

5 Thread the yarn onto a needle and make a few stitches through the knot. Gently remove the circles. Shake and trim the pompom, but do not cut the tie strands. Suspending a wool pompom in steam will make it even fuller (hang it at the end of a long needle for safety).

CARE OF CROCHET

As you have invested so much time and effort in making your crocheted projects, take care when cleaning and storing them. Taking proper care of your projects will prolong their lives. Start by referring to the care instructions on the labels that were supplied with the yarn.

CARE OF YOUR PROJECT

Keep a thorough record of all projects, to include the pattern, the tension swatch, a small winding of the yarn/s, and most importantly a yarn label for each of the yarns used. Care instructions for any special ready-made trimming, ribbons, zips, or press studs should also be included. If you are giving a crochet project as a gift, it is important to attach care information so that the recipient can look after it properly.

Preparing for washing

Remove any special buttons or trims that can be damaged by water or dry-cleaning. To retain the shape of openings, tack them closed using a fine cotton yarn that can be easily pulled out when dry. Measure the piece in all directions and record these dimensions, so you can mould it into the correct shape when it is still damp.

It is often a good idea to sew a care label to your crocheted items for convenience. This works best for larger items such as blankets and garments. Labels can be bought from craft shops, yarn shops, and online. Write the care instructions on the label with a permanent ink pen before attaching it. The label can then be attached securely with a sewing needle and some matching sewing thread.

Washing

Refer to your yarn label for washing instructions. Yarns labelled "superwash" or "machine washable" can be washed in a washing machine on a gentle cycle and at a cool temperature. Many yarn labels, however, recommend hand washing.

Wash your animal fibre crochet with great care, avoiding friction (rubbing), agitation (swirling the water), and hot water, which can cause felting in wool yarns and damage other fibres.

Dissolve a mild detergent in a large sink full of lukewarm water. Submerge a single item and gently press up and down on it. Soak for a few minutes, then rinse to remove the soapy water.

Squeeze out the water very gently, pressing the item against the sink. Do not wring. Supporting the damp item, move it onto a large towel. Roll in the towel to remove more moisture.

Drying

Dry washed crochet flat on a fresh towel, turning over occasionally to speed up the process and avoid damage by mildew.

Large items, such as throws, can be dried on the floor; cover the floor first with a large plastic sheet, then lay towels on top of this before positioning the throw.

It may be necessary to replace the towels every so often with dry ones if the item is particularly large or thick, in order to help it dry more quickly.

Mould damp crochet into its correct size and shape before leaving to dry, and never leave in direct sunlight or near a heating source. Once completely dry, you can block and steam the piece if necessary, see p.68.

Never hang up a crocheted item to dry; the weight will cause it to become permanently misshapen, and no amount of blocking will restore it to its original shape and size.

Storing and moth control

Check regularly for telltale holes. If storing all summer, place an anti-moth product in the drawer or closet with your wool crochet and renew it as directed.

Before repairing a hole in a moth-infested item, place it in the freezer overnight to kill any eggs. Crochet that is too large for the freezer, such as a throw, can be placed all day in the sun to achieve the same result.

When a crocheted item is not being used, store it flat. If you hang it up, the stitches will become stretched and any damage will be irreversible. If your crochet is to be stored for any length of time, wrap it in acid-free tissue paper, placing the paper between the folds as well as around the outside.

STITCH TECHNIQUES

The basic crochet stitches can be combined in various ways to create endless textures and sculptured effects. Not all the vast range of crochet stitch techniques can be included, but the most commonly used are explained here in detail. When attempting the stitch patterns on pp.82–83, refer back to these step-by-step instructions to see more clearly how to achieve the textures.

SIMPLE TEXTURES

The simplest and most subtle crochet textures are created by working into various parts of the stitches or between the stitches in the row below. Before trying out any of these techniques, learn about the parts of the stitches so you can identify them easily.

> **PARTS OF STITCHES**

Double crochet stitches: Work two rows of double crochet (see pp.34–35) and fasten off. Look closely at your sample and make sure you can identify all the parts of the stitch labelled above. If your crochet pattern tells you to work into the stitch below, always insert the hook under BOTH loops (the front loop and the back loop) at the top of the stitch as explained on p.35 for double crochet, unless it tells you to do otherwise.

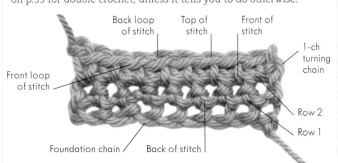

Back loop of stitch · Top of stitch · Front of stitch · Front loop of stitch · 1-ch turning chain · Row 2 · Row 1 · Foundation chain · Back of stitch

Treble crochet stitches: Work two rows of treble crochet (see pp.44–45) and fasten off. Again, make sure you can identify all the parts of the stitch labelled above. As for double crochet and all other crochet stitches, if your crochet pattern tells you to work into the stitch below, always insert the hook under both loops at the top of the stitch, unless it tells you to do otherwise.

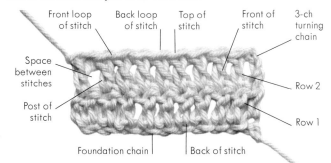

Front loop of stitch · Back loop of stitch · Top of stitch · Front of stitch · 3-ch turning chain · Space between stitches · Post of stitch · Row 2 · Row 1 · Foundation chain · Back of stitch

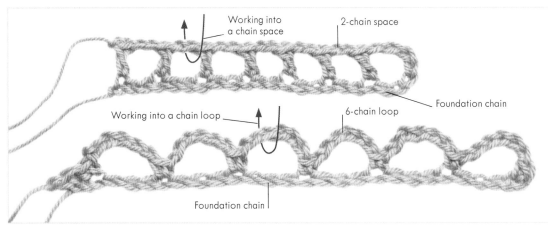

Working into a chain space · 2-chain space · Working into a chain loop · 6-chain loop · Foundation chain · Foundation chain

Chain spaces and chain loops: In many stitch patterns, chain stitches are introduced between basic stitches to create holes or spaces in the fabric. Spaces formed by short chains are called chain spaces, and those formed by long chains are called chain loops. When a crochet pattern instructs you to work into a chain space (or loop), always insert your hook from front to back through the space and not into the actual chain stitches.

WORKING INTO THE BACK LOOP OF A DOUBLE CROCHET

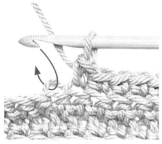

Ridge effect: Working into only the back loops of the stitches in every row of double crochet creates a deep, ridged effect. The ridges are formed by the unworked loops.

WORKING INTO THE FRONT LOOP OF A DOUBLE CROCHET

Smooth effect: Working into only the front loop of each double crochet in the row below, on every row, creates a less pronounced texture than working into only the back loop.

WORKING INTO THE BACK LOOP OF A TREBLE CROCHET

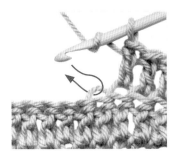

Treble ridge: The same techniques shown for working into the back or front of a double crochet can be used on all crochet stitches to create ridges. The fabric looks the same on both sides.

WORKING INTO SPACES BETWEEN STITCHES

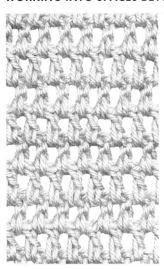

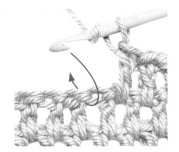

Treble space: Another way to achieve a subtly different texture with basic stitches is to work the stitches into the spaces between the stitches in the row below, instead of into the tops of the stitches.

WORKING INTO A CHAIN SPACE

Simple texture: Tweed stitch illustrates the simplest of all textures created by working into a chain space. Here, double crochet stitches are worked in the 1-chain spaces between the stitches in the row below, instead of into the tops of the stitches.

Tweed stitch pattern
Because it is such a popular stitch and a perfect alternative to basic double crochet, the pattern for it is given here. (See p.81 for abbreviations.) Start with an even number of chains.
Row 1: 1 dc in second ch from hook, *1 ch, miss next ch, 1 dc in next ch; rep from * to end, turn.
Row 2: 1 ch (does NOT count as a stitch), 1 dc in first dc, 1 dc in next 1-ch sp, *1 ch, 1 dc in next 1-ch sp; rep from * to last dc, 1 dc in last dc, turn.
Row 3: 1 ch (does NOT count as a stitch), 1 dc in first dc, *1 ch, 1 dc in next 1-ch sp; rep from * to last 2 dc, 1 ch, miss next dc, 1 dc in last dc, turn.
Rep rows 2 and 3 to form patt.

SCULPTURAL TEXTURES

These easy raised and grouped crochet stitch techniques produce attractive sculptural textures. Although they can be used to create fairly dense stitch patterns (see pp.82–83), they are also found in lace stitches (see pp.111–113).

❯ FRONT POST TREBLE

Working around the post is used to make a fabric that imitates knitted ribbing, but it can also be used on its own in rows to create a ridged effect.

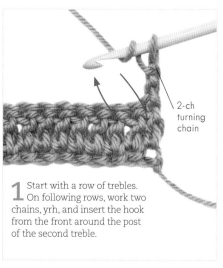

1 Start with a row of trebles. On following rows, work two chains, yrh, and insert the hook from the front around the post of the second treble.

2-ch turning chain

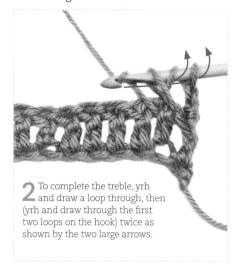

2 To complete the treble, yrh and draw a loop through, then (yrh and draw through the first two loops on the hook) twice as shown by the two large arrows.

3 Work a treble around each of the following trebles in the row below in the same way. At the end of the row, work a treble into the top of the turning chain. Repeat the second row to form a ridged texture.

❯ BACK POST TREBLE

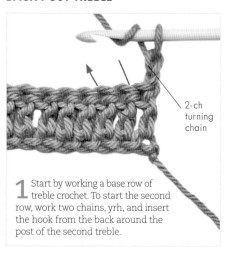

1 Start by working a base row of treble crochet. To start the second row, work two chains, yrh, and insert the hook from the back around the post of the second treble.

2-ch turning chain

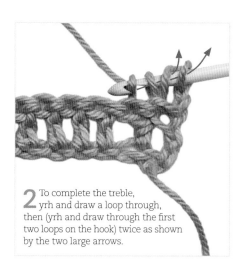

2 To complete the treble, yrh and draw a loop through, then (yrh and draw through the first two loops on the hook) twice as shown by the two large arrows.

3 Work a treble around each of the trebles in the row below in the same way. Continue as for step 3 of Front post treble (above).

❯ SHELLS

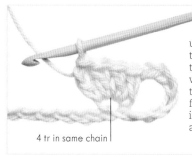

4-tr shell: Shells are the most frequently used of all crochet stitch techniques. Usually made with trebles, they are formed by working several stitches into the same stitch or space. Here four trebles have been worked into the same chain to form a 4-tr shell.

4 tr in same chain

5-tr shell: Here five trebles have been worked into the same chain to form a 5-tr shell. Any number of trebles can be used to form a shell, but the most commonly used crochet shells have two, three, four, five, or six stitches. Shells can also be made with half trebles and taller basic stitches.

5 tr in same chain

BOBBLES

Joining effect: Bobbles are formed using the shell technique and the cluster technique so that the stitches are joined together at the top and the bottom.

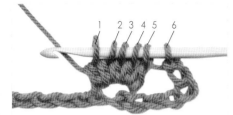

1 To work a 5-tr bobble, work five incomplete trebles (as for a cluster) into the same stitch (as for a shell. There are now six loops on the hook.

2 Wrap the yarn around the hook and draw a loop through all six loops on the hook.

3 This completes all of the trebles at the same time and joins them at the top. Some bobbles are completed with an extra chain as shown by the large arrow. Bobbles are usually made with three, four, or five trebles. Bobbles made with half trebles are called puff stitches.

CLUSTERS

Crocheted clusters look like upside down shells. They are made by joining the tops of several stitches (each worked into a different stitch below) into a single top.

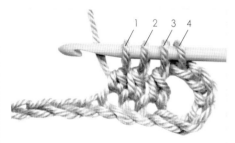

1 To make a 3-tr cluster, work a treble up to the last yrh that completes the treble. Then work an incomplete treble into each of the next two stitches in the same way. There are now four loops on the hook.

2 Wrap the yarn around the hook and draw a loop through all four loops on the hook.

3 This completes all of the trebles at the same time and joins them at the top. Clusters can be made with two, three, four, five, six, or more trebles, and with half trebles or taller basic stitches as well.

POPCORNS

1 Popcorns are started like shells. To make a 5-tr popcorn, begin by working five trebles in the same stitch.

2 Remove the hook from the loop and insert it from back to front through the top of the first treble of the group. Draw the working loop through the top of the first treble as shown by the large arrow.

3 This pulls the tops of the shells together to form a bobble-type shape. Unlike the top of a bobble, the top of a popcorn protrudes forwards because of the method of construction. Popcorns are usually made with three, four, or five trebles.

FLOWER GARLAND

Flower motifs are quick and easy projects for using all of the stitches you have learned up until now. The use of all the different heights of the stitches together creates curves that are perfect for petals.

TECHNIQUES USED Double crochet **p.34**, Half treble crochet **p.38**, Treble crochet **p.44**, Double treble crochet **p.48**, Working into a chain space **p.75**

SIZE
Small: 4.5cm (1¾in) in diameter; Medium: 5cm (2in) in diameter; Large: 5.5cm (2¼in) in diameter

YARN
DMC Natura Just Cotton – 50g/155m/169yds (100% cotton; any 4-ply yarn or crochet thread will substitute here or use different weight yarns for various sizes of flower)

A x 1   B x 1   C x 1

HOOK
3mm hook

NOTIONS
Yarn needle

TENSION
Exact tension is not essential

PATTERN
Note: Make three of each colour in every size of flower, making nine of each in total.

BIG FLOWER (MAKE 9)
Work 5 ch, ss in first ch to form a ring.
Round 1: 1 ch, work 16 dc into ring, join round with a ss into first ch.
Round 2: 4 ch, (1 dtr, 2 ch) into next st, *1 dtr into next st, (1 dtr, 2 ch) into next st; rep from * to end of round, join round with a ss into top of 4 ch.

Round 3: 1 ch, (1 htr, 2 tr, 1 dtr, 2 tr, 1 htr) all into next 2-ch sp, *1 dc in between next 2 dtr, (1 htr, 2 tr, 1 dtr, 2 tr, 1 htr) all into next 2-ch sp; rep from * to end of round, join round with a ss into first ch. Fasten off yarn, weave in ends.

MEDIUM FLOWER (MAKE 9)
Work 5 ch, ss in first ch to form a ring.
Round 1: 1 ch, work 12 dc into ring, join round with a ss into first ch.
Round 2: 3 ch, (1 tr, 2 ch) into next st, *1 tr into next st, (1 tr, 2 ch) into next st; rep from * to end of round, join round with a ss into top of ch 3.
Round 3: 1 ch, (1 htr, 3 tr, 1 htr) all into next 2-ch sp, *1 dc in between next 2 tr, (1 htr, 3 tr, 1 htr) all into next 2-ch sp; rep from * to end of round, join round with a ss into first ch. Fasten off yarn, weave in ends.

SMALL FLOWER (MAKE 9)
Work 4 ch, ss in first ch to form a ring.
Round 1: 1 ch, work 10 dc into ring, join round with a ss into first ch.
Round 2: 3 ch, (1 tr, 2 ch) into next st, *1 tr into next st, (1 tr, 2 ch) into next tr; rep from * to end of round, join round with a ss into top of ch 3.
Round 3: 1 ch, (1 htr, 3 tr, 1 htr) all into next 2-ch sp, *1 dc in between next 2 tr, (1 htr, 3 tr, 1 htr) all into next 2-ch sp; rep from * to end of round, join round with a ss into first ch. Fasten off yarn, weave in ends.

FINISHING
Work a chain of desired length, threading through the middle of the flowers to create a garland. Alternatively, mount individual flowers onto a safety pin or brooch back to create a corsage.

1 Work around the central circle to create five petals. Work a double crochet into the space between the next two double treble crochets after each petal.

2 Crochet a series of stitches around each flower for petals. You will need double crochet, half treble, and treble stitch. Work the same number of stitches into each chain space.

FOLLOWING SIMPLE STITCH PATTERNS

Working a project from a crochet pattern for the first time can seem difficult for a beginner, especially if an experienced crocheter is not at hand as a guide. The best way to prepare for a crochet pattern is to first practise crocheting rectangles of various stitch patterns using simple stitch techniques. This is a good introduction to following abbreviated written row instructions and symbol diagrams.

UNDERSTANDING WRITTEN INSTRUCTIONS

As long as you know how to work all the basic stitches and can work them from the simple patterns on pp.66–67 and have reviewed pp.74–77 where special stitch techniques are explained, there is nothing stopping you from trying to work the simple textural stitch patterns on pp.82–83. Simply consult the list on the opposite page for the meanings of the various abbreviations and follow the written row instructions one step at a time.

Begin by making the required number of chains for the foundation chain, using your chosen yarn and one of the hook sizes recommended for this yarn weight on p.14. Crochet a swatch that repeats the pattern only a few times to test it out. (If you decide to make a blanket or cushion cover with the stitch later, you can adjust the hook size before starting it to obtain the exact flexibility of fabric you desire for your project.)

Work each row of the stitch pattern slowly and mark the right side of the fabric (if there is one) as soon as you start, by tying a contrasting coloured thread to it. Another good tip is to tick off the rows as you complete them or put a sticky note under them, so you don't lose your place in the pattern. If you do get lost in all the stitches, you can pull out all the rows and start the pattern from the foundation chain again.

UNDERSTANDING STITCH SYMBOL DIAGRAMS

Crochet stitch patterns can also be given in symbols (see opposite). These diagrams are usually even easier to follow than directions with abbreviations because they create a visual reference of approximately how the finished stitch will look. Each basic stitch on the chart is represented by a symbol that resembles it in some way. The position of the base of each stitch symbol indicates which stitch or chain space it is worked into in the row below. If the symbols are joined at the base, this means that they are worked into the same stitch in the row below.

The beginning of the foundation chain will be marked as your starting point on the diagram. Read each row on the diagram either from right to left or left to right following the direction of the arrow. Although you can consult the written instructions for how many chains to make for a foundation chain and how to repeat the stitch repeat across a row (or a row repeat up the fabric), it is easy to work these out yourself from the diagram once you become proficient in reading diagrams. But to begin with, work from the written instructions and use the diagram as a visual aid. Once you have completed the first few rows of the pattern, you can dispense with the written instructions altogether and continue with the diagram as your sole guide. If the stitch is an easy one, you will very quickly be able to work it without looking at any instructions at all.

This symbol diagram for the open shell stitch (see p.111) is a good introduction to working from a symbol diagram. Start at the bottom of the diagram and follow it row by row with the aid of the numbered tips.

SAMPLE STITCH PATTERN

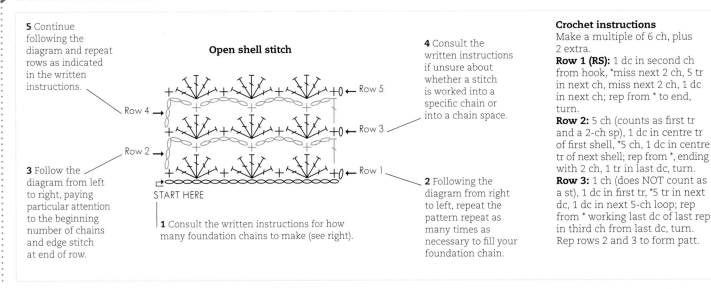

5 Continue following the diagram and repeat rows as indicated in the written instructions.

Open shell stitch

← Row 5

Row 4 →

← Row 3

Row 2 →

← Row 1

START HERE

3 Follow the diagram from left to right, paying particular attention to the beginning number of chains and edge stitch at end of row.

1 Consult the written instructions for how many foundation chains to make (see right).

4 Consult the written instructions if unsure about whether a stitch is worked into a specific chain or into a chain space.

2 Following the diagram from right to left, repeat the pattern repeat as many times as necessary to fill your foundation chain.

Crochet instructions
Make a multiple of 6 ch, plus 2 extra.
Row 1 (RS): 1 dc in second ch from hook, *miss next 2 ch, 5 tr in next ch, miss next 2 ch, 1 dc in next ch; rep from * to end, turn.
Row 2: 5 ch (counts as first tr and a 2-ch sp), 1 dc in centre tr of first shell, *5 ch, 1 dc in centre tr of next shell; rep from *, ending with 2 ch, 1 tr in last dc, turn.
Row 3: 1 ch (does NOT count as a st), 1 dc in first tr, *5 tr in next dc, 1 dc in next 5-ch loop; rep from * working last dc of last rep in third ch from last dc, turn.
Rep rows 2 and 3 to form patt.

CROCHET ABBREVIATIONS

These are the abbreviations most commonly used in crochet patterns. The abbreviations for the basic stitches are listed first and the other abbreviations found in crochet patterns follow. Any special abbreviations in a crochet pattern will always be explained in the pattern.

Abbreviations for basic stitches

Note: The names for the basic crochet stitches differ in the UK and the US. This book uses UK crochet terminology, so if you have learned to crochet in the US, be sure to take note of the difference in terminology.

ch	chain	**cm**	centimetre(s)	**sp**	space(s)
ss	slip stitch	**cont**	continu(e)(ing)	**st(s)**	stitch(es)
dc	double crochet (US single crochet – sc)	**dc2tog**	work 2 dc together	**TBL**	through back loop
		dc3tog	work 3 dc together, see also p.313	**TFL**	through front loop
htr	half treble (US half double crochet – hdc)	**dec**	decreas(e)(ing)	**tog**	together
		foll	follow(s)(ing)	**tr2tog**	work 2 tr together
tr	treble (US double crochet – dc)	**g**	gram(s)	**tr3tog**	work 3 tr together, see also p.313
dtr	double treble (US treble crochet – tr)	**htr2tog**	work 2 htr together	**WS**	wrong side
trtr	triple treble (US double treble crochet – dtr)	**htr3tog**	work 3 htr together, see also p.313	**yds**	yard(s)
		in	inch(es)	**yrh**	yarn round hook (US yarn over hook – yo)
qtr	quadruple treble (US triple treble crochet – trtr)	**inc**	increas(e)(ing)		
		m	metre(s)	*	repeat instructions after asterisk or between asterisks as many times as instructed
quintr	quintuple treble (US quadruple treble – quadtr)	**mm**	millimetre(s)		
		oz	ounce(s)		
		patt(s)	pattern(s)	( )	repeat instructions inside round brackets as many times as instructed
Other abbreviations		**rem**	remain(s)(ing)		
alt	alternate	**rep**	repeat(s)(ing)		
beg	begin(ning)	**RS**	right side	[ ]	used for a repeat within a repeat

CROCHET STITCH SYMBOLS

These are the symbols used in this book, but crochet symbols are not universal so always consult the key with your crochet instructions for those used in your pattern.

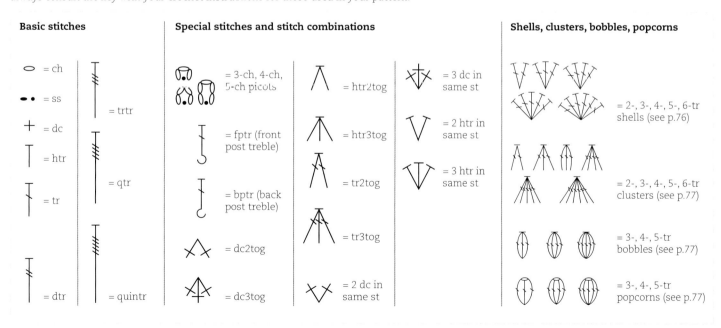

Basic stitches

◯ = ch

•─• = ss

+ = dc

T = htr

↑ = tr

↑ = dtr

↑ = trtr

↑ = qtr

↑ = quintr

Special stitches and stitch combinations

= 3-ch, 4-ch, 5-ch picots

= fptr (front post treble)

= bptr (back post treble)

= dc2tog

= dc3tog

= htr2tog

= htr3tog

= tr2tog

= tr3tog

= 2 dc in same st

= 3 dc in same st

= 2 htr in same st

= 3 htr in same st

Shells, clusters, bobbles, popcorns

= 2-, 3-, 4-, 5-, 6-tr shells (see p.76)

= 2-, 3-, 4-, 5-, 6-tr clusters (see p.77)

= 3-, 4-, 5-tr bobbles (see p.77)

= 3-, 4-, 5-tr popcorns (see p.77)

SIMPLE TEXTURAL STITCH PATTERNS

Selected for how easy they are to work, these stitch patterns cover an array of textures. Beginner crocheters should follow the written instructions for the first few rows, referring to the symbols for clarification and p.81 for simple stitch patterns. Where there is no right or wrong side marked in the instructions of a stitch (see rib stitch and close shells stitch, below), it looks the same on both sides and the fabric is reversible.

❯ CROCHET RIB STITCH

Crochet diagram

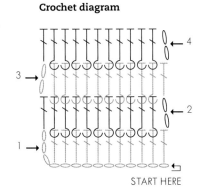

START HERE

Crochet instructions
Make a multiple of 2 ch.
Row 1: 1 tr in fourth ch from hook, 1 tr in each of rem ch, turn.
Row 2: 2 ch (counts as first st), miss first tr, *1 tr around post of next tr from front, 1 tr around post of next tr from back; rep from * to end, 1 tr in top of turning ch at end, turn.
Rep row 2 to form patt.

❯ SIMPLE CROSSED STITCH

Crochet diagram

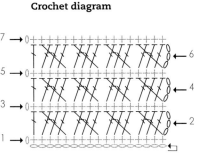

START HERE

Crochet instructions
Make a multiple of 4 ch, plus 2 extra.
Row 1: 1 dc in second ch from hook, 1 dc in each of rem ch, turn.
Row 2 (RS): 3 ch (counts as first tr), miss first dc, 1 tr in each of next 3 dc, yrh and insert hook from front to back in first dc (the missed dc), yrh and draw a long loop through (extending the loop so that it reaches back to position of work and does not squash 3-tr group just made), (yrh and draw through first two loops on hook) twice (called long tr), *miss next dc, 1 tr in each of next 3 dc, 1 long tr in last missed dc; rep from * to last dc, 1 tr in last dc, turn.
Row 3: 1 ch (does NOT count as a st), 1 dc in each tr to end (do NOT work a dc in 3-ch turning chain), turn.
Rep rows 2 and 3 to form patt.

❯ CLOSE SHELLS STITCH

Crochet diagram

START HERE

Crochet instructions
Make a multiple of 6 ch, plus 2 extra.
Row 1: 1 dc in second ch from hook, *miss next 2 ch, 5 tr in next ch, miss next 2 ch, 1 dc in next ch; rep from * to end, turn.
Row 2: 3 ch (counts as first tr), 2 tr in first dc, *miss next 2 tr, 1 dc in next tr, 5 tr in next dc (between shells); rep from *, ending last rep with 3 tr in last dc (instead of 5 tr), turn.
Row 3: 1 ch (does NOT count as a st), 1 dc in first tr, *5 tr in next dc (between shells), miss next 2 tr, 1 dc in next tr; rep from *, working last dc in top of 3-ch at end, turn.
Rep rows 2 and 3 to form patt.

CLUSTER AND SHELL STITCH

Crochet diagram

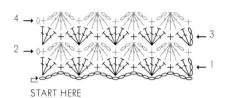

START HERE

Crochet instructions
Note: cluster (also called dc5tog) = over next 5sts (which include 2 tr, 1 dc, 2 tr) work (yrh and insert hook in next st, yrh and draw a loop through, yrh and draw through first two loops on hook) five times (six loops now on hook), yrh and draw through all six loops on hook (see p.77). Make a multiple of 6 ch, plus 4 extra.
Row 1 (RS): 2 tr in fourth ch from hook, miss next 2 ch, 1 dc in next ch, *miss next 2 ch, 5 tr in next ch, miss next 2 ch, 1 dc in next ch; rep from * to last 3 ch, miss next 2 ch, 3 tr in last ch, turn.
Row 2: 1 ch (does NOT count as a st), 1 dc in first tr, *2 ch, 1 cluster over next 5 sts, 2 ch, 1 dc in next tr (centre tr of 5-tr group); rep from *, working last dc of last rep in top of 3 ch at end, turn.
Row 3: 3 ch (counts as first tr), 2 tr in first dc, miss next 2 ch, 1 dc in next st (top of first cluster), *5 tr in next dc, miss next 2 ch, 1 dc in next st (top of next cluster); rep from *, ending with 3 tr in last dc, turn.
Rep rows 2 and 3 to form patt.

SIMPLE BOBBLE STITCH

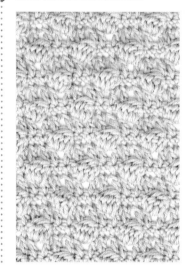

Crochet diagram

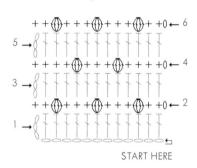

START HERE

Crochet instructions
Note: bobble = (yrh and insert hook in specified st, yrh and draw a loop through, yrh and draw through first two loops on hook) four times all in same st (five loops now on hook), yrh and draw through all five loops on hook (see p.77). Make a multiple of 4 ch, plus 3 extra.
Row 1 (WS): 1 tr in fourth ch from hook, 1 tr in each of rem ch, turn.
Row 2 (RS): 1 ch (does NOT count as a st), 1 dc in each of first 2 tr, *1 bobble in next tr, 1 dc in each of next 3 tr; rep from * to last 2 tr, 1 bobble in next tr, 1 dc in next tr, 1 dc in top of 3 ch at end, turn.
Row 3: 3 ch (counts as first tr), miss first dc and work 1 tr in each st to end, turn.
Row 4: 1 ch (does NOT count as a st), 1 dc in each of first 4 tr, *1 bobble in next tr, 1 dc in each of next 3 tr; rep from *, ending with 1 dc in top of 3 ch at end, turn.
Row 5: Rep row 3.
Rep rows 2–5 to form patt, ending with a patt row 5.

SHELLS AND CHAINS

Crochet diagram

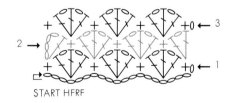

START HERE

Crochet instructions
Make a multiple of 6 ch, plus 2 extra.
Row 1 (RS): 1 dc in second ch from hook, *miss next 2 ch, work (1 tr, 1 ch, 1 tr, 1 ch, 1 tr) all in next ch, miss next 2 ch, 1 dc in next ch; rep from * to end, turn.
Row 2: 4 ch (counts as 1 tr and a 1-ch sp), 1 tr in first dc, miss next tr, 1 dc in next tr (centre tr of shell), *work (1 tr, 1 ch, 1 tr, 1 ch, 1 tr) all in next dc (between shells), miss next tr, 1 dc in next tr (centre tr of shell); rep from *, ending with [1 tr, 1 ch, 1 tr] in last dc, turn.
Row 3: 1 ch (does NOT count as a st), 1 dc in first tr, *work (1 tr, 1 ch, 1 tr, 1 ch, 1 tr) all in next dc, miss next tr, 1 dc in next tr (centre tr of shell); rep from *, working last dc of last rep in third of 4-ch made at beg of previous row, turn.
Rep rows 2 and 3 to form patt.

EMBELLISHMENTS FOR CROCHET

There are many ways to add subtle or bold embellishments to your crochet. Although it may seem unimportant, choosing the right buttons when they are required comes top of the list, so always select buttons carefully and take your finished crochet along to try them out before purchasing any. Other adornments that will dress up your crochet include beads, ribbons, pompoms and fringe, edgings, and embroidery.

BEADED CROCHET

Beads can be sewn onto your finished crochet if you are only adding a few. But for an all-over effect, work the beads into the fabric as you crochet. The most common beaded crochet technique uses double crochet as the background to the beads.

❯ WORKING BEADED DOUBLE CROCHET

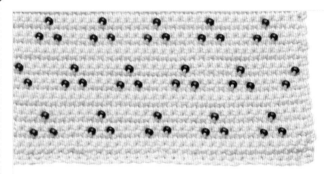

Beaded crochet is suitable for a range of simple, spaced-out, all-over geometric patterns. But beware of using too many beads on the crochet or beads that are too big, as they can add so much extra weight to the fabric that they stretch it out.

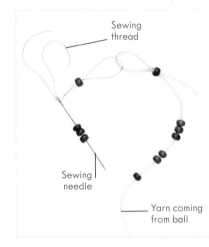

Sewing thread

Sewing needle

Yarn coming from ball

1 Beaded double crochet is usually worked from a chart that shows the positions of the beads on the fabric. The chart is read as for a chart for colourwork (see p.116), and the key provided with the chart indicates which stitches are worked as plain double crochet and which have beads. Loop the end of the yarn into a loop of sewing thread as shown, then thread the beads onto the needle and down onto the yarn.

2 Follow the chart for the bead pattern, sliding the beads along the yarn until they are needed. The beads are always positioned on wrong-side rows. When a bead position is reached, work the next double crochet up to the last yrh – there are now two loops on the hook. Slide a bead up close to the crochet and wrap the yarn around the hook.

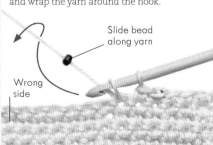

Slide bead along yarn

Wrong side

3 Draw a loop through both loops on the hook to complete the double crochet.

4 Complete the double crochet tightly, so that the bead sits snugly against the fabric on the right side of the crochet.

EMBROIDERY ON CROCHET

Because double crochet creates such a firm fabric, it is easy to work embroidery onto it. Many embroidery stitches are suitable for crochet and a few of the most popular ones are given here. Use the same yarn for the embroidery as the yarn used for the crochet, or a slightly thicker yarn, so that the stitches will show up well. Always work the stitches with the same type of blunt-ended yarn needle that is used for seams.

❯ BLANKET STITCH

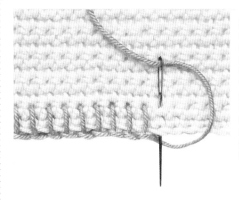

Edging: Blanket stitch creates an excellent crisp, decorative finish. Secure the yarn with two or three overcast stitches worked at the edge of the crochet. Then make evenly spaced stitches from left to right, as shown here.

❯ CHAIN STITCH

Motif: Chain stitch is perfect for curved motifs. Hold the yarn on the wrong side of the fabric and draw loops through with the hook. To fasten off, pull the yarn end through the last loop and then back to the wrong side over the loop. Darn in the ends on the wrong side.

❯ CROSS STITCH

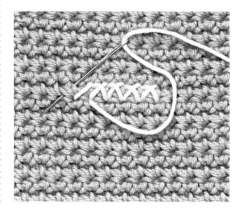

1 Work each individual cross stitch on double crochet over a single double crochet stitch. Complete each cross stitch before moving on to the next. Keep the stitches fairly loose so they don't distort the crochet.

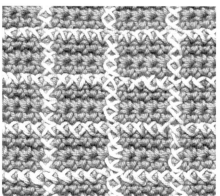

2 Adding lines of cross stitches is an effective way to create an interesting plaid pattern on a base of plain double crochet. This is the perfect technique for dressing up a simple piece of double crochet.

EDGINGS ON CROCHET

Several styles of edging patterns are provided on pp.88–93 because they are excellent, simple adornment for your crochet. Some edgings can be worked directly onto your crochet (see p.86), and others made separately and then sewn on, as shown below.

❯ ADDING EDGINGS

Attach an edging: To sew an edging in place, use a yarn that matches the base crochet and a blunt-ended yarn needle. Secure the yarn at the right-hand end of the seam with two or three overcast stitches. Then work evenly spaced overcast stitches through both the base crochet and the edging, as shown.

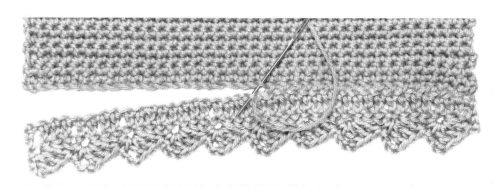

TECHNIQUES

FINISHING DETAILS

Finishings require slightly different crochet techniques. Some of the techniques most frequently used are shown here. Take your time with all finishings, and practise the methods on small swatches before adding them to your completed pieces.

DOUBLE CROCHET EDGING

Along top or bottom of a piece of crochet: Adding a simple double crochet edging is a good way to tidy up the edges of a piece of crochet. To work a double crochet edging along the top or bottom of a piece of crochet, join the yarn to the first stitch with a slip stitch, work 1 ch, 1 dc in the same place as the slip stitch, then work 1 dc in each stitch below all along the edge.

Along row-ends of a piece of crochet: A double crochet edging is worked the same way along the row-ends of a piece of crochet, but it is not as easy to achieve an even edging. To create a perfect result, experiment with how many stitches to work per row-end. If the finished edging looks flared, try working fewer stitches per row-end; and if it looks puckered, try working more stitches per row-end.

CROCHETING EDGING DIRECTLY ONTO EDGE

Any of the edgings starting with a row of double crochet on pp.88–93 can easily be worked directly onto the crochet.

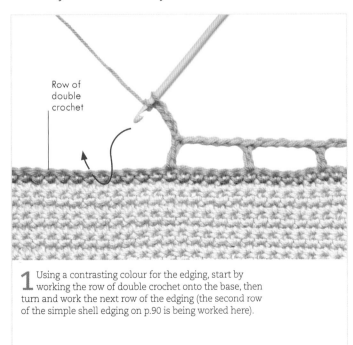

Row of double crochet

1 Using a contrasting colour for the edging, start by working the row of double crochet onto the base, then turn and work the next row of the edging (the second row of the simple shell edging on p.90 is being worked here).

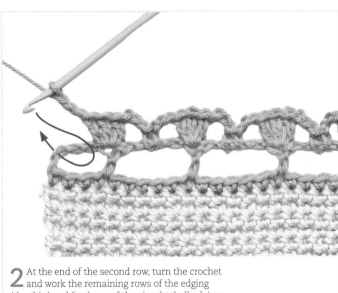

2 At the end of the second row, turn the crochet and work the remaining rows of the edging (the third and final row of the simple shell edging is being worked here).

ROUND BUTTONS

Making matching crochet buttons is a great finishing detail. Experiment with different yarn and hook sizes to make round buttons of the desired size. The buttons here are made using a superfine cotton yarn and a 2mm (US size 5 steel or B-1) hook for a button approximately 1.5cm (½in) in diameter.

Insert stuffing

Extend loop to prevent button from unravelling

1 Make each button as follows: Make 4 ch and join with a ss to first ch to form a ring.
Round 1 (RS): 1 ch, 8 dc in ring (working over yarn tail while working dc into ring), join with a ss to first dc. (Do not turn at end of rounds, but work with RS always facing.)
Round 2: 1 ch, 1 dc in same dc as last ss, 2 dc in next dc, (1 dc in next dc, 2 dc in next dc) three times, join with a ss to first dc. (12 dc)
Round 3: 1 ch, 1 dc in each dc to end, join with a ss to first dc.
Round 4: 1 ch, 1 dc in same dc as last ss, (dc2tog over next 1 dc, 1 dc in next dc) three times, dc2tog over last 2 dc, join with a ss to first dc. (8 dc) Take the loop off the hook and extend it to prevent the button from unravelling. Push the yarn tail from round 1 into the inside of the button and fill it firmly with toy stuffing.

2 Slip the loop back on the hook and tighten it. Continue the button as follows:
Round 5: 1 ch, dc2tog over first 2 dc (same dc as last ss and next dc), (2 dc over next 2 dc) three times, join with a ss to first dc. (4 dc) Fasten off, leaving a long loose end at least 20cm (8in) long. Push more stuffing inside if necessary. Then, using a blunt-ended needle and the long yarn tail, sew the opening at the back of the button closed.

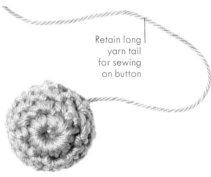

3 Do not cut off the yarn tail, but keep it for sewing on the button.

Retain long yarn tail for sewing on button

BUTTON LOOPS

Button loops are very easy to make along the edge of a cushion cover, the front of a cardigan, or for closings on baby garments.

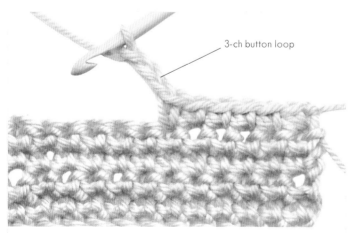

3-ch button loop

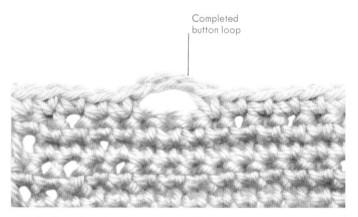

Completed button loop

1 Work in double crochet to the position of the button loop. Make two, three, or more chains, depending on the size of the button.

2 Skip the same number of stitches on the edge and work the next double crochet in the next stitch. Test the size of the first completed button loop with the button and adjust the number of chains if necessary.

3 Continue along the edge, working double crochet and button loops until the edging is complete. To make stronger loops, work a second row of double crochet along the first row, working the same number of double crochet stitches as chains into each loop.

SIMPLE EDGING PATTERNS

Adding a decorative crochet edging to an otherwise mundane-looking piece of crochet can transform it from a simple project into an eye-catching piece of stitching with a touch of elegance. All the simple crochet edgings that follow are worked widthwise, so you start with a length of chain roughly equivalent to the length of edging you need. Suitable even for beginners, these edgings are perfect for dressing up towel ends, throws, baby blankets, necklines, and cuffs. When making an edging that will encircle a blanket, be sure to add extra for turning the corners; the edging can then be gathered at each corner to allow for the turning. Use a short test swatch to calculate how much extra you will need at each corner. See p.81 for abbreviations and symbols.

CHAIN FRINGE

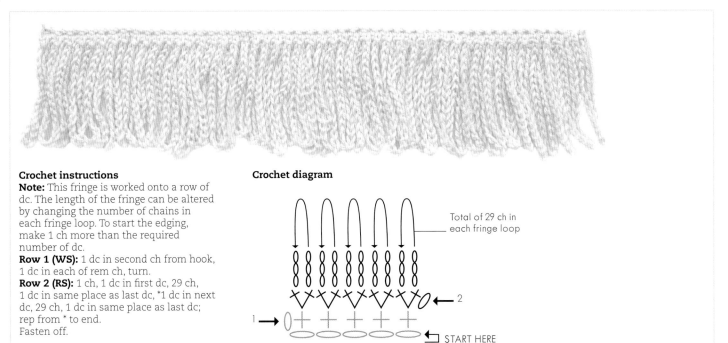

Crochet instructions

Note: This fringe is worked onto a row of dc. The length of the fringe can be altered by changing the number of chains in each fringe loop. To start the edging, make 1 ch more than the required number of dc.

Row 1 (WS): 1 dc in second ch from hook, 1 dc in each of rem ch, turn.

Row 2 (RS): 1 ch, 1 dc in first dc, 29 ch, 1 dc in same place as last dc, *1 dc in next dc, 29 ch, 1 dc in same place as last dc; rep from * to end.

Fasten off.

Crochet diagram

Total of 29 ch in each fringe loop

START HERE

STEP EDGING

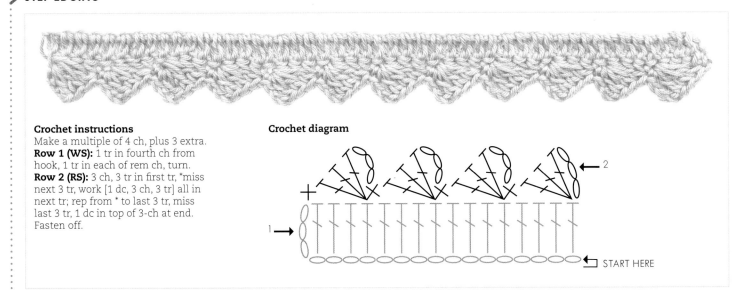

Crochet instructions

Make a multiple of 4 ch, plus 3 extra.

Row 1 (WS): 1 tr in fourth ch from hook, 1 tr in each of rem ch, turn.

Row 2 (RS): 3 ch, 3 tr in first tr, *miss next 3 tr, work [1 dc, 3 ch, 3 tr] all in next tr; rep from * to last 3 tr, miss last 3 tr, 1 dc in top of 3-ch at end.

Fasten off.

Crochet diagram

START HERE

› PICOT SCALLOP EDGING

Crochet instructions
Make a multiple of 4 ch, plus 2 extra.
Row 1 (WS): 1 dc in second ch from hook, *5 ch, miss next 3 ch, 1 dc in next ch; rep from * to end, turn.
Row 2 (RS): 1 ch, *work (4 dc, 3 ch, 4 dc) all in next 5-ch loop; rep from * to end. Fasten off.

Crochet diagram

› DOUBLE LOOP EDGING

Crochet instructions
To start edging, make a multiple of 5 ch, plus 2 extra.
Row 1 (WS): 1 dc in second ch from hook, 1 dc in next ch, *5 ch, miss next 2 ch, 1 dc in each of next 3 ch; rep from * to last 4 ch, 5 ch, miss next 2 ch, 1 dc in each of last 2 ch, turn.
Row 2 (RS): 1 ch, 1 dc in first dc, *8 ch, 1 dc in centre dc of next group of 3-dc (at other side of 5-ch loop); rep from * working last dc in last dc of row 1.
Fasten off.

Crochet diagram
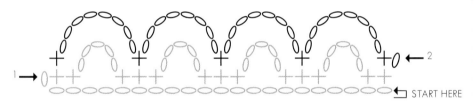

› GRAND EYELET EDGING

Crochet instructions
Make a multiple of 7 ch, plus 2 extra.
Row 1 (WS): 1 dc in 2nd ch from hook, 1 dc in each of rem ch, turn.
Row 2 (RS): 1 ch, 1 dc in first dc, 1 htr in next dc, 1 tr in next dc, 1 dtr in next dc, *5 ch, miss next 3 dc, 1 dc in next dc, 1 htr in next dc, 1 tr in next dc, 1 dtr in next dc; rep from * to last 4 dc, 5 ch, miss next 3 dc, 1 dc in last dc.
Fasten off.

Crochet diagram
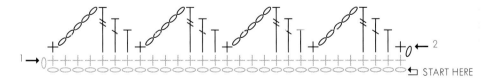

TECHNIQUES

❯ PILLAR EDGING

Crochet instructions
Make a multiple of 10 ch, plus 2 extra.
Row 1 (WS): 1 dc in second ch from hook, 1 dc in each
of rem ch, turn.
Row 2 (RS): 1 ch, 1 dc in first dc, *2 ch, miss next dc, 1 tr
in next dc, (2 ch, miss next dc, 1 dtr in next dc) twice, 2 ch,
miss next dc, 1 tr in next dc,
2 ch, miss next dc, 1 dc in next dc; rep from * to end.
Fasten off.

Crochet diagram

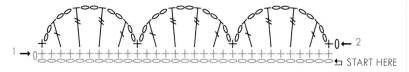

❯ SIMPLE SHELL EDGING

Crochet instructions
Make a multiple of 6 ch, plus 2 extra.
Row 1 (RS): 1 dc in second ch from hook, 1 dc in each of
rem ch, turn.
Row 2: 5 ch, miss first 3 dc, 1 tr in next dc, *5 ch, miss
next 5 dc, 1 tr in next dc; rep from * to last 3 dc, 2 ch, miss
next 2 dc, 1 tr in last dc, turn.
Row 3: 1 ch, 1 dc in first tr, 3 ch, 3 tr in next tr, *3 ch, 1 dc
in next 5-ch space, 3 ch, 3 tr in next tr; rep from *, ending
with 3 ch, miss first 2 ch of last 5 ch, 1 dc in next ch.
Fasten off.

Crochet diagram

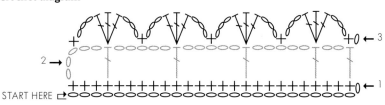

❯ TWIRL FRINGE

Crochet instructions
Note: The fringe will twirl naturally; do not press out
the twirls.
To start edging, make a multiple of 2 ch.
Row 1 (WS): 1 dtr in fourth ch from hook, *1 ch, miss next
ch, 1 dtr in next ch; rep from * to end, turn.
Row 2 (RS): 1 ch, 1 dc in first dtr, *24 ch, 1 dc in second ch
from hook, 1 dc in each of rem 22 ch, 1 dc in next dtr; rep
from * to end.
Fasten off.

Crochet diagram

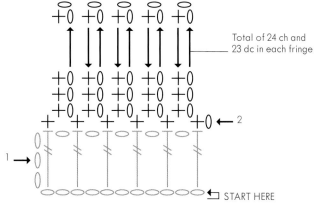

Total of 24 ch and
23 dc in each fringe

❯ TRIPLE PICOT EDGING

Crochet instructions
Make a multiple of 6 ch, plus 2 extra.
Row 1 (WS): 1 dc in second ch from hook, 1 dc in each of rem ch, turn.
Row 2 (RS): 5 ch, work (1 dc, [5 ch, 1 dc] twice) all in first dc, *4 ch, miss next 5 dc, (1 dc, [5 ch, 1 dc] three times) all in next dc; rep from * to end.
Fasten off.

Crochet diagram

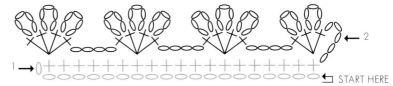

❯ CLUSTER AND SHELL EDGING

Crochet instructions
Make a multiple of 8 ch, plus 4 extra.
Row 1 (WS): 1 tr in fourth ch from hook, *miss next 3 ch, 6 tr in next ch (to make a shell), miss next 3 ch, work (1 tr, 1 ch, 1 tr) all in next ch; rep from * to last 8 ch, miss next 3 ch, 6 tr in next ch, miss next 3 ch, 2 tr in last ch, turn.
Row 2 (RS): 1 ch, miss first tr, 1 dc in next tr, *4 ch, (yrh, insert hook in next tr, yrh and draw a loop through, yrh and draw through first 2 loops on hook) six times (once into each of 6 tr of shell), yrh and draw through all seven loops on hook to complete cluster, 6 ch, 1 ss in top of cluster just made, 4 ch, 1 dc in next 1-ch sp (between 2 tr); rep from * to end, working last dc of last rep in top of 3 ch at end.
Fasten off.

Crochet diagram

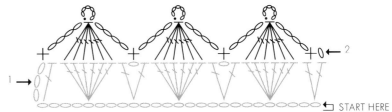

❯ BOLD SCALLOP EDGING

Crochet instructions
Make a multiple of 10 ch, plus 2 extra.
Row 1 (RS): 1 dc in second ch from hook, 1 dc in each of rem ch, turn.
Row 2: 1 ch, 1 dc in first dc, 2 ch, miss next 2 dc, 1 dc in next dc, 7 ch, miss next 3 dc, 1 dc in next dc, *6 ch, miss next 5 dc, 1 dc in next dc, 7 ch, miss next 3 dc, 1 dc in next dc; rep from * to last 3 dc, 2 ch, miss next 2 dc, 1 dc in last dc, turn.
Row 3: 1 ch, 1 dc in first dc, 13 tr in 7-ch loop, *1 dc in next 6-ch sp, 13 tr in next 7-ch loop; rep from *, ending with 1 dc in last dc.
Fasten off.

Crochet diagram

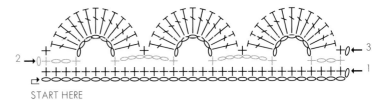

LONG LOOP EDGING

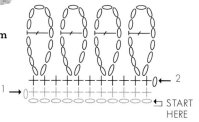

Crochet instructions

Make a multiple of 3 ch.
Row 1 (WS): 1 dc in second ch from hook, 1 dc in each of rem ch, turn.
Row 2 (RS): 1 ch, 1 dc in first dc, 9 ch, 1 tr in sixth ch from hook, 4 ch,
*1 dc in each of next 3 dc, 9 ch, 1 tr in sixth ch from hook, 4 ch;
rep from * to last dc, 1 dc in last dc.
Fasten off.

Crochet diagram

DIAMOND EDGING

Crochet instructions

Make a multiple of 6 ch, plus 2 extra.
Row 1 (RS): 1 dc in 2nd ch from hook, *4 ch, yrh twice and insert hook in
same place as last dc, (yrh and draw first two loops on hook) twice, yrh
twice, miss next 5 ch and insert hook in next ch, (yrh and draw first two
loops on hook) twice, yrh and draw through all three loops on hook (called
dtr2tog), 4 ch, 1 dc in same place as last dtr; rep from * to end, turn.
Row 2: 5 ch, 1 dtr in first dtr2tog, 4 ch, 1 dc in same place as last dtr, *4 ch,
dtr2tog over last dtr worked into and next dtr, 4 ch, 1 dc in same place as last
dtr; rep from *, 4 ch, yrh twice and insert hook in same place as last dc, (yrh
and draw first two loops on hook) twice, yrh three times and insert hook in
last dc in previous row, (yrh and draw first two loops on hook) three times,
yrh and draw through all three loops on hook.
Fasten off.

Crochet diagram

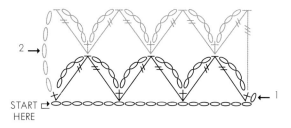

DOUBLE SCALLOP EDGING

Crochet instructions

Make a multiple of 5 ch, plus 2 extra.
Row 1 (RS): 1 dc in second ch from hook, 1 dc in each of rem ch, turn.
Row 2: 6 ch, miss first 2 dc, 1 dc in next dc, *5 ch, miss next 4 dc, 1 dc in
next dc; rep from * to last 3 dc, 3 ch, miss next 2 dc, 1 tr in last dc, turn.
Row 3: 3 ch, 3 dc in first 3-ch sp, 1 dc in next dc (between loops), *work
(3 dc, 3 ch, 3 dc) all in next 5-ch loop, 1 dc in next dc; rep from *, ending
with (3 dc, 3 ch, 1 dc) in last 6-ch loop, turn.
Row 4: 1 ch, 1 dc in first 3-ch picot, *5 ch, 1 dc in next 3-ch picot; rep
from * to end, turn.
Row 5: 1 ch, 1 dc in first dc, *1 ch, 6 tr in next 5-ch loop, 1 ch, 1 dc in
next dc; rep from * to end.
Fasten off.

Crochet diagram

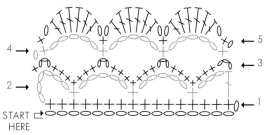

SIMPLE MULTIPLE-STITCH EDGING

Crochet instructions
Make a multiple of 8 ch, plus 2 extra.
Row 1 (WS): 1 dc in second ch from hook, 1 dc in each of rem ch, turn.
Row 2 (RS): 1 ch, 1 ss in first dc, *1 dc in next dc, 1 htr in next dc, 1 tr in next dc, 3 dtr in next dc, 1 tr in next dc, 1 htr in next dc, 1 dc in next dc, 1 ss in next dc; rep from * to end. Fasten off.

Crochet diagram

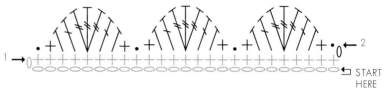

PETAL EDGING

Crochet instructions
Make a multiple of 14 ch, plus 2 extra.
Row 1 (RS): 1 dc in second ch from hook, 1 dc in each of rem ch, turn.
Row 2: 1 ch, 1 dc in first dc, *6 ch, miss next 6 dc, work (2 tr, 2 ch, 2 tr) all in next dc, 6 ch, miss next 6 dc, 1 dc in next dc; rep from * to end, turn.
Row 3: 1 ch, 1 dc in first dc, *6 ch, work (2 tr, 2 ch, 2 tr) all in next 2-ch sp, 6 ch, 1 dc in next dc; rep from * to end. Fasten off.
Note: When blocking this edging, pin out each point at each 2-ch sp to achieve the correct shape.

Crochet diagram

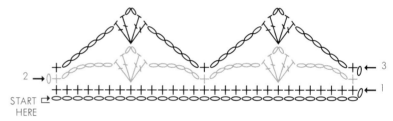

CIRCLES EDGING

Crochet instructions
Make a multiple of 6 ch.
Row 1 (RS): 1 dc in ninth ch from hook, *7 ch, miss next 5 ch, 1 dc in next ch; rep from * to last 3 ch, 3 ch, miss next 2 ch, 1 dc in last ch, turn.
Row 2: 1 ch, 1 dc in first tr, 2 ch, 1 tr in next dc, *5 ch, 1 tr in next dc; rep from *, ending with 2 ch, 1 dc in fourth ch from last dc in previous row, turn.
Row 3: 1 ch, 1 dc in first dc, *3 ch, 1 tr in next tr, 3 ch, 1 dc in 7-ch loop of row 1 (catching 5-ch loop in previous row inside dc); rep from * to end working last dc of last rep in last dc of row 2.
Fasten off.

Crochet diagram

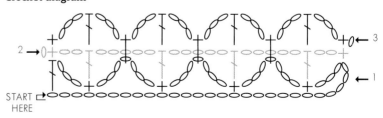

WORKING CROCHETED EDGES

Crocheted edgings are extremely versatile as you can work them separately or as
an integral part of your fabric. If you work the edge separately, in a strip or ribbon, you must then
attach the edge to your piece by simply sewing it to the fabric with a whip or overcast stitch
(see p.85). Working an edging directly onto the main fabric is usually preferable, as it creates
a seamless, unified fabric with less finishing.

EDGINGS WORKED INTO WOVEN FABRICS

Non-knitted/crocheted fabrics can also be edged in crochet. Towels, cushions, pillowcases, napkins, and tea
towels with a fancy crocheted edge elevate the everyday household items into desirable decorative interior
pieces. Woven fabric may need a bit more preparation before an edge is worked, especially with a tight weave
or an edge likely to fray. To prevent fraying under the crochet when using a fabric ground, you may need to
hem the material first, before attempting to edge it. If the fabric is not too dense, you may be able to insert
the hook straight through it on the first row. However, a neater, more even finish can be achieved when you
prepare the edge first. You can do this in various ways with differing results to the finished edge.

> **ATTACHING A CROCHETED EDGING USING THE PUNCHED HOLE METHOD**

1 First mark where you want the hook to be inserted, at regular intervals along the seam or selvedge.

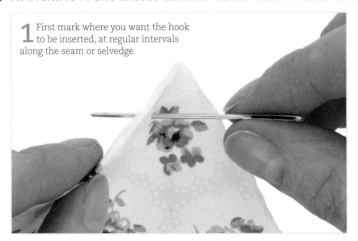

2 Make a series of holes in the edge of the fabric by using the tip of the hook, a large darning needle, or a fabric eyelet hole punch if you are using bulky yarn and a large hook. Ensure that you make the appropriate multiple of holes required for the edge.

3 Join the yarn to the first space with a slip stitch (see p.28), and then work one chain stitch.

4 Work one double crochet (see p.34) into the first hole. Do not pull the yarn tightly or the fabric will ruck up.

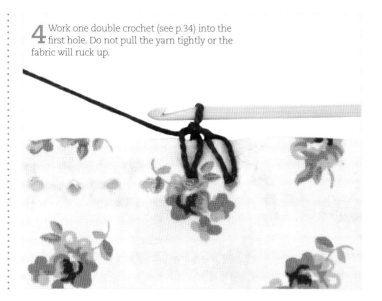

5 Then work one double crochet into each hole evenly along the edge, making sure to keep the stitching quite loose.

ATTACHING A CROCHETED EDGING USING THE BLANKET STITCH METHOD

1 Choose a sewing or embroidery thread, or the crochet thread you intend to use for the edge. This could be the same colour as the edging or a complementary shade. A contrasting colour to both the edge and the fabric can also look effective.

2 Sew an even, traditional blanket stitch (see p.85) along the edge of the fabric. Ensure that the number of stitches used is a multiple that works with the stitches in the edge to create a neat finish.

3 Attach the edging yarn to the horizontal top edge of the first blanket stitch.

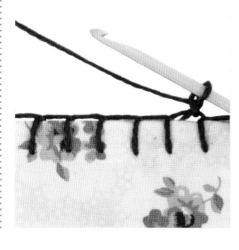

4 Work the first double crochet row into the blanket stitches.

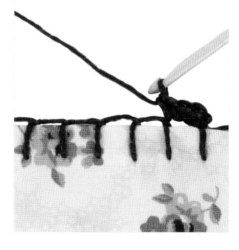

5 Ensure that you work the same multiple of edge stitches into each blanket stitch, around the top horizontal line of each. Fasten off the yarn and weave in all ends.

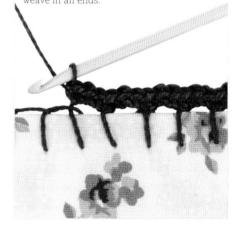

CROCHET-EDGED CUSHIONS

Level of difficulty ✳✳✳

Adding an attractive crocheted embellishment to a cushion, bolster, or pillow is a quick and easy way to personalize shop-bought home furnishing. Turn to pp.94–95 for detailed information about working a crocheted edge.

TECHNIQUES USED Double crochet **p.34**, Treble crochet **p.44**, Working into a chain space **p.75**, Clusters **p.77**, Working crocheted edges **p.94**

SIZE
To fit the length of your cushion

YARN
DMC Petra Crochet Cotton Perle No. 5 – 100g/400m/437yds (100% cotton; any cotton yarn will suit a fine print or silky fabric. You can use a DK yarn for a heavier weight edging)

x 1

HOOK
2.5mm hook

NOTIONS
Yarn needle
Cushion cover ready to embellish

TENSION
Exact tension is not essential

SPECIAL ABBREVIATIONS
3-tr cluster: 3-treble cluster. (Yrh, insert hook into ch sp, yrh and draw a loop through, yrh and draw through first two loops on hook) three times in next 6-ch sp, four loops now on hook, yrh and draw through all four loops on hook to close 3 tr group.

PATTERN
Either make your own cushions or use bought ones with a matching or contrasting thread for the edging.

CLUSTER SCALLOP CUSHION
Prepare the edge to be embellished by making holes at regular intervals along the edge, approx 5mm (¼in) from the edge. You will need a multiple of eight, plus one hole for this edging to work. See diagram below. With right side (RS) facing, attach yarn to the edge to be embellished, work 1 ch.
Row 1: Work 1 dc into each hole along the edge.
Row 2: 1 ch, 3 dc, *6 ch, miss next 3 dc, 5 dc; rep from * to last 6 dc, 6 ch, miss next 3 dc, 1 dc in each of last 3 dc, turn.
Row 3: 3 ch, 1 3-tr cluster in next 6 ch sp, *4 ch, one 3-tr cluster in same ch sp, 4 ch, one 3-tr cluster in same ch sp, but do not close the cluster (leave last four loops on hook), one 3-tr cluster in next 6-ch sp and close this cluster and last cluster at the same time by drawing the loop through all seven loops on hook; rep from * to last 6-ch sp, (4 ch, one 3-tr cluster in same ch sp) twice, 1 tr in last dc.
Fasten off.

TRIPLE PICOT VARIATION CUSHION
Prepare the edge to be embellished by working a blanket stitch along the RS of the edge, using the yarn you will be edging with. Make a multiple of four blanket stitches. See diagram below.
Attach yarn to the first blanket stitch, with wrong side (WS) facing.
Row 1: Work 4 dc into the first blanket stitch, then work 3 dc into each of next blanket stitches along edge, turn.
Row 2: 5 ch, work (1 dc, [5 ch, 1 dc] twice) all in first dc, *4 ch, miss next 5 dc, dc into next dc, 4 ch, miss next 5 dc, (1 dc, [5 ch, 1 dc] three times) all in next dc; rep from * to end.
Fasten off.

Cluster scallop diagram

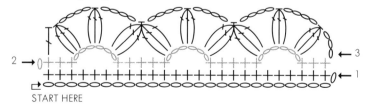

START HERE

Triple picot variation diagram

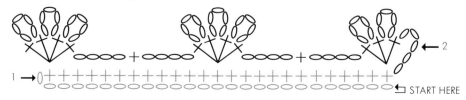

START HERE

CIRCULAR CROCHET

Crochet can be worked not only back and forth in rows, but round and round in circles to form tubes or flat shapes started from the centre (called motifs). The basic techniques for crocheting in the round are very easy to learn, even for a beginner, so it is not surprising that many popular crochet accessories are made with circular crochet, including flowers and Afghan motifs, as well as seamless toys, hats, mittens, containers, and bags.

CROCHETING TUBES

Tubular crochet is started on a long chain of foundation stitches that are joined at the ends to form a ring. The subsequent rounds of stitches are then worked around this foundation ring. The easiest of all crochet cylinders is a double crochet tube, shown below, which is worked in a spiral without turning chains.

> STARTING A TUBE

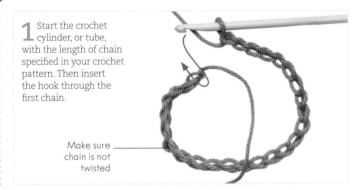

1 Start the crochet cylinder, or tube, with the length of chain specified in your crochet pattern. Then insert the hook through the first chain.

Make sure chain is not twisted

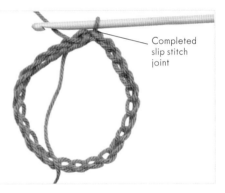

2 Draw a loop through the chain and at the same time through the loop on the hook to complete the slip stitch. This joins the chain into a ring. Work the first and following rounds as directed in your pattern.

Completed slip stitch joint

> DOUBLE CROCHET SPIRAL TUBE

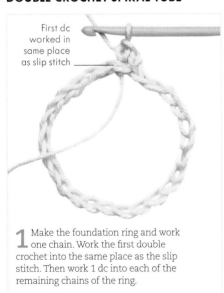

First dc worked in same place as slip stitch

1 Make the foundation ring and work one chain. Work the first double crochet into the same place as the slip stitch. Then work 1 dc into each of the remaining chains of the ring.

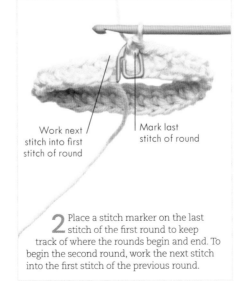

Work next stitch into first stitch of round

Mark last stitch of round

2 Place a stitch marker on the last stitch of the first round to keep track of where the rounds begin and end. To begin the second round, work the next stitch into the first stitch of the previous round.

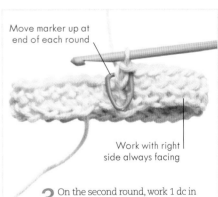

Move marker up at end of each round

Work with right side always facing

3 On the second round, work 1 dc in each dc in the round below. At the end of the round, move the stitch marker up onto the last stitch of this round. (As the spiral grows, the beginning of the round moves gradually to the right.) Continue round and round in the same way until the crochet tube is the required length.

> **TREBLE CROCHET TUBE WITHOUT TURNS**

When basic stitches taller than double crochet are used to make crochet tubes, each round is started with a turning chain.

1 To work a treble crochet tube with the right side of the work always facing (without turns), begin with three chains. Then work 1 tr into the next chain and each of the remaining chains around the ring.

Three chains count as first stitch of round

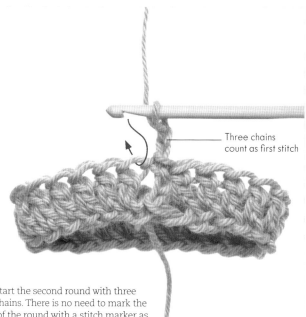

Three chains count as first stitch

3 Start the second round with three chains. There is no need to mark the end of the round with a stitch marker as the turning chain shows where each round begins. Continue around the tube again, working 1 tr into each tr in the previous round. At the end of the second round, join the last stitch to the top of the turning chain with a slip stitch. Continue in the same way, beginning all following rounds with three chains.

Join with a slip stitch to top of three chains

2 At the end of the round, join the last stitch to the top of the turning chain at the beginning of the round by working a slip stitch into the third of the three chains.

> **TREBLE CROCHET TUBE WITH TURNS**

If a treble crochet tube needs to match crochet worked in rows in other parts of an item, then the work can be turned at the end of each round.

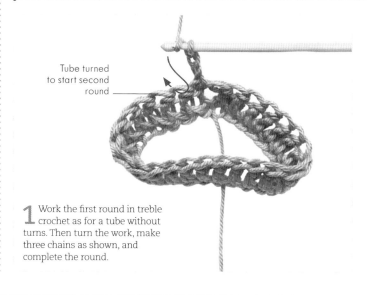

Tube turned to start second round

1 Work the first round in treble crochet as for a tube without turns. Then turn the work, make three chains as shown, and complete the round.

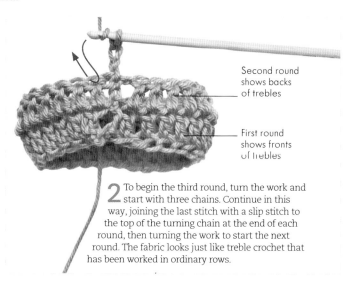

Second round shows backs of trebles

First round shows fronts of trebles

2 To begin the third round, turn the work and start with three chains. Continue in this way, joining the last stitch with a slip stitch to the top of the turning chain at the end of each round, then turning the work to start the next round. The fabric looks just like treble crochet that has been worked in ordinary rows.

TECHNIQUES

A BASIC GRANNY SQUARE

If you are new to crochet, the granny square, or motif (also called an Afghan square), is an excellent practice project, and a great way to perfect your treble stitch. If you are a seasoned crocheter, there are many variations on the basic granny square that you can try.

Practice square: Use a different colour for each round until you are confident about making motifs.

1 Work 6 ch and join with a ss to form a ring. For round one, work 3 ch, then 2 tr in the ring, then 3 more ch; *then 3 tr in the ring and 3 ch.

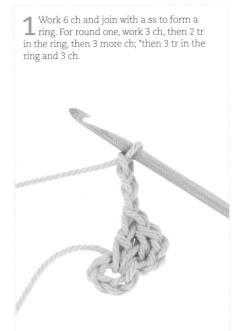

2 Rep from * two more times. Join the round with a ss to the top of the first chain. Break off yarn at the end of this and every round for a striped motif, adding different colours for each round.

3 For round two, join new yarn in any 3-ch sp, ch 3, work 2 tr, ch 3 and work 3 tr in the same sp; *chain 1, work 3 tr, ch 3 and work 3 tr all in the next 3-ch sp. Repeat from * two more times, then ch 1. Join round with a ss to the top of the first chain.

4 For round three, join the yarn in any 3-ch sp, ch 3, work 2 tr, ch 3 and work 3 tr in the same sp. Ch 1, work 3 tr in the next 1-ch sp; *ch 1, work 3 tr, ch 3 and work 3 tr all in the next 3-ch sp for the corner. Ch 1, work 3 tr in the next 1-ch sp. Repeat from * around, then ch 1. Join round with a ss to the top of the first chain.

Turn the motif as you work.

> JOINING MOTIFS

Flat slip-stitch seam: Working seams with crochet stitches is the simplest way to join motifs. For a slip-stitch seam, lay the two motifs side by side. Work each slip stitch through only one loop (the back loop) of the top of a stitch on each motif. (Use a hook one size smaller than the hook used for the motifs, but work the stitches very loosely.)

Right sides together

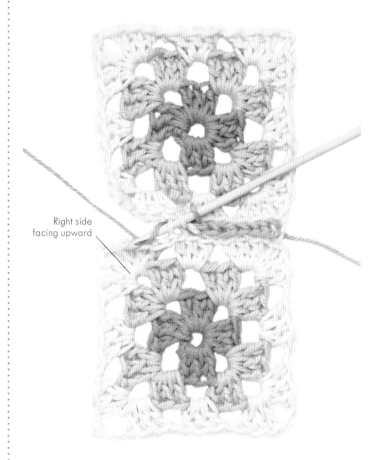

Right side facing upward

Double-crochet seam: A double-crochet seam is also quick to work. It forms a ridge, which can either be a feature on the right side, or hidden on the wrong side of the work. Place the two motifs together, either wrong side to wrong side (ridge on right side), or right side to right side (ridge on wrong side). Then work each double crochet through only one loop of the top of a stitch on each square (the loop closest to you on the top square and the loop farthest from you on the bottom square).

> THE JOIN-AS-YOU-GO METHOD

When you are making motifs, you can create a neat and practically invisible seam by joining each motif to the others as you work. To demonstrate the technique, a traditional granny square method is described, but you can apply the same technique to other types of motif. First, crochet one complete motif, then work the second motif up to the penultimate round, but don't fasten off. Work along the edge of the second motif, right up until you are about to make the corner chain. Work one chain and attach with a slip stitch into one of the corner chains on the first motif, and finish off the corner space with one chain and a group of three trebles into the corner space.

Instead of working one chain before the next group of trebles, join with a slip stitch into the next 1-chain space on the first motif. Work the next group of trebles along the edge of your second motif, before joining it to the first motif with a slip stitch as before.

Continue in this way until you get to the next corner, then join the corner chain of the second motif to the corner chain of the first in the same way as before. Now continue around the edges to complete the second motif. Once you have completed the second motif, fasten off. Repeat for all following motifs, noting that some will need to be joined along two edges.

SIMPLE MOTIF PATTERNS

Making crochet motifs is a great way to use up yarn scraps, and this was probably the reason they became so popular. You can stitch motifs together to form small items, such as bags or cushion covers, or to form larger items, such as throws and baby blankets. Joined motifs also make great scarves and shawls, especially when made in gossamer mohair. But if you are a beginner, stick to less hairy yarns when making your first motifs as it is easier to learn the technique with a smooth, standard lightweight or medium-weight wool yarn. When following diagrams, use colours as explained in the written instructions. The symbol tones used in the diagram are used to distinguish the rows and do not indicate colour changes. (See p.81 for a list of crochet abbreviations and basic stitch symbols.) Join on new colours (see p.57). Do not turn the motifs at the end of the rounds, but work with the right side always facing.

❯ TRADITIONAL AFGHAN SQUARE

Crochet diagram

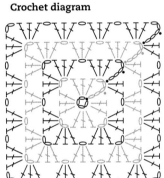

Crochet instructions

This square is worked in four colours (A, B, C, D), a different colour for each round.
With A, work 4 ch, ss to first ch to form a ring.
Round 1 (RS): With A, 5 ch (counts as 1 tr and a 2-ch sp), (3 tr in ring, 2 ch [these 2 ch form a corner sp]) 3 times, 2 tr in ring, join with a ss to third of 5 ch. Fasten off A.
Round 2: With B, join with a ss to a 2-ch corner sp, 5 ch, 3 tr in same corner sp, *1 ch, (3 tr, 2 ch, 3 tr) in next 2-ch corner sp; rep from * twice more, 1 ch, 2 tr in same corner sp as 5 ch at beg of round, join with a ss to 3rd of 5-ch. Fasten off B.
Round 3: With C, join to a 2-ch corner sp, 5 ch, 3 tr in same corner sp, *1 ch, 3 tr in next 1-ch sp, 1 ch, (3 tr, 2 ch, 3 tr) in next 2-ch corner sp; rep from * twice more, 1 ch, 3 tr in next 1-ch sp, 1 ch, 2 tr in same sp as 5-ch at beg of round, join with a ss to 3rd of 5-ch. Fasten off C.
Round 4: With D, join to a 2-ch corner sp, 5 ch, 3 tr in same corner sp, *(1 ch, 3 tr in next 1-ch sp) twice, 1 ch, (3 tr, 2 ch, 3 tr) in next 2-ch corner sp; rep from * twice more, (1 ch, 3 tr in next 1-ch sp) twice, 1 ch, 2 tr in same sp as 5 ch at beg of round, join with a ss to third of 5 ch.
Fasten off.

❯ PLAIN SQUARE

Crochet diagram

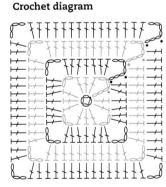

Crochet instructions

This square is worked in four colours (A, B, C, D).
With A, work 4 ch, ss to first ch to form a ring.
Round 1 (RS): 5 ch (counts as 1 tr and a 2-ch sp), (3 tr in ring, 2 ch) 3 times, 2 tr in ring, join with a ss to third of 5 ch.
Round 2: With B, join with a ss to any 2-ch sp, 7 ch (counts as 1 tr and a 4-ch sp), 2 tr in same 2-ch corner sp, *1 tr in each of next 3 tr, (2 tr, 4 ch, 2 tr) in next 2-ch corner sp; rep from * twice more, 1 tr in each of next 3 sts (working last of these tr in top of turning ch at beg of previous round), 1 tr in same sp as 7 ch at beg of round, join with a ss to third of 7 ch. Fasten off B.
Round 3: With C, join to a 4-ch corner sp, 7 ch, 2 tr in same corner sp, *1 tr in each of tr along this side of square, (2 tr, 4 ch, 2 tr) in next 4-ch corner sp; rep from * twice more, 1 tr in each of tr along this side of square (working last of these tr in top of turning ch at beg of previous round), 1 tr in same sp as 7 ch at beg of round, join with a ss to third of 7-ch. Fasten off B.
Round 4: With D, rep round 3.
Fasten off.

FLOWER HEXAGON

Crochet diagram

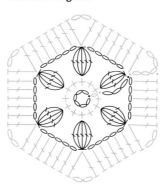

Crochet instructions
Note: bobble = (yrh and insert hook in dc, yrh and draw a loop through, yrh and draw through first two loops on hook) five times all in same dc (six loops now on hook), yrh and draw through all six loops on hook.
This hexagon is worked in two colours (A, B).
With A, work 6 ch, ss to first ch to form a ring.
Round 1 (RS): 1 ch, 12 dc in ring, join with a ss to first dc.
Round 2: 3 ch, (yrh and insert hook in same dc as last ss, yrh and draw a loop through, yrh and draw through first two loops on hook) four times all in same dc (five loops now on hook), yrh and draw through all five loops on hook (counts as first bobble), *5 ch, miss next dc, 1 bobble in next dc; rep from * 4 times more, 5 ch, join with a ss to top of first bobble. Fasten off A.
Round 3: With B, join with a ss to top of a bobble, 5 ch (counts as 1 tr and a 2-ch sp), 1 tr in same place as ss, *5 tr in next 5-ch sp, (1 tr, 2 ch, 1 tr) in top of next bobble; rep from * 4 times more, 5 tr in next 5-ch sp, join with a ss to third of 5 ch at beg of round.
Fasten off.

SIMPLE HEXAGON

Crochet diagram

Crochet instructions
Note: cluster = (yrh and insert hook in sp, yrh and draw a loop through, yrh and draw through first two loops on hook) three times all in same sp (four loops now on hook), yrh and draw through all four loops on hook.

This hexagon is worked in two colours (A, B).
With A, work 6 ch, ss to first ch to form a ring.
Round 1 (RS): 3 ch, tr2tog (counts as first cluster), (3 ch, 1 cluster in ring) 5 times, 1 ch, join with 1 htr in top of first cluster.
Round 2: 3 ch, tr2tog in sp formed by 1-htr, *3 ch, (1 cluster, 3 ch, 1 cluster) in next 3-ch sp; rep from * 4 times more, 3 ch, 1 cluster in next 1-ch sp, 1 ch, join with 1 htr in top of first cluster changing to B with last yrh of htr. Cut off A.
Round 3: With B, 3 ch, tr2tog in sp formed by 1-htr, *3 ch, (1 cluster, 3 ch, 1 cluster) in next 3-ch sp, 3 ch, 1 cluster in next 3-ch sp; rep from * 4 times more, 3 ch, (1 cluster, 3 ch, 1 cluster) in next 3-ch sp, 1 ch, join with 1 htr in top of first cluster changing to C with last yrh of htr. Cut off B.
Round 4: With A, 3 ch, 1 tr in sp formed by 1-htr, *3 tr in next 3-ch sp, (3 tr, 2 ch, 3 tr) in next 3-ch sp, 3 tr in next 3-ch sp; rep from * 4 times more, 3 tr in next 3-ch sp, (3 tr, 2 ch, 3 tr) in next 3-ch sp, 1 tr in next 1-ch sp, join with a ss to third of 3 ch at beg of round.
Fasten off.

CIRCLE

Crochet diagram

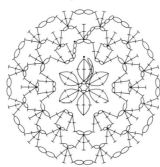

Crochet instructions
Cluster: Work three half finished trebles into the next stitch, then finish them off together. Yrh, insert into st, pull loop through, yrh, pull through two loops, *yrh, insert into same st, pull loop through, yrh, pull through two loops*, rep from * to * once, four loops on hook, yrh and pull through all loops. With yarn A, 5 ch, join into round with ss.
Round 1: 3 ch, *1 cl in ring, 2 ch; rep from * 5 more times, join round with ss. (6cl, 6ch sp). Change to yarn B, attaching to any 2-ch sp.
Round 2: 3 ch, (1 tr, 2 ch, 2 tr) in same 2-ch sp, 2ch, *(2 tr, 2 ch, 2 tr) in next 2 ch sp, 2 ch; rep from * to end, join round with ss. (12 tr groups, 12 ch sp) Change to yarn C, attaching to any 2-ch sp.
Round 3: 3 ch, 2 tr in same 2 ch sp, 2 ch, (3 tr, 2 ch) into each ch sp to end, join round with ss. (12 tr groups, 12 ch sp). Change to yarn D, attaching to any ch sp.
Round 4: As round 3.
Fasten off.

⟩ TRIANGLE

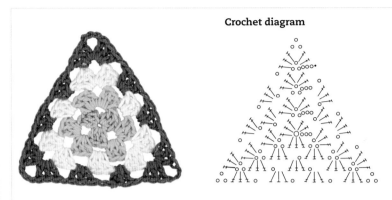

Crochet diagram

Crochet instructions
With yarn A, work 5 ch, ss in first ch to join round.
Round 1: 3 ch, (2 tr, 3 ch) into ring, (3 tr, 2 ch) twice in ring, join round with ss. Change to yarn B, attaching to any 3-ch sp.
Round 2: 3 ch, (2 tr, 3 ch, 3 tr) into same ch sp, *1 ch, (3 tr, 3 ch, 3 tr) into next ch sp; rep from * twice, 1ch, join round with ss. Change to yarn C, attaching to any 3 ch sp.
Round 3: 3 ch, (2 tr, 3 ch, 3 tr) in same ch sp, 1 ch, 3 tr in next 1-ch sp, 1 ch, *(3 tr, 3 ch, 3 tr) into next ch sp, 1 ch, 3 tr in next 1-ch sp, 1 ch; rep from * to end, join round with ss. Change to yarn D, attaching to any 3-ch sp.
Round 4: 3 ch, (2 tr, 3 ch, 3 tr) in same ch sp, 1 ch, (3 tr in next 1-ch sp, 1 ch) twice, *(3 tr, 3 ch, 3 tr) into next ch sp, 1 ch, (3 tr in next 1-ch sp, 1 ch) twice; rep from * to end, join round with ss. Fasten off.

SIMPLE FLOWER PATTERNS

Crochet flowers are very attractive – even simple ones like these, which are all easy and very quick to make. You may want to try them out right away but wonder what to do with them. First, they make great individual brooches, which, in turn, are perfect gifts. Just sew brooch pins to the back and maybe a button or an artificial pearl to the flower centre. Crochet flowers and leaves can also be used to decorate crocheted hats, the ends of scarves, glove cuffs, or bags. Sprinkled over a cushion cover, they will make a bold statement in a room as well. When following diagrams, use colours as explained in the written instructions. The symbol tones are used to distinguish the rows and do not indicate colour changes. (See p.81 for a list of crochet abbreviations and basic stitch symbols.) Join on new yarn colours as explained on p.57. Do not turn at the end of the rounds, but work with the right side of the flowers always facing.

⟩ HEPTAGON FLOWER

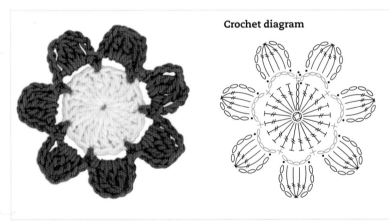

Crochet diagram

Crochet instructions
Note: cluster = (yrh twice and insert hook in sp, yrh and draw a loop through, [yrh and draw through first two loops on hook] twice) four times all in same sp (five loops now on hook), yrh and draw through all five loops now on hook. This flower is worked in two colours (A, B).
With A, work 4 ch, ss to first ch to form a ring.
Round 1 (RS): 4 ch (counts as first dtr), 20 dtr in ring, join with a ss to 4th of 4 ch. Fasten off A.
Round 2: With B, join with a ss to same place as last ss, 1 ch (does NOT count as a st), 1 dc in same place as last ss, (5 ch, miss next 2 dtr, 1 dc in next dtr) six times, 5 ch, join with a ss to first dc of round.
Round 3: *Work (1 ss, 4 ch, 1 cluster, 4 ch, 1 ss) all in next 5-ch loop; rep from * six times more, join with a ss to last dc in round 2. Fasten off.

⟩ SHORT LOOP FLOWER

Crochet diagram

Crochet instructions
This flower is worked in two colours (A, B).
With A, work 4 ch, ss to first ch to form a ring.
Round 1 (RS): 1 ch (does NOT count as a st), 8 dc in ring, join with a ss to first dc of round.
Round 2: 1 ch (does NOT count as a st), 2 dc in same place as ss, *2 dc in next dc; rep from * to end, join with a ss to first dc of round. 16 dc. Fasten off A.
Round 3: With B, join with a ss to a dc, 1 ch, work (1 dc, 9 ch, 1 dc) all in the same position as last ss, 1 dc in next dc, *work (1 dc, 9 ch, 1 dc) all in next dc, 1 dc in next dc; rep from * six times more, join with a ss to first dc of round. Fasten off.

❯ LONG LOOP FLOWER

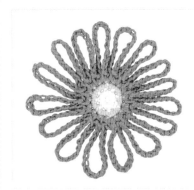

Crochet diagram

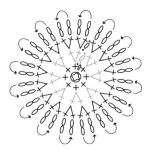

Crochet instructions

This flower is worked in three colours (A, B, C).
With A, work 4 ch, ss to first ch to form a ring.
Round 1 (RS): 1 ch (does NOT count as a st), 8 dc in ring, join with a ss to first dc of round. Fasten off A.
Round 2: With B, join with a ss to a dc, 1 ch (does NOT count as a st), 2 dc in same place as last ss, *2 dc in next dc; rep from * to end, join with a ss to first dc of round. 16 dc. Fasten off B.
Round 3: With C, join with a ss to a dc, 1 ch, work (1 dc, 17 ch, 1 dc) all in same place as last ss, *work (1 dc, 17 ch, 1 dc) all in next dc; rep from * 14 times more, join with a ss to first dc of round.
Fasten off.

❯ PENTAGON FLOWER

Crochet diagram

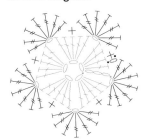

Crochet instructions

This flower is worked in two colours (A, B).
With A, work 5 ch, ss to first ch to form a ring.
Round 1 (RS): 3 ch (counts as first tr), 4 tr in ring, (1 ch, 5 tr in ring) four times, 1 ch, join with a ss to top of 3 ch at beg of round. Fasten off A.
Round 2: With B, join with a ss to a centre tr of a 5-tr group, 1 ch, 1 dc in same place as last ss, (7 dtr in next 1-ch sp, 1 dc in centre tr of next 5-tr group) four times, 7 dtr in next 1-ch sp, join with a ss to first dc of round.
Fasten off.

❯ SQUARE PETAL FLOWER

Crochet diagram

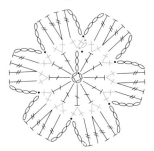

Crochet instructions

This flower is worked in three colours (A, B, C).
With A, work 4 ch, ss to first ch to form a ring.
Round 1 (RS): 3 ch (counts as first tr), 11 tr in ring, join with a ss to top of 3 ch at beg of round. Fasten off A.
Round 2: With B, join with a ss same place as last ss, 1 ch (does NOT count as a st), 2 dc in same place as last ss, 2 dc in each tr to end, join with a ss to first dc of round. 24 dc.
Fasten off B.
Round 3: With C, join with a ss to a dc, *4 ch, 1 dtr in next dc, 2 dtr in next dc, 1 dtr in next dc, 4 ch, ss in next dc; rep from * 5 times more, working last ss in same place as first ss of round.
Fasten off.

❯ SIMPLE LEAF

Crochet diagram

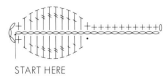

START HERE

Crochet instructions

Note: The leaf is worked in one row, around both sides of the foundation chain.
To begin leaf and stem, make 23 ch.
Row 1 (RS): Working into only one loop of each foundation chain, work 1 dc in 2nd ch from hook, 1 dc in each of next 10 ch (this completes the stem), 1 htr in next ch, 1 tr in each of next 2 ch, 1 dtr in each of next 4 ch, 1 tr in each of next 2 ch, 1 htr in next ch, 1 dc in next ch (this is the last ch), 3 ch, then continue working around other side of foundation ch (working into other loop of each ch) as follows: 1 dc in first ch, 1 htr in next ch, 1 tr in each of next 2 ch, 1 dtr in each of next 4 ch, 1 tr in each of next 2 ch, 1 htr in next ch, ss in next ch.
Fasten off. Press stem flat.

OPENWORK

Whether worked with fine threads for lace collars, pillow edgings, and tablecloths or with soft wools for shawls, throws, and scarves, openwork crochet has an enduring appeal. As illustrated by the easy techniques on this page and the next, these airy lace textures are produced by working chain spaces and chain loops between the basic stitches.

SIMPLE LACE TECHNIQUES

A few of the openwork stitch patterns on pp.111–113 are explained here to provide an introduction to some popular openwork crochet techniques – chain loops, shells, and picots. Refer to the instructions for the stitches when following the steps that are shown here.

> CHAIN LOOP MESH

1 After working the first row of chain loops into the foundation chain as explained (see p.111), work the 5-chain loops of the following rows into the loops below, joining them on with a dc as shown here.

2 Remember to work the last dc of each row into the space inside the turning chain made at the beginning of the previous row. If you don't, your lace will become narrower.

> SHELL MESH STITCH

1 On the shell row of this stitch (see p.112), start each shell with a dc in a chain loop. Then work all the tr of the shell into a single dc as shown.

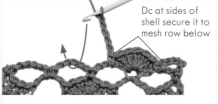

Dc at sides of shell secure it to mesh row below

2 Complete the shell with a dc worked into the following chain loop. Then work a chain loop and join it to the next chain loop with a dc as shown.

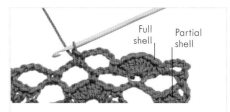

Full shell   Partial shell

3 Continue alternating shells and chain loops to complete the shell row. Work mesh and shell rows alternately, working partial shells at ends on alternate shell rows.

> PICOT NET STITCH

1 In this stitch pattern (see p.111), work four chains for each picot. Close the picot-ring by working a slip stitch in the fourth chain from the hook as shown.

2 Work 3 dc between each of the picots in each picot row as shown.

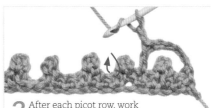

3 After each picot row, work a 2-chain space above each picot and a tr between the picots as shown.

FILET CROCHET

Filet crochet is the easiest of all the openwork techniques. Once you learn how to work the simple structure of the open filet mesh and the solid filet blocks, all you need to do is follow a simple chart to form the motifs and the repeating patterns.

⟫ MAKING BASIC FILET MESH

When working the foundation chain for the basic filet mesh, there is no need to start with an exact number of chains, just make an extra long chain and unravel the unused excess later when finishing your crochet.

Filet mesh in symbols and words: The diagram provides the best explanation of how filet mesh is worked. If in doubt, work a mesh from the written pattern as follows: Make a multiple of 3 ch (3 ch for each mesh square needed), plus 5 extra (to form the right-side edge and top of the first mesh square of the first row).
Row 1: 1 tr in eighth ch from hook, *2 ch, miss next 2 ch, 1 tr in next ch; rep from * to end.
Row 2: 5 ch, miss first tr, 1 tr in next tr, *2 ch, 1 tr in next tr; rep from * working last tr in third ch from last tr in row below.

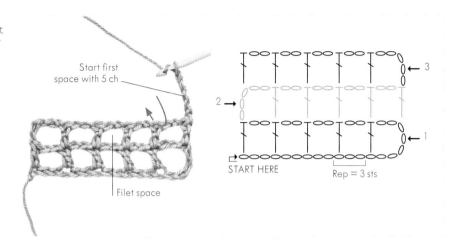

⟫ MAKING FILET BLOCKS

The pattern motifs on filet crochet are created by filling in some of the mesh squares and leaving others empty. In other words, the designs are built up with solid squares and square holes. Having learned how to work the filet mesh, understanding how to fill them in to form blocks is easy.

Filet blocks in symbols: The diagram illustrates how the blocks are made – instead of working two chains to form an empty square, work two trebles to fill in the square. An individual block consists of a treble on each side and two trebles in the centre. To work a block above a filet space, work the two centre trebles into the 2-chain space. To work a block above another block, work a treble into each of the trebles below.

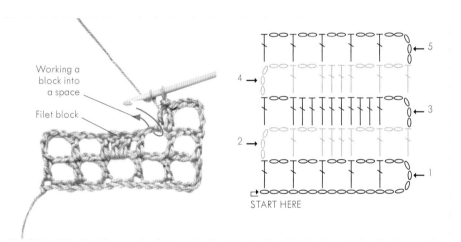

⟫ READING FILET CHARTS

This chart on the right shows the simple motif in the block symbol diagram above. Although actual filet charts are bigger and have elaborate patterns (see pp.108–110), the principle is the same as for this tiny chart. Each square on the chart represents either a filet space or a filet block. Please note that left-handed crocheters will need to work the diagram and instructions in a mirror image.
    To start working from a chart, make three chains for each of the squares along the bottom row of the chart, plus five chains extra. (You can work the chart stitch-repeat as many times as desired.) Working the chart from the bottom upwards, make the blocks and spaces on the chart, while reading the first row and all following odd-numbered rows from right to left, and the even-numbered rows from left to right.

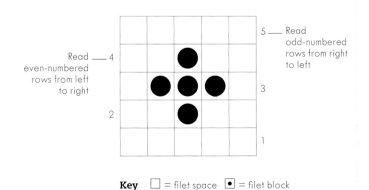

Key ☐ = filet space ▣ = filet block

FILET STITCH PATTERNS

Follow the instructions on p.107 to work filet crochet from these charts. The best yarn to use for filet lace is a superfine cotton yarn and a suitably small size crochet hook (see recommended hook sizes on p.14). This technique forms patterns by filling in parts of a chain stitch mesh with treble crochet stitches. Because filet crochet is reversible, it makes great curtains. It can also be used for edgings along the ends of pillowcases and hand towels, or even wall hangings.

➤ SPECIAL NOTE AND SYMBOL KEY

Repeat the charted motifs as many times as desired widthwise, and work across the stitches in rows until the chart is complete. To continue the pattern upwards, start at row 1 again.

Key ☐ = filet space   ▣ = filet block

➤ DIAMONDS BORDER

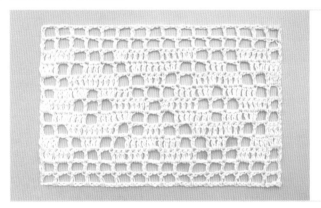

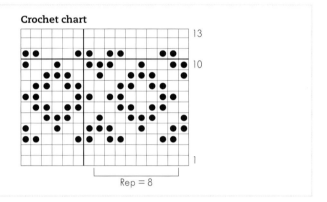

Crochet chart

➤ FLOWERS AND CIRCLES

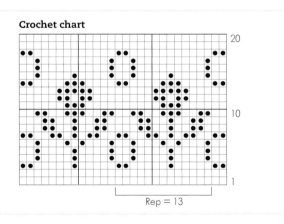

Crochet chart

➤ ZIGZAG BORDER

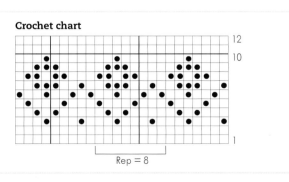

Crochet chart

> **APPLE**

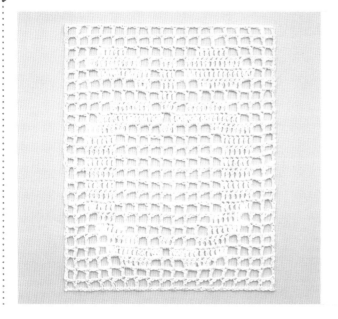

Crochet chart

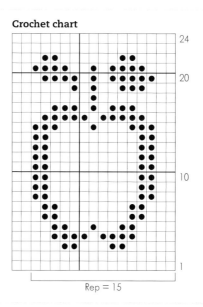

Rep = 15

> **BLOOM**

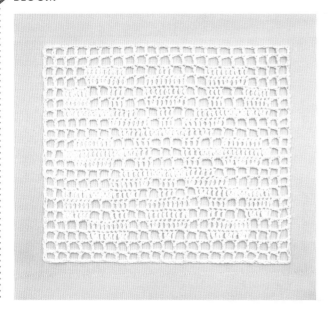

Crochet chart

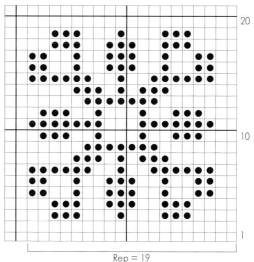

Rep = 19

> **CROSSES BORDER**

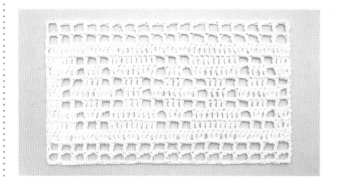

Crochet chart

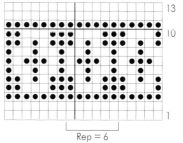

Rep = 6

TECHNIQUES

HEART

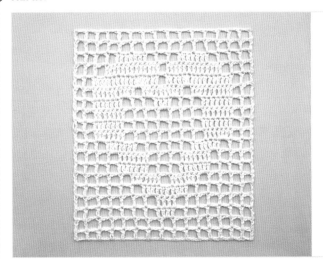

Crochet chart

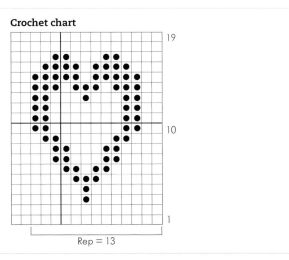

Rep = 13

DOG

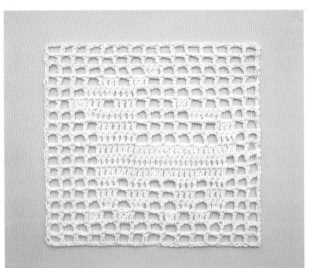

Crochet chart

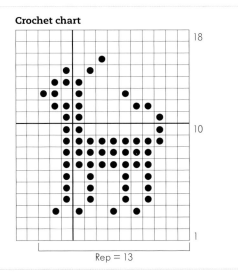

Rep = 13

BIRD

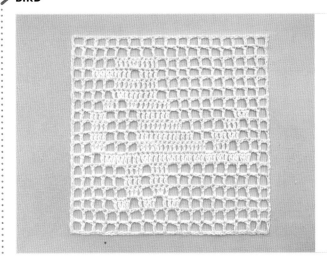

Crochet chart

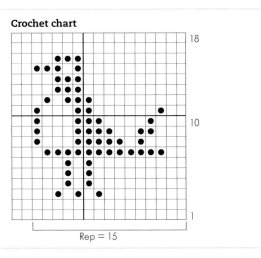

Rep = 15

SIMPLE OPENWORK STITCH PATTERNS

Openwork crochet stitches are popular because of their lacy appearance (see scarf on pp.114–115), and because they are quicker to work than solid crochet textures. The written instructions below explain how many chains to start with. So if working from the diagram, consult the written instructions to make the foundation chain. When working a wide piece, such as a blanket, it is difficult to count and keep track of the number of foundation chains being made. In this case, make a chain a few centimetres longer than the correct length and unravel the excess later.

CHAIN LOOP MESH

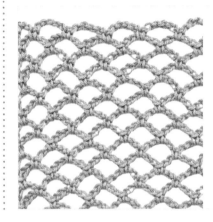

Crochet diagram

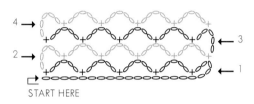

START HERE

Crochet instructions
Make a multiple of 4 ch, plus 2 extra.
Row 1: 1 dc in sixth ch from hook, *5 ch, miss next 3 ch, 1 dc in next ch; rep from * to end, turn.
Row 2: *5 ch, 1 dc in next 5-ch loop; rep from * to end, turn.
Rep row 2 to form patt.

PICOT NET STITCH

Crochet diagram

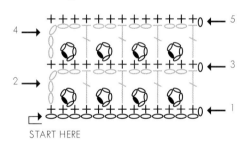

START HERE

Crochet instructions
Make a multiple of 3 ch, plus 2 extra.
Row 1 (RS): 1 dc in second ch from hook, 1 dc in next ch, *4 ch, 1 ss in fourth ch from hook (called 1 picot), 1 dc in each of next 3 ch; rep from * omitting 1 dc at end of last rep, turn.
Row 2: 5 ch (counts as 1 tr and a 2-ch sp), miss first 3 dc (which includes 2 dc before picot and 1 dc after picot), 1 tr in next dc, *2 ch, miss next 2 dc (which includes 1 dc on each side of picot), 1 tr in next dc; rep from * to end, turn.
Row 3 1 ch (does NOT count as a st), 1 dc in first tr, *work (1 dc, 1 picot, 1 dc) all in next 2-ch sp, 1 dc in next tr; rep from * working last dc of last rep in third ch from last tr, turn.
Rep rows 2 and 3 to form patt.

OPEN SHELL STITCH

Crochet diagram

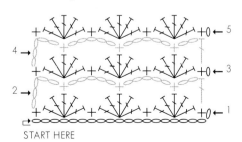

START HERE

Crochet instructions
Make a multiple of 6 ch, plus 2 extra.
Row 1 (RS): 1 dc in second ch from hook, *miss next 2 ch, 5 tr in next ch, miss next 2 ch, 1 dc in next ch; rep from * to end, turn.
Row 2: 5 ch (counts as first tr and a 2-ch sp), 1 dc in centre tr of first shell, *5 ch, 1 dc in centre tr of next shell; rep from *, ending with 2 ch, 1 tr in last dc, turn.
Row 3: 1 ch (does NOT count as a st), 1 dc in first tr, *5 tr in next dc, 1 dc in next 5-ch loop; rep from * working last dc of last rep in third ch from last dc, turn.
Rep rows 2 and 3 to form patt.

ARCHED MESH STITCH

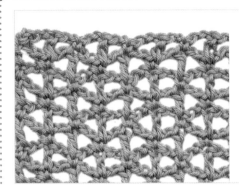

Crochet diagram

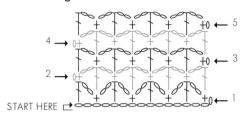

START HERE

Crochet instructions

Make a multiple of 4 ch.
Row 1: 1 dc in second ch from hook, 2 ch, miss next ch, 1 tr in next ch, *2 ch, miss next ch, 1 dc in next ch, 2 ch, miss next ch, 1 tr in next ch; rep from * to end, turn.
Row 2: 1 ch (does NOT count as a st), 1 dc in first tr, 2 ch, 1 tr in next dc, *2 ch, 1 dc in next tr, 2 ch, 1 tr in next dc; rep from * to end, turn.
Rep row 2 to form patt.

BANDED NET STITCH

Crochet diagram

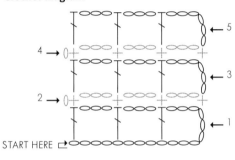

START HERE

Crochet instructions

Make a multiple of 4 ch, plus 2 extra.
Row 1 (RS): 1 tr in tenth ch from hook, *3 ch, miss next 3 ch, 1 tr in next ch; rep from * to end, turn.
Row 2: 1 ch (does NOT count as a st), 1 dc in first tr, *3 ch, 1 dc in next tr; rep from *, ending with 3 ch, miss next 3 ch, 1 dc in next ch, turn.
Row 3: 6 ch (counts as 1 tr and a 3-ch sp), miss first dc and first 3-ch sp, 1 tr in next dc, *3 ch, 1 tr in next dc; rep from * to end, turn.
Rep rows 2 and 3 to form patt.

SHELL MESH STITCH

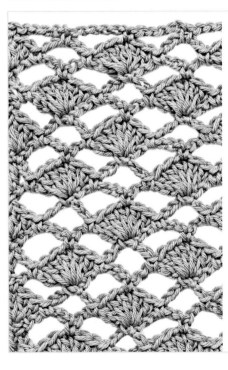

Crochet diagram

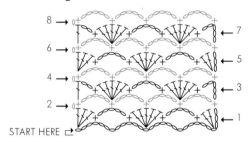

START HERE

Crochet instructions

Make a multiple of 12 ch, plus 4 extra.
Row 1 (RS): 2 tr in fourth ch from hook, *miss next 2 ch, 1 dc in next ch, 5 ch, miss next 5 ch, 1 dc in next ch, miss next 2 ch, 5 tr in next ch; rep from *, ending last rep with 3 tr (instead of 5 tr) in last ch, turn.
Row 2: 1 ch (does NOT count as a st), 1 dc in first tr, *5 ch, 1 dc in next 5-ch loop, 5 ch, 1 dc in third tr of next 5-tr shell; rep from * working last dc of last rep in top of 3-ch at end, turn.
Row 3: *5 ch, 1 dc in next 5-ch loop, 5 tr in next dc, 1 dc in next 5-ch loop; rep from *, ending with 2 ch, 1 tr in last dc, turn.
Row 4: 1 ch (does NOT count as a st), 1 dc in first tr, *5 ch, 1 dc in third tr of next 5-tr shell, 5 ch, 1 dc in next 5-ch loop; rep from * to end, turn.
Row 5: 3 ch (counts as first tr), 2 tr in first dc, *1 dc in next 5-ch loop, 5 ch, 1 dc in next 5-ch loop, 5 tr in next dc; rep from * ending last rep with 3 tr (instead of 5 tr) in last dc, turn.
Rep rows 2–5 to form patt.

❯ BLOCKS LACE

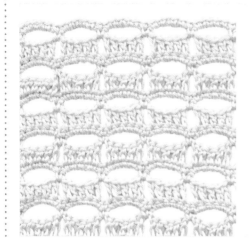

Crochet diagram

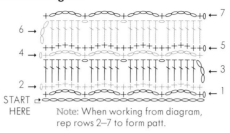

Note: When working from diagram, rep rows 2–7 to form patt.

Crochet instructions
Make a multiple of 5 ch, plus 2 extra.
Row 1 (RS): 1 dc in second ch from hook, *5 ch, miss next 4 ch, 1 dc in next ch; rep from * to end, turn.
Row 2: 1 ch (does NOT count as a st), 1 dc in first dc, *5 dc in next 5-ch loop, 1 dc in next dc; rep from * to end, turn.
Row 3: 3 ch (counts as first tr), miss first dc, 1 tr in each of next 5 dc, *1 ch, miss next dc, 1 tr in each of next 5 dc; rep from * to last dc, 1 tr in last dc, turn.
Row 4: 1 ch (does NOT count as a st), 1 dc in first tr, *5 ch, 1 dc in next 1-ch sp; rep from * working last dc of last rep in top of 3 ch at end, turn.
Rep rows 2–4 to form patt.

❯ TIARA LACE

Crochet diagram

Crochet instructions
Make a multiple of 12 ch.
Row 1 (WS): 1 dc in second ch from hook, *5 ch, miss next 3 ch, 1 dc in next ch; rep from * to last 2 ch, 2 ch, miss next ch, 1 tr in last ch, turn.
Row 2 (RS): 1 ch (does NOT count as a st), 1 dc in first st, miss next 2-ch sp, 7 tr in next 5-ch loop, 1 dc in next 5-ch loop, *5 ch, 1 dc in next 5-ch loop, 7 tr in next 5-ch loop, 1 dc in next 5-ch loop; rep from *, ending with 2 ch, 1 dtr in last dc, turn.
Row 3: 1 ch (does NOT count as a st), 1 dc in first dtr, 5 ch, 1 dc in second of next 7-tr shell, 5 ch, 1 dc in sixth tr of same shell, *5 ch, 1 dc in next 5-ch loop, 5 ch, 1 dc in second of next 7-tr shell, 5 ch, 1 dc in sixth tr of same shell; rep from *, ending with 2 ch, 1 dtr in last dc, turn.
Rep rows 2 and 3 to form patt.

❯ FANS STITCH

Crochet diagram

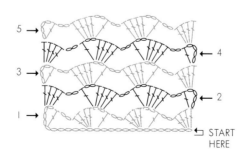

Crochet instructions
Make a multiple of 7 ch, plus 4 extra.
Row 1: 1 tr in fifth ch from hook, 2 ch, miss next 5 ch, 4 tr in next ch, *2 ch, 1 tr in next ch, 2 ch, miss next 5 ch, 4 tr in next ch; rep from * to end, turn.
Row 2: 4 ch, 1 tr in first tr, *2 ch, miss next 2-ch sp and work (4 tr, 2 ch, 1 tr) all in following 2-ch sp; rep from * to last 2-ch sp, miss last 2-ch sp and work 4 tr in 4-ch loop at end, turn.
Rep row 2 to form patt.

SHELL MESH SCARF

This openwork scarf, using lace crochet techniques and fine yarn, is warm but delicate enough to carry you through autumn to spring. Turn to pp.111–113 for a collection of alternative openwork stitch patterns.

Level of difficulty

TECHNIQUES

TECHNIQUES USED Double crochet **p.34**, Treble crochet **p.44**, Making a tassel **p.71**, Shells **p.76**, Simple lace techniques **p.106**

SIZE
Approx 125 x 14cm/49¼ x 5½in, with 10cm (4in) tassels

YARN
Rowan Fine Lace – 50g/400m/437yds (80% baby alpaca and 20% merino wool; use any fine merino for the same effect)

x 1

HOOK
3.5mm hook

NOTIONS
Yarn needle

TENSION
Exact tension is not essential

PATTERN
Work 64 ch (any multiple of 12sts plus 4 extra will work).
Row 1: 2 tr in fourth ch from hook. *miss 2sts, 1 dc in next st, 5 ch, miss 5sts, 1 dc in next st, miss 2sts, 5 tr in next st. Repeat from * and ending last repeat with 3 tr (instead of 5) in last st. Turn.
Row 2: 1 ch, 1 dc in first tr, *5 ch, 1 dc in next ch sp, ch 5, 1 dc in third tr of next 5 tr shell, repeat from * and work last dc of last repeat in top of ch at end. Turn.
Row 3: *5 ch, 1 dc in next ch sp, 5 tr in next dc, 1 dc in next ch sp. Repeat from * and ending with 2 ch, 1 tr in last dc. Turn.
Row 4: 1 ch, 1 dc in first tr, *5 ch, 1 dc in third tr of next 5 tr shell, 5 ch, 1 dc in next ch sp. Repeat from * to end. Turn.
Row 5: 3 ch (counts as first tr), 2 tr in first dc, *1 dc in next ch sp, 5 ch, 1 dc in next ch sp, 5 tr in next dc. Repeat from * ending last repeat with 3 tr (instead of 5) in last dc. Turn.
Repeat rows 2–5 to form pattern until the scarf is the required length.
Fasten off, weave in ends.

MAKING THE TASSELS
Cut the yarn into 25cm (10in) lengths. Tie bundles of 15 lengths together in an overhand knot through each chain loop space at the ends of the scarf – this scarf has 10 tassels at either end.

1 To crochet the shell pattern used for this scarf, insert your hook into the double crochet stitch from the row below.

2 Work the treble stitches for the shell, see pattern above, into the double crochet stitch. Complete the shell by working five trebles into the same double crochet stitch.

3 Encourage the shell to "fan out" within the scarf by working a double crochet stitch into the next chain space before working the next shell sequence.

COLOURWORK

One-colour crochet has its charms, but using your imagination to combine colours
is more challenging and rewarding. All of the crochet colourwork techniques are easy to master
and worth experimenting with. They include colourwork stitch patterns (see pp.117–119), stripes,
tapestry, intarsia (see p.39 and below), and corner to corner crochet (see p.120).

TAPESTRY AND INTARSIA COLOURWORK

Tapestry and intarsia crochet are both worked in double crochet stitches. Tapestry is usually worked with only
two colours in a row; the colour not in use is carried across the top of the row below and stitches are worked
over it to enclose it. When a colour is used only in an area of the crochet rather than across the entire row, the
intarsia technique is required; a different length of yarn is used for each section of colour.

❯ COLOURWORK CHARTS

The charted crochet design
will reveal which technique
to use – tapestry or intarsia.
If the pattern on the chart
shows two colours repeated
across each horizontal row
of squares, then the tapestry
technique is required. Motifs
worked in isolation require
the intarsia technique.
Each square on the charts
represent one double crochet.

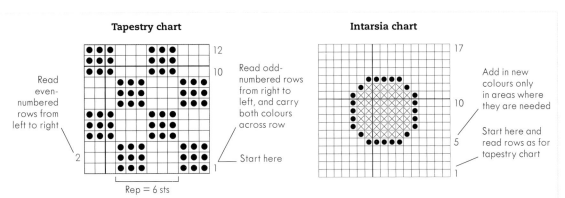

Tapestry chart

Read
even-
numbered
rows from
left to right

Read odd-
numbered rows
from right to
left, and carry
both colours
across row

Start here

Rep = 6 sts

Intarsia chart

Add in new
colours only
in areas where
they are needed

Start here and
read rows as for
tapestry chart

Corner to corner crochet chart
Start at the bottom right-hand corner and progress
diagonally across the chart working right to left then
left to right alternately. Sometimes the chart can get
confusing to follow, so it may help to turn the page to
the direction you are working from and cross out each
row as it is worked.

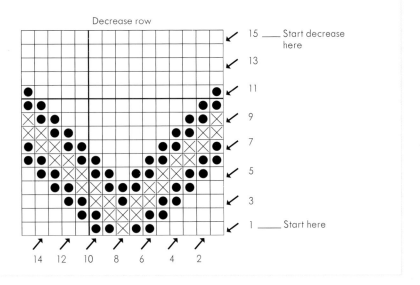

Decrease row

Start decrease
here

Start here

❯ TAPESTRY TECHNIQUE

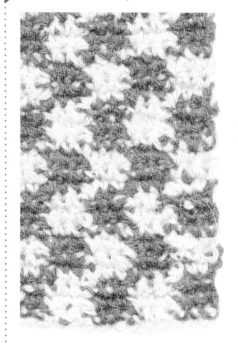

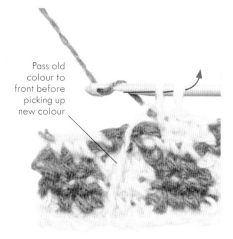

Pass old colour to front before picking up new colour

Enclose colour not in use inside stitches

1 To change to a new colour in tapestry, work up to the last yrh of the double crochet stitch before the colour change, then pass the old colour to the front of the work over the top of the new colour and use the new colour to complete the stitch.

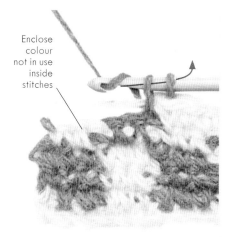

2 Work the next stitch in the new colour in the usual way, but keep the old yarn positioned along the top of the row below so that the double crochet stitches in the new colour enclose it.

❯ INTARSIA TECHNIQUE

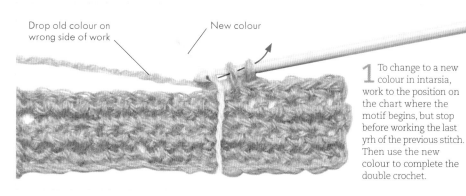

Drop old colour on wrong side of work

New colour

1 To change to a new colour in intarsia, work to the position on the chart where the motif begins, but stop before working the last yrh of the previous stitch. Then use the new colour to complete the double crochet.

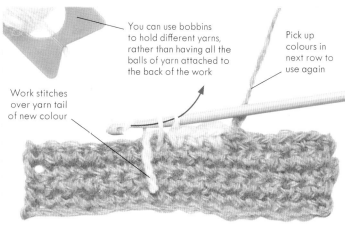

You can use bobbins to hold different yarns, rather than having all the balls of yarn attached to the back of the work

Pick up colours in next row to use again

Work stitches over yarn tail of new colour

2 Work all the required stitches in the new colour as shown. Then join on another ball (or length of yarn) for the next area of background colour. Use a separate yarn for each area of colour.

INTARSIA CUSHION

This striking bolster cushion is worked in two pieces and has an attractive diamond and stripe intarsia pattern. The pattern includes the option for a double-sided cushion or for stitching one side in plain crochet.

TECHNIQUES USED Double crochet **p.34**, Blocking and seams **p.68**, Colourwork charts **p.116**, Intarsia colourwork **p.117**

SIZE
30 x 50cm (12 x 19¾in)

YARN
Rowan Pure Wool DK – 50g/130m/142yds
  (100% wool; any DK wool will be
  suitable for this project)

A x 4   **B** x 2

HOOK
4mm hook

NOTIONS
Yarn needle

TENSION
15sts x 20 rows per 10cm (4in) square

› PATTERN
Note: When changing yarn colour: with yarn A insert hook into next st, pull through a loop, change to yarn B, yrh and crochet both loops on hook. Work the next stitch in yarn B. Changing the yarn is completed in the final step of the previous stitch.

CUSHION FRONT
With yarn A, work 76 ch.
Row 1: dc into second ch from hook, dc to end. (75sts)
Row 2: 1 ch, dc to end of row.
Rows 3–9: Repeat row 2.
Row 10: With yarn B, 1 ch, dc to end of row.
Row 11: Repeat row 10.
Row 12: With yarn A, 1 ch, dc to end of row.

Row 13: Repeat row 12.
Row 14–17: With yarn B, 1 ch, dc to end of row.
Row 18–21: With yarn A, 1 ch, dc to end of row.
Row 22: See chart below for the colourwork intarsia design. Working in intarsia and changing yarn colour before the final stage in the last stitch, with yarn A (referred to as A) 1 ch, 10 dc, yarn B (referred to as B) 1 dc, *A17 dc, B1 dc; repeat from * two more times, A10 dc.
Row 23: Repeat row 22.
Row 24: With A, 1 ch, 9 dc, B3 dc, *A15 dc, B3 dc; repeat from * two more times, A9 dc.
Row 25: Repeat row 24.
Row 26: With A, 1 ch, 8 dc, B2 dc, A1 dc, B2 dc, *A13 dc, B2 dc, A1 dc, B2 dc; repeat from * two more times, A8 dc.
Row 27: Repeat row 26.
Row 28: With A, 1 ch, 7 dc, B2 dc, A3 dc, B2 dc, *A5 dc, B1 dc, A5 dc, B2 dc, A3 dc, B2 dc; repeat from * two more times, A7 dc.
Row 29: Repeat row 28.
Row 30: With A, 1 ch, 6 dc, B2 dc, A2 dc, B1 dc, A2 dc, B2 dc, *A3 dc, B3 dc, A3 dc, B2 dc, A2 dc, B1 dc, A2 dc, B2 dc; repeat from * two more times, A6 dc.
Row 31: Repeat row 30.
Row 32: Repeat row 28.
Row 33: Repeat row 32.
Row 34: Repeat row 26.

Row 35: Repeat row 34.
Row 36: Repeat row 24.
Row 37: Repeat row 36.
Row 38: Repeat row 22.
Row 39: Repeat row 38.
Row 40: With A, 1 ch, dc to end of row.
Rows 41–43: Repeat row 40.
Rows 44–47: With B, 1 ch, dc to end of row.
Rows 48–49: With A, 1 ch, dc to end of row.
Rows 50–51: With B, 1 ch, dc to end of row.
Rows 52–60: With A, 1 ch dc to end of row.
Fasten off.

CUSHION BACK
Repeat instructions for cushion front. For the plain version, work as follows:
With yarn A, work 76 ch.
Row 1: Dc into second ch from hook, dc to end of row. (75sts)
Row 2: 1 ch, dc to end of row.
Rows 3–60: Repeat row 2.
Fasten off.

FINISHING
With right sides together, sew the cushion, leaving one shorter side open. Turn inside out and insert cushion pad. Either sew edges together or insert a zip.

Intarsia pattern

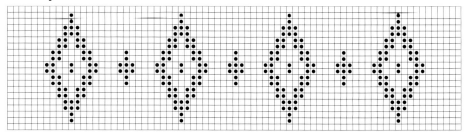

CORNER TO CORNER CROCHET (C2C)

In this style of crochet, each block is essentially made up of three chains and three trebles. The blocks are slip stitched to three-chain spaces of blocks from the previous row. Increases are made at the beginning of each row until the maximum desired diagonal width is reached. Then the work is decreased back down.

❯ INCREASING SEQUENCE

The most common stitch used to make C2C blocks is the treble, but half trebles can also be used. The trebles work up more quickly, while the half trebles allow for more detailed colourwork designs as the resulting blocks are smaller and denser.

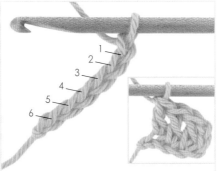

1 Make six chain stitches (the foundation for an increase). Work one treble in the fourth chain from the hook and then work one treble in each of the next two chain stitches. That's one block made and this counts as row 1.

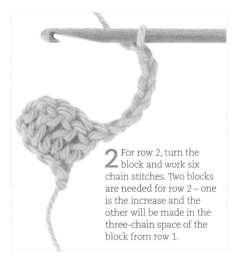

2 For row 2, turn the block and work six chain stitches. Two blocks are needed for row 2 – one is the increase and the other will be made in the three-chain space of the block from row 1.

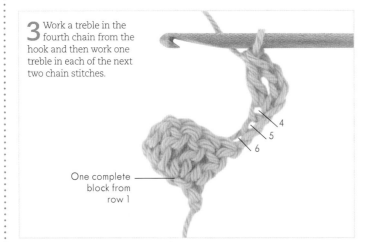

3 Work a treble in the fourth chain from the hook and then work one treble in each of the next two chain stitches.

One complete block from row 1

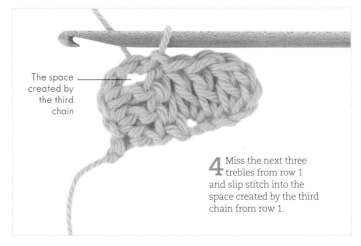

The space created by the third chain

4 Miss the next three trebles from row 1 and slip stitch into the space created by the third chain from row 1.

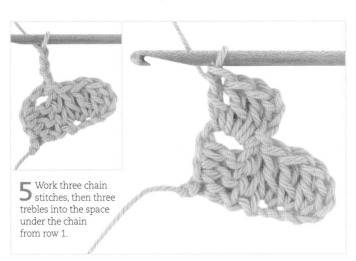

5 Work three chain stitches, then three trebles into the space under the chain from row 1.

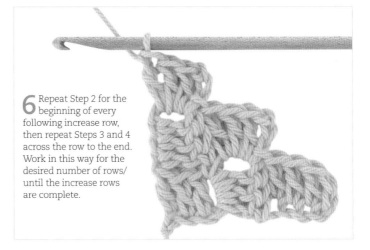

6 Repeat Step 2 for the beginning of every following increase row, then repeat Steps 3 and 4 across the row to the end. Work in this way for the desired number of rows/until the increase rows are complete.

❯ DECREASING SEQUENCE

1 Now, to start the decreasing. Slip stitch across the top of the three trebles you've just worked and into the three-chain space. This is where your row will now begin.

2 Work three chain stitches, make three trebles in the chain space and then repeat Steps 3 and 4, as before, across the row.

3 At the end of each row, make a slip stitch into the last third chain space but don't make a block. Turn the work and slip stitch across the trebles as before, ready to start the next row.

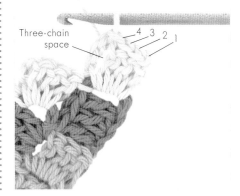

Three-chain space   4 3 2 1

❯ CHANGING COLOUR IN CORNER TO CORNER CROCHET

To make working easier, for each section of colour you'll need a ball, twist, or bobbin of yarn in that colour. The more complex the design, the more balls of yarn you'll have to juggle. Those more challenging patterns will have many colour changes, so it's worth getting used to making the twists you need in advance. You can also carry yarn strands over multiple blocks, if needed, and much of this can be hidden by crocheting over the strands.

The principle of C2C colourwork remains the same: just finish the current block, then drop the current yarn and pick up the new yarn to pull through the loop on the hook. This method ensures the block is square.

Yarn pulled through the loop

CRAFTER'S WRAP

Wow friends and family with this technicolour geometric wrap, with sewn fabric interior to keep all your crochet kit neat, tidy, and handy whenever you need it.

Level of difficulty

TECHNIQUES USED Chain stitch **p.26**, Treble crochet **p.44**, Working into a chain space **p.75**, Corner to corner crochet **p.120**

TECHNIQUES

SIZE
23.5 x 28cm (9¼ x 11in)

YARN
Paintbox Cotton DK – 50g/125m/137yds (100% cotton; you can use any cotton DK to achieve a similar effect)

A x 1   **B** x 1   **C** x 1   **D** x 1

E x 1   **F** x 1

HOOK
2.5mm hook

NOTIONS
2 fat quarters of fabric and iron-on interfacing
Disappearing ink pen and ruler
Sewing machine, optional

TENSION
8 blocks = 10cm (4in)

PATTERN

Note: Change colour after a block is complete: slip stitch new colour through to begin the next block. When a colour change happens on the edge of the work, you can change colour halfway through the last st before the new row.

With yarn A, work 6 ch.
Row 1 (RS): 1 tr in fourth ch from hook, 1 tr in each of next 2 ch, turn. (1 block)
Row 2: 6 ch, 1 tr in fourth ch from hook, 1 tr in each of next 2 ch, ss to 3-ch sp of row 1, 3 ch, 3 tr in same 3-ch sp, turn. (2 blocks)
Row 3: 6 ch, 1 tr in fourth ch from hook, 1 tr in each of next 2 ch, *ss in next 3-ch sp of previous row, 3 ch, 3 tr in same 3-ch sp; rep from * to end, turn. (3 blocks)
Rows 4–19: Repeat row 3 following chart for colour changes. (19 blocks)
Row 20 (WS): Ss into last 3sts made and into the first 3-ch sp, 3 ch, 3 tr in 3-ch sp, *ss in next 3-ch sp of previous row, 3 ch, 3 tr in same 3-ch sp; rep from * to end, turn. (19 blocks)

CORNER TO CORNER CHART

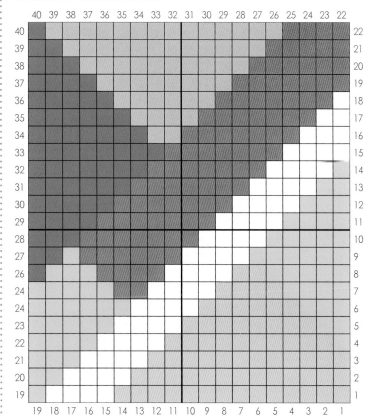

Following the chart
Start at the bottom right corner with block 1 and progress diagonally across the chart, working right to left and then left to right alternately. It may help to photocopy or turn the page to the direction you are working from and cross out each row as it is worked. Square number 1 is the top right corner of the finished piece.

Colour blocks When you view the crocheted fabric as a whole you can see how the pattern breaks down into a series of blocks. Once you've got the hang of one block, it's just a case of repeating that and switching colours.

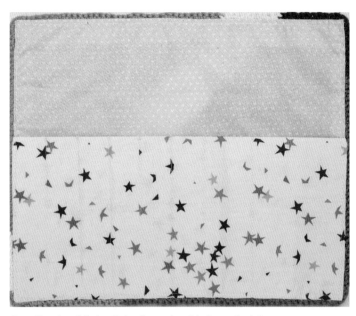

Coordinating fabrics Enjoy browsing fabrics to find the best prints and plains to partner the vibrant crocheted outer. Sewing on a sewing machine will be quicker and more secure, but hand sewing can work, too.

Row 21: 6 ch, 1 tr in fourth ch from hook, 1 tr in each of next 2 ch *ss in next 3-ch sp of previous row, 3 ch, 3 tr in same 3-ch sp; rep from * to last 3-ch sp, end with 1 ss in the last 3-ch sp, turn. (19 blocks)

Row 22: Repeat row 20

Row 23: Ss into last 3sts made and into the first 3-ch sp, *3 ch, 3 tr in same 3-ch sp, ss in next 3-ch sp; rep from * to end, finishing with 1 ss in last 3-ch sp, turn. (18 blocks)

Rows 24–40: Repeat row 23. (decreases by 1 block per row)

Do not cut yarn in use, weave in all other ends.

Edging: 1 ch (does not count as a stitch), 3 dc to corner, *2 dc around post of tr, 1 dc in next 3 tr; rep from* around all four sides changing colour to match main piece. Fasten off and weave in ends.

TIES

With right side (RS) facing, turn the work through 90 degrees anticlockwise, so that the yarn D section is on the right-hand side. Attach yarn D to the ninth block up from the bottom on the right-hand side, work 61 ch, turn, ss into the back bump of the 2nd ch from hook, ss in the back bump of each ch to the beginning, 2 dc in the edge of main piece, work 61 ch, turn, ss into the back bump of the 2nd ch from hook, ss in the bump of each ch to the beginning, ss into the next 2sts.

Fasten off, and weave in ends.

FINISHING

Measure your crochet piece. Cut the main piece of lining fabric so that it has a 1cm (⅜in) seam allowance around both short sides and the top. Cut interfacing minus the seam allowance. Iron the interfacing, lining up the bottom of both pieces. Press the seam allowance around the three edges.

For the pocket, cut fabric to the same size as the main piece, press in half lengthways, wrong sides (WS) together, leaving a 1cm (⅜in) overhang. Press the 1cm (⅜in) overhang. Folded, place the pocket on top of the main piece lining it up with the raw edge of the lining of the main piece. Fold the pressed overhang behind the raw edge. Pin fabrics together.

With a disappearing ink pen and ruler, mark where you want the long pockets with a minimum of 2.5cm (1in) between each. Sew down the marked lines.

Top stitch around all four sides with 0.5cm (³⁄₁₆in) seam allowance. Pin to the WS of the crochet piece and hand stitch in place.

SIMPLE COLOURWORK STITCH PATTERNS

Crochet colourwork stitch patterns are great fun and easy to work. This selection of stitches includes an array of textures, so you are sure to find one that catches your eye. Although some of the stitches have a right and wrong side, the back and front of these fabrics still look very similar. The reversibility of crochet is one of its best features. If you want to make a scarf, shawl, baby blanket, throw, or cushion cover with one of these stitches, take your time to choose the right colour combination. See p.81 for abbreviations and basic stitch symbols. Any special symbols are given with the individual diagram.

SPIKE STITCH STRIPES

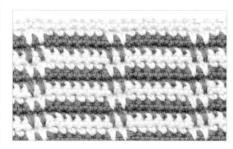

Crochet diagram

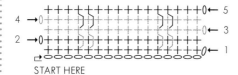

START HERE

KEY

spike st in st
one row below
next st

Crochet instructions

NOTE: spike st = do not work into next st, but instead insert hook front to back through top of st one row below this st, yrh and draw a loop through, lengthening the loop to the height of the row being worked (and enclosing the missed st), yrh and draw through both loops on hook to complete an elongated dc. This pattern is worked in two colours (A, B). With A, make a multiple of 8 ch, plus 1 extra.

Row 1 (RS): With A, 1 dc in second ch from hook, 1 dc in each of rem ch, turn.

Row 2: With A, 1 ch (does NOT count as a st), 1 dc in each dc to end, turn.

Row 3: With B, 1 ch (does NOT count as a st), *1 dc in each of next 3 dc, (1 spike st in top of st one row below next st) twice, 1 dc in each of next 3 dc; rep from * to end, turn.

Row 4: With B, rep row 2.

Row 5: With A, rep row 3.
Rep rows 2–5 to form patt.

TRIANGLES SPIKE STITCH

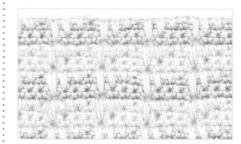

Crochet diagram

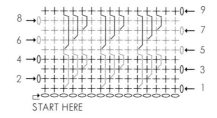

START HERE

KEY

spike st in st
one row below
next st

spike st in st
2 rows below
next st

spike st in st
3 rows below
next st

Crochet instructions

NOTE: spike st = do not work into next st, but instead insert hook front to back through top of st 1, 2, or 3 rows below this st, yrh and draw a loop through, lengthening the loop to the height of the row being worked (and enclosing the missed st), yrh and draw through both loops on hook to complete an elongated dc.
This pattern is worked in two colours (A, B). With A, work a multiple of 4 ch.

Row 1 (RS): With A, 1 dc in second ch from hook, 1 dc in each of rem ch, turn.

Row 2: With A, 1 ch (does NOT count as a st), 1 dc in each dc to end, turn.

Rows 3 and 4: With A, (rep row 2) twice.

Row 5 (RS): With B, 1 ch (does NOT count as a st), 1 dc in first dc, *1 dc in next dc, 1 spike st in top of dc one row below next dc, 1 spike st in top of dc 2 rows below next dc, 1 spike st in top of dc 3 rows below next dc; rep from * to last 2 dc, 1 dc in each of last 2 dc, turn.

Rows 6, 7, and 8: With B, (rep row 2) three times.

Row 9 (RS): With A, rep row 5.
Rep rows 2–9 to form patt, ending with a patt row 5 or 9.

SIMPLE ZIGZAG STITCH

Crochet diagram

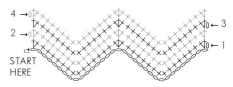

START HERE

Note: When working from diagram, rep rows 2 and 3 for stitch pattern.

Crochet instructions

This pattern is worked in three colours (A, B, C). With C, make a multiple of 16 ch, plus 2 extra.

Row 1 (RS): With A, 2 dc in second ch from hook, *1 dc in each of next 7 ch, miss next ch, 1 dc in each of next 7 ch, 3 dc in next ch; rep from * to end, working 2 dc (instead of 3 dc) in last ch, turn.

Row 2: With A, 1 ch (does NOT count as a st), 2 dc in first dc, *1 dc in each of next 7 dc, miss next 2 dc, 1 dc in each of next 7 dc, 3 dc in next dc; rep from * to end, working 2 dc (instead of 3 dc) in last dc, turn.

Rows 3 and 4: With B, rep row 2.

Rows 5 and 6: With C, (rep row 2) twice.

Rows 7 and 8: With A, (rep row 2) twice.
Rep rows 3–8 to form patt.

UNUSUAL STITCHES

If you want to try some stitches that are a little more unusual, you could choose either Tunisian simple stitch or broomstick stitch. While they are not difficult stitches to work, it is best to make sure you have mastered the basics of crochet before you try them out.

TUNISIAN CROCHET

Tunisian crochet combines elements of both knitting and crochet. It produces a fabric that looks very similar to either a woven fabric or knitted stocking stitch, depending on the stitch variation. A row is completed by working two "passes" (a "forward" and a "return" pass) as opposed to one regular row in crochet, and these are worked with a special hook (see p.19). This is because you need room for the many loops on the hook during one of the passes of each row.

Tunisian crochet: Tunisian simple stitch is the easiest Tunisian stitch and produces a dense fabric. Always work with the RS facing you.

1 Tunisian crochet begins with a regular chain, after which each row is composed of two passes. The first row is the foundation row. Insert the hook into the first chain, yrh and draw a loop through, leaving this loop on the hook.

2 Repeat the last step for each chain to the end. You will have the same number of loops on the hook as the number of chains you began with. The foundation forward pass is now complete.

3 Now begin the return pass of the foundation row. When you get to the end of the first forward pass, do not turn, but simply work one chain.

4 Then yrh and pull through the first two loops on the hook.

5 Repeat this, working off the loops in pairs until one loop is left on the hook. The foundation, or first row (a forward and a return pass), is complete.

6 For the forward pass of row two (the first regular row), do not work a turning chain – the loop on the hook counts as the first stitch. Miss the vertical stitch directly under the hook and insert the hook into the next vertical stitch from right to left.

7 Yrh and pull through the stitch, then repeat, pulling a loop through each vertical stitch to the end of the row, leaving each loop on the hook. Work each following forward pass of every row in this way. Now work the return pass for this (and every following) row in the same way as for steps 3 and 4. Continue working Tunisian Simple stitch in this way until the project is the desired length.

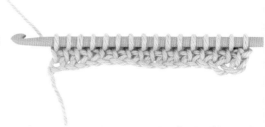

BROOMSTICK CROCHET

Broomstick crochet was originally made using a broom handle to create the lacy effect. Basic broomstick stitch is normally worked using a regular hook and a 20mm–25mm (¾in–1in) diameter knitting needle to create the large, lacy loops typical of this stitch.

Broomstick combination: Also known as peacock eye crochet, this stitch can be combined with regular crochet stitches to create pattern variations.

1 Make a chain as usual, making the last chain larger by pulling up with the hook, and placing it onto the knitting needle.

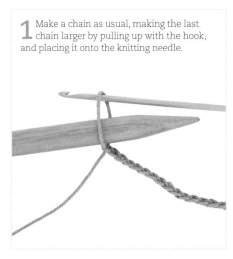

2 Insert the hook into the next chain, yrh, and pull a loop through.

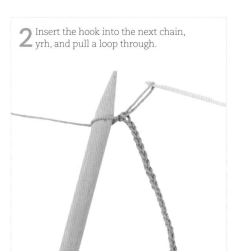

3 Place the loop onto the knitting needle.

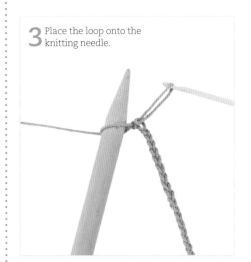

4 Continue to work Steps 2 and 3 until all the loops are on the knitting needle.

5 Slide the hook through the first groups of loops (the pattern will tell you how many), and pull them off the needle.

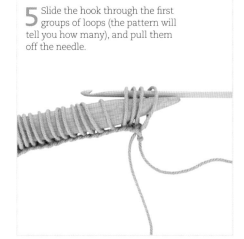

6 Yrh and pull through all the loops on the hook, then work a multiple of dc stitches into the group of loops (again, the pattern will indicate how many).

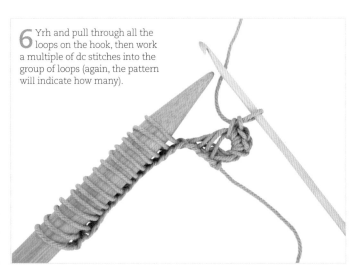

7 Continue in this way until all the loops have been crocheted into, and this completes a row of broomstick lace. You can continue in the same way, drawing up loops through each stitch, or continue in regular crochet, or a mixture of both to create beautiful broomstick lace patterns.

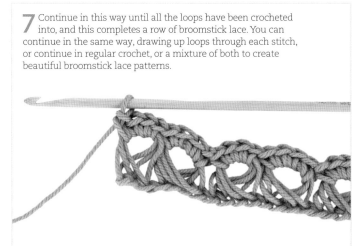

UNUSUAL YARNS

Make a change from working with wool yarns by trying out some unusual materials. String, wire, and rag strips are great fun to crochet with, and the materials used can be recycled ones. To take you through the techniques involved, a quick-to-make item is shown with each of these "yarns". It isn't advisable to try to learn to crochet with unusual yarns, so make sure you are deft at forming double crochet stitches before attempting to work with them.

STRING CROCHET

Tightly crocheted string forms a sturdy fabric suitable for containers. Because it is usually neither too thick nor too thin, garden twine is a good choice for a first string crochet project. It is also easy to obtain and forms a fabric that holds its shape well.

> **CROCHETING A ROUND STRING CONTAINER**

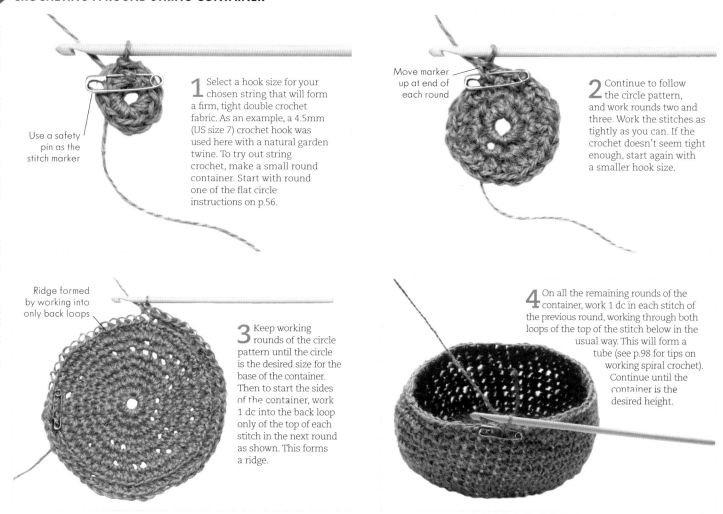

Use a safety pin as the stitch marker

1 Select a hook size for your chosen string that will form a firm, tight double crochet fabric. As an example, a 4.5mm (US size 7) crochet hook was used here with a natural garden twine. To try out string crochet, make a small round container. Start with round one of the flat circle instructions on p.56.

Move marker up at end of each round

2 Continue to follow the circle pattern, and work rounds two and three. Work the stitches as tightly as you can. If the crochet doesn't seem tight enough, start again with a smaller hook size.

Ridge formed by working into only back loops

3 Keep working rounds of the circle pattern until the circle is the desired size for the base of the container. Then to start the sides of the container, work 1 dc into the back loop only of the top of each stitch in the next round as shown. This forms a ridge.

4 On all the remaining rounds of the container, work 1 dc in each stitch of the previous round, working through both loops of the top of the stitch below in the usual way. This will form a tube (see p.98 for tips on working spiral crochet). Continue until the container is the desired height.

WIRE CROCHET

As long as it is fine enough, wire is easy to crochet with even though it takes a little practice to produce even stitches. As with string crochet, it is best to stick to simple double crochet for wire – more exotic stitches are difficult to distinguish among the bendy, airy wire loops. Adding beads to wire crochet is the best way to jazz it up and turn it into simple jewellery, such as the easy-to-make, bendy bangle shown here.

> ## CROCHETING A BEADED WIRE BANGLE

The easiest wire thickness to crochet with is a 0.3mm (28 gauge) copper wire, which can be obtained online from craft shops or shops that sell jewellery supplies. For this wire size you will need a 3mm (US size D-3) crochet hook.

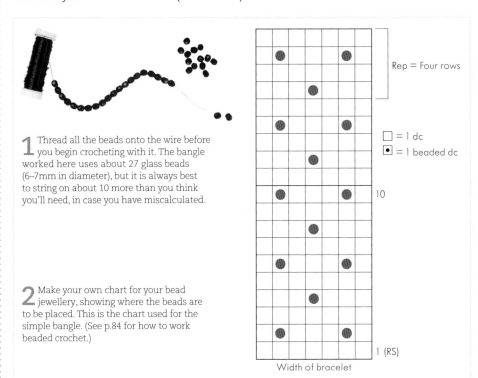

1 Thread all the beads onto the wire before you begin crocheting with it. The bangle worked here uses about 27 glass beads (6–7mm in diameter), but it is always best to string on about 10 more than you think you'll need, in case you have miscalculated.

2 Make your own chart for your bead jewellery, showing where the beads are to be placed. This is the chart used for the simple bangle. (See p.84 for how to work beaded crochet.)

Rep = Four rows

☐ = 1 dc
⊡ = 1 beaded dc

10

1 (RS)

Width of bracelet

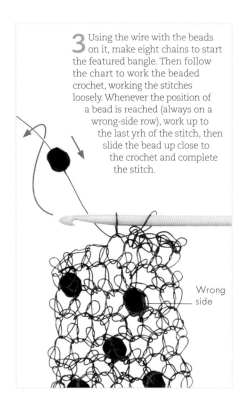

3 Using the wire with the beads on it, make eight chains to start the featured bangle. Then follow the chart to work the beaded crochet, working the stitches loosely. Whenever the position of a bead is reached (always on a wrong-side row), work up to the last yrh of the stitch, then slide the bead up close to the crochet and complete the stitch.

Wrong side

4 Work the bangle until it is the desired length. End with a right-side (non-bead) row so that the wrong side will be facing for the next row. Place the other end of the bangle behind the next row and work the last row through both layers of the bangle by inserting the hook through the foundation chain of the second layer as shown.

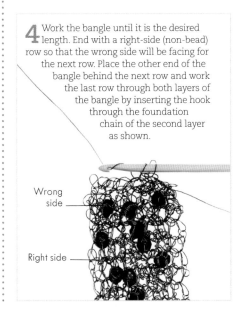

Wrong side

Right side

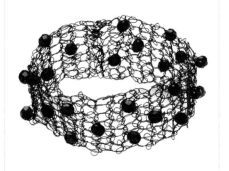

5 After completing the double crochet seam, cut the wire and fasten off. Darn in the wire tails along the double crochet seam, using a blunt-ended yarn needle and wrapping the wire tightly a few times around the edge of the crochet. Then cut off the remaining wire close to the bangle. Turn the bangle right side out.

> ## ALTERNATIVE BANGLE

You can also make plain wire crochet bangles and decorate them once they have been completed. This bangle has been worked plain without any beads. Buttons have been sewn along the centre of the bangle with a light contrasting silk button thread.

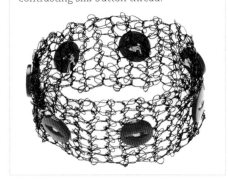

RAG-STRIP CROCHET

The biggest advantage of rag-strip crochet is its limitless colour palette – the "yarn" can be made from any cotton shirt-weight or patchwork-weight fabric. To try out the technique, work circles with rag strips and make them into a bag.

> PREPARING FABRIC STRIPS

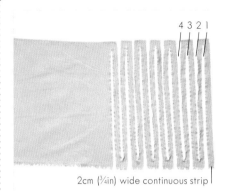

4 3 2 1

2cm (¾in) wide continuous strip

1 To make a continuous fabric strip 2cm (¾in) wide, cut or tear the fabric from selvedge to selvedge, stopping each tear/cut about 1.5cm (½in) from the edge.

2 As you tear the strips, wind them into balls. Rag crochet uses up a lot of fabric. To start your project, you can prepare some rag yarn in each of the colours you need and make more later as required.

> CROCHETING TWO CIRCLES FOR A BAG

1 For a firm crochet fabric, use a 10mm (US size N-15) crochet hook and 2cm (¾in) wide patchwork-weight fabric cotton strips. Simple double crochet is the best stitch to use for rag crochet. To begin a circle for a bag, work round 1 of the flat circle pattern on p.56 (but leave the yarn tail at the back of the work and do not attempt to work the stitches of this round over it).

A large paper clip is the best stitch marker for rag-strip crochet

2 Continuing to follow the circle pattern, introduce new colours for stripes as desired. Work the circle until it is the size you want for a bag front. Then work a second circle the same size. Using the hook, pull any yarn tails through a few stitches on the wrong side (WS) to secure them and trim off the ends.

Change to a new colour with last yrh of a round

3 Line the two circles with a harmonizing fabric print. (The edge of the lining should reach the base of the tops of the double crochet stitches of the last row.)

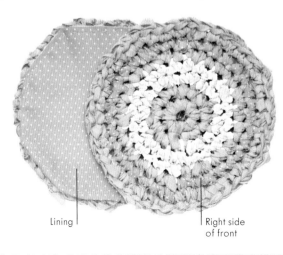

Lining

Right side of front

4 With the WS facing, pin the bag front and back together. Then using a sewing needle and matching thread or thin cotton yarn, stitch the seam just under the tops of the double crochet stitches of the last round, leaving an opening at the top. For a bag strap, make a long plait with some of the fabric strip yarn or use a long ready-made cord.

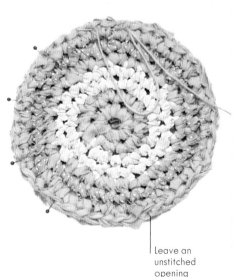

Leave an unstitched opening

CROCHETED TOYS

Although crocheted toys look difficult, they are relatively easy to make, and quick as well. This step-by-step guide to crocheting a toy provides tips for making the pieces, doing the stuffing, stitching the parts together, and adding facial features (see pp.135–137 for the pattern).

TOY TECHNIQUES

This cute teddy bear has been designed for intermediate crocheters, and its pattern on pp.135–137 has an easy-to-follow style. Because the toy has a step-by-step guide, it is an ideal first toy project. Being able to see what the pieces look like before they are stuffed will give you confidence that your crochet toy is turning out the shape it should.

The tips in the steps apply to crocheted toys in general. Start your toy project by selecting the yarns and hook required. For the sample teddy bear, you only need two colours of yarn. Select a crochet hook that will produce a tight double crochet fabric, one to two sizes smaller than the size recommended for the yarn weight category (see p.14).

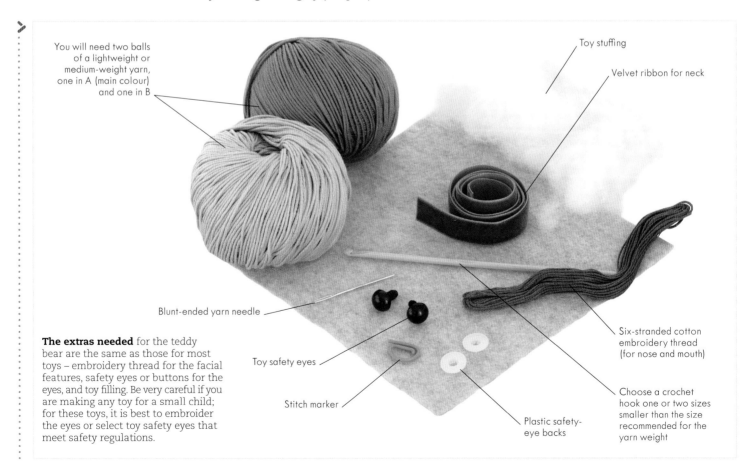

You will need two balls of a lightweight or medium-weight yarn, one in A (main colour) and one in B

Toy stuffing

Velvet ribbon for neck

Blunt-ended yarn needle

Six-stranded cotton embroidery thread (for nose and mouth)

The extras needed for the teddy bear are the same as those for most toys – embroidery thread for the facial features, safety eyes or buttons for the eyes, and toy filling. Be very careful if you are making any toy for a small child; for these toys, it is best to embroider the eyes or select toy safety eyes that meet safety regulations.

Toy safety eyes

Stitch marker

Plastic safety-eye backs

Choose a crochet hook one or two sizes smaller than the size recommended for the yarn weight

CROCHETING A TEDDY

1 Place a stitch marker or scrap of different coloured yarn as you crochet at the position for each eye, so that when you have finished making the head, you will be able to attach the safety eyes symmetrically.

2 Begin stuffing the head just after you have begun decreasing, when the opening is still large enough to do so easily. Make sure you insert enough toy stuffing to fill the head completely.

3 When you have finished the head, there will be a small hole left. To sew this up, ensure you leave a long tail of yarn for sewing. Thread the yarn tail all round the opening with a yarn needle.

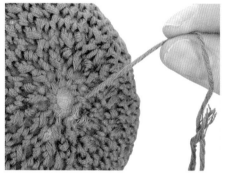

4 Now pull tightly on the thread to close the hole. Secure the closure with a few stitches to ensure that it does not open. You can also use this long tail to sew the body onto the head; if you wish to do so, do not fasten it off.

5 Attach the safety eyes and then sew the muzzle onto the face by sewing with a whip or overcast stitch (see p.68) in the same colour as the muzzle.

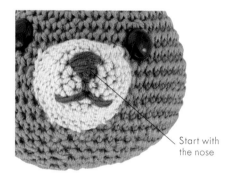

Start with the nose

6 Using the embroidery thread, embroider a mouth and nose onto the muzzle as shown, or to your own design, creating an individual personality for the teddy.

7 Attach the head to the body using neat stitches (mattress stitch works well – see p.69), taking a stitch from the body then the head alternately as you go round, but use any neat technique you are comfortable with, ensuring that the head is on securely and does not flop over.

Push stuffing down with crochet hook

8 To stuff the limbs, use the blunt end of the crochet hook or any long object, such as a knitting needle, to push down the toy filling. Ensure that the stuffing is pushed right down to the bottom. Use this technique to insert more stuffing and ensure that the limbs are stuffed tightly.

9 Attach the limbs to the body in the position shown, in a similar way to the head. While ensuring that you attach securely so that the limbs do not fall off, also make sure that they are not sewn so that they are immovable. Sew from one small spot at the side of the arm or leg, rather than at the tip, to the body to allow them to move.

TEDDY BEAR

You never forget your first bear and this one is sure to become a true keepsake. Worked in the round using adjustable rings for neatly curved paws and feet, this project is quick and satisfying to make.

TECHNIQUES USED Double crochet **p.34**, Double crochet increases **p.50**, Double crochet decreases **p.52**, Making a simple adjustable ring **p.57**, Crochet toys **p.130**

SIZE
Approx 28 x 16cm (11 x 6¼in)

YARN
Rico Design Essential Cotton DK – 50g/
   130m/142yds (100% mercerized cotton;
   you can use any DK weight yarn)

A x 1   **B** x 1

HOOK
3.75mm hook

NOTIONS
Two stitch markers
Yarn needle
12mm (½in) black safety toy eyes
Brown embroidery thread and needle
Brown felt for inner ears
Toy stuffing
1cm (⅜in)-wide velvet ribbon

TENSION
Exact tension is not essential

SPECIAL ABBREVIATIONS
Adjustable ring: Wind the yarn twice
   around your finger. Insert the hook
   and wrap the yarn around it. Pull the
   hook back through and work a chain.
   Work the first round of sts into the
   "ring", then pull the tail of yarn gently
   to close it, before joining the sts into
   a round using a ss.

PATTERN
Follow this pattern and then refer to
pp.128–129 when assembling your toy.

Note: The teddy bear is worked in spirals.
Do not join rounds, but place a marker
at first stitch of the round, moving it
each round to mark the beginning of
the next round.

HEAD
With yarn A, make an adjustable ring and
work 6 dc into the ring. (6sts)
Round 1: 2 dc into each st to the end. (12sts)
Round 2: *1 dc, 2 dc in the next st; rep from
* to end. (18sts)
Round 3: *2 dc, 2 dc in the next st; rep from
* to end. (24sts)
Round 4: *3 dc, 2 dc in the next st; rep from
* to end. (30sts)
Round 5: *9 dc, 2 dc in the next st; rep from
* to end. (33sts)
Round 6: *10 dc, 2 dc in the next st; rep
from * to end. (36sts)
Round 7: *11 dc, 2 dc in the next st; rep
from * to end. (39sts)
Round 8: *12 dc, 2 dc in the next st; rep
from * to end. (42sts)
Round 9: *13 dc, 2 dc in the next st; rep
from * to end. (45sts)
Place two stitch markers on the next row
10sts apart to mark where you will put
the toy eyes.
Round 10: *14 dc, 2 dc in next st; rep from *
to end. (48sts)
Round 11: *15 dc, 2 dc in next st; rep from *
to end. (51sts)
Round 12: *16 dc, 2 dc in next st; rep from *
to end. (54sts)
Rounds 13–14: Dc in each st to end.
Round 15: *dc2tog, 7 dc; rep from *
to end. (48sts)

Round 16: *dc2tog, 6 dc; rep from *
to end. (42sts)
Round 17: *dc2tog, 5 dc; rep from *
to end. (36sts)
Round 18: *dc2tog, 4 dc; rep from *
to end. (30sts)
Round 19: *dc2tog, 3 dc; rep from *
to end. (24sts)
Round 20: *dc2tog, 2 dc; rep from *
to end. (18sts)
Round 21: *dc2tog, 1 dc; rep from *
to end. (12sts)
Add some stuffing to the head now.
Round 22: *dc2tog; rep from* to end. (6sts)
Put the working loop on a stitch holder and
attach the toy eyes to the head in the places
you marked on round 10.
Finish stuffing the head. Weave the cut yarn
through the last 6sts, pull to close the hole
at the base of the head.
Weave in yarn to secure and cut off any
loose ends.

MUZZLE
With yarn B, make an adjustable ring and
work 6 dc into the ring. (6sts)
Round 1: 2 dc into each st to end. (12sts)
Round 2: *3 dc, 2 dc in the next st; rep from *
to end. (15sts)
Round 3: Dc in each st to end.
Round 4: *4 dc, 2 dc in next st; rep from *
to end. (18sts)
Rounds 5–6: Dc in each st to end.
Round 7: *5 dc, 2 dc in next st; rep from *
to end. (21sts)
Round 8: Dc in each st to end.
Cut the yarn leaving a long tail and pull
through loop to secure.
Position the muzzle carefully and sew
it onto the face. Use brown embroidery
thread to sew the nose and mouth detail
on the muzzle.
Weave in and cut off any loose ends.

BODY

With yarn A, make an adjustable ring and work 6 dc into the ring. (6sts)
Round 1: 2 dc into each st to end. (12sts)
Round 2: *3 dc, 2 dc in next st; rep from * to end. (15sts)
Round 3: *4 dc, 2 dc in next st; rep from * to end. (18sts)
Round 4: Dc in each st to end.
Round 5: *5 dc, 2 dc in next st; rep from * to end. (21sts)
Round 6: Dc in each st to end.
Round 7: *6 dc, 2 dc in next st; rep from * to end. (24sts)
Round 8: Dc in each st to end.
Round 9: *7 dc, 2 dc in next st; rep from * to end. (27sts)
Round 10: Dc in each st to end.
Add some stuffing to the body now.
Round 11: *8 dc, 2 dc in next st; rep from * to end. (30sts)
Round 12: Dc in each st to end.
Round 13: *9 dc, 2 dc in next st; rep from * to end. (33sts)
Round 14: Dc in each st to end.
Round 15: *10 dc, 2 dc in next st; rep from * to end. (36sts)
Round 16: Dc in each st to end.
Round 17: *dc2tog, 10 dc; rep from * to end. (33sts)
Round 18: *dc2tog, 9 dc; rep from * to end. (30sts)
Round 19: *dc2tog, 3 dc; rep from * to end. (24sts)
Round 20: *dc2tog, 2 dc; rep from * to end. (18sts)
Round 21: *dc2tog, 1 dc; rep from * to end. (12sts)
Round 22: *dc2tog; rep from * to end. (6sts)
Cut the yarn leaving a long tail and pull through loop to secure. Finish stuffing the body. Thread the cut yarn onto a yarn needle and weave through the last 6sts, pull the yarn to close the hole at the top of the body. Sew the body firmly to the head. Weave in and cut off any loose ends.

ARMS (MAKE 2)

Stuff the arms as you go along.
With yarn A, make an adjustable ring and work 6 dc into the ring. (6sts)
Round 1: 2 dc into each st to end. (12sts)
Round 2: *1 dc, 2 dc in the next st; rep from * to end. (18sts)
Round 3: *2 dc, 2 dc in the next st; rep from * to end. (24sts)
Rounds 4–6: Dc in each st to the end.
Round 7: *dc2tog, 2 dc; rep from * to end. (18sts)
Round 8: *dc2tog, 4 dc; rep from * to end. (15sts)

Round 9: *dc2tog, 3 dc; rep from * to end. (12sts)
Rounds 10–19: Dc in each st to end.
Round 20: Dc2tog, dc in each st to end. (11sts)
Rounds 21–25: Dc in each st to end.
Round 26: Dc2tog, dc in each st to end. (10sts)
Rounds 27–28: Dc in each st to end.
Cut the yarn leaving a long tail and pull through loop to secure.
Finish stuffing the arm firmly.
Thread the cut yarn onto a wool needle and weave through the last 10sts, pull the yarn to close the hole at the top of the arm, weave in yarn to secure. Position the arms carefully in place and sew them onto the body.

LEGS (MAKE 2)

Stuff the legs as you go along.
With yarn A, make an adjustable ring and work 6 dc into the ring. (6sts)
Round 1: 2 dc into each st to end. (12sts)
Round 2: 2 dc, 2 dc in the next st, 2 dc, 3 htr in the next st, 2 htr, 3 htr in the next st, 2 dc, 2 dc in the last st. (18sts)
Round 3: 3 dc, 2 dc in the next st, 2 dc, 1 htr, 2 htr in the next st, 4 htr, 2 htr in the next st, 1 htr, 1 dc, 2 dc in the next st, 2 dc. (22sts)
Round 4: 2 dc in the first st, 8 dc, 3 htr in the next st, 5 htr, 3 htr in the next st, 6 dc. (27sts)
Round 5: Dc in each st to end.
Round 6: 1 dc, dc2tog, 8 dc, dc2tog, 6 dc, dc2tog, 6 dc. (24sts)

The legs are worked from the feet upwards. Start with an adjustable ring (see p.57) and maintain even tension as you increase the number of stitches on each round. Stuff the legs as they evolve.

Round 7: 11 dc, htr3tog, 3 htr, htr3tog, 4 dc. (20sts)
Round 8: 3 dc, dc2tog, 4 dc, dc2tog, 1 dc, dc2tog, 1 dc, dc2tog, 3 dc. (16sts)
Round 9: 8 dc, dc2tog, 1 dc, dc2tog, 3 dc. (14sts)
Round 10: Dc in each st to end.
Round 11: Dc2tog, dc in each st to end. (13sts)
Rounds 12–16: Dc in each st to end.
Round 17: Dc2tog, dc in each st to end. (12sts)
Rounds 18–22: Dc in each st to end.
Round 23: Dc2tog, dc in each st to end. (11sts)
Rounds 24–28: Dc in each st to end.
Round 29: Dc2tog, dc in each st to end. (10sts)
Cut the yarn leaving a long tail and pull through loop to secure.
Finish stuffing the legs firmly.
Thread the cut yarn onto a wool needle and weave through the last 10sts, pull the yarn to close the hole at the top of the leg, weave in yarn to secure. Position the legs carefully and sew onto the body.

EARS (MAKE 2)

With yarn A, make an adjustable ring and work 6 dc into the ring. (6sts)
Round 1: 2 dc into each st to end. (12sts)
Round 2: *1 dc, 2 dc in next st; rep from * to end. (18sts)
Round 3: Dc in each st to end.
Round 4: *2 dc, 2 dc in next st; rep from * to end. (24sts)
Round 5: Dc in each st to end.
Round 6: *3 dc, 2 dc in next st; rep from * to end. (30sts)
Rounds 7–8: Dc in each st to end.
Round 9: Dc2tog, dc in each st to end. (29sts)
Round 10: Dc2tog, dc in each st to end. (28sts)
Cut the yarn, leaving a long tail, and secure. Cut two pieces of felt and stitch them inside the ears using running stitch. Try not to allow the stitches to go through to the outer ear. Sew the ears onto the head. Weave in and cut off any loose ends. Tie a velvet ribbon around the bear's neck.

FELTED CROCHET

When felted, crochet shrinks, and it is not possible to control the exact amount of shrinkage. Luckily, there are many things you can make from felted crochet that do not require precise sizes, from cushion covers to simple bags. Motifs cut from felt also make great brooches or decoration on other crochet.

FELTING BASICS

If you are a beginner, avoid attempting a felted garment pattern until you have gained some experience with felting smaller items. Before taking the plunge into a specific project, read all about the felting basics below and discover some helpful tips. The best yarns for felted crochet are 100 per cent wool yarns and other animal fibre yarns that have not been too tightly spun, such as roving yarns. As a rule, the longer the fibres of a yarn, the more easily they felt. A mixed fibre yarn with at least 50 per cent wool or feltable animal fibre will felt to varying degrees, and it is best to try a test swatch first to see if a yarn felts, as some wools have been treated to avoid felting. Always avoid wool yarns marked "machine washable", as these will not felt.

➤ PREPARING A SWATCH FOR TEST-FELTING

By testing a swatch of your yarn, you can determine how much it will shrink when felted. But keep in mind that felting is not an exact science because of all these variables – washing machine agitation, water temperature, detergent type, and yarn fibre content, spin, and colour.

Work a swatch in double crochet that is approximately 20cm (8in) square; accurate shrinkage measurements cannot be obtained with smaller swatches as they shrink more than is usual.

To measure the tension before and after felting, tie yarn markers around stitches in the crochet using a different-coloured yarn, which preferably does not felt. Place them about 20 stitches apart on one row horizontally and about 20 rows apart vertically, making a note of how many stitches are in between. You then have obvious markers once the piece has been felted, so that you can take a measurement of distance between stitches and rows. As you know the number of rows and stitches within those markers, you can calculate the tension per cm/in and therefore the amount that your swatch has shrunk.

Prepare a swatch as explained above, then put it in your washing machine and add in a large hand towel. (The towel increases the agitation in the water to enable the felting process and should always be put in with your felting.) Add half the amount of laundry detergent normally used for a full load. Use a water temperature of about 40°C (104°F) for yarn that contains any mohair, and about 60°C (140°F) for 100 per cent wool yarns.

Wash the sample using the full washing cycle and the full spin for that cycle. Tug the washed swatch gently in both directions, then lay it right-side up on your ironing board and pat it into a rectangular shape.

Leave it to dry completely – the shrinkage is only complete when the felt is totally dry. If necessary, do more tests with new swatches, altering the temperature or the length of the wash cycle. Keep detailed records of your testing, listing tension, hook size, sizes of pre-felted and felted swatch, machine setting, and the type and amount of detergent.

Yellow markers measure the horizontal shrinkage after felting

Red markers measure the vertical shrinkage after felting

TIPS FOR FELTING

• If you are trying out felting for the first time, make several test swatches in different weights of yarn and felt them together in the same washing-machine load, so you can get a feel for the different thicknesses of crocheted felt.

• Do not tightly crochet your projects before felting because they will felt better with more room to move within the stitches, as agitation is the most important part of creating a well-felted item.

• When using highly contrasting colours in the same piece of crochet or putting them in the same felting load, put a colour catcher in the washing machine. This absorbs loose dye and will prevent colours from running.

• Wool will fade slightly when felted, due to the high temperatures and the detergent, but this adds an attractive quality to the felt.

• Clean your washing machine after a felting load by wiping it out with a damp cloth to remove any stray fibres.

❯ BEFORE AND AFTER FELTING

Crochet changes character when it is felted, softening and shrinking – sometimes more widthways than lengthways, but it depends on the yarn. Integrated decorative effects can be achieved with crocheted stripes or embroidery worked onto the crochet prior to felting.

Double crochet swatches

You can see that the felted swatch is considerably smaller than the unfelted, but when compared to the half treble swatch below, it is not as completely felted. You can still see the stitches quite clearly. This happens for two reasons: first, a double crochet is a small, tight stitch, so the yarn within the fabric has very little room to move and create the desired amount of friction to aid felting. Second, the sample is striped, and different colours have a bearing on felting. Two yarns of different colours may felt slightly differently, due to the diverse chemical make-up in the dyes, and because the yarn might have already felted slightly during the dye process.

Double crochet swatch before felting
Width = 20cm (8in);
Length = 20cm (8in)

Double crochet swatch after felting
Width = 16.5cm (6½in);
Length = 18.5cm (7¼in)

Half treble swatches

The half treble stitch is a looser, taller stitch, with more gaps in the fabric than a double crochet stitch. This has resulted in a much more tightly felted fabric than the double crochet test swatch (above), as the yarn has more room to create the desired amount of friction. You can work out the amount that your final project will felt from this test, by working out the ratio of shrinkage in the measurements.

Remember that if your project is made of different pieces sewn together, you must do this first as each piece will felt slightly differently and unevenly – this can be seen in the irregular edges at the bottom of the double crochet felted swatch. Also, the sewing up of the pieces might affect the felting. Felting is always an unknown quantity, and the test swatching is purely for a guide to tension.

Half treble crochet swatch before felting
Width = 20cm (8in);
Length = 20cm (8in)

Half treble crochet swatch after felting
Width = 16cm (6¼in);
Length = 17cm (6¾in)

PROJECTS

BLANKETS AND CUSHIONS

A square- or rectangular-shaped item makes an appealing first project. Colourful designs featuring the classic granny square, chevrons, and flowers will brighten any interior scheme.

FLOWER BLANKET

Level of difficulty

This vibrant update of the vintage-inspired flower blanket is crocheted together, not sewn, so it looks great from both sides without any ugly seams. This blanket is an ideal project for using up oddments of yarn.

TECHNIQUES USED Treble crochet **p.44**, Working in the round **p.56**, Joining on a new colour **p.57**, Working into a chain space **p.75**, The join-as-you-go method **p.101**

SIZE
Approx 80 x 120 (90 x 170:100 x190)cm/
31½ x 47¼ (35½ x 67:39½ x 74¾)in

YARN
Sirdar Snuggly DK – 50g/165m/180yds (55% nylon and 45% acrylic; you can use any DK yarn, wool or acrylic, or a mix will work well, or use oddments of DK)

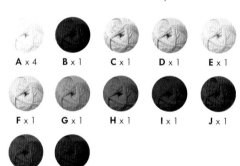

A x 4   B x 1   C x 1   D x 1   E x 1

F x 1   G x 1   H x 1   I x 1   J x 1

K x 1   L x 1

HOOK
4mm hook

NOTIONS
Yarn needle

TENSION
Exact tension is not essential

SPECIAL ABBREVIATIONS
Puff: (Yrh, insert hook into st, yrh and pull through loop, drawing it up to height of htr) four times, nine loops on hook, yrh and pull through all loops on hook.
Popcorn: See p.77

PATTERN
FLOWER MOTIFS
Round 1: With any contrast shade, work 3 ch to count as first tr, work 1 tr into third ch from hook, then work 10 further tr into same chain. Join round with a ss. Change colour.
Round 2: 2 ch, work 1 puff into first tr, 1 ch, *1 puff, 1 ch; rep from * to end of round, join round with a ss. Change colour.
Round 3: 3 ch, work popcorn into bottom of chain, 3 ch, *work popcorn into next 1-ch sp, 3 ch; rep from * to end of round, join round with a ss.
Make enough flower motifs in the same way for the desired size of blanket. For a small blanket, work 96 flowers; for a medium blanket, work 153 flowers; for a large blanket work 190 flowers.

JOINING THE MOTIFS
With the border shade, work a final row around one flower motif as follows:
Join yarn to any 3-ch sp. 3 ch, (1 tr, 3 ch, 2 tr) all into same sp, *(2 tr, 1 ch, 2 tr) into next 3-ch sp twice, (2 tr, 3 ch, 2 tr) into next 3-ch sp; rep from * twice more, (2 tr, 1 ch, 2 tr) into next 3-ch sp twice, join round with a ss.
To join the next flower to the first finished motif, work border around the next flower as follows:
With the border shade, join yarn to any 3-ch sp. 3 ch, (1 tr, 3 ch, 2 tr) all into same sp, (2 tr, 1 ch, 2 tr) into next 3-ch sp twice, (2 tr, 1 ch) into next 3-ch sp, work a ss into the central ch of any 3-ch corner sp of first

motif to join the corners, 1 ch, 2 tr back into original 3-ch sp of second motif. *2 tr into next 3-ch sp, ss into next 1-ch sp of first motif, 2 tr back into original 3-ch sp of second motif; rep from * once more, (2 tr, 1 ch) into next 3-ch sp, ss into central ch of next corner ch of first motif, 1 ch, 2 tr back into original 3-ch sp of second motif, (2 tr, 1 ch, 2 tr) into next 3-ch sp twice, (2 tr, 3 ch, 2 tr) into next 3-ch sp, (2 tr, 1 ch, 2 tr) into next 3-ch sp twice, join round with a ss.
Work all following motifs from first row in the same way as this, joining each subsequent flower to the previous motif along one side. On the second row of motifs, join first flower of the row to the motif below in the same way as previously stated. For all following motifs, join along two sides to the motifs immediately adjacent and below it in the same way as before.
For a small blanket arrange eight motifs wide by 12 motifs long. For a medium blanket, arrange nine motifs wide by 17 motifs long. For a large blanket, arrange 10 motifs wide by 19 motifs long.

FINISHING
With the border shade, attach yarn to any corner of blanket.
3 ch, 4 tr into same corner sp, continue around the whole blanket working (2 tr, 1 ch, 2 tr) into every 1-ch sp, (2 tr, 1 ch, 2 tr) into each joining sp of two motifs and 5 tr into each corner sp. Join round with a ss. Weave in all ends and block very lightly to shape, being careful not to flatten the 3D nature of the flower motifs.

LAP BLANKET

Level of difficulty ✳✳✳

This warm and cosy blanket works up surprisingly quickly due to the super bulky yarn and large hook. The tweed stitch is simply composed of double crochet and chain stitch, creating a luxurious texture with minimal effort.

TECHNIQUES USED Chain stitch **p.26**, Slip stitch **p.28**, Double crochet **p.34**, Working into a chain space/tweed stitch pattern **p.75**, Double crochet edging **p.86**

SIZE
Approx 98 x 120cm (38½ x 47¼in)

YARN
Sirdar Big Softie – 50g/45m/49yds
(51% wool and 49% acrylic; any
super-bulky-weight wool or acrylic
yarn will substitute. Try alpaca for
a heavyweight blanket)

A x 17   **B** x 3

HOOK
10mm hook

NOTIONS
Yarn needle

TENSION
Exact tension is not essential

SPECIAL ABBREVIATIONS
Crab stitch: Means simply working dc in
reverse, working round the row, or round
in this case, from left to right, instead
of right to left. After completing a row
of dc, do not turn the work around; work
1 ch, *insert the hook into the next stitch
to the right, not in the stitch you just
completed, but the next one. Draw a
loop through. Yrh as normal and pull
through both loops on the hook;
rep from * across row.

PATTERN
With yarn A, work 81 ch.
Row 1: 1 dc into second ch from hook,
(1 ch, miss 1 ch, dc in next ch) to end.
Row 2: 1 ch, dc in first dc, dc in ch sp,
(1 ch, 1 dc into ch sp) to end, dc into last dc.
Row 3: 1 ch, dc in first dc, (1 ch, dc into ch
sp) to last ch sp, miss next dc, dc in last dc.
Rep last two rows until work measures
approximately 120cm (47¼in) long, or
desired length. Fasten off yarn.

FINISHING
Block blanket lightly.
Attach yarn B to any point around edge
and work evenly in dc around entire
edge, working 3 dc into each corner.
Join round with a ss, but do not turn;
instead, work one row in crab stitch.
Fasten off yarn, weave in ends, and
block edge lightly.

Adding a trim around the blanket will give
your project a professional finish, with an
even edge around all sides. See pp.180 and
242 for more projects with crab stitch edging.

COLOURFUL GRANNY BLANKET

Level of difficulty ✱✱✱

This rainbow blanket uses the bright tones of the yarn to great effect. The join-as-you-go technique, using the white yarn, creates a pretty border and saves time, which is great when creating a large item such as this.

TECHNIQUES USED Treble crochet **p.44**, Working into a chain space **p.75**, The join-as-you-go method **p.101**, Plain square **p.104**

SIZE
Approx 180 x 110cm (71 x 43½in)

YARN
Sirdar Snuggly Baby Bamboo DK – 50g/ 95m/104yds (80% bamboo and 20% wool; any weight or fibre content will work here. Try wool for a warmer look. Change the hook to suit the yarn and remember that the blanket may come out a different size or texture)

A x 4   B x 4   C x 4   D x 4

E x 4   F x 4   G x 9

HOOK
4mm hook

NOTIONS
Yarn needle

TENSION
Exact tension is not essential

PATTERN
Work 4 ch, join with a ss to form a ring.
Round 1: 3 ch (counts as first tr), 2 tr in ring, 3 ch, *3 tr in ring, 3 ch; rep from * twice. Join round with ss to top of first ch.
Round 2: Ss to next corner sp, 3 ch, (1 tr, 3 ch, 2 tr) into corner sp, 3 tr, *(2 tr, 3 ch, 2 tr) into next corner sp, 3 tr; rep from * to end of round. Join round with ss to top of first ch.
Round 3: Ss to next corner sp, 3 ch, (1 tr, 3 ch, 2 tr) into corner sp, 1 tr into each tr to next corner sp, *(2 tr, 3 ch, 2 tr) into next corner sp, 1 tr into each tr to next corner sp; rep from * to end of round. Join round with ss to top of first ch.
Rep last round twice.
Fasten off yarn.
Make 14 squares of each colour; 84 squares in total. Block all pieces lightly.

JOINING THE SQUARES
Arrange each set of colours in order as in the photograph. Attach yarn G to corner sp of first square and complete next round as round three. Take next square and work round two sides as per round three, when you get to the corner sp, work 2 tr, 1 ch into corner, then attach square two to square one with a ss to the corresponding corner, 1 ch, 2 tr into corner, ss to the corresponding st of square one, then *work 3sts along the next side as usual, ss to the corresponding st of square one; rep from * to next corner, 2 tr, 1 ch into corner, join to the corresponding corner ch, then work along the remaining side as normal without a join. Two squares are joined.

Turn to pp.100–104 for more information about the classic granny square, plus additional patterns for different squares, triangles, and other motifs.

Continue joining the first row of seven squares in the same way, then join each square of the next row to the top of the first in the same way; you will need to join along two sides of some squares from this row.

EDGING
Join yarn G to any corner space. Work one row of trebles all around, working (2 tr, 3 ch, 2 tr) into the corner spaces as before.

BABY BLANKET

This charming throw is made using the "join-as-you-go" method, so that you don't have all the squares to join at the end. Plan the colour scheme for your blanket before buying any yarn.

TECHNIQUES USED Treble crochet **p.44**, Working into a chain space **p.75**, Working into spaces between stitches **p.75**, A basic granny square **p.100**

BLANKETS AND CUSHIONS

SIZE
Approx 92 x 107cm (36¼ x 42in)

YARN
Rowan Pure Wool DK – 50g/125m/137yds
(100% wool; you can use any DK wool
or wool mix to achieve a similar effect)

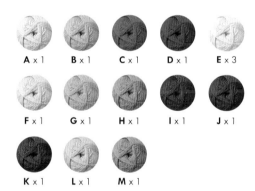

A x 1   B x 1   C x 1   D x 1   E x 3

F x 1   G x 1   H x 1   I x 1   J x 1

K x 1   L x 1   M x 1

HOOK
4mm hook

NOTIONS
Yarn needle

TENSION
Exact tension is not essential

SPECIAL ABBREVIATIONS
Working between posts/stitches: Rather
than inserting your hook under the top
"V" of the stitch of the previous round
(in this case, a treble) you will insert your
hook underneath the actual stitch and
therefore between the posts of the stitches
of the previous round. This is done so
that the "petals" will open up and
separate once the square is complete.

Slip Stitch Join for Join-As-You-Go:
Holding one square, which has been
completed up to and including round
two, to a complete square (up to and
including round three) to join as you
go, you replace the 3-ch corner sp with
1 ch, 1 ss join, 1 ch, after making the
first cluster for that corner. Replace
the 1-ch sp between clusters along the
side with 1 ss join.
To complete the stitch: Insert the hook
into the sp (either 3-ch corner sp or 1-ch
edge sp), yrh, bring yarn from back of
ch sp to the front, and also through
the loop on the hook.
Slip Stitch Join: Put hook into stitch,
yrh, bring wool through stitch, and
loop on hook.

⟩ PATTERN
Make 168 squares in total for a blanket
of the same size as the one shown here.

FOR ALL SQUARES
Foundation With your choice of colour,
4 ch, ss into first st to form a ring.
Round 1: 3 ch (counts as a tr), 11 tr into
ring. Join with a ss to third ch of 3 ch.
Fasten off. (12sts)
Round 2: With a second colour, join new
colour working between the posts/stitch
of the stitches of round 1 throughout,
3 ch (counts as a treble) and 1 tr into
same sp between posts, 2 tr in each sp
to end, join with a ss to third ch of 3 ch.
Fasten off. (24sts)

This project contains a vast array of colours and you need to
make sure that the shades work together before splashing out
on expensive balls of yarn. Make a colour sketch to suit your
palette and then crochet a few squares as samples.

Each granny square, or motif, starts with a foundation ring. Turn to p.28 for more information about how to use slip stitches to form a foundation ring.

FOR FIRST SQUARE ONLY
Round 3: With a third colour, join new colour working between the posts/stitch of the stitches of round two throughout, 3 ch (counts as a treble), 2 tr into same place, 3 ch (corner sp), 3 tr into same place (forms a corner), *1 ch, miss 3sts from round two, 3 tr in next sp,1 ch, miss 3sts from round two, 3 tr, 3 ch, 3 tr into next sp, repeat from * two times, ch 1, miss 3sts from round two, 3 tr in next sp, 1 ch, join with a ss into third ch of 3 ch.
Fasten off, weave in ends.

FOR ALL OTHER SQUARES
Hold unfinished square against a finished (to round three) square, right side (RS) facing.

WHEN JOINING TO 1 COMPLETED SQUARE
Round 3: When joining to 1 completed square, with your third colour choice join new colour, work between the posts/stitch of the stitches of round two throughout, 3 ch (counts as a treble), 2 tr into same place, 1 ch, 1 ss join into 3-ch corner sp of completed square, 1 ch, 3 tr into same place (forms a corner), 1 ss join into next 1-ch sp of completed square, miss 3 sts from round two, 3 tr in next sp, 1 ss join into next 1-ch sp of completed square, miss 3 sts from round two, 3 tr in next sp, 1 ch, 1 ss join into 3-ch corner sp of completed square, 1 ch, 3 tr into same sp, *1 ch, miss 3 sts from round two, 3 tr in next sp, 1 ch, miss 3 tr from round two, 3 tr, 3 ch, 3 tr into next sp, repeat from * once, 1 ch, miss 3 sts from round two, 3 tr into next sp, 1 ch, join with a ss into third ch of 3 ch.
Fasten off, weave in ends.

WHEN JOINING TO 2 SQUARES
Hold the unfinished square against the finished squares, RS facing (one square above, one square to the left of that square).
Round 3: Join new colour and work between the posts/stitch of the stitches of round two throughout, 3 ch (counts as a treble), 2 tr into same place, 1 ch, 1 ss join into 3-ch corner sp of completed square above, 1 ch, 3 tr into same place (forms a corner), 1 ss join into next 1-ch sp of completed square above, miss 3sts from round two, 3 tr in next sp, 1 ss join into 3-ch corner sp of completed square above, 1 ss join into 3-ch corner sp of completed square to top left, 1 ch, 3 tr in same sp, *1 ch, miss 3sts from round 2, 3 tr in next sp, 1 ch, miss 3 tr from round 2, 3 tr, 3 ch, 3 tr into next sp, repeat from * once, 1 ch, miss 3 sts from round 2, 3 tr into next sp, 1 ch, join with a ss into third ch of 3 ch.
Fasten off, weave in ends.

WHEN JOINING TO 3 COMPLETED SQUARES
Hold the unfinished square against the finished squares, RS facing (one square above, one square to the left of that square, one square to the left of this square).
Round 3: Join new colour and work between the posts/stitch of the stitches of round two throughout, 3 ch (counts as a treble), 2 tr into same place, 1 ch, 1 ss join into 3-ch corner sp of completed square above, 1 ch, 3 tr into same place (forms a corner), 1 ss join into next 1-ch sp of completed square above, miss 3sts from round two, 3 tr in next sp, 1 ss join into next 1-ch sp of completed square above, miss 3 sts from round two, 3 tr in next sp, 1 ss join into 3-ch corner sp of completed square above, 1 ss join into 3-ch corner sp of completed square to top left, 1 ss join into 3-ch corner sp of completed square to left, 3 tr in same sp, 1 ss join into next 1-ch sp of completed square to left, miss 3sts from round two, 3 tr in next sp, 1 ss join into next 1-ch sp of completed square to left, miss 3 tr from round two, 3 tr in next sp, 1 ch, 1 ss join into 3-ch corner sp of completed square to left, 1 ch, 3 tr into same sp, 1 ch, miss 3sts from round two, 3 tr in next sp, 1 ch, miss 3sts from round two, 3 tr, 3 ch, 3 tr in next sp, 1 ch, miss 3 sts from round 2, 3 tr into next sp, 1 ch, join with a ss into third ch of 3 ch.
Fasten off and weave in ends.

EDGING
Row 1: With yarn E, or your choice of colour, join in any 3-ch corner sp. 3 ch, 2 tr, 3 ch, 3 tr, 1 tr in each tr along each edge, 1 tr in each 1-ch sp and 2 tr into each 3-ch corner sp from square below, 3 tr, 3 ch, 3 tr in each 3-ch corner sp, join with a ss and fasten off.
Row 2: With yarn A, join in any 3-ch corner sp, 3 ch, 2 tr, 3 ch, 3 tr, 1 tr in each tr along each edge, 3 tr, 3 ch, 3 tr in each 3-ch corner sp, join with a ss and fasten off.

CHEVRON CUSHION

Working chevrons in stripes produces a striking fabric with little effort. Regular shaping creates the peaks and troughs, while the crisp cotton makes for well-defined zigzags.

TECHNIQUES USED Chain stitch **p.26**, Double crochet **p.34**, Shaping crochet **p.50**, Blocking and seams **p.68**

Level of difficulty

BLANKETS AND CUSHIONS

SIZE
Approx 35cm square (13¾in square)

YARN
Twilleys Freedom Sincere DK – 50g/
115m/126yds (100% organic cotton;
any DK yarn will substitute here – try
a wool mix for a cosy alternative) and
Rico Design Baby Cotton Soft DK –
50g/125m/137yds (50% cotton and
50% acrylic)

A x 1   **B** x 1   **C** x 1

HOOK
4mm hook

NOTIONS
Yarn needle
35cm (13¾in) square cushion pad
Two black buttons

TENSION
Exact tension is not essential

PATTERN
With yarn A, work 73 ch.
Row 1: 1 dc into second ch from hook, 1 dc
in each ch to end. Turn. (72sts)
Row 2: 1 ch, 1 dc into same st, 7 dc, miss
next 2 dc, 7 dc, *2 dc in each of next 2sts,
7 dc, miss next 2 dc, 7 dc; rep from * to
last st, 2 dc in last st. Turn.
Row two forms pattern, rep for desired length
of fabric, changing colour after every four
rows in this order:
yarn A
yarn B
yarn C
When fabric measures approx 75cm (29½in),
ending with four rows of yarn A, fasten off
yarn and weave in ends.

FINISHING
Block piece lightly to shape.
Wrap piece around cushion pad, with an
overlap halfway down the back of the pad.
Ensure the starting edge of the piece is on
top, and is overlapping the bottom of the
piece. Sew up the bottom two side seams
of the cushion, then sew down the top two
side seams, overlapping the bottom seam.
Fasten the opening of the cushion by sewing
buttons on the bottom edge of the piece,
corresponding to the missed dc sts next
to the end of each point. These will form
the buttonholes.

To ensure that the crochet doesn't stretch
after the cushion pad is inserted, make a couple
of overstitches underneath the buttons to join
the two white zigzags on the flap and the
backing of the cushion cover.

GRANNY CUSHION

This chic update on the humble granny square is quick to make but has high impact, and produces a stylish cushion that is simple for beginners to follow.

Level of difficulty ✱✱✱

TECHNIQUES USED Chain stitch **p.26**, Slip stitch **p.28**, Treble crochet **p.44**, Working in the round **p.56**, A basic granny square **p.100**

SIZE
40cm (15¾in) square

YARN
Debbie Bliss Cotton DK – 50g/84m/92yds (100% cotton; you can substitute any DK weight yarn for this project)

A × 2   **B** × 2   **C** × 4   **D** × 2

HOOK
3.75mm hook

NOTIONS
Yarn needle
40cm (15¾in) square cushion pad

TENSION
Rounds 1–3 measure 8cm (3in)

PATTERN (MAKE 2)
Always work with right side (RS) facing. With yarn A, 4 ch, ss in first ch to form a ring.
Round 1: 4 ch (counts as 1 tr and 1 ch), *3 tr into ring, 1 ch, rep from * twice, 3 tr into ring, join with a ss to third of 4 ch. Fasten off A.
Round 2: Join B into any ch sp, 3 ch (counts as first tr), 2 tr, 2 ch, 3 tr in same ch sp, 1 ch, *3 tr, 2 ch, 3 tr in next ch sp, 1 ch; rep from * twice, join with a ss in top of initial 3 ch. Fasten off B.
Round 3: Join C into any corner ch sp, 3 ch (counts as first tr), 2 tr, 2 ch, 3 tr in same ch sp, 1 ch, 3 tr in next ch sp, 1 ch, *3 tr, 2 ch, 3 tr in next ch sp, 1 ch, 3 tr in next ch sp, 1 ch; rep from * twice, join with a ss in top of initial 3 ch. Fasten off C.
Round 4: Join D into any corner ch sp, 3 ch (counts as first tr), 2 tr, 2 ch, 3 tr in ch sp, 1 ch, 3 tr in next ch sp, 1 ch, 3 tr in next ch sp, 1 ch, *3 tr, 2 ch, 3 tr in next ch sp, 1 ch, 3 tr in next ch sp, 1 ch, 3 tr in next ch sp, 1 ch; rep from * twice, join with a ss in top of initial 3 ch. Fasten off D.
Continue working each round in colour sequence as follows, working as round four; each round will have one extra 3 tr in ch sp worked on each side of the square, corners remain the same.
Rounds 5 and 6: Yarn C.
Round 7: Yarn A.
Rounds 8 and 9: Yarn C.
Rounds 5 and 6: Yarn C.
Round 7: Yarn A.
Rounds 8 and 9: Yarn C.
Round 10: Yarn B.
Rounds 11 and 12: Yarn C.
Round 13: Yarn D.
Round 14: Yarn C.
Round 15: Yarn A.
Where two rounds are worked consecutively in C, you may prefer to

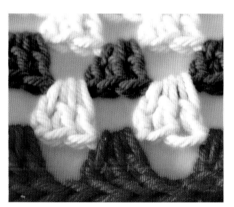

The open nature of this giant granny square means that the cushion pad will show through the crochet fabric. The white cushion pad shown here works well because the main colour is white. However, if you prefer to make your cushion in different shades, you may wish to choose a coloured insert or cover the pad before inserting it inside the crocheted cover.

ss to next corner space instead of fastening off and rejoining yarn.
Fasten off yarn, weave in ends.

FINISHING
Press front and back according to ballband instructions. Place front and back with wrong sides together, rejoin A to top left corner space, and working through front and back, join on three sides as follows:
1 dc in ch sp, *1 dc in top of each of next 3 tr, 1 dc in ch sp; rep from * to corner, 3 dc in corner ch sp; rep from * to next corner sp, 3 dc in corner ch sp; rep from * to top right-hand corner. Leaving the top of the cushion open, insert cushion pad and close by continuing in dc to first st, ss into top of first dc.
Fasten off yarn, weave in ends.

OWL CUSHION

Level of difficulty

This colourful toy owl is made in Tunisian simple stitch.
You can practise the technique, which uses a long crochet hook, on
a sample square before attempting the shaping used for this project.

TECHNIQUES USED Chain stitch **p.26**, Double crochet **p.34**, Treble crochet **p.44**, Tunisian crochet **p.127**

SIZE
38 x 31cm (15 x 12¼in)

YARN
Rowan Handknit Cotton – 50g/85m/93yds
   (100% cotton; you can use any DK weight
   yarn for a similar look to this project)

A x 3   **B** x 1   **C** x 1   **D** x 1

E small amount   **F** small amount

HOOKS
4mm and 5mm hook
5.5mm Tunisian hook

NOTIONS
Yarn needle
50cm (20in) cotton fabric suitable
   for a cushion pad
Approx 220g (8oz) toy stuffing

TENSION
17sts x 16 rows to 10cm (4in)

SPECIAL ABBREVIATIONS (SEE P.127)
TSS: Tunisian simple stitch: Chain any
   number to length desired.
Foundation row: Forward pass: insert hook
   into first ch sp from hook. Yrh and pull up
   a loop. *Insert into next, yrh and pull up a
   loop. Repeat from * keeping all loops
   on hook.

Return pass: Yrh and pull back through
one loop.
* Yrh and pull through two loops.
Repeat from * until one loop remains
on hook.
Rows: Forward pass: working forward
   again, *insert hook from side to side
   under next vertical bar (behind front
   bar and in front of back bar), yrh and
   draw up a loop. Repeat from * to last,
   keeping all loops on hook. Pull up a
   loop from the last st. Return pass: Yrh
   and pull back through one loop.
   * Yrh and pull through two loops.
   Repeat from * until one loop remains
   on hook. Repeat the second row. In the
   pattern, the forward pass and return
   pass are written as one row.
Increase: on the forward pass, put your
   hook under the horizontal bar between
   the normal vertical pick-up points.
   Yrh, and pull the new loop on the
   hook, inc complete.
Decrease: on the forward pass, put your
   hook under two vertical loops, yrh, and
   pull through both loops, dec complete.
Tying in colours: this is done on the
   return pass of the row. When you
   have the last loop of yarn A on the
   hook, put your yarn over colour B so
   the yarns are twisted, then return
   pass as normal in B.

PATTERN
FRONT
Row 1: With the Tunisian hook and yarn A,
25 ch; pick up the loops (25 loops on hook),
work return pass.
Row 2: Pick up a st (two loops on the hook)
inc, pick up the next 21 st, inc, pick up last
2 st (27 loops on hook). Return pass.
Row 3: As row 2, inc between the second
and third st, and between third and second st
at the other end (29 loops). Return pass.
Row 4: As row 2. (31 loops)
Row 5: As row 2. (33 loops)
Row 6 start wings: Wind off 25 grams
of yarn C so you have two balls of yarn C.
Take yarn A off the hook, with yarn C make
a slip knot and 3 ch, pick up two loops.
(three loops of yarn C on hook) pick up the
loop in yarn A, pick up the rest of the row
in yarn A. In yarn C, make a slip knot and
3 ch, pick up 2 st. (3 yarn C sts on hook).
(3C, 33A, 3C = 39sts). Return pass.
See "tying in colours" instructions (left)
for this and subsequent rows when
taking off loops.
Row 7: With yarn C, pick up three loops
(four loops on hook), pick up 31 loops of A,
and 4 in C (4C, 31A, 4C = 39sts). Work return
pass in colour sequence from now on.
Row 8: With yarn C, pick up a loop, inc, pick
up two more loops in C, 31 in A, 2 in C, inc,
pick up last two loops (5C, 31A, 5C = 41sts).
Fasten off A.
Row 9: Pick up so you have 6C on the hook,
29D and 6C. (41sts)
Row 10: Inc between second and third st,
and third and second st at the other end.
Pick up so you have 7C, 29D, and 7C. (43sts)
Row 11: Pick-up 8C, 27D, and 8C. (43sts)
Row 12: Inc as row 10, 10C, 25A, 10C. (45sts)
From now on you will be given the colour
sequence needed on the hook for each
row, and inc as row 10.
Row 13: C10, A25, C10. (45sts)

Row 14: Inc row C12, A23, C12. (47sts)
Row 15: Inc row C13, A23, C13.
Fasten off A. (49sts)
Row 16: C13, D23, and C13. (49sts)
Row 17: C13, D23, and C13. (49sts)
Row 18: Inc row C14, D23, C14.
Fasten off D. (51sts)
Row 19: C14, A23, C14. (51sts)
Row 20: C14, A23, C14. (51sts)
Row 21: Inc row C15, A23, C15. (53sts)
Row 22: C15, A23, C15. Fasten off A. (53sts)
Row 23: C15, D23, C15. (53sts)
Row 24: As row 23.
Row 25: C14, D25, C14. Fasten off D. (53sts)
Row 26: C13, A27, C13. (53sts)
Row 27: C13, A27, C13. (53sts)
Row 28: C13, A27, C13. (53sts)
Row 29: C12, A29, C12. Fasten off A. (53sts)
Row 30: C12, D29, C12. (53sts)
Row 31: C12, D29, C12. (53sts)
Row 32: Start dec at outer edges, (see "decrease" instructions, p.158). The end of the row dec is done 3sts from the end, then pick up the last st as usual. In C pick up first st, dec, pick up eight more sts in C, 31 in D, 8 in C, dec, pick up last st. (C10, D31, C10 = 51sts). Fasten off D.
Row 33: C10, A31, C10. (51sts)
Row 34: Dec either end as before, C8, A33, C8. (49sts)
Row 35: C8, A33, C8. (49sts)
Row 36: You will now be starting the head. Dec either end. C6, A10, B15, (start with a second ball of A) A10, C6. (47sts)
Row 37: C5, A9, B19, A9, C5. (47sts)
Row 38: Dec either end C3, A8, B23, A8, C3. (45sts)
Row 39: Dec either end C2, A6, B27, A6, C2. (43sts)
Return pass: you will also be working dec on this part of the row. Yrh, and pull through two loops, take off in the normal manner until you have three loops on the hook, yrh and in C pull through all three loops. Fasten off C. (41sts)
Row 40: With yarn A, pull a loop through the last C st, A5, B31, A5. (41sts)
Row 41: Dec either end, A2, B35, A2. Fasten off A. (39sts)
Row 42: Put your hook under the edge A loop and pull B loop through, dec, pick up 33 loops in B, dec, pick up last loop. (37sts)
Row 43: Dec either end. (35sts)
Row 44: Dec either end. (33sts)
Row 45: Dec either end. (31sts)
Row 46: Dec either end. (29sts)
Rows 47–53: TSS. (29sts)
Row 54: Inc either end. (31sts)
Row 55: Inc either end. (33sts)
Row 56 Start ears: Pick up 12st (13 loops on hook). Return pass. (13sts)

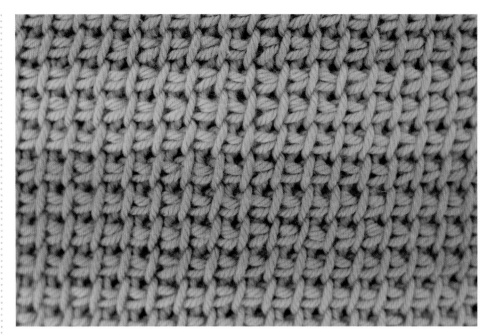

Neat stripes in blue and oatmeal represent this owl's chest plumage. For more information on changing yarn colour, turn to p.39; for more colourwork techniques, refer to pp.116–119.

Row 57: Pick up seven loops (eight loops on hook). Return pass.
Rows 58–63: Pick up one less st each row (2sts left on row 63).
Change to 5mm hook and, putting hook under vertical bars, work in ss down the ear and across the head until there are 12sts left on row 56. Change back to Tunisian hook and pick up the rest of the row (12sts). Return pass.
Row 57: Ss across four loops, pick up so you have eight loops on the hook. Return pass.
Rows 58–63: Work a dec at the beginning of each row. Fasten off B. Weave in all ends.

BACK (WORK COMPLETELY IN A)
Rows 1–5: As front.
Row 6: 3 ch, pick up two loops, then 33 loops from body, with a spare length of A, 3 ch, pick up these loops (39 loops on the hook). Return pass.
Rows 7–38: Work as for front, inc and dec where stated. You will have the total number of loops on the hook for each row.
Row 39: Dec either end, work return pass as normal. (43sts)
Row 40: Dec either end. (41sts)
Row 41: Dec either end. (39sts)
Row 42: Dec either end. (37sts)
Rows 43–63: As front, fasten off, weave in ends.

EYES (MAKE 2)
With yarn F and 4mm hook, make a slip knot from the tail, 3 ch, 12 tr into the first ch, fasten off with an invisible join, leaving a 15cm (6in) tail for sewing onto the face. Pull up the tail so there is no hole in the centre of the eye and sew firmly. With yarn B, add a V shape in the centre of each eye.

BEAK
With yarn E and 4mm hook.
Row 1: Make a slip knot and 2 ch, dc in the first ch turn. (1 dc)
Row 2: 1 ch, 2 dc in dc. (2sts)
Row 3: 1 ch, 2 dc in the first dc, dc in the next dc. (3sts)
Row 4: 1 ch, 2 dc in the first dc, dc in next 2sts. (4sts)
Next row: Working down the side of the triangle, 1 ch, 5 dc down the first side, 2 ch, 5 dc down the second side, 1 ch, dc in each dc. (14 dc)
Fasten off with an invisible join leaving a 20cm (8in) tail for sewing the beak to the face. Sew the eyes and the beak to the head.

FEET (MAKE 2)
With yarn B and 4mm hook.
Row 1: Make a slip knot and 7 ch, dc in second ch from the hook, dc in the rest of the ch. Turn. (6 dc)

Row 2: 1 ch, 2 dc in the first dc, dc in the next 4sts, 2 dc in the last dc. Turn. (8sts)

Row 3: 3 ch, tr in the same st, tr in the next 2sts, 2 tr in each of the next 2sts, tr in the next 2sts, 2 tr in the last st. (12sts)

Row 4 first claw: 2 ch, tr in the same st, tr in next 2sts, turn. (3sts)

Row 5: 2 ch, tr dec, fasten off.

2nd claw: Join yarn to next st on row three.

Row 4: 3 ch, tr dec twice, tr in the next st, turn. (3sts)

Row 5: 2 ch, tr dec, fasten off.

3rd claw: Join yarn to the next st on row three.

Row 4: 3 ch, tr in next st, 2 tr in top of 3 ch, turn. (3sts)

Row 5: 2 ch, tr dec, fasten off.

Dc round claw: Start at foundation ch, work 10 dc up the first side, 2 ch, 5 dc down second side, ss into next st.

Middle claw: 6 dc up the first side, 2 ch, 6 dc down other side, ss into next st.

3rd claw: 5 dc up first side, 2 ch, 10 dc down second side, 1 ch, dc along foundation ch, ss into first dc, fasten off leaving a 15cm (6in) tail for sewing to the body.

MAKING THE CUSHION PAD

Using the front of the owl as a guide, draw round the owl, cut out the template 1cm (½in) larger than the outline. Cut two pieces of material to the correct shape and sew together, stuffing the cushion before you sew the bottom closed.

FINISHING

With 5mm hook and the appropriate colour, put the wrong sides of the owl together with the front facing you, and starting at the bottom of the wing, dc all round, putting in the cushion pad before you dc the bottom of the cushion. Sew feet to the bottom of the cushion. Fasten off yarn, weave in ends.

The dense effect of Tunisian simple stitch makes this owl appear very neat and compact, with its raspberry pink wings folded into its body. Its feet are worked in regular crochet stitches and sewn on.

HOME AND GIFTS

With trend-led colourways of yarn, there are opportunities galore for updating your home – from useful baskets to a contemporary chunky rug – and for crocheting a handmade gift.

DESKTOP STORAGE POTS

Level of difficulty

An ideal project for beginners, these colourful and practical storage pots are quick and easy to make and can be used for storing anything from pens and stationery to jewellery. The pots are worked in a spiral and vary in size.

TECHNIQUES USED Chain stitch **p.26**, Double crochet **p.34**, Changing colours **p.39**, Double crochet increases **p.50**, Working in the round **p.56**

HOME AND GIFTS

SIZE
Tall: 7 x 10cm (2¾ x 4in); Small: 6.5 x 4cm (2½ x 1½in); Wide: 12 x 7cm (4¾ x 2¾in)

YARN
Texere Yarns C4 Linen – 200g/450– 600m/492–656yds spool (100% linen; you can try coloured string or any thick plant fibre, such as linen or cotton, for a non-fluffy look)

A x 1   **B** x 1

HOOK
5mm hook

NOTIONS
Stitch marker
Yarn needle

TENSION
Ensure that tension is tight to create a 3D pot that does not sag

PATTERN

Note: Place a stitch marker in the first stitch of each round, moving the marker up as each round is completed.

TALL POT
With yarn A, work 2 ch, 6 dc in second ch from hook.
Round 1: 2 dc in each st. (12sts)
Round 2: *2 dc in next st, dc in next st; rep from * to end. (18sts)
Round 3: *2 dc in next st, dc in next 2sts; rep from * to end. (24sts)
Round 4: *2 dc in next st, dc in next 3sts; rep from * to end. (30sts)
Round 5: Working in back loops only, dc in each st to end.
Continue working even rounds through both loops (1 dc in each st to end) until piece measures 10cm (4in) from round 5. With yarn B, work even rounds for three rounds or until work reaches desired height. Fasten off, weave in ends.

SMALL POT
With yarn B, work as for tall pot to end of round five.
Continue working even rounds through both loops (1 dc in each st to end) until piece measures 5cm (2in) from round 5, or desired height.
Fasten off, weave in ends.

WIDE POT
With yarn B, work as for tall pot to end of round 4.
Round 5: *2 dc in next st, dc in next 4sts; rep from * to end. (36sts)
Round 6: *2 dc in next st, dc in next 5sts; rep from * to end. (42sts)

For double strength, each storage pot is made rigid by working with double strands of yarn. When your pot has reached the diameter you require, begin working upwards and end at your preferred height.

Round 7: *2 dc in next st, dc in next 6sts; rep from * to end. (48sts)
Round 8: Working in back loops only, dc in each st to end.
Continue working even rounds through both loops (1 dc in each st to end) for four rounds. With yarn A, work even rounds for four rounds or until work reaches desired height.
Fasten off, weave in ends.

STRUCTURED BASKETS

Using such bulky yarns means these baskets work up quickly. The yarn is recycled so can vary from cone to cone. Adjust your hook as necessary for the thickness of the yarn, and crochet tightly for a rigid fabric.

TECHNIQUES USED Changing colours **p.39**, Double crochet increases **p.50**, Working in the round **p.56**, Working into the back loop of a double crochet **p.75**

SIZE

Large: approx 20 x 17cm (8 x 6¾in);
    Medium: approx 15 x 15cm (6 x 6in);
    Small: approx 14 x 10cm (5½ x 4in)

YARN

DMC Hoooked Zpagetti yarn –
    850g/120m/131yds (100% recycled
    T-shirt yarn; any super-bulky yarn will
    work here. You could even try making
    your own yarn from old T-shirts and
    jersey fabric)

A x 1   **B** x 1

HOOK

12mm hook

NOTIONS

Stitch marker
Large-eyed yarn needle

TENSION

Exact tension is not essential

PATTERN

Note: These baskets are worked in spirals. Do not join rounds, but place a marker at the first stitch of the round, moving it up as each round is completed.

LARGE BASKET
With yarn A, work 2 ch and work 6 dc into second ch from hook, join round with a ss to first st.
Round 1: 1 ch, work 2 dc in each st around, do not join round, place marker. (12sts)
Round 2: *2 dc in next st, 1 dc in next dc, rep from * to end. (18sts)
Round 3: *2 dc in next st, 1 dc in next 2 dcs, rep from * to end. (24sts)
Round 4: *2 dc in next st, 1 dc in next 3 dcs, rep from * to end. (30sts)
Round 5: *2 dc in next st, 1 dc in next 4 dcs, rep from * to end. (36sts)
Round 6: *2 dc in next st, 1 dc in next 5 dcs, rep from * to end. Join round with a ss. (42sts)
Round 7: 1 ch, 1 dc TBL into each st around. Join with ss.
Round 8: 1 ch, 1 dc into each st around. Do not join round.
Work last round five times.
Round 14: 3 ch, tr into bottom of same st, miss next st, *2 tr into next st, miss next st; rep from * to end of round, join to top of first ch with a ss.
Round 15: Work as round 8.
Round 16: 1 ch, 7 dc, 7 ch, miss next 7 dc, 14 dc, 7 ch, miss next 7 dc, dc to end.
Round 17: 1 ch, (dc to 7-ch sp, 7 dc into ch sp) twice, dc to end, join round with a ss. Fasten off yarn, weave in ends.

MEDIUM BASKET
With yarn A, work as for large basket to round 5. (36sts)
Round 6: 1 ch, 1 dc TBL into each st around. Join with ss.
Round 7: 1 ch, 1 dc into each st around.

Do not join round.
Work last round three times, then change to yarn B and work two rounds.
Round 13: 1 ch, 6 dc, 6 ch, miss next 6 dc, 12 dc, 6 ch, miss next 6 dc, dc to end.
Round 14: 1 ch, (dc to 6 ch sp, 6 dc into ch sp) twice, dc to end, join round with a ss. Fasten off yarn, weave in ends.

SMALL BASKET
With yarn B, work as for large basket to round 4. (30sts)
Round 5: 1 ch, 1 dc TBL into each st around. Join with ss.
Change to yarn A.
Round 6: 1 ch, 1 dc into each st around. Do not join round.
Work last round four times. Join round with a ss.
Fasten off yarn, weave in ends.

For smart storage, this trio of baskets stack neatly inside each other. Easy-to-grasp handles are crocheted into the larger two baskets for carrying.

HANGING TOY BASKET

This pretty accessory will be at home in any child's room. Constructed in spirals using double crochet, it can easily be tackled by a beginner. Instructions are given for a medium and a large toy basket.

TECHNIQUES USED Using slip stitch to form a foundation ring **p.28**, Changing colours **p.39**, Double crochet increases **p.50**, Double crochet decreases **p.52**

SIZE
25 (30) x 40 (45)cm/9¾ (12) x 15¾ (17¾)in

YARN
Sirdar Simply Recycled Aran – 50g/93m/102yds (51% recycled cotton and 49% acrylic; any aran weight or cotton blend could be used here)

A x 2   **B** x 1   **C** x 1

HOOK
3.5mm hook

NOTIONS
Stitch marker
Yarn needle

TENSION
14sts x 16 rows per 10cm (4in)

PATTERN
Note: Worked in the round in a spiral, do not turn and do not join at end of each round.

With yarn A, ch 4 and join with a ss to form a ring.
Round 1: 1 ch (does not count as stitch), 6 dc into ring, place marker to indicate last st of round (move marker up at end of each round, so it always indicates last st). (6sts)
Round 2: 2 dc into each st. (12sts)
Round 3: *1 dc in next st, 2 dc in next st, rep from * to end. (18sts)
Round 4: *1 dc in next 2sts, 2 dc in next st, rep from * to end. (24sts)
Round 5: *1 dc in next 3 sts, 2 dc in next st, rep from * to end. (30sts)
Round 6: *1 dc in next 4sts, 2 dc in next st, rep from * to end. (36sts)
Round 7: *1 dc in next 5sts, 2 dc in next st, rep from * to end. (42sts)
Round 8: *1 dc in next 6sts, 2 dc in next st, rep from * to end. (48sts)
Round 9: *1 dc in next 7sts, 2 dc in next st, rep from * to end. (54sts)
Round 10: *1 dc in next 8sts, 2 dc in next st, rep from * to end. (60sts)
Round 11: *1 dc in next 9sts, 2 dc in next st, rep from * to end. (66sts)
Round 12: *1 dc in next 10sts, 2 dc in next st, rep from * to end. (72sts)
Round 13: *1 dc in next 11sts, 2 dc in next st, rep from * to end. (78sts)
Round 14: *1 dc in next 12sts, 2 dc in next st, rep from * to end. (84sts)
Round 15: *1 dc in next 13sts, 2 dc in next st, rep from * to end. (90sts)
Round 16: *1 dc in next 14sts, 2 dc in next st, rep from * to end. (96sts)

Large size only
Next round: *1 dc in next 15sts, 2 dc in next dc, rep from * to end. (102sts)
Continue without shaping until piece measures 16cm (6¼in) for small size and 18cm (7in) for large size from round 1.

Large size only
Next round: *1 dc in next 15sts, dc2tog, rep from * to end. (96sts)

Both sizes
Next round: *1 dc in next 14sts, dc2tog, rep from * to end. (90sts)
Next round: *1 dc in next 13sts, dc2tog, rep from * to end. (84sts)
Next round: *1 dc in next 12sts, dc2tog, rep from * to end. (78sts)
Next round: *1 dc in next 11sts, dc2tog, rep from * to end. (72sts)
Change to B and work six (eight) rounds in dc as set.
Change to C and work two (two) rounds in dc as set.

HANGING LOOP
At start of next round, make 20 ch, miss 12sts, dc to end of round. (60sts and 20ch)
Next round: 1 dc in each ch and 1 dc in each st to end of round. (80sts)
Work four (five) rounds in dc as set.
Final round 1 ss in each dc to end.
Fasten off yarn, weave in ends. Block lightly according to instructions on ballband.

CHUNKY RUG

This stylish rug is worked in rounds and makes an eye-catching addition to any room. The chunky yarn is soft and warm underfoot and works up quickly on a large crochet hook.

Level of difficulty

TECHNIQUES USED Half treble crochet **p.38**, Treble crochet **p.44**, Treble crochet decreases **p.53**, Working in the round **p.56**, Working into a chain space **p.75**

SIZE
90cm (35½in) in diameter

YARN
Cygnet Seriously Chunky – 100g/48m/52yds (100% acrylic; any super-chunky yarn, with a high synthetic content is suitable)

x 6

HOOK
12mm hook

NOTIONS
Yarn needle

TENSION
Rounds 1–2 measure 15cm (6in) diameter

SPECIAL ABBREVIATIONS
Treble clusters worked as follows, depending on pattern instruction:

HTRCL: half treble cluster (htr2tog). Insert hook into st, yrh, draw through, yrh and draw through one loop, insert hook into st, yrh, draw through, yrh and draw through all three loops on hook.

TRCL: treble cluster (tr2tog). Yrh, insert hook into st, yrh, draw through, yrh and draw through two loops, yrh, insert hook into st, yrh, draw through, yrh and draw through two loops, yrh and draw through remaining three loops on hook.

DTRCL: double treble cluster (tr3tog). Yrh twice, insert hook into st, yrh, draw through, yrh and draw through two loops twice, yrh twice, insert hook into st, yrh, draw through, yrh and draw through two loops twice, yrh and draw through rem three loops on hook.

Treble cluster pair: tr2tog, 1 ch, tr2tog all in the same ch sp.

PATTERN
Work 4 ch, ss into first ch to make a ring.
Round 1: 2 ch, 1 htr into ring, 1 ch, *htrcl into ring, 1 ch, repeat from * six more times, ss into top of first htr to close round. (8 htrcl)
Round 2: Ss into next ch sp, 3 ch, 1 tr into ch sp, 2 ch, *tr2tog in next ch sp, 2 ch, repeat from * to end of round, ss into top of first tr to close round. (8 tr2tog)
Round 3: Ss into next ch sp, 3 ch, 1 tr into ch sp, 1 ch, trcl in same ch sp, 1 ch, *tr2tog, 1 ch, tr2tog, in next ch sp, 1 ch, repeat from * to end, ss into top of first tr to close round. (8 tr cluster pairs)
Round 4: Ss into next ch sp, 3 ch, 1 tr into ch sp, 1 ch, *tr2tog in next ch sp, 1 ch, repeat from * to end, ss into top of first tr to close round. (16 tr2tog)
Round 5: Ss into next ch sp, 3 ch, 1 tr into ch sp, 1 ch, tr2tog into same ch sp, 1 ch, *tr2tog, 1 ch, tr2tog in next ch sp, 1 ch, repeat from * to end, ss into top of first tr to close round. (16 tr cluster pairs)
Round 6: Ss into next ch sp, 3 ch, 1 tr into ch sp, 1 ch, *tr2tog in next ch sp, 1 ch, repeat from * to end, ss into top of first tr to close round. (32 tr2tog)
Round 7: Ss into next ch sp, 3 ch, 1 tr into ch sp, 1 ch, tr2tog into same ch sp, 1 ch, tr2tog in next ch sp, ch 1 *tr2tog, 1 ch, tr2tog in next ch sp, 1 ch, tr2tog in next ch sp, 1 ch, repeat from * to end, ss into top of first tr to close round. (16 tr2tog and 16 tr cluster pairs)

Round 8: As round 6. (48 tr clusters)
Round 9: Ss into next ch sp, 5 ch, *1 dtr in next ch sp, 1 ch, repeat from * to end, join with a ss into fourth ch of 5 ch.
Round 10: Ss into next ch sp, 3 ch, 1 tr into ch sp, 1 ch, tr2tog into same ch sp, 1 ch, tr3tog in next ch sp, 1 ch, *tr2tog, 1 ch, tr2tog in next ch sp, 1 ch, tr3tog in next ch sp, 1 ch, repeat from * to end, ss into top of first tr to close round. (24 tr cluster pairs and 24 large tr clusters made)
Round 11: As round 6. (72 tr2tog)
Round 12: 1 ch, *1 dc in top of tr2tog, 1 dc into ch sp, repeat from * to end, ss into 1 ch to close round.

FINISHING
Weave in all ends securely on reverse. Pin rug to a flat surface and spray lightly with water, shape to a flat circle, and leave to dry.
A non-slip backing can be sewn to the reverse of the rug, if desired.

The treble clusters and half treble clusters in this project create an attractive mesh pattern towards the outside of the rug and this contrasts well with the tighter stitches at the edge, and the nice neat finish given by the final row of double crochet.

HOME AND GIFTS

ROUND STOOL COVER

Level of difficulty

The vibrant colours of this stool cover add interest to a practical project. Worked in the round using trebles and double crochet, this is an ideal project for someone with some experience of crochet.

TECHNIQUES USED Double crochet **p.34**, Treble crochet **p.44**, Double crochet decreases **p.52**, Working in the round **p.56**, Joining on a new colour **p.57**

SIZE
27cm (10½in) in diameter

YARN
Rowan Pure Wool Aran – 100g/170m/
  186yds (100% wool; any aran weight,
  preferably superwash wool, will give
  a similar texture and finish)

A x 1   **B** x 1   **C** x 1   **D** x 1

E x 1   **F** x 1

HOOK
4.5mm hook

NOTIONS
Yarn needle

TENSION
Rounds 1–3 measure 10cm (4in)
  in diameter

PATTERN
With yarn A, work 4 ch, join with a ss to form a ring (see p.56).
Round 1: 3 ch, 1 tr, *1 ch, 2 tr, rep from * four times, 1 ch, join with a ss into top of 3 ch, (6 tr pairs made), fasten off A.
Round 2: Join B into any ch sp, 3 ch, 1 tr, 1 ch, 2 tr in same ch sp, *1 ch, (2 tr, 1 ch, 2 tr) in next ch sp, rep from * four times, 1 ch, join with a ss into top of 3 ch. (6-tr pairs and 12-ch sp) Fasten off B.
Round 3: Join C into any ch sp, 3 ch, 2 tr into same ch sp, *1 ch, 3 tr into next ch sp, rep from * to end, 1 ch, join with a ss into top of 3 ch, fasten off C. (12 3-tr and 12-ch sp)
Round 4: Join D into any ch sp, work as for round 3, fasten off D. (12 3-tr and 12-ch sp)
Round 5: Join E into any ch sp, 3 ch, 1 tr, 1 ch, 2 tr in same ch sp, *1 ch, (2 tr, 1 ch, 2 tr) in next ch sp, rep from * 10 times, 1 ch, join with a ss into top of 3 ch, fasten off E. (12-tr pairs and 24-ch sp)
Round 6: Join F into any ch sp, work as for round 3, fasten off F. (24 3-tr and 24-ch sp)
Round 7: Join A into any ch sp, work as for round 3, fasten off A. (24 3-tr and 24-ch sp)
Round 8: Join B into any ch sp, work as for round 3, fasten off B. (24 3-tr and 24-ch sp)
Round 9: Join C into any ch sp, work as for round 3, but work 2 ch between each 3 tr, fasten off C. (24 3-tr and 24-ch sp)
Round 10: Join D into any ch sp, 1 ch, * work 1 dc into top of each tr, 1 dc in ch sp, repeat from * to end, join with a ss into top of 1 ch (96 dc), do not turn work, do not fasten off yarn. Continue to work in rounds decreasing as follows:
Round 11: 1 ch, *1 dc in each of next 6 dc, dc2tog, repeat from * to end, join with a ss in top of 1 ch. (84sts)
Round 12: 1 ch, 1 dc in each dc to end of round, join with a ss in top of ch 3.

Treble crochet gives a lovely openwork finish to the top of this cover, but the underneath is much more dense because it is worked in double crochet. This will ensure that the cover fits snugly over the stool, preventing it from slipping.

Round 13: As round 12.
Round 14: 1 ch, *1 dc in each of next 5 dc, dc2tog, repeat from * to end, join with a ss in top of 1 ch. (72sts)
Round 15: As round 12.
Round 16: 1 ch, * 1 dc in each of next 4 dc, dc2tog, repeat from * to end. (60sts)
Round 17: As round 12. Fasten off yarn, weave in ends.

RUSTIC POUFFES

These simple pouffes are a great way to bring a touch of colour into your home. The size is simple to adjust by working more, or fewer, increase rounds.

HOME AND GIFTS

TECHNIQUES USED Chain stitch **p.26**, Working in the round **p.56**, Blocking and seams **p.68**, Darning in yarn **p.70**, Working into the back loop of a double crochet **p.75**

SIZE

Large: 40cm (15¾in) in diameter;
    Small: 30cm (12in) in diameter

YARN

Hoopla yarn – 500g/100m/109yds (95–100% cotton and 0–5% lycra; a super-bulky cotton or stretchy jersey fabric yarn will be suitable for this project)

A x 4   **B** x 5

HOOK

8mm hook

NOTIONS

Stitch marker
Large-eyed yarn needle
Two round box cushions, approx 40 x 15cm (15¾ x 6in) and 30 x 8cm (12 x 3in); or a low-tog duvet to fill the large pouffe

TENSION

Rounds 1–3 measures approx 12cm (5in) in diameter

PATTERN

Note: The top of each pouffe is made first, then the sides. The base is made as a separate piece and sewn on. This allows the cushion filling to be removed for washing.

TOP

With 8mm hook, work 6 ch, ss in the first ch to form a ring.
Round 1: 6 dc into ring. Do not join or turn, continue working in a spiral with right side (RS) facing, using stitch marker to indicate the last st of each round (remove and replace after last dc of each round). (6sts)
Round 2: 2 dc in each dc. (12sts)
Round 3: (1 dc, 2 dc in next dc) to end. (18sts)
Round 4: (2 dc, 2 dc in next dc) to end. (24sts)
Continue increasing as set, working 1 more dc between each increase, making six increases evenly on each round until work measures 30 (40)cm/12 (15¾)in. Make a note of the stitch count as this will be needed for making the base of the pouffe.
Next round: 1 dc TBL in each dc to end.
Next and subsequent rounds: 1 dc in each st to end, continue to work in a spiral, without increasing until the sides measure 8 (15)cm/3 (6)in.
Fasten off yarn and weave in ends. Sew all loose ends of yarn securely in place as, due to the nature of the yarn, they can work loose over time and may fray.

BASE

Work as for top, increasing as set until stitch count matches stitch count noted for top. Fasten off yarn, weave in ends.

FINISHING

Fill the pouffe with a cushion pad or duvet. Attach bottom to sides by sewing through last round of sides and last round of bottom to secure. Weave in loose ends securely. Shape gently to give a rounded appearance.

Stretchy jersey or cotton yarn (a by-product of the textile industry) is popular with crocheters. Its chunkiness means that your pouffes will grow rapidly, while its texture creates a lovely knotted effect.

OCTOPUS MOBILE

Level of difficulty ✱✱✱

Transform a little one's room into an underwater scene with this gorgeously cute hanging octopus. Dangle it safely out of the grasp of little fingers by simply adjusting the length of the attaching chain.

TECHNIQUES USED Double crochet **p.34**, Half treble crochet **p.38**, Treble crochet **p.44**, Shaping **p.50–52**, Making a simple adjustable ring **p.57**, Toy techniques **p.132–33**

SIZE
33cm (13in) long, including tentacles

YARN
Paintbox Yarns Cotton DK – 50g/125m/
137yds (100% cotton, any DK weight
cotton yarn will work here)

A x 2   **B** x 1   **C** x 1   **D** x 1

HOOK
3mm hook

NOTIONS
Stitch marker
2 x 10mm (½in) safety eyes
Toy stuffing

TENSION
Exact tension is not essential – crochet
tightly to ensure that the stuffing does
not show through stitches

SPECIAL ABBREVIATIONS
DCBLO: Double crochet in back loop only:
work a dc in back loop only of next st.

PATTERN
Note: Main body of octopus is worked in the round in spirals. Do not join each round or use turning chains unless indicated; instead place a marker at the start of the round, moving upwards each round to denote beginning of rounds.
1ch at beg of round does not count as a stitch.

OCTOPUS BODY
With yarn A, make an adjustable ring.
Round 1: Work 6 dc in ring, pull up to tighten, do not join round but place marker for working in spirals, move marker up every round.
Round 2: 2 dc in each dc around. (12sts)
Round 3: (1 dc in next dc, 2 dc in next dc) around. (18sts)
Round 4: (2 dc into each of next 2 dc, 2 dc in next dc) around. (24sts)
Round 5: (3 dc, 2 dc in next dc) around. (30sts)
Round 6: (4 dc, 2 dc in next dc) around. (36sts)

Round 7: (5 dc, 2 dc in next dc) around. (42sts)
Round 8: 1 dcblo in each st around.
Rounds 9–11: 1 dc in each st around.
Round 12: (6 dc, 2 dc in next dc) around. (48sts)
Round 13: dc in each st around. Place safety eyes now on top of row 13, 13 stitches apart, at front of octopus. Work four rounds straight in dc.
Round 18: (7 dc, 2 dc in next dc) around (54sts)
Work three rounds straight in dc.
Round 22: (8 dc, 2 dc in next dc) around (60sts)
Work three rounds straight in dc.
Round 26: (8 dc, dc2tog) around (54sts)
Work three rounds straight in dc.

Begin stuffing the body now before the hole gets too small to stuff.

Round 30: (7 dc, dc2tog) around (48sts)
Work two rounds straight in dc.

Cute facial features
The eyes sit low down on the face and the mouth is simple and small. These features add to the cuteness of amigurumi crocheted toys – a Japanese style of crocheting small animals that often have anthropomorphic features.

Round 33: (6 dc, dc2tog) around. (42sts)
Work one round straight in dc.
Round 35: (5 dc, dc2tog) around. (36sts)
Work one round straight in dc.
Round 37: (4 dc, dc2tog) around. (30sts)
Round 38: (3 dc, dc2tog) around. (24sts)
Round 39: (2 dc, dc2tog) around. (18sts)
Round 40: (1 dc, dc2tog) around. (12sts)
Round 41: dc2tog around. (6sts)
Fasten off leaving a long tail. Thread the long tail onto a yarn needle and pass around top opening, pull up tightly to close hole, and secure.

TENTACLES

Reattach yarn A to bottom of octopus, joining into any unworked loop of round 8.
Round 1: 1 ch, (1 dc, 2 dc in next st) around, join round with ss. (63sts)
Round 2: 2 ch (counts as 1 htr), 1 htr in same st, 1 htr in each st around, join round with ss. (64sts)
Round 3: 1 ch, *1 dc, 1 htr, 3 tr, 1 htr, 1 dc, 1 ss; rep from * around. (64sts)
Round 4: 1ch, *1 dc in each st to next tr, 42 ch, 2 tr in 3rd ch from hook, 3 tr in each of next 4 ch, 2 tr in each of next 27 ch, 1 tr in each of next 8 ch, 1 dc in next htr from round 3; rep from * a further four times, **1 dc in each st to next tr, 47 ch, 2 tr in 3rd ch from hook, 3 tr in each of next 4 ch, 2 tr in each of next 32 ch, 1 tr in each of next 8 ch, 1dc in next htr from round 3; rep from ** twice more, 1dc in each st to end, join round with ss. (8 tentacles)

BOTTOM OF TENTACLES

With yarn B, make an adjustable ring.
Round 1: Work 6 dc in ring, pull up to tighten, do not join round but place marker for working in spirals, move marker up every round.
Round 2: 2 dc in each dc around (12sts)
Round 3: (1 dc in next dc, 2 dc in next dc) around (18sts)
Round 4: (2 dc into each of next 2 dc, 2 dc in next dc) around. (24sts)
Round 5: (3 dc, 2 dc in next dc) around. (30sts)
Round 6: (4 dc, 2 dc in next dc) around. (36sts)
Round 7: (5 dc, 2 dc in next dc) around. (42 dc)
Round 8: 1 ch, (1 dc in next st, 2 dc in next st) around, join round with ss. (63sts)
Round 9: 2ch (counts as 1 htr), 1 htr in same st, 1 htr in each st around, join round with ss (64sts).
Round 10: 1 ch, *1 dc, 1 htr, 3 tr, 1 htr, 1 dc, 1 ss; rep from * around. (64sts)

Spiralled tentacles
The tentacles are formed of neat ruffles, which are made by simply increasing lots of stitches very quickly along the row, causing the fabric to buckle and curl.

Round 11: 1ch, *1 dc in each st to next tr, 42 ch, 2 tr in 3rd ch from hook, 3 tr in each of next 4 ch, 2 tr in each of next 27 ch, 1 tr in each of next 8 ch, 1 dc in next htr from round 3; rep from * a further four times, **1 dc in each st to next tr, 47 ch, 2 tr in 3rd ch from hook, 3 tr in each of next 4 ch, 2 tr in each of next 32 ch, 1 tr in each of next 8 ch, 1dc in next htr from round 3; rep from ** twice more, 1 dc in each st to end, join round with ss. (8 tentacles)

Sew bottom of tentacles to the bottom of the octopus body, with RSF each other, then join the top and bottom of the tentacles as follows:
With top of yarn A tentacles facing, join yarn B to the st to the left of any tentacle, 1 ch, insert hook through same stitch and corresponding yarn B stitch below, work 1 dc. Work 1 dc through all corresponding pairs of sts in same way around to next tentacle, then work evenly in dc all down the right side of tentacle, working 1 dc through corresponding pairs of stitches – these will be the unworked bottom loops of the starting chain of the tentacles. Fasten off yarn when you get to the bottom of the chain of the tentacle.
Rejoin yarn to left of next tentacle and work in the same way – repeating until all 8 tentacles have been joined on one side.

STARFISH (MAKE 1 EACH IN YARNS B, C, AND D; OPTIONAL)

With desired yarn colour, make adjustable ring, *work 2 ch, 1dc in 2nd ch from hook, ss into adjustable loop; rep from * four more times, join round with ss and pull up loop to close hole.
Fasten off yarn.

FINISHING

Weave in all ends neatly and embroider a little mouth at the front of body, on the 3rd row up on octopus body, in the central stitch between the eyes.
Fasten starfish, if using, to the top left of the octopus head as shown.
Join yarn A to top of octopus head and make a chain of desired length for hanging. Fasten off.
Arrange tentacles by twisting the ruffles to fall in the intended direction, so they fall in neat spirals from the body.

Optional extras Sew some cute and simple little starfish decorations to the top of the octopus head for added colour and interest. You can make as many of these as desired, adding some to the tentacles, too, if you wish.

CAT BASKET

This colourful cat basket makes good use of the increasingly popular T-shirt yarn, which is a by-product of the clothing industry. It is satisfying to make as the thickness of the yarn means that you get very quick results.

TECHNIQUES USED Working in the round **p.56**, Adjustable ring **p.57**, Working into the back loop of a double crochet **p.75**

SIZE
Approx 44cm (17½in) in diameter

YARN
Hoooked Zpagetti – 850g/120m/131yds (100% recycled T-shirt yarn; you can use super bulky weight T-shirt yarn, cotton, or felted wool to achieve a similar effect. You may need to use the yarns double to make the basket rigid enough)

A x 1   **B** x 1   **C** x 1

HOOK
10mm hook

NOTIONS
Stitch marker
Large-eyed yarn needle
Circular cushion, optional

TENSION
Exact tension is not essential

SPECIAL ABBREVIATIONS
Adjustable ring: Wind the yarn twice around your finger. Insert the hook and wrap the yarn around it. Pull the hook back through and work a chain. Work the first round of sts into the "ring", then pull the tail of yarn gently to close it, before joining the sts into a round using a ss.

Crab stitch: Means simply working dc in reverse, working round the row, or round in this case, from left to right, instead of right to left. After completing a row of dc, do not turn the work around; work 1 ch, *insert the hook into the next stitch to the right, not in the stitch you just completed, but the next one. Draw a loop through. Yrh as normal and pull through both loops on the hook; rep from * across row.

➤ PATTERN

Note: The basket is worked in a spiral. Do not join at end of round. Mark the first stitch of each round with a stitch marker or length of coloured yarn, in order to keep track of rounds and stitches.

With yarn A, make an adjustable ring and work 6 dc into ring. (6sts)
Round 1: 2 dc in each dc to end. (12sts)
Round 2: *1 dc in next st, 2 dc in next st, rep from * to end. (18sts)
Round 3: With yarn B, *1 dc in next 2sts, 2 dc in next st, rep from * to end. (24sts)
Round 4: With yarn A, *1 dc in next 3sts, 2 dc in next st, rep from * to end. (30sts)
Round 5: *1 dc in next 4sts, 2 dc in next st, rep from * to end. (36sts)
Round 6: With yarn B, *1 dc in next 5sts, 2 dc in next st, rep from * to end. (42sts)
Round 7: With yarn A, *1 dc in next 6sts, 2 dc in next st, rep from * to end. (48sts)
Round 8: *1 dc in next 7sts, 2 dc in next st, rep from * to end. (54sts)
Round 9: With yarn B, *1 dc in next 8sts, 2 dc in next st, rep from * to end. (60sts)
Round 10: With yarn A, *1 dc in next 9sts, 2 dc in next st, rep from * to end. (66sts)

Round 11: *1 dc in next 10 sts, 2 dc in next st, rep from * to end. (72sts)
Round 12: With yarn B, *1 dc in next 11sts, 2 dc in next st, rep from * to end. (78sts)
Round 13: With yarn A, *1 dc in next 12sts, 2 dc in next st, rep from * to end. (84sts)
Round 14: *1 dc in next 13sts, 2 dc in next st, rep from * to end. (90sts)
Round 15: 1 dc TBL in each st to end.
Round 16: 1 dc in each st (front and back loops) to end.
Round 17: With yarn B, 1 dc in each st to end.
Rounds 18–19: With yarn A, 1 dc in each st to end.
Round 20: With yarn B, 1 dc in each st to end.
Rounds 21–22: With yarn A, 1 dc in each st to end.
Round 23: With yarn C, crab st in each st to end. Ss at end of round to join.
Fasten off, weave in ends.
Place a circular cushion inside (optional).

Keeping it simple with a double crochet stitch gives a pleasing, even effect. The yarn needs to be as non-stretchy as possible to keep the basket rigid, and the diameter and height can be adjusted by adding or subtracting increases and rounds.

FILIGREE BOOKMARKS

Level of difficulty ✳✳✳

A very simple, quick-to-make project, these delicate bookmarks are perfect for using up ends of yarn. Use the thicker yarn to make a bookmark for a coffee-table book and the finer yarn to make a bookmark for a novel.

TECHNIQUES USED Chain stitch **p.26**, Slip stitch **p.28**, Double crochet **p.34**, Treble crochet **p.44**

SIZE

Approx 18 x 2cm (7in x ¾in), with an 18cm (7in) tassel

YARN

DMC Petra Crochet Cotton Perle No. 5 – 100g/400m/437yds (100% cotton; try small amounts of fine crochet cotton for this project) and DMC Petra Crochet Cotton Perle No. 3 – 100g/280m/306yds (the bookmark will get slightly bigger or smaller, depending on the thickness)

A x 1   **B** x 1

HOOKS

2mm hook
2.5mm hook

NOTIONS

Yarn needle
Assorted beads, if desired

TENSION

Exact tension is not essential

PATTERN

With the 2mm hook, if working with the finer No. 5 yarn, or the 2.5mm hook, if using the thicker No. 3 yarn, work 42 ch.

Round 1: 6 dc into second ch from hook, miss next ch, 1 dc into next ch, miss next ch, *6 dc into next ch, miss next ch; 1 dc into next ch, miss next ch; rep from * to last ch, work (6 dc, 1 ch, 6 dc) into last ch, do not turn. Now rotate your work 180 degrees and continue working back into the unworked loop of each ch as follows: *miss next ch, dc into next ch, miss next ch, 6 dc into next ch; rep from * to end, 1 ch, ss to first dc to join round.

Round 2: 4 ch (counts as 1 tr, 1 ch), tr into second dc from the first round, (1 ch, 1 tr) into each of next 3 dc, miss next 3 dc, *(tr, 1 ch) into each of next 3 dc, 1 tr into next dc, miss 3 dc; rep from * to last 6 dc group, (tr, 1 ch) into each of next 4 dc, tr into next dc, 3 ch, **(tr, 1 ch) into each of next 4 dc, tr into next dc, miss next 3 dc; rep between * and **, join round with a ss.
Fasten off, weave in ends.

FINISHING

Cut two lengths of yarn 36cm (14¼in) long, and fold in half. Insert the loop through the 3-ch sp at one end of the bookmark. Push the end of the lengths through the loop and pull tight to make a tassel, braiding the yarn if desired. Thread assorted beads onto the end of the tassel and secure with a knot.

The main strip is worked in the round by crocheting into both sides of the starting chain. Note the difference between the sizes of the bookmarks – this is achieved by using different thicknesses of crochet yarn and sizes of hook.

BOOK COVER

Level of difficulty ✱✱✱

This practical, crocheted book cover is quick to work both in the round and in rows, and will protect your book from damage when you're out and about. It closes with a button-and-loop fastening for easy access.

TECHNIQUES USED Half treble crochet **p.38**, Simple stripes **p.39**, Working in the round **p.56**, Working into a chain space **p.75**, Button loops **p.87**

HOME AND GIFTS

SIZE
Approx. 21 x 16cm (8¼ x 6¼in)

YARN
Sirdar Hayfield Bonus Chunky –
100g/137m/150yds (100% acrylic; you
can use any chunky weight yarn to
complete this project; some synthetic
fibre is preferable, for durability)

A x 1   **B** x 1

HOOK
5.5mm hook

NOTIONS
Yarn needle
3cm (1¼in) button, in tonal colour

TENSION
13sts x 9.5 rows per 10cm (4in) square in
half treble crochet

PATTERN
In yarn A, work 20 ch.
Row 1: Work 1 htr in second ch from hook,
work 1 htr in each st to end. (19sts)
Continue to work 1 htr in each st on the
back side of the foundation chain to end.
(38sts)
Begin working in rounds. Do not turn or join.
Rounds 2–12: 1 htr in each st.
Change to yarn B.
Rounds 13–18: 1 htr in each st.
Round 19: 1 htr in each st, ch 1, turn.
Begin working in rows.
Row 1: 1 htr in next 19sts, ch 1, turn. (19sts)
Row 2: 1 htr in each st, ch 1, turn.
Rows 3–7: Repeat row 2.
Row 8: 1 htr in first 8sts, ch 3, miss 3sts,
1 htr in last 8sts, ch 1, turn.
Row 9: 1 dc in first 8sts, 3 dc in ch loop,
1 dc in last 8sts.
Fasten off, weave in ends.

FINISHING
Place your book in the cover and close the
flap to mark the position of the button.
Attach the button securely with a strand
of yarn.

Half treble crochet, worked in a chunky
yarn, creates a dense fabric that is ideal for
this book cover. A stylish button adds a
decorative closure and gives the cover
a modern look.

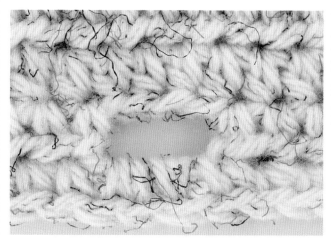

Buttonhole up close
Ensure that your chosen
button is larger than the
buttonhole. The stretchy
properties of the yarn and
stitches will ensure the
hole stretches to fit the
button. If the hole is too
large, the button may not
fasten properly.

FLOWER PIN CUSHION

Level of difficulty

This colourful pin cushion is worked in spirals for the base, and the use of the different crochet stitches creates pretty patterns with minimal fuss.

TECHNIQUES USED Slip stitch **p.28**, Shaping **p.50**, Working in the round **p.56**, Joining on a new colour **p.57**, Working into the back and front loops of a double crochet **p.75**

SIZE
Approx 8cm (3in) in diameter

YARN
DMC Petra Cotton Perle No. 3 – 100g/
   280m/306yds (100% cotton; any small
   amount of crochet thread will
   substitute here)

A x 1   **B** x 1   **C** x 1   **D** x 1   **E** x 1

HOOK
2.5mm hook

NOTIONS
Stitch marker
Yarn needle
Toy stuffing

TENSION
Exact tension is not essential

PATTERN

Note: Do not join rounds, but place a marker at the first stitch of the round, moving it up as each round is completed to mark the beginning of each round. 1 ch at beg of non-spiral rounds does not count as a stitch.

With yarn A, work 2 ch.
Round 1: 6 dc into second ch from hook, join round with a ss.
Round 2: 1 ch, 2 dc into each st around, join round with a ss. (12sts)
Round 3: 1 ch, 1 dc in each st around, join round with a ss. (12sts)
Round 4: 1 ch, 1 dc, (3 tr into next st, 1 dc) 5 times, 3 tr into last st, join round with a ss. Fasten off.
Change to yarn B, attaching to any central tr of 3-tr group.
Round 5: 1 ch, *3 dc into tr, 1 tr into next tr, 1 dtr into dc, 1 tr into next tr; rep from * to end of round. Join round with a ss. (36sts)
Round 6: 1 ch, 1 dc, (2 dc into next st, 5 dc) to end of round, ending with 4 dc only, join round with a ss. Fasten off. (42sts)
Change to yarn C, attaching to the first dc of a pair.
Round 7: 1 ch, (1 dc, 1 ch, 1 dc, 1 htr, 1 tr, 3 tr into next st, 1 tr, 1 htr) around. Join round with a ss, fasten off. (54sts)
Change to yarn D, attaching yarn to central tr of any 3-tr group.
Round 8: 1 ch, *3 dc into central tr, 1 dc, 1 htr, 1 tr, miss 1 dc, 1 dtr in ch sp, miss 1 dc, 1 tr, 1 htr, 1 dc; rep from * to end of round. (60sts)
Round 9: 1 ch, 1 dc into each st to end of round.
Work the next round TFL of every stitch.
Round 10: 2 ss, 1 ch, *2 dc, 1 htr, 1 tr, 3 tr into next st, 1 tr, 1 htr, 2 dc, 1 ss; rep from * to end of round. Fasten off.
Change to yarn E, attaching to the back loop of any stitch from round 9.

Round 11: 1 ch, 1 dc TBL into each st around. (60sts)
Work six rounds straight in regular dc, working in spirals, placing a marker at the beg of each round and moving it up as you go.
Round 18: (8 dc, dc2tog) around. (54sts)
Round 19: (7 dc, dc2tog) around. (48sts)
Round 20: (6 dc, dc2tog) around. (42sts)
Continue in this way, decreasing 6sts per round by working one less dc in between decreases, until there are 6sts left. Stuff the cushion before the hole gets too small. Fasten off yarn, thread through remaining stitches, and pull up tight to close hole. Weave in all ends.

To crochet in the round, you will first need to make a foundation row that is joined into a ring. Refer to p.28 for more information about working slip stitch and using slip stitches to form a foundation ring.

HATS AND SCARVES

Crocheted hats and scarves are particularly toasty, and there's an array of crochet stitches in this selection of cosy makes – plus, plenty of scope for adding pompoms and tassels.

BABY BONNET

This bonnet has a simple construction – a rectangle folded and sewn to create a cute pixie point at the back. Create your own stripe sequence and textures by changing stitches for each stripe, as here, or use the same stitch all the way up.

Level of difficulty ✱✱✱

TECHNIQUES USED Simple stripes **p.39**, Treble crochet **p.44**, Double crochet decreases **p.52**, Blocking and seams **p.68**, Double crochet edging **p.86**

SIZE
To fit a baby, aged 0–3 (3–6) months

YARN
Debbie Bliss Baby Cashmerino – 50g/ 125m/137yds (55% merino wool, 33% acrylic, and 12% cashmere; any DK weight yarn will substitute here. Baby yarns are preferable for their softness and easy-to-wash fibres)

A x 1   **B** x 1   **C** x 1

HOOK
4mm hook

NOTIONS
Yarn needle
15mm (½in) pink button

TENSION
18 dc to 10cm (4in) square

PATTERN
With yarn A, work 56 (62) ch.
Row 1: 1 htr in third ch from hook, 1 htr in each ch to end. (54(60)sts)
Row 2: 2 ch, 1 htr in each st to end.
Row 3: As row 2.
Change to yarn B.
Row 4: 1 ch, 1 dc in each st to end of row.
Rows 5–7: As row 4.
Change to yarn C.
Row 8: 3 ch, 1 tr in each st to end of row.
Row 9: As row 8.
Rows 10–18: Rep rows 1–9 stripe sequence.
Change to yarn A.
Rows 19–21: 2 ch, 1 htr in each st to end. Change to yarn B and work straight in dc until piece measures approx 15(16)cm/6(6¼)in.

FINISHING
Fold piece in half lengthways to create the bonnet, sewing along top seam, which will become the back of bonnet, to close it.
Round 1: With yarn C, work 20 ch for chin strap, attach chain to bottom corner of the hat and work evenly in dc all around face opening, working 3 dc into corner sp to get round, then work in dc evenly along bottom of the bonnet for neck opening, join round with a ss.
Round 2: Work 1 dc into each ch of chin strap, working 3 dc into last ch, then turn work around 180 degrees and work back into unworked bottom loops of chain. Complete the face opening evenly in dc, then work (dc2tog, 1 dc) along the neck opening to decrease, work 1 dc into each dc along chin strap, to centre dc of 3 dc, 3 ch, miss next dc, dc in each dc to end of chin strap. Fasten off yarn and weave in all ends. Sew button to bottom corner of bonnet, corresponding to buttonhole of chin strap.

Turn to pp.68–70 for seam techniques. Use the same coloured yarn for sewing up as the surrounding yarn of the seam, so that the stitching does not show.

CHILD'S HAT WITH EARS

Level of difficulty ✳✳✳

This hat is the cutest headgear ever – worked in the round as one dome, the contrasting ears are then crocheted in two pieces and sewn on.

TECHNIQUES USED Chain stitch **p.26**, Slip stitch **p.28**, Double crochet **p.34**, Half treble crochet **p.38**, Working in the round **p.56**

SIZE
To fit a child aged 1–5 years

YARN
Rowan Kid Classic – 50g/140m/153yds (70% wool, 22% mohair, and 8% polyamide; you can use any wool or wool mix DK yarn for this project) and Rowan Pure Wool DK, 50g/125m/137yds (100% wool)

A x 1   **B** x 1

HOOK
4.5mm hook

NOTIONS
Stitch marker
Yarn needle

TENSION
15 htr x 12 rows per 10cm (4in)

➤ PATTERN
With yarn A, work 3 ch and 8 htr into third ch from hook, ss into first st to join.
Round 1: Work 2 htr into each htr, join round with a ss to first st. (16sts)
Round 2: 2 ch, *work 2 htr into next st, 1 htr into next st, rep from * to end of round, join round with a ss to first st. (24sts)
Round 3: 2 ch, *work 1 htr in next st, 2 htr into next st, 1 htr into next st, rep from * to end of round, join round with a ss to first st. (32sts)
Round 4: 2 ch, *work 1 htr in next 2sts, 2 htr into next st, 1 htr into next st, rep from * to end of round, join round with a ss to first st. (40sts)
Round 5: 2 ch, *work 1 htr in next 3sts, 2 htr into next st, 1 htr into next st, rep from * to end of round, join round with a ss to first st. (48sts)
Continue in this way, working extra sts between each inc until there are 72sts. Work straight without increasing (1 htr in each st) for approx 10cm (4in). Fasten off yarn. Join yarn B to bottom round of hat crown and work 1 row of dc all round, join round with a ss. Fasten off yarn, weave in ends.

EARS (MAKE 2)
With yarn A, work in spirals, placing a marker at end of each round, moving it up each round.
Work 2 ch and 6 dc into second ch from hook, join round with a ss to first st. Continue in spirals for remainder of ear piece.
Round 1: 1 ch, 2 dc into each dc, do not join round. (12sts)
Round 2: *1 dc in next dc, 2 dc in next dc, rep from * to end of round. (18sts)
Round 3: *1 dc in next 2 dc, 2 dc in next dc, rep from * to end of round. Join round with a ss. (24sts)
Fasten off yarn. With yarn B, make two more ears the same up to round 2.

FINISHING
Block hat pieces lightly.
Sew each yarn A ear piece to a yarn B ear piece, with wrong sides facing each other and yarn B at front.
Sew an ear to either side of the hat crown.

Make a tight ring at the centre of each ear piece for a neat finish. Turn to p.56 for more details about crocheting flat circles.

MEN'S BEANIE HAT

This classic beanie-style hat is made in the round, from crown to rim. Made entirely in double crochet, the stripes add classic style. The ribbing at the edge is made by working around the double crochet posts on the round below.

TECHNIQUES USED Chain stitch **p.26**, Double crochet **p.34**, Changing colours **p.39**, Double crochet increases **p.50**

SIZE
To fit an adult man

YARN
Debbie Bliss Bluefaced Leicester British Wool – 50g/75m/82yds (100% wool; you can use any aran-weight wool or wool-mix yarn to achieve a similar effect)

A x 1   B x 1   C x 1

HOOKS
4.5mm hook
5mm hook

NOTIONS
Stitch marker
Yarn needle

TENSION
17sts x 20 rows per 10cm (4in)

SPECIAL ABBREVIATIONS
RDCF: raised double crochet front. At the front of the work, insert hook from right to left, around the post of the dc on the previous row, yrh, draw through, yarn around hook, draw through two loops on hook, therefore making a dc.

RDCB: raised double crochet back. At the back of the work, insert hook from right to left, around the post of the dc on the previous row, yrh, draw through, yarn around hook, draw through two loops on hook, therefore making a dc.

PATTERN
Note: Do not join rounds, but place a marker at the first stitch of the round, moving it up as each round is completed to mark the beginning of each round.

With yarn A and 5mm hook, work 2 ch.
Round 1: 9 dc in second ch from hook, place marker. (9sts)
Round 2: 2 dc in each dc to marker. (18sts)
Round 3: *1 dc, 2 dc in next dc, rep from * to marker. (27sts)
Round 4: *2 dc, 2 dc in next dc, rep from * to marker. (36sts)
Round 5: *3 dc, 2 dc in next dc, rep from * to marker. (45sts)
Round 6: Dc in each st to marker.

Combining colours as stripes is more challenging than crocheting in just one colour, but it's well worth the effort and easy once you've mastered the technique. Turn to p.39 for more details.

Round 7: *4 dc, 2 dc in next dc, rep from * to marker. (54sts)
Round 8: Dc in each st to marker.
Round 9: *5 dc, 2 dc in next dc, rep from * to marker. (63sts)
Round 10: Dc in each st to marker.
Round 11: *6 dc, 2 dc in next dc, rep from * to marker. (72sts)
Round 12: Dc in each st to marker.
Round 13: *7 dc, 2 dc in next dc, rep from * to marker. (81sts)
Work straight in continuous rounds of dc until hat measures 10.5cm (4¼in).
With yarn B, work two rounds in dc.
With yarn C, work two rounds in dc.
With yarn B, work two rounds in dc.
With yarn A, work two rounds in dc.
With yarn B, work two rounds in dc.
With yarn C, work two rounds in dc.
With yarn B, work two rounds in dc.
With yarn A, work two rounds in dc.
Next round: With yarn B and 4.5mm hook, dc2tog, dc in each st to end. (80sts)
Next round: *rdcf, rdcb, rep from * to end, ss in next 2sts.
Fasten off, weave in ends.

CHILD'S HAT WITH EARFLAPS

Level of difficulty ***

This simple and fun project will keep your little one cosy all winter – in fact, they might never want to take it off! Worked in the round from the top, the hat uses half treble stitches to give superb warmth.

TECHNIQUES USED Half treble crochet **p.38**, Changing colours **p.39**, Working in the round **p.56**, Adjustable ring **p.57**, Double crochet edging **p.86**

SIZE

To fit a child, aged 3–4 (4–5:5–6); the hat circumference measures 45cm (17¾in), 47cm (18½in), and 48cm (19in)

YARN

Debbie Bliss Cashmerino DK – 50g/110m/ 120yds (55% merino wool, 33% acrylic, and 12% cashmere; any DK weight yarn with a high merino wool content will achieve a similar effect)

A x 1   **B** x 1

HOOK

3.5mm hook

NOTIONS

Yarn needle

Two circles cut from cardboard, with an outer diameter of 6cm (2¼in) and a ring cut from the middle with a diameter of 2.5cm (1in) to make the pompom (or a pompom maker)

TENSION

19sts x 8 rows per 10cm (4in)

SPECIAL ABBREVIATIONS

Adjustable ring: See p.130

❯ PATTERN

Turn to p.233 for how to work htr2tog.

Round 1: Using the adjustable ring method (see p.130) of starting and yarn A, work 2 ch (counts as a stitch at the start of each round) and then 6 htr into the ring. Close the

ring and join into a round with a ss. (7sts)
Round 2: 2 ch, 1 htr into same st, 2 htr into each st to end, join into a round with a ss. (14sts)
Round 3: 2 ch, *2 htr into next st, 1 htr into next st; rep from * to last st, 2 htr into next st, join into a round with a ss. (21sts)
Round 4: 2 ch, *2 htr into next st, 1 htr into each of next 2sts; rep from * to last 2sts, 2 htr into next st, 1 htr into next st, join into a round with a ss. (28sts)
Continue in this way, increasing 7sts on each round until nine rounds in total have been worked. (63sts)
Round 10: 2 ch, 1 htr into each st to end, join into a round with a ss.
Round 11: 2 ch, *2 htr into next st, 1 htr into each of next 8 sts; rep from * to last 8sts, 2 htr into next st, 1 htr into each of next 7sts, join into a round with a ss. (70sts)
Round 12: 2 ch, *2 htr into next st, 1 htr into each of next 9sts; rep from * to last 9sts, 2 htr into next st, 1 htr into each of next 8sts, join into a round with a ss. (77sts)
Round 13: 2 ch, 1 htr into each st to end, join into a round with a ss.
Round 14: 2 ch, *2 htr into next st, 1 htr into each of next 10sts; rep from * to last 10sts, 2 htr into next st, 1 htr into each of next 9sts, join into a round with a ss. (84sts)

Medium and large sizes only

Round 15: 2 ch, 1 htr into each st to end, join into a round with a ss.
Round 16: 2 ch, *2 htr into next st, 1 htr into each of next 11sts; rep from * to last 11sts, 2 htr into next st, 1 htr into each of next 10sts, join into a round with a ss. (91sts)

Large size only

Round 17: 2 ch, 1 htr into each st to end, join into a round with a ss.
Round 18: 2 ch, *2 htr into next st, 1 htr into each of next 12sts; rep from * to last 12sts, 2 htr into next st, 1 htr into each of next

11sts, join into a round with a ss. (98sts)

All sizes

Work straight (as per round 10) until the depth of the hat measures 15 (16:17)cm/ 6 (6¼:6¾)in from the beginning.
Next round: With yarn B, 1 ch, 1 dc into each st to end, join into a round with a ss.
Next round: With yarn A, 2 ch, 1 htr into each st to end, join into a round with a ss.
Next round: With yarn B, 1 ch, 1 dc into each st to end, join into a round with a ss. Break off yarn B.
Next round: With yarn A, 2 ch, 1 htr into each st to end, join into a round with a ss. Break off yarn A.

MAKING THE EARFLAPS

Rejoin yarn A at 15(15:16)sts after the end of the last round. 2 ch, 1 htr into each of the next 14(15:16)sts. Turn.
Row 1: 2 ch, htr2tog, work 1 htr into each st to the last 2sts, htr2tog. 12(13:14)sts. Turn.
Repeat row one until 2(1:2)sts remain.
Fasten off yarn. Make the second earflap on the other side of the hat to match.

EDGING

Join yarn B to the end of the last complete round worked.
Work 1 ch. 1 dc into each st.
At the first earflap, work 2 dc into each end of row to the point of the earflap.
Work 26 ch, then turn and, starting from the third ch from hook, work 1 dc into each ch.
Work 2 dc into each end of row.
Work 1 dc into each st along the base of hat.
Work the second earflap in the same way as the first.
Work 1 dc into each st to the end of the round. Join with a ss. Fasten off yarn.

FINISHING

Make a 6cm (2¼in) pompom in yarn B and attach to the top of the hat.
Weave in all ends.

STRIPED BERET

The beret is quick and easy to make and will make a perfect gift for a friend. It is worked in the round, in ombre greys, starting at the centre and then adding each row.

Level of difficulty

TECHNIQUES USED Chain stitch **p.26**, Using slip stitch to form a foundation ring **p.28**, Treble crochet **p.44**, Working in the round **p.56**, Bobbles **p.77**

SIZE
To fit an adult woman

YARN
Rico Essentials Merino DK – 50g/120m/ 131yds (100% merino wool; you can use any DK wool yarn for a similar effect)

A x 1 **B** x 1 **C** x 1

HOOK
4mm hook

NOTIONS
Yarn needle

TENSION
8 bobbles per 10cm (4in)

SPECIAL ABBREVIATIONS
Beg bobble: 3 ch (yrh and insert hook in st, yrh and draw a loop through, yrh and draw through first two loops on hook) three times all in same st, yrh and draw a loop through all four loops on hook.

Bobble stitch: (yrh and insert hook in st, yrh and draw a loop through, yrh and draw through first two loops on hook) four times all in same st, yrh and draw a loop through all five loops on hook.

Dec 1 bobble: (yrh and insert hook in st, yrh and draw a loop through, yrh and draw through first two loops on hook) four times all in same st, rep in next st, yrh and draw a loop through all nine loops on hook.

Crab stitch: See p.146.

PATTERN
Note: Every round after round 2 has to start in the top of a bobble and every bobble is worked into an existing bobble – not a chain. You can safely pass the yarn up from row to row, which makes for a much neater finish.

With yarn A, work 4 ch, ss in last ch from hook to form a ring.

Round 1: 3 ch (counts as 1 tr), 11 tr into centre ring. (12sts)

Round 2: 3 ch (counts as 1 tr), in next st work a beg bobble, 1 bobble into each of the foll 11sts, ss in top of 3 ch to join. (12 bobbles) Continue in rounds of alternate colours.

Round 3: With yarn B, ss into top of next bobble, (beg bobble, 1 bobble) into same bobble, work 2 bobbles into each of foll 11 bobbles, ss in top of 3 ch to join. (24 bobbles)

Round 4: With yarn C, ss into top of next bobble, beg bobble into same bobble, 1 ch, (1 bobble into next bobble, 1 ch) 23 times, ss in top of 3 ch to join. (24 bobbles)

Round 5: With yarn A, ss into top of next bobble, (beg bobble, 1 bobble) into same bobble, (1 bobble into next bobble, 2 bobbles into next bobble) 11 times, 1 bobble into last bobble, ss in top of 3 ch to join. (36 bobbles)

Round 6: With yarn B, ss into top of next bobble, beg bobble into same bobble, 1 ch, (1 bobble into next bobble, 1 ch) to end, ss in top of 3 ch to join. (36 bobbles)

Round 7: With yarn C, ss into top of next bobble, (beg bobble, 1 bobble) into same bobble, 1 bobble into each of the next 2 bobbles, (2 bobbles into next bobble, 1 bobble into each of the next 2 bobbles) 11 times, ss in top of 3 ch to join. (48 bobbles)

Round 8: With yarn A, work as for round 6. (48 bobbles)

Round 9: With yarn B, ss into top of next bobble, (beg bobble, 1 bobble) into same bobble, 1 bobble into each of next 3 bobbles, (2 bobbles into next bobble, 1 bobble into each of next 3 bobbles) 11 times, ss in top of 3 ch to join. (60 bobbles)

Round 10: With yarn C, work as for round 6. (60 bobbles)

Round 11: With yarn A, rep round 10.

Round 12: With yarn B, rep round 10.

Round 13: With yarn C, rep round 10.

Round 14 (dec round): With yarn A, ss into top of next bobble, 3 ch, (yrh and insert hook into same bobble, draw a loop through, yrh and draw through first two loops on hook) three times, (yrh and insert hook into next bobble, draw a loop through, yrh and draw through first two loops on hook) four times, yrh and draw through all 8 loops on hook, 1 ch, (1 bobble in next bobble, 1 ch) 3 times, *dec 1 bobble, 1 ch, (1 bobble in next bobble, 1 ch) three times, rep from * a further 10 times, ss in top of 3 ch to join. (48 bobbles)

Round 15: With yarn B, work as for round 6. (48 bobbles) Break off yarn B.

Round 16 (dec round): With yarn C, ss into top of next bobble, 3 ch, (yrh and insert hook into same bobble, draw a loop through, yrh and draw through first two loops on hook) three times, (yrh and insert hook into next bobble, draw a loop through, yrh and draw through first two loops on hook) four times, yrh and draw through all eight loops on hook, 1 ch, (1 bobble in next bobble, 1 ch) twice, *dec 1 bobble, 1 ch, (1 bobble in next bobble, 1 ch) twice, rep from * a further 10 times, ss in top of 3 ch to join. (36 bobbles) Break off yarn C.

Round 17: With yarn A, ss in next bobble, 1 ch (does not count as 1 dc), 1 dc into top of same bobble, 1 dc into each ch and bobble to end, ss in top of 1st dc to join. (72sts)

Rounds 18–19: 1 ch (does not count as 1dc), 1 dc into same st, 1 dc into each dc to end, ss in top of 1st dc to join.

Round 20: 1 ch, now work in crab stitch, ss in 1 ch to join. Fasten off, weave in ends.

LACY SCARF

This pretty and feminine scarf uses multiple increases to create ruffles. The pattern is worked in a round, but working into both sides of the starting chain. It can easily be adapted for a longer or shorter scarf.

TECHNIQUES USED Making a foundation chain **p.26**, Treble crochet **p.44**, Double treble crochet, **p.28**, Treble crochet increases **p.50**

SIZE
Approx 150 x 10cm (59 x 4in)

YARN
Rowan Kidsilk Haze – 25g/210m/230yds (70% super kid mohair and 30% silk; for the same light and airy feel, use any fine mohair, or you can use any lace-weight yarn with varying effect)

x 3

HOOK
4.5mm hook

NOTIONS
Yarn needle

TENSION
Exact tension is not essential

PATTERN

Make a length of chain approx 10cm (4in) shorter than desired scarf.

For this 150cm (59in) long scarf, a chain of approx 140cm (55in) was worked. Now work 3 ch extra (counts as first treble on round 1).

Round 1: 2 tr into fourth ch from hook, 1 tr in each ch to end, do not join or turn, work 3 tr into the last ch, then turn your work 180 degrees and work 1 tr into the unworked bottom loop of each ch to end, join round with a ss to top of first ch.

Round 2: 3 ch, 1 tr into bottom of ch, 3 tr into central tr of 3-tr group of round 1, 2 tr into each tr to other end of scarf, work 3 tr into central tr of 3 tr gp, 2 tr into each tr to end, join round with a ss to top of first ch.

Round 3: 4 ch, 1 dtr into bottom of ch, 2 dtr into each tr to centre tr of 3-tr group of round 2, 3 dtr into central tr, 2 dtr into each tr to other end of scarf, 3dtr into central tr, 2dtr into each tr to end, join round with a ss to top of first ch.

Round 4: 5 ch (counts as 1 dtr, 1 ch), (1 dtr, 1 ch), into bottom of ch, (1 dtr, 1 ch) into each dtr to centre dtr of 3-dtr group of round 3, (1 dtr, 1 ch, 1 dtr, 1 ch, 1 dtr) into central dtr; (1 dtr, 1 ch) into each dtr to other end of scarf, (1 dtr, 1ch, 1dtr, 1ch, 1dtr) into central dtr, (1 dtr, 1 ch) into each dtr to end, join round with a ss to top of first ch.

You can now continue to make rounds in the same way if you wish – work an increase round working 2 tr into each st or ch sp, or work a plain round or whatever type of ruffle round you wish until the desired width of ruffle is reached.

Fasten off, weave in ends. Do not block the scarf as it may flatten the ruffle.

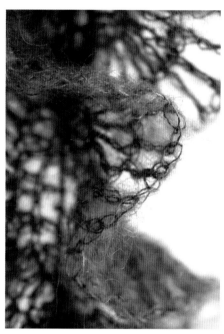

Work additional stitch increases in each round for a more highly ruffled scarf, or work plain rows in between increases for a less ruffled one.

BROOMSTICK LACE SHAWL

Level of difficulty

What better accessory for a wedding or summer party in the garden than this delicate, threadlike shawl? Crocheted with a long broomstick and using gossamer fine yarn, the stunning result hides how easy it is to make.

TECHNIQUES USED Making a foundation chain **p.26**, Simple lace techniques **p.106**, Broomstick crochet **p.128**

SIZE
Approx 60 x 150cm (23½ x 59in)

YARN
Rowan Kidsilk Haze – 25g/210m/230yds (70% super kid mohair and 30% silk; any lace-weight mohair yarn will give a similar effect. This pattern is also suitable for using with any DK yarn for a more solid shawl. Non-fluffy yarns will produce a robust shawl)

x 5

HOOKS
4.5mm hook
20mm x 35 or 40cm (¾ x 14 or 16in) long broomstick or knitting needle

NOTIONS
Yarn needle

TENSION
Six groups of four loops (24 dc) and four rows to 10cm (4in)

PATTERN
Note: The shawl is a straight piece of broomstick crochet, but half of it is worked on one side of the foundation row of double crochet, referred to here as the "spine", and half of it is worked on the other side. This gives a symmetrical look to the finished shawl. If you find it hard to insert the hook into the top of the dc to put the next loop on the broomstick, use a smaller, pointed-ended hook – remember to use the 4.5mm hook to work the dc sts.

FOUNDATION SPINE AND FIRST SIDE
Work 144 ch making sure they are kept nice and loose. Leave a long tail in case you miscount and need to make a few extra chains to get the right number of stitches on the foundation row.
Insert hook under back bump only of first ch, 1 dc. Insert hook in same way, 1 dc in each ch to end. (144sts)

PATTERN ROW
Pick up a loop onto the broomstick in each dc across. (144 loops)
Take off loops in groups of four, placing 4 dc in each group. (144sts = 36 groups)
Rep pattern row for half of required length. Fasten off.

SECOND SIDE
Join yarn to end of initial spine of dc farthest away from the tail of yarn and work pattern row as for first side.

FINISHING
Weave in all ends.
Avoid heavy blocking of this shawl or you will flatten the beautiful, fluffy texture of the yarn. Pin out to the required size, lightly spritz with water, and allow to dry naturally.

Construction pattern

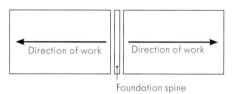

Foundation spine

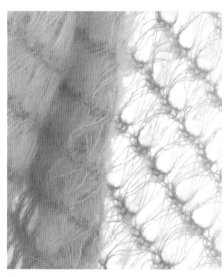

Work the foundation row of double crochet into the back bump only of the initial chain, to provide balanced loops to work each side of the shawl outwards, from the centre back foundation "spine".

TWEED STITCH COWL

Level of difficulty

This warm and cosy cowl is made in the round using the shape of a Möbius strip. By making one twist, the loop appears never-ending, and each round of crochet increases both the top and the bottom of the piece.

TECHNIQUES USED Chain stitch **p.26**, Slip stitch **p.28**, Double crochet **p.34**, Working into a chain space/tweed stitch pattern **p.75**

SIZE
92 x 18cm (36 x 7in)

YARN
Rowan Felted Tweed Aran – 50g/87m/
   95yds (50% wool, 25% alpaca, and
   25% viscose; any aran weight yarn
   with high wool content will produce
   a similar effect)

x 4

HOOK
5.5mm hook

NOTIONS
Stitch marker
Yarn needle

TENSION
16sts x 18 rows per 10cm (4in)

PATTERN
Work 148 ch.
Foundation row: Starting in the third ch from hook, *1 dc into next st, 1 ch, miss next st; rep from * to last st, 1 dc into last st. Join with a ss into the last ch from hook (that is, the base of the first st), making one twist (which means that round one will be worked in the base of the sts on the foundation row).
Mark the first st with the stitch marker or safety pin. (This is purely to help you see easily where the round has started; the double-sided nature of the cowl and the fabric can sometimes make this tricky.)
Round 1: 1 ch, *work 1 dc into the ch sp on the row below, 1 ch, miss next st; rep from * to end, join with a ss.
Round 2: 3 ch, *miss next st, work 1 dc into the ch sp on the row below, 1 ch; rep from * to last st, work 1 dc into the last st, join with a ss.
Repeat these two rows seven more times (16 rows in total).
Fasten off, weave in ends.

Tweed stitch is an easy crochet stitch that is also known as seed stitch. It creates a dense-textured fabric, which is ideal for a winter warmer.

CHUNKY SCARF

Level of difficulty

This cosy scarf is made up and down along the length of the scarf, rather than back and forth across its width. A half treble stitch is worked between the stitches and the addition of tassels provides more length.

TECHNIQUES USED Making a foundation chain **p.26**, Half treble crochet **p.38**, Simple stripes **p.39**, Making a tassel **p.71**, Working into spaces between stitches **p.75**

SIZE
17 x 230cm (6¾ x 90½in)

YARN
Debbie Bliss Rialto Chunky – 50g/60m/ 66yds (100% extra-fine superwash merino wool; you can use any chunky-weight, merino wool yarn to achieve a similar effect)

A x 2   **B** x 2   **C** x 2   **D** x 2

HOOK
6.5mm hook

NOTIONS
Yarn needle

TENSION
8sts x 9.5 rows per 10cm (4in)

PATTERN
With yarn A, work 182 ch.
Row 1: 1 htr in third ch from hook, htr in each ch to end, turn.
Row 2: 2 ch, *htr in the space between the first 2sts, rep from * to end, turn.
With yarn B, rep row 2 twice.
With yarn C, rep row 2 twice.
With yarn D, rep row 2 twice.
With yarn A, rep row 2 twice.
With yarn B, rep row 2 twice.
With yarn C, rep row 2 twice.
With yarn D, rep row 2 twice.
Fasten off, weave in yarn ends as you work along the rows.

TASSELS
With matching yarn, place one tassel at the end of each row on both ends of the scarf as follows:
Cut four 25cm (9¾in) long pieces of yarn, fold in half, feed loop through end of row, bring ends through loop, pull to fasten in place (see p.71).

By working half treble stitch in the spaces between stitches to create tiny "pockets", and by using chunky yarn, this scarf is sure to keep the wearer toasty by trapping warm air within the scarf.

GLOVES, SOCKS, AND SLIPPERS

Wear crochet from top to toe. Banish cold fingers and toes with this selection of ultra-warm patterns; there's something for every member of the family.

CHILD'S WRISTWARMERS

Level of difficulty

Worked in double crochet, these simple striped wristwarmers are an ideal way to practise changing colours. With no shaping, the thumb slit is worked by leaving part of the seam open when sewing up.

TECHNIQUES USED Chain stitch **p.26**, Double crochet **p.34**, Half treble crochet **p.38**, Changing colours **p.39**, Overcast stitch (or whip stitch) seam **p.68**, Shells **p.76**

GLOVES, SOCKS, AND SLIPPERS

SIZE
To fit a child, aged 8–10 years

YARN
King Cole Merino Blend DK –
50g/104/m/114yds (100% wool; any DK weight wool-blend yarn, preferably machine washable, can be substituted)

A x 1   **B** x 1   **C** x 1

HOOKS
5mm hook
6mm hook

NOTIONS
Yarn needle

TENSION
14sts x 18 rows per 10cm (4in) in
double crochet

PATTERN (MAKE 2)

Note: When working colour changes, yarn should be changed on last yrh of last dc in the row; yarn should be cut and not "carried".

With yarn A and 6mm hook, work 27 ch. Change to 5mm hook for the remainder of the pattern.
Row 1 (WS): Dc into second ch from hook, 1 dc in each st to end, change to yarn B, turn. (20sts)
Row 2 (RS): 1 ch, dc in each st to end, turn.
Row 3: As row 2, change to yarn C at end of row.
Continue working in double crochet in the following colour sequence:
Rows 4 and 5: Yarn C.
Rows 6 and 7: Yarn A.
Rows 8 and 9: Yarn B.
Rows 10 and 11: Yarn C.
Rows 12 and 13: Yarn A.
Rows 14 and 15: Yarn B.
Rows 16 and 17: Yarn C.
Rows 18 and 19: Yarn A.
Rows 20 and 21: Yarn B.
Rows 22 and 23: Yarn C.
Rows 24 and 25: Yarn A.
Fasten off yarn, weave in all ends.

Rejoin yarn C to top right-hand corner of row 1, work shell trim as follows:
dc in first st, ss in next dc, *5 htr in next dc, miss 1 dc, ss in next dc, rep from * to end. Fasten off yarn C (8 htr shells made).
Turn work 180 degrees and rejoin C to top right-hand edge, repeat shell trim.

FINISHING
With RS facing, fold piece in half and sew a seam along row edges, leaving 2cm (¾in) unworked for thumb slit.
Optional extra: you could work a round of dc evenly all around the thumbhole slit to neaten and reinforce it.
Weave in any remaining ends.
Press according to ballband instructions.

The cuffs of each wristwarmer are decorated with half treble shells. Refer to pp.38–39 for information about half treble crochet and simple stripes.

CHILD'S MITTENS WITH STRING

Level of difficulty

Simple stitches in bright colours create the perfect accessory for little boys or girls. Constructed in spirals of double crochet, these mittens work up in next to no time and are ideal for beginners.

TECHNIQUES USED Double crochet **p.34**, Simple stripes **p.39**, Double crochet increases **p.50**, Double crochet decreases **p.52**, Working in the round **p.56**

SIZE
To fit a child, aged 6–10 years

YARN
Debbie Bliss Baby Cashmerino – 50g/
125m/137yds (55% merino wool, 33% acrylic, and 12% cashmere; you can use any soft 4-ply to DK weight yarn with a synthetic content for durability to achieve a similar effect)

A x 1   **B** x 1   **C** x 1

HOOK
3.25mm hook

NOTIONS
Stitch marker
Yarn needle

TENSION
Exact tension is not essential

PATTERN (MAKE 2)

Note: You may find it useful to mark the last st of first four rounds with a stitch marker. Do not join rounds, but place a marker at the first stitch of the round, moving it up as each round is completed to mark the beginning of each round.

With yarn A, work 4 ch, ss in first ch to form a ring.
Round 1: 6 dc into ring. (6sts)
Round 2: 2 dc in each st. (12sts)
Round 3: *1 dc in next st, 2 dc in next st, rep from * to end of round. (18sts)
Round 4: *1 dc in next 2sts, 2 dc in next st, rep from * to end of round. (24sts)
Round 5 onwards: Continue to work in dc until piece measures 8cm (3in).

THUMB OPENING
Next round: 6 ch, miss 6 dc, dc to end of round (this is first of 6 ch).

Next round: 1 dc in each of 6 ch, dc to end. Work dc in each st for three further rounds. Fasten off A.
Join B into any dc, work two rounds of dc in B, fasten off B.
Join C into any dc, work two rounds of dc in C, fasten off C.
Rejoin A to any dc, work three rounds of dc in A.
Fasten off yarn, weave in ends.

THUMB
Join A to any point around thumb opening. Work 12 dc evenly around gap.
Working in dc, continue to work in a spiral until thumb measures 3.5cm (1⅜in).
Next round: Dc2tog to end of round. (6sts)
Cut off yarn leaving a long tail, thread tail onto a yarn needle then thread through remaining stitches, pull tight, and fasten off.
Join A into a dc on last round of first mitten, make 100 ch (or to desired length), ss into any st on last round of second mitten.
Fasten off yarn, weave in ends.

The joining string is 100 chain stitches long, but you can lengthen or shorten it to suit the height of your child simply by adding or omitting stitches.

WOMEN'S WRISTWARMERS

Level of difficulty

These vibrant and practical wristwarmers have a pretty, three-dimensional texture created by treble puff stitches and a crochet rib using raised trebles.

TECHNIQUES USED Half treble crochet **p.38**, Treble crochet **p.44**, Double crochet increases **p.50**, Overcast stitch (or whip stitch) seam **p.68**, Sculptural textures **p.76**

SIZE
Approx. 20 (22:24)cm/8 (8¾:9½)in

YARN
Cascade 220 Superwash – 100g/200m/ 219yds (100% wool; any DK weight yarn will substitute here

x 1

HOOKS
3.75mm hook
4mm hook

TENSION
18 tr x 14 rows to 10cm (4in) square

NOTIONS
Yarn needle

SPECIAL ABBREVIATIONS
RTRF: raised treble front. At the front of the work, yrh, insert hook from right to left, around the post of the treble stitch on the previous row, yrh, draw through, yrh, draw through two loops on hook, yrh, draw through last two loops on hook, therefore making a treble stitch.

RTRB: raised treble back. At the back of the work, yrh, insert hook from right to left, around the post of the treble stitch on the previous row, yrh, draw through, yrh, draw through two loops on hook, yrh, draw through last two loops on hook, therefore making a treble stitch.

Treble puff stitch: *yrh, insert hook into st, yrh, draw back through, yrh, draw through two loops on hook, rep from * three times more (five loops on hook), yrh and pull through all loops. Puff completed.

PATTERN
Using 4mm hook, work 40 (44:48) ch. Change to 3.75mm hook.
Row 1: 1 tr into fourth ch from hook (first 3 ch count as 1 tr), 1 tr and into each ch to end. Turn. (37 (39:43)sts)
Row 2: 3 ch (counts as first rtrb), *1 rtrf, 1 rtrb; rep from * to end of row.
Row 3: 3 ch (counts as first rtrf), *1 rtrb, 1 rtrf; rep from * to end of row.
Rep last two rows until rib measures approx. 8cm (3in), or desired length.

RIGHT WRISTWARMER
Row 1 (RS): 2 ch (counts as 1 htr), 1 htr in each st to end, turn.
Rep last row twice more.
Row 4: 3 ch (counts as 1 tr throughout), (1 puff, 1 tr) nine (nine:10) times, htr to end of row, turn.
Rep row 1 three times.
Row 8: 3 ch, (1 tr, 1 puff) eight (eight:nine) times, htr to end of row, turn.
Rep row 1 three times.
Row 12: As row 4.
Row 13: As row 1.
Fasten off yarn, leaving long end for sewing up seam.

LEFT WRISTWARMER
Row 1 (RS): 2 ch (counts as 1 htr), 1 htr in each st to end, turn.
Rep last row twice more.

Row 4: 3 ch (counts as 1 tr throughout), htr to last 19 (19:21)sts, (1 puff, 1 tr) nine (nine:10) times, 1 tr into last st, turn.
Rep row 1 three times.
Row 8: 3 ch, htr to last 17 (17:19)sts, (1 puff, 1 tr) eight (eight:nine) times, 1 tr into last st, turn.
Rep row 1 three times.
Row 12: As row 4.
Row 13: As row 1.
Fasten off yarn, leaving long end for sewing up seam.

FINISHING
Fold each wristwarmer in half lengthways so that right sides face each other, then sew up side seam 5cm (2in) down from top, fasten off yarn, and reattach approx 6cm (2½in) further down the seam, to allow space for thumb, checking that the distance is correct to fit your hand. Sew up remainder of seam down to bottom of rib.

These wristwarmers are made from two basic rectangles sewn together with gaps left for thumb holes. Turn to pp.68–69 for details about seams.

NORDIC FINGERLESS MITTS

Level of difficulty

You'll never have to take gloves on and off again – simply flip over the mitt top to reveal fingers, ready for any delicate task. These Scandi-style gloves will stretch slightly for a snug and comfortable fit.

TECHNIQUES USED Chain stitch **p.26**, Double crochet **p.34**, Shaping **p.50–52**, Working into the back loop of a double crochet **p.75**, Tapestry colourwork **p.117**

SIZE

Small (Medium:Large); gloves are approx.
15(16:17)cm (6 (6⅓:6⅜)in) long and
19(22:24)cm (7½(8⅜:9½)in) around widest part of hand
Length can be adapted slightly to fit perfectly, see pattern notes.

YARN

Millamia Naturally Soft Aran – 50g/80m/
87yds (100% merino wool; any aran weight yarn will work here; make sure the yarn is soft and warm to ensure the gloves' comfort and thermal properties)

A x 3   **B** x 1

HOOKS

3.5mm and 4.5mm hooks

NOTIONS

Stitch marker
2 x 10mm (½in) diameter buttons

TENSION

19sts and 18 rows in double crochet using 4.5mm hook

SPECIAL ABBREVIATIONS

Button loop: 5 ch, ss to bottom of chain.
DCBLO: Double crochet in back loop only: work a dc in back loop only of next st.
DC3TOG: Double crochet 3sts together: draw up a loop in each of next 3sts, four loops on hook, yoh and draw through all loops at once to decrease 2sts.

PATTERN

Note: Glove cuffs are worked straight, in rows, then joined into a ring.
Hand of gloves is worked in the round in spirals. Do not join each round or use turning chains unless indicated; instead place a marker at the start of the round, moving upwards each round to denote beginning of rounds.
Work hand and then thumb to desired length where indicated; keep trying on the glove to obtain the perfect fit. Repeat this process when working the flap.
Main body for hand is worked in tapestry crochet "rice" stitch, but the thumb is worked without colourwork – however, on colourwork rounds, carry the contrast yarn inside the working yarn when hooking the thumb so that it is in the right place to pick up again when needed.
1ch at beg of round does not count as stitch.

LEFT GLOVE
Cuff
Using yarn A and 3.5mm hook, work 13 ch.
Row 1: 1 dc in 2nd ch from hook and each ch to end, turn. (12sts)
Row 2: 1ch, 1 dcblo in each st across, turn. (12sts)
Repeat row 2 till strip is 36(42:48) rows long. Do not fasten off. Join two short ends of strip with a slip stitch crochet join.
Turn cuff on its side and change to larger 4.5mm hook.
Round 1: Work 30(36:42) dc evenly around top, join round with ss. (30(36:42)sts)
Round 2: 1 ch, 1 dc in each dc around, do not join round but place marker and begin to work in spirals, moving marker up every round. (30(36:42)sts)

Thumb gusset shaping
Round 1: work row 1 of chart, adding in yarn B where needed and repeating the 6sts repeat all around.

RICE STITCH CHART

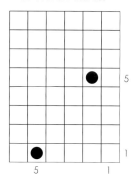

Continue to follow the chart from now on, working three plain rows and then a rice stitch row as outlined in the chart (see above), working all thumb gusset stitches (sts beween the increases) in yarn A, without rice stitch.
Round 2: 6 dc, 2 dc in next st, 1 dc, 2 dc in next st, 1 dc in each st to end. (32(38:44)sts)
Round 3: 1 dc in each st around.
Round 4: 6 dc, 2 dc in next st, 3 dc, 2 dc in next st, 1 dc in each st to end. (34(40:46)sts)
Round 5: 7 dc working in pattern from round 5 of chart, work in yarn A across next 5sts (thumb stitches), holding yarn B inside the work as usual for tapestry crochet, then after these 5sts, work in rice stitch pattern from st 3 of round 5 of chart as normal
Round 6: 6 dc, 2 dc in next st, 5 dc, 2 dc in next st, 1 dc in each st to end. (36(42:48)sts)
Round 7: 1 dc in each st around.
Round 8: 6 dc, 2 dc in next st, 7 dc, 2 dc in next st, 1 dc in each st to end. (38(44:50)sts)
Round 9: 7 dc, working in pattern from round 1 of chart, work in yarn A across next 9 thumb sts, holding yarn B inside the work as usual for tapestry crochet, then after these 9sts, work in rice stitch pattern from st 3 of round 1 of chart as normal
Round 10: 6 dc, inc, 9 dc, inc, 1 dc in each st to end. (40(46, 52)sts)

Round 11: 1 dc in each st around.
Round 12: 6 dc, 2 dc in next st, 11 dc, 2 dc in next st, 1 dc in each st to end. (42(48:54)sts)
Round 13: 1 dc in each st around, working in pattern from round 5 of chart and in yarn A across 13 thumb sts as before
Round 14: 6 dc, 2 dc in next st, 13 dc, 2 dc in next st, 1 dc in each st to end. (44(50:56)sts)
Round 15: 1 dc in each st around.
Round 16: 6 dc, 2 dc in next st, 15 dc, 2 dc in next st, 1 dc in each st to end. (46(52:58)sts)

Sizes M and L only
Round 17: 1 dc in each st around, working in pattern from round 1 of chart and in yarn A across 17 thumb sts as before
Round 18: 6 dc, 2 dc in next st, 17 dc, 2 dc in next st, 1 dc in each st to end. (54(60) dc)

All sizes
If desired, you can now try on the mitt and keep working straight in rice st with a yarn A thumb pattern if necessary until desired length to where the thumb meets the hand.

Hand
Next round: 7 dc in pattern as set, 1 ch, miss next 17(19:19)sts for thumb, 1 dc in each dc in pattern as set to end. (30(36:42)sts)
Next round: 7 dc in pattern, 1 dc in 1ch, dc in pattern to end of round. (30(36:42)sts)
Flap set up round: 9(10:12) dc in pattern, continuing in rice stitch pattern, work next 12(15:18) dc through blo, then work 1 dc in each st to end in pattern.
Continue working straight in pattern for three (four:five) rows or until hand is desired length to bottom of fingers.
Fasten off.

Thumb
Rejoin yarn A with 4.5mm hook to thumb sts, in the dc to the right of 1 ch from hand sts, dc3tog inserting hook in st that yarn was joined to, into bottom loop of 1ch from hand, and into next thumb st, then work 14 (16:16) dc around rem thumb sts; do not join round but place marker for working in spirals and move marker up on each round. (15 (17:17)sts)
Work straight on these sts until thumb measures desired length minus 2.5cm (1in).
Next round: [3 dc, dc2tog] three times, dc 0(2:2). (12(14:14)sts)
Work two rounds straight.

Next round: [2 dc, dc2tog] three times, dc 0(2:2). (9(11:11)sts)
Work one round straight.
Next round: [1 dc, dc2tog] three times, dc 0(2:2). (6(8:8)sts)
Fasten off, leaving long tail. Thread long tail onto a yarn needle and pass around top of thumb opening, pull up tightly to draw in top of thumb and secure neatly.

RIGHT GLOVE
Work as for left glove from cuff to start of thumb gusset shaping.

Thumb gusset shaping
Use a 4.5mm hook.
Round 1: Work row 1 of chart (see p.217), adding in yarn B where needed and repeating the 6sts repeat all around. Continue to follow the chart from now on, working three plain rows and then a rice st row as outlined in the chart, working all thumb gusset stitches in yarn A without rice sts.
Round 2: 1 dc in each st to last 9sts, 2 dc in next st, 1 dc, 2 dc in next st, 1 dc in each st to end. (32(38:44)sts)
Round 3: 1 dc in each st around.
Round 4: 1 dc in each st to last 11sts, 2 dc in next st, 3 dc, 2 dc in next st, 1 dc in each st to end. (34(40:46)sts)
Round 5: 1 dc working in pattern from round 5 of chart, in each st to last 12 dc, work in yarn A across 5 thumb sts, holding yarn B inside the work as usual for tapestry crochet, then after these 5sts, work in rice stitch pattern from st 3 of round 5 of chart as normal
Continue in this way, increasing on every other row at thumb gusset as for left glove and working thumb solely in yarn A until there are 46(54:60) dc.
If desired, you can now try on the mitt and keep working straight in rice st with a yarn A thumb pattern if necessary until desired length to where the thumb meets the hand.

Hand
Next round: 22(28:34) dc in pattern as set, 1ch, miss next 17(19:19) sts for thumb, 1 dc in each dc in pattern as set to end. (30(36:42)sts)
Next round: 22(28:34) dc in pattern, 1 dc in 1ch, dc in pattern to end of round. (30(36:42)sts)
Flap set up round: 9 (10:12) dc in pattern, continuing in rice stitch pattern, work next 12(15:18) dc through blo, then work 1 dc in each st to end in pattern.

Continue working straight in pattern for 3(4, 5) rows or until hand is desired length to bottom of fingers.
Fasten off.
Work thumb as for left glove.

Flap – work the same for both gloves
With yarn A and 4.5mm hook, work 19(22:25) chain.
Round 1: 1 dc in 2nd ch from hook and each ch to end (18(21:24) dc), then work 1 dc in each unworked front loop only from flap set up round at back of hand, join round with ss. (30(36:42)sts)
Round 2: 1 ch, work one round straight in pattern as set from main glove, do not join round but place marker for working in spirals, moving marker up each round. Continue straight in pattern until flap measures 5cm (2in) less than desired length to tallest fingertip, ending with a rice st colourwork row.
Shape top – continue to work the rest of flap in yarn A only
Round 1: 1 dc in each st around in yarn A.
Round 2: [3(4:5) dc, dc2tog] around. (24(30:36)sts)
Round 3:: 1 dc in each st around.
Round 4: [2(3:4) dc, dc2tog] around. (18(24:30)sts)
Round 5: 1 dc in each st around.
Round 6: [1(2:3) dc, dc2tog] around. (12(18:24)sts)
Round 7: [0(1:2) dc, dc2tog] around. (6(12:18)sts)

Sizes M and L only
Round 8: [0(1)dc, dc2tog] around. (6(12)sts)

Size L only
Round 9: [dc2tog] around. (6sts)

All sizes
Fasten off, leaving long tail. Thread long tail onto a yarn needle and pass around top of flap opening, pull up tightly to draw in top and secure neatly.
With 4.5mm hook join yarn B to top of flap, work 5 ch button loop (see p.217), fasten off.

FINISHING
Weave in all ends and sew buttons to cuff to work with button loops.

MARY-JANE BOOTIES

Level of difficulty

These little shoes would make the perfect baby shower gift. They are worked up in a single piece in a round, from the middle of the sole and up to the sides, with the strap added after. A contrasting colour trim and a button complete the look.

TECHNIQUES USED Double crochet **p.34**, Half treble crochet **p.38**, Shaping **p.50–52**, Working in the round **p.56**, Making a simple adjustable ring **p.57**

SIZE
To fit a baby, aged 0–3
(3–6) months

YARN
Rowan Wool Cotton DK – 50g/113m/
124yds (50% wool and 50% cotton;
any DK weight yarn with some cotton
content for added structure will be
perfect here)

A x 1   **B** x 1

HOOK
3.5mm hook

NOTIONS
Yarn needle

TENSION
10sts x 5cm (2in)

PATTERN
After completing round 7, measure the
length of the sole – it should be approx.
9–10cm (3½–4in) long (10–11cm/4–4¼in
long). Ss into starting ch at end of each round.

1 ch at beginning of round does not count as
dc. 2 ch at beginning of round counts as htr.

SOLE
With yarn A, work 9 ch.
Round 1: Starting in second ch from hook,
7 dc, 3 dc in next st, do not turn, continue
in back loops of foundation ch, 6 dc, 2 dc in
last st, ss in first st. (18sts)

Round 2: 1 ch, 2 dc in next st, 6 dc, 2 htr
in next st 3 times, 6 dc, 2 dc in next 2sts,
ss in first st. (24sts)
Round 3: 1 ch, 1 dc, 2 dc in next st, 6 dc, (1 htr,
2htr in next st), three times, 6 dc, (1 dc, 2 dc
in next st) twice, ss in first st. (30sts)
Round 4: 1 ch, 2 dc, 2 dc in next st, 6 dc,
(2 dc(htr), 2 dc(htr) in next st) three times,
6 dc, (2 dc, 2 dc in next st) three times, ss in
first st. (36sts)
Round 5: 1 ch, 3 dc, 2 dc in next st, 6 dc,
(3 dc(htr), 2 dc(htr) in next st) three times,
6 dc, (3 dc, 2 dc in next st) twice, ss in first
st. (42sts)
Round 6: 1 ch, 4 dc, 2 dc in next st, 6 dc,
(4 dc(htr), 2 dc(htr) in next st) three times,
6 dc, (4 dc, 2 dc in next st) twice, ss in first
st. (48sts)

Larger size only:
Round 7: 1 ch, 5 dc, 2 dc in next st, 6 dc,
(5 htr, 2 htr in next st) three times, 6 dc,
(5 dc, 2 dc in next st) twice, ss in first st.
(54sts)

SIDES
Round 7(8): 1(2) ch, 48 dc (53sts),
ss into second ch. (48:54sts)
Round 8(9). 2 ch, 10(12) htr, htr2tog,
15(17) htr, htr2tog, 14(15) htr, htr2tog,
2(3) htr, ss into second ch. (45:51sts)
Round 9(10): 2 ch, 10(12) htr, htr2tog,
14(16) htr, htr2tog, 13(14) htr, htr2tog,
1(2) htr, ss into second ch. (42:48sts)
Round 10(11): 2 ch, 10(12) htr, htr3tog,
12(14) htr, htr3tog, 11(12) htr, htr2tog,
0(1) htr, ss into second ch. (37:43sts)
Round 11(12): 1 ch, 11(13) dc, dc3tog,
10(12) dc, dc3tog, 8(10) dc, dc2tog, ss into
first st. (32:38sts)
Fasten off.

STRAPS
For the right shoe, count 3sts from the left
side dc3tog from last round then attach

yarn A. For the left shoe, count 1st from the
right side dc3tog from row 12, then attach
yarn A.
Row 1: 1 ch, 2 dc. (2sts)
Rows 2–12: Turn work, 1 ch, 2 dc.
Row 13: 8 ch, ss into last st to make a loop.
Fasten off.

TRIM
With yarn B, work an even trim of reverse
double crochet, or crab stitch, (see p.146)
along the top edge of the shoe, going all
around the strap.

BUTTON (MAKE 2)
With yarn B, make an adjustable ring
(see p.134).
Round 1: 6 dc into the ring, pull ring
tight. (6sts)
Round 2: 2 dc in each st. (12sts)
Round 3: Dc in each st.
Round 4: Dc2tog across all sts. (6sts)
Sew up button opening and sew to shoes.
Weave in loose ends.

These booties are decorated with a
trim of reverse double crochet, or crab
stitch. Refer to p.146 for information
on how to create this stitch, and see
pp.174 and 242 for other projects that
use crab stitch.

MINI-TRAINER BOOTIES

Level of difficulty ✷✷✷

These booties are worked in a round, with a raised contrast colour strip separating the sole from the sides and a chunky strap to keep them on tiny feet. Using Velcro® to fasten makes them really easy to put on and take off, too.

TECHNIQUES USED Chain stitch **p.26**, Double crochet **p.34**, Half treble crochet **p.38**, Shaping **p.50–52**, Working in the round **p.56**, Sculptural textures **p.76**

GLOVES, SOCKS, AND SLIPPERS

SIZE
To fit a baby, aged 0–3 (3–6) months

YARN
Rowan Wool Cotton DK – 50g/113m/ 124yds (50% merino wool and 50% cotton; you can use any DK weight yarn with some cotton content for structure)

A x 1 **B** x 1

HOOK
3.5mm hook

NOTIONS
Yarn needle
Two small pieces of Velcro®
Sewing needle and thread

TENSION
10sts per 5cm (2in)

SPECIAL ABBREVIATIONS
Raised double crochet back (RDCB):
See p.195

⟩ PATTERN
After completing round 7, measure the length of the sole – it should be approx. 9–10cm (3½–4in) long (10–11cm/4–4¼in long). Ss into starting ch at end of each round.

1ch at beginning of round does not count as dc. 2ch at beginning of round counts as htr.

SOLE
With yarn A, work 9 ch.
Round 1: Starting in second ch from hook, 7 dc, 3 dc in next st, rotate 180 degrees and continue along the back loop of the chains, 6 dc, 2 dc in last st, ss in first st. (18sts)
Round 2: 1 ch, 2 dc in next st, 6 dc, 2 htr in next st three times, 6 dc, 2 dc in each of last 2 dc, ss in first st. (24sts)
Round 3: 1 ch, 1 dc, 2 dc in next st, 6 dc, (1 htr, 2 htr in next st) three times, 6 dc, (1 dc, 2 dc in next st) twice, ss in first st. (30sts)
Round 4: 1 ch, 2 dc, 2 dc in next st, 6 dc, (2 dc(htr), 2 dc(htr) in next st) three times, 6 dc, (2 dc, 2 dc in next st) three times, ss in first st. (36sts)
Round 5: 1 ch, 3 dc, 2 dc in next st, 6 dc, (3 dc(htr), 2 dc(htr) in next st) three times, 6 dc, (3 dc, 2 dc in next st) twice, ss in first st. (42sts)
Round 6: 1 ch, 4 dc, 2 dc in next st, 6 dc, (4 dc(htr), 2 dc(htr) in next st) three times, 6 dc, (4 dc, 2 dc in next st) twice, ss in first st. (48sts)

Larger size only:
Round 7: Change to yarn B, 1 ch, 5 dc, 2 dc in next st, 6 dc, (5 htr, 2 htr in next st) three times, 6 dc, (5 dc, 2 dc in next st) twice, ss in first st. (54sts)

SIDES
Round 7(8): 1 ch, 48(54) rdcb, ss into first st. (48:54 sts)
Round 8(9): 1 ch, 48(54) rdcb, ss into first st.
Round 9(10): Change to yarn A, 1 ch, 48(54) dc, ss into first st.
Round 10(11): 1 ch, 48(54) dc, ss into first st.
Round 11(12): 1 ch, 11(13) dc, (htr2tog, 3 htr) four times htr2tog, 13(17) dc, dc2tog. (42:48 sts)
Round 12(13): 1 ch, 11(13) dc, (htr2tog, 2 htr) four times, htr2tog, 11(15) dc, dc2tog. (36:42 sts)

Round 13(14): 1 ch, 11(13) dc, (htr2tog, 1 htr) four times, htr2tog, 9(13) dc, dc2tog. (30:36 sts)
Round 14(15): 1 ch, 11(13) dc, 5 dc(htr)2tog, 9(13) dc, ss into first st. (25:31 sts)
Fasten off.

STRAPS
With yarn A, work 9 ch.
Row 1: Starting in second ch from hook, 8 dc. (8sts)
Rows 2–12: Turn work, ch 1, 8 dc.
Row 13: Dc2tog, 4 dc, dc2tog. (6sts)
Row 14: Dc2tog, 2 dc, dc2tog. (4sts)
Row 15: 2 dc2tog. (2sts) Fasten off.
Add some surface crochet stripes in chain stitch on the rounded edge for decoration, in yarn B.

FINISHING
Sew the straps onto the shoes. Cut two small squares of Velcro® and sew on to secure the rounded edge of the strap down. Weave in loose ends.

For a rigid shoe, use a cotton-based yarn that will create a stiff fabric. For a softer feel, try a pure merino yarn. Refer to p.50 for instructions on how to work double crochet increases.

WOMEN'S SOFT PUMPS

A simple but stylish way to keep your toes cosy indoors.

Play with colour and brighten up dull days with a splash of neon

or choose neutral shades for understated elegance.

Level of difficulty

TECHNIQUES USED Double crochet **p.34**, Half treble crochet **p.38**, Treble crochet **p.44**, Working in the round **p.56**, Working into the back loop of a double crochet **p.75**

SIZE
To fit an adult woman,
shoe size UK 3–4 (5:6)

YARN
Artesano Chunky – 100g/105m/115yds
(100% wool; you can use any aran
chunky-weight yarn for a similar look
for this project)

A x 1   **B** x 1

HOOK
5mm hook

NOTIONS
Two stitch markers
Yarn needle

TENSION
11sts x 14 rows per 10cm (4in)

➤ PATTERN
Notes: The sole is worked in spirals; do not
join at end of each round and do not turn.
When the sole is done, fasten off yarn A and
join yarn B into the same stitch to make the
upper. Turn to p.233 for how to work htr2tog.

SOLE (MAKE 2)
Round 1: With yarn A, work 18 (20:22) ch,
3 dc in third ch from hook, 10 (12:14) dc,
4 tr, 5 tr into last ch, place marker in top of
third tr (remove and replace this marker on
subsequent rounds as indicated), do not
turn but work into the opposite side of the
foundation ch for rem sts, 4 tr, 10 (12:14) dc,

2 dc in same st as initial 3 dc. Do not join
and do not turn, place a second marker in
last st (remove and replace on subsequent
rounds to mark last st). (38(42:46)sts)
Round 2: 3 htr, dc to first before first
marker, 2 htr into next st, 3 tr into next st
(remove and replace marker in centre tr),
2 htr into next st, dc to last 2sts, 2 htr, do
not join or turn, place marker in last htr.
(42(46:50)sts)
Round 3: 3 htr into next st, 2 htr into next st,
3 htr, dc to 2sts before marker, 1 htr, 2 tr into
next st, remove marker, 3 tr into next st
(replace marker in centre tr), 2 tr into next
st, 1 htr, dc to last 4sts, 3 htr, 2 htr in next st.
Do not join and do not turn. (50(54:58)sts)
Round 4: 1 htr, 3 htr into next st, 1 htr in
next st, 2 htr in next st, 3 htr, dc to 6sts
before marker, 3 htr, (2 htr into next st) two
times, 2 tr into next st, remove marker, 3 tr
into next st (replace marker in centre st),
2 tr into next st, (2 htr into next st) two times,
3 htr, dc to last 4sts, 3 htr, 2 htr in next st.
Do not join and do not turn. (62(66:70)sts)
Ss into next 3sts, fasten off A.

UPPER (MAKE 2)
Join B into last ss.
Round 1: 1 dc in each st to end, join with
a ss to top of first dc. (62(66:70)sts)
Round 2: 1 ch (does not count as a stitch),
1 dc TBL in each dc to end, join to top of
first dc. (62(66:70)sts)
Round 3: 2 ch (counts as first htr), 6 (7:8) htr,
16 dc, 2 (3:4) htr, (htr2tog) two times, htr3tog
place marker to indicate centre toe stitch,
(htr2tog) two times, 2 (3:4) htr, dc to last
8(9:10)sts, 8 (9:10) htr, join to top of first htr.
(56(60:64)sts)
Round 4: 1 ch (does not count as a st), 1 dc
in same sp as 1 ch, 2 dc, (dc2tog) three
times, dc to last 8sts, (dc2tog) three times,
dc to end (remove and replace marker
when you reach it), join with a ss to top
of first dc. (50(54:58)sts)

Round 5: 1 ch (does not count as st), dc to
7sts before marker, 4 htr, htr2tog, htr3tog,
(remove and replace marker), htr2tog, 4 htr,
dc to end, join to top of first dc. (46(50:54)sts)
Round 6: 1 ch (does not count as a st), 3 dc,
(dc2tog) two times, dc to 3sts before marked
stitch, htr2tog, htr3tog, htr2tog, dc to last
5sts, (dc2tog) two times, dc to end. Join to
top of first dc. (38(42:46)sts)

Shoe sizes 5 and 6 only
Round 7: 2 ch (counts as stitch), htr to one st
before marker, htr3tog, htr to end. (40(44)sts)

All sizes
Round 8: Dc to end.
Round 9: (optional for narrow feet) Work
1 ss into each dc to end.
Fasten off yarn, weave in ends.
Block lightly by spraying with water and
stuffing with cotton to create shape.

These slippers are designed to be snug at
first because the wool will "give" with wear. If
in doubt about which size to make, opt for the
smaller size. Choose a dark colour for the sole
as it's more practical than a lighter shade.

WOMEN'S ANKLE SOCKS

Level of difficulty ✱✱✱

GLOVES, SOCKS, AND SLIPPERS

These pretty, comfortable socks are worked in the round from the cuff down, using an alternating pattern of double crochet and treble crochet stitches. The tip of the toe and the heel are reinforced by using double crochet.

TECHNIQUES USED Chain stitch **p.26**, Double crochet **p.34**, Half treble crochet **p.38**, Treble crochet **p.44**, Double crochet decreases **p.52**, Working in the round **p.56**

SIZE
To fit an adult woman, UK shoe sizes 4–7

YARN
Regia Angora Merino 4-ply – 50g/200m/219yds (65% merino wool, 25% nylon, and 10% angora; you can substitute any DK weight sock yarn for this project, preferably with nylon)

x 1

HOOKS
2.5mm hook
3mm hook

NOTIONS
Two stitch markers
Yarn needle

TENSION
23sts x 22 rows per 10cm (4in)

PATTERN (MAKE 2)
Work the cuff-ribbing sideways.

CUFF-RIBBING (WORKED SIDEWAYS)
With 2.5mm hook, work 10 ch.
Row 1: 1 htr in third ch from hook, 1 htr in each ch to end, turn. (8sts)
Row 2: 1 htr TBL in each st to end, turn. Rep row 2 a further 28 times. (30 rows) Using ss all along row, join first row to last row to form a large ring.

CUFF TO HEEL
Turn ribbing 90 degrees, so you are working into the sides of the rows on the cuff.

Round 1: With 3mm hook, work 45 dc evenly around the cuff, place marker to indicate end of round.
You are now working in continuous rounds.
Round 2: *1 dc, 1 tr, rep from * to marker, 1 dc.
Round 3: *1 tr, 1 dc, rep from * to marker, 1 tr. Rep rounds 2 and 3 until sock measures 19cm (7½in), making sure to end on a round 3.

HEEL
Row 1: 22 dc, turn.
Row 2: 1 ch, 22 dc, turn.
Work in rows of dc until heel flap measures 5cm (2in).

TURN THE HEEL
Row 1: 1 ch, 13 dc, dc2tog, 1 dc, turn.
Row 2: 6 dc, dc2tog, 1 dc, turn.
Row 3: Dc to 1st from end of prev row, dc2tog (your second st of the dc2tog will be the next dc, which is two rows below), 1 dc, turn. Rep row 3, five times. (14sts)

FOOT
Round 1: 14 dc, evenly work 10 dc in side of heel rows, place marker, 1 dc, *1 tr, 1 dc, rep from * across to other side of heel, place marker, evenly work 12 dc into sides of heel rows, place marker to indicate end of round. (59sts)
Round 2: 20 dc, (dc2tog) twice, 1 tr, *1 dc, 1 tr, rep from * to marker, 1 dc, (dc2tog) twice, dc to end marker. (55sts)
Round 3: (1 dc, 1 tr) nine times, dc2tog, tr2tog, 1 dc, *1 tr, 1 dc, rep from * to marker, tr2tog, dc2tog, (1 tr, 1 dc) twice, 1 tr. (51sts)
Round 4: (1 tr, 1 dc) eight times, tr2tog, dc2tog, 1 tr, *1 dc, 1 tr, rep from * to marker, dc2tog, tr2tog, (1 dc, 1 tr) twice. (47sts)
Remove all but ending marker.
Round 5: *1 dc, 1 tr, rep from * to last st, 1 dc.
Round 6: *1 tr, 1 dc, rep from * to last st, 1 tr. Rep last two rounds until sock measures 23cm (9in).

TOE
Round 1: 16 dc, dc2tog, place marker, 23 dc, place marker, dc to end of round. (46sts)
Round 2: *dc to 3sts from marker, dc2tog, 1 dc, slip marker, 1 dc, dc2tog, rep from * once, dc to end of round. (42sts)
Rep round 2, three times. (On the last round there will be no dc after the last dc2tog). (30sts)
Remove end marker.
Round 3: *dc to 3sts from marker, dc2tog, 1 dc, slip marker, 1 dc, dc2tog, rep from * once. (26sts)
Round 4: Rep round 3. (22sts)
Fasten off, leaving a long end.

FINISHING
Turn sock inside out and using the end left from fastening off, ss across both thicknesses of toe sts to seam together. Weave in ends.

Adjust the size of these socks by adding or subtracting stitches in multiples of two, in the round, to change the foot circumference, or by working the foot longer or shorter to adjust the length.

MEN'S CHUNKY SOCKS

Level of difficulty ✳✳✳

These cosy socks are made in the round, worked from the cuff down, with a contrasting colour used on the ribbing, heel, and toe, and worked in stripes to add extra detailing.

TECHNIQUES USED Chain stitch **p.26**, Double crochet **p.34**, Half treble crochet **p.38**, Double crochet decreases **p.52**, Working in the round **p.56**

SIZE
To fit an adult man, UK shoe sizes 9–11

YARN
Regia 6-ply DK – 50g/125m/137yds (75% wool and 25% nylon; you can use any DK weight wool/acrylic blend yarn to achieve a similar effect)

A x 1   **B** x 1

HOOKS
2.5mm hook
3mm hook

TENSION
19sts x 14 rows per 10cm (4in)

NOTIONS
Two stitch markers
Yarn needle

SPECIAL ABBREVIATIONS
LHTR: linked half treble. On starting st, insert hook into second ch of starting ch, yrh, draw through, insert hook into st, yrh, draw through st, yrh, draw through all loops on hook. For each st after that as follows: insert hook into horizontal bar in st before, yrh, draw through, insert hook into st, yrh, draw through st, yrh, draw through all loops on hook.
LHTR2TOG: linked half treble 2 together. Insert hook into horizontal bar in st before, yrh, draw through, insert hook into next st, yrh, draw through st, insert hook into next st, yrh, draw through st, yrh, draw through all loops on hook.

PATTERN (MAKE 2)
Adjust the size by adding or subtracting stitches in the round to change the circumference, or by working the foot longer or shorter to adjust the length.

CUFF RIBBING (WORKED SIDEWAYS)
With 2.5mm hook and yarn B, work 14 ch.
Row 1: 1 htr in third chain from hook, 1 htr in each ch to end, turn (12sts)
Row 2: 1 htr TBL in each st to end, turn. Rep row 2 a further 46 times. (48 rows) Using ss all along row, join first row to last row to form a large ring.

CUFF TO HEEL
Turn ribbing 90 degrees, so you are working into the sides of the rows on the cuff.
Round 1: With 3mm hook and yarn A, 2 ch, 1 lhtr in each row side to end, change to yarn B, join, place stitch marker to indicate end of round. (48sts)
Round 2: 2 ch, lhtr in each st to end, change to yarn A, join.
Round 3: 2 ch, lhtr2tog, lhtr in each st to 2sts from marker, lhtr2tog, change to yarn B, join. (46sts)
Round 4: Rep round 2, change to yarn A.
Round 5: Rep round 2, change to yarn B.
Round 6: Rep round 3. (44sts)
Round 7: Rep round 2, change to yarn A.
Round 8: Rep round 2, do not join.
From now on, work in continuous rounds throughout.
Round 9: 1 lhtr, lhtr2tog, lhtr in each st to 2sts from marker, lhtr2tog. (42sts). Work straight in continuous rounds of lhtr until sock measures 17cm (6¾in) from cuff edge.

HEEL
Row 1: 22 lhtr (do NOT fasten off yarn A, as you will pick this up again later on the foot). With yarn B, 20 dc, turn.
Row 2: 1ch, 1 dc in each dc to end of yarn B sts, turn.

Rep row 2 until heel measures 6cm (2½in).

TURN THE HEEL
Row 1: 1 ch, 12 dc, dc2tog, 1 dc, turn.
Row 2: 1 ch, 6 dc, dc2tog, 1 dc, turn.
Row 3: Dc to 1 st from end of prev row, dc2tog (your second st of the dc2tog will be the next dc which is two rows below), 1 dc, turn. Rep row 3 until you reach the end of the heel stitches, there will be no dc after the dc2tog at the end of your last two rows. (12sts). Fasten off.

FOOT
Round 1: With yarn A, left in place at beginning of heel, 2 ch, work 8 lhtr evenly up the side of the heel, 1 lhtr in each of the sts from the heel turn and 8 lhtr evenly placed down the other side of the heel flap; place marker, work lhtr in each lhtr across the front of foot, place marker. (50sts) You are now working in continuous rounds of lhtr again.
Round 2: Lhtr2tog, 1 lhtr, lhtr2tog, 18 lhtr, lhtr2tog, 1 lhtr, lhtr2tog, slip marker, lhtr in each st to next marker. (46sts)
Round 3: Lhtr2tog, 1 lhtr, lhtr2tog, 14 lhtr, lhtr2tog, 1 lhtr, lhtr2tog, remove marker, lhtr in each st to next marker. (42sts)
Round 4: Lhtr in each st to end of round. Work in continuous rounds of lhtr until sock measures 25cm (10in) from heel.

TOE
Round 1: With yarn B, 21 dc, place marker, dc to end of round.
Round 2: Dc2tog, *dc to 2sts from marker, dc2tog**, slip marker, dc2tog, rep from between * and **. (38sts). Rep round 2, six times. (14sts). Fasten off, leaving a long end.

FINISHING
Turn sock inside out and using the end left from fastening off, ss across both thicknesses of toe sts to seam together. Weave in ends.

WHAT TO
WEAR

With a host of patterns for crocheted cardigans, hoodies, and jumpers, you can kit out the whole family's wardrobe. Your projects will soon become new favourite outfits.

BABY'S CROSSOVER CARDIGAN

Level of difficulty

This sweet, wrap-around cardigan is worked in half treble stitch and crosses over from left to right, as well as right to left. The crocheted ties can be altered as your child grows to extend the life of your lovingly made garment.

TECHNIQUES USED Chain stitch **p.26**, Half treble crochet **p.38**, Blocking and seams **p.68–70**, Double crochet edging **p.86**

SIZE
To fit a child, aged 12–18 months

YARN
Debbie Bliss Baby Cashmerino – 50g/ 125m/137yds (55% wool, 33% acrylic, and 12% cashmere; you can use any wool or wool mix, 4-ply to sportweight yarn for this project)

x 4

HOOK
4mm hook

NOTIONS
Safety pins
Yarn needle

TENSION
18sts x 13 rows to 10cm (4in)

SPECIAL ABBREVIATIONS
Half treble decrease (htr2tog)**:** yrh, put hook in next st, and pull through yarn (three loops on the hook), yrh, insert hook in the next st, and pull through yarn (five loops on the hook), yrh, and pull through all loops.

PATTERN
The fronts and back of this cardigan are worked in one piece.

FRONT AND BACK
Row 1: Work 150 ch, htr into the third ch from the hook, htr into the rest of the ch. (148sts, 2 ch)
Row 2: 2 ch, htr in each htr, no htr into top of 2 ch. (148sts)
Row 3: 2 ch, htr2tog, htr in the rest of the htr, no htr into top of 2 ch. (146sts)
Repeat row three until you have 108 htr. Start dividing, keep in pattern.

FIRST FRONT
Row 23: 2 ch, htr2tog, htr in the next 24sts. (25sts)
Row 24: 2 ch, htr to end, no htr into top of 2 ch. (24sts)
Row 25: 2 ch, htr2tog, htr into each htr, htr into 2 ch. (23sts)
Repeat rows 24–25 until you have 11sts.
Row 38: 2 ch, htr in the same place as 2 ch, htr to end, not in top of 2 ch. (11sts)
Fasten off leaving a 30cm (12in) tail for sewing up.

BACK
Miss 4sts on row 22 from edge of first front. Rejoin yarn.
Row 23: 2 ch, htr in the same st, htr in the next 48sts, turn. (49sts)
Row 24: 2 ch, htr in the same st, htr to the end, no htr into the top of the 2 ch. (49sts)
Rows 25–38: Rep row 24.

NECK SHAPING
Row 39: 2 ch, htr in the same st, htr in the next 9 htr. (10sts)
Fasten off.
Miss 29 htr, rejoin yarn.
2 ch, htr in the same st, htr in the next 9 htr. (10sts)
Fasten off.

Half treble crochet makes a thick, dense fabric that is perfect for clothes. Lightweight, soft baby yarn, as used here, also makes this cardigan both a great summer and a winter cover-up.

WHAT TO WEAR

SECOND FRONT

Miss 4sts on row 22 from edge of back. Rejoin yarn.

Row 23: 2 ch, htr in the same st, htr to end. (25sts)

Row 24: 2 ch, htr2tog, htr to end, no htr into top of 2 ch. (23sts)

Row 25: 2 ch, htr in the same st, htr to end. (23sts)

Repeat rows 24–25 until you have 11sts.

Row 38: 2 ch, htr in the next 10 htr. (10sts)

Fasten off leaving a 30cm (12in) tail for sewing up.

SLEEVES (MAKE 2)

Row 1: Make 31 ch, htr in third ch from the hook, htr in each ch, turn. (29sts)

Row 2: 2 ch, htr in same st, htr in each htr, do not htr in top of 2 ch throughout. (29sts)

Row 3: As row 2. (29sts)

Row 4: 2 ch, 2 htr in same st (inc made), htr in each htr to end. (30sts)

Repeat rows 2–4 until you have 35sts.

Row 20: Rep row 2. (35sts)

Row 21: Rep row 2. (35sts)

Row 22: 2 ch, 2 htr in same st, htr in each htr to last st, 2 htr in last st. (37sts)

Repeat rows 20–22 once. (39sts)

Row 26: Rep row 2. (39sts)

Row 27: 1 ch, ss across 6 st, 2 ch, htr in next 27 htr, turn. (27sts)

Row 28: 2 ch, htr2tog, htr in each htr to last 2sts, htr2tog, turn. (24sts)

Repeat row 28 until you have 12sts.

Fasten off.

FINISHING

Sew the shoulder seams together using back stitch. Whip stitch the sleeve seams together.

With safety pins, pin the sleeve into the arm hole. The first pin should have the sleeve seam between the missed st on row 23 and the middle of the sleeve cap in line with the shoulder seam. Ease the rest of the sleeve in place, then whip st the two pieces together.

Repeat for the other sleeve.

EDGING

Join the yarn to the centre back of the neck and work dc all around the garment, working 3 dc to two rows of htr on the fronts, joining to the first dc with a ss. Work dc round the bottom of the sleeve joining to the first dc with a ss.

TIES

Attach yarn to first st on the bottom of the garment, work 40 ch, fasten off, weave in ends. Repeat at the last st. Make a 40-ch tie 25cm (9¾in) from the beginning ch and 25cm (9¾in) from the other end, and also on row 20, where fronts cross over.

The beauty of crocheting the ties on this cardigan is that you will avoid the need to sew on ribbons or strips of fabric that tiny fingers might pull off. Work your chain stitches with an even tension (see pp.26–27) for a neat finish.

CHILD'S PONCHO

A bit like a giant patterned square, this poncho is colourful and cosy with a square in the middle to go over the head. This is the perfect accessory for children to layer over any outfit.

TECHNIQUES USED Chain stitch **p.26**, Treble crochet **p.44**, Working into a chain space **p.75**, Working into spaces between stitches **p.75**

SIZE
To fit a child, aged 4–9 years

YARN
Artesano Superwash Merino DK –
   50g/112m/122yds (100% merino wool;
   you can use any DK yarn for a similar
   look to this project)

A x 2   **B** x 2   **C** x 2   **D** x 2

E x 3   **F** x 3

HOOK
4.5mm hook

NOTIONS
Four stitch markers
Yarn needle

TENSION
4 x 3 tr groups to 10cm (4in), nine rows
   to 10cm (4in)

PATTERN

Row 1: With yarn A, make a slip knot 10cm (4in) from the end of the yarn, work 75 ch, tr into the fourth ch from the hook (first 4 ch count as a tr st), tr in the next ch, *1 ch, tr in the next 3 ch, repeat from * to the end (24 x 3 tr groups), 1 ch, ss to the top of the 3 ch. Make sure you do not twist the row, fasten off and weave in end. With the 10cm (4in) tail, join to the fourth ch and sew in end.
Put stitch markers in first, seventh, 13th, and 19th ch sp leaving 5-ch sp between each two markers. These mark where the corners will be.

Row 2: Join yarn B at first marked ch sp, work (3 ch, 2 tr, 3 ch, 3 tr) in same ch sp to make the first corner, 1 ch, *(3 tr in next ch sp, 1 ch) five times**, (3 tr, 3 ch, 3 tr) in next ch sp, 1 ch; repeat from * twice, then from * to ** once, ss into the top of the 3 ch at the beginning of the round, fasten off and sew in ends. (20 x 3 tr groups and four corner groups)

Row 3: Join yarn C to 3-ch corner sp, work (3 ch, 2 tr, 3 ch, 3 tr) in same ch sp, 1 ch, *(3 tr in next ch sp, 1 ch) to next corner**, (3 tr, 3 ch, 3 tr) in 3-ch corner sp, 1 ch; rep

from * twice, then from * to ** once, ss to top of 3 ch and fasten off. Weave in ends. (6 x 3 tr groups between corners)

Rows 4–16: Repeat row 3 in following colours. You will have one more 3 tr group on each side of the square on each row.

Row 4: Yarn D. (7 x 3 tr)
Row 5: Yarn E. (8 x 3 tr)
Row 6: Yarn A. (9 x 3 tr)
Row 7: Yarn B. (10 x 3 tr)
Row 8: Yarn F. (11 x 3 tr)
Row 9: Yarn C. (12 x 3 tr)
Row 10: Yarn E. (13 x 3 tr)
Row 11: Yarn A. (14 x 3 tr)
Row 12: Yarn D. (15 x 3 tr)
Row 13: Yarn B. (16 x 3 tr)
Row 14: Yarn C. (17 x 3 tr)
Row 15: Yarn E. (18 x 3 tr)
Row 16: Yarn F. (19 x 3 tr)
Rows 17–32: Repeat colour sequence again.
Row 33: With yarn A, work in dc all around the edges, working 5 dc at the corners, fasten off with an invisible join.

Using a yarn that is 100 per cent wool makes this a warm and snuggly garment for a child. Choose colours carefully for a harmonious effect and use the same colour for the neckline and the double crochet edging along the bottom to lend a coherent feel.

STRIPY SWEATER

This versatile garment is made in the round, working from the bottom up. The sleeves are then joined to the body and the yoke is shaped using raglan style decreases (see pp.52–53).

Level of difficulty ✳✳✳

TECHNIQUES USED Chain stitch **p.26**, Double crochet **p.34**, Simple stripes **p.39**, Treble crochet **p.44**, Shaping **p.50–52**, Slip stitch seam **p.70**, Circular crochet **p.98**

SIZE
To fit a child, aged 3–4 (4–5:6–7) years

YARN
Debbie Bliss Baby Cashmerino DK – 50g/
125m/137yds (55% wool, 33% acrylic,
and 12% cashmere; you can use any DK
weight merino-mix yarn to achieve a
similar effect)

A x 3 (3:5) **B** x 1 (1:1) **C** x 1 (2:2)

HOOKS
3.5mm and 4mm hooks

NOTIONS
Eight stitch markers
Yarn needle

TENSION
16sts x 8.5 rows per 10cm (4in)

PATTERN
This garment is given in three sizes with
the smallest size first. The larger sizes are
shown in brackets.

BODY
With yarn A and 4mm hook, work
108 (112:116) ch, being careful not to twist,
join first ch to last ch with ss to create
a large ring.
Round 1: With 3.5mm hook, 1 ch, 1 dc in
each ch to end, join to top of ch 1 with ss,
place stitch marker to indicate end of
round. (108(112:116)sts)
Round 2: 1 ch, 1 dc in each st to end, join.
Rep round 2 until piece measures
3cm (1¼in).
Next round: 3 ch, 1 tr, in each st to end of
round, join.
Rep last round a further two (four:four) times.
Continuing to work in straight rounds of tr,
work as follows:
One round in yarn B.
Two rounds in yarn C.
One round in yarn B.
Six (seven:seven) rounds in yarn A.
One round in yarn B.
Two rounds in yarn C.
One round in yarn B.
One (one:two) rounds in yarn A.
Fasten off.

SLEEVES (MAKE 2)
With yarn A and 4mm hook, work
28(29:29) ch, being careful not to twist,
join first ch to last ch with ss, to create
a large ring.
Round 1: With 3.5mm hook, 1 ch, 1 dc in
each ch to end, join. (28(29:29)sts)
Round 2: 1 ch, 1 dc in each st to end, join.
Rep round 2 until piece measures
3cm (1¼in).

To check whether this sweater will fit your
child, the exact measurements are as follows:
to fit chest size 58.5 (61:63.5)cm/23 (24:25)in,
and with a sleeve length of 27 (28:29)cm/10½
(11:11½)in.

The attractive neckline, worked in dense double crochet, contrasts beautifully with the more open treble stitches used in the body of the sweater.

MAIN SLEEVE
Place stitch marker at start of round, and move it up for each row.
Round 1: 3 ch, 1 tr in each st to end, join.
Round 2: 3 ch, 2 tr in next st, 1 tr in each st to 2sts from marker, 2 tr in next st, 1 tr, join. (30(31:31)sts)
Rep last two rounds once. (32(33:33)sts)
Rep round 1.
With yarn B, rep round 2. (34(35:35)sts)
With yarn C, rep rounds 1 and 2.
(36(37:37)sts)
With yarn B, rep round 1.
With yarn A, rep round 2. (38(39:39)sts)
Rep rounds 1 and 2, two (three:three) times.
(42(45:45)sts)

Size 3–4 years only
Rep round 1.

All sizes
With yarn B, rep round 1.
With yarn C, rep round 2. (44 (47:47)sts)
With yarn C, rep round 1.
With yarn B, rep round 2. (46(49:49)sts)
With yarn A, rep round 1.

Size 6–7 years only
Rep round 2. (51sts)

All sizes
Fasten off.

JOINING SLEEVES TO BODY
From fasten off point on body, count 4sts and place marker in the next st, from marker count 8(9:9)sts counter clockwise and place marker (leaving 8(9:9)sts between markers).
From first marker placed, count 44(45:47) sts and place marker (leaving 44(45:47)sts between markers), from this third marker, count 8(9:9)sts and place marker (leaving 8(9:9)sts between markers).
Around the body you should now have marked st, 44(45:47)sts, marked st, 8(9:9)sts, marked st, 44(45:47)sts, marked st, 8(9:9)sts.

From fasten off point on each sleeve, count 4sts to the right and place marker in next st, from marker count 8(9:9)sts counter clockwise and place marker in next st. (8(9:9)sts between markers.)

JOINING ROUND
Line up the right sleeve to the right underarm of the body, with a beg slip knot on the hook, insert hook in marked stitches of both the body and the sleeve together at the back of the sweater and ss to join, 3 ch (counts as tr), tr in each st across the back of the body to second marked stitch, *inserting hook through both layers of marked sts of body and other sleeve, work 1 tr, tr across sts of sleeve* to marker, working through both layers, 1 tr in marked sts of sleeve and body, tr across front to next marker, rep between * and * and ss to top of ch 3 to join. Remove underarm st markers. (164(170:178)sts)
Round 1: 3 ch, tr2tog, 40 (41:43) tr, tr2tog, 1 tr, place marker, *1 tr, tr2tog, 30 (32:34) tr, tr2tog, 1 tr, ** place marker, 1 tr, tr2tog, 40 (41:43) tr, tr2tog, 1 tr, place marker, rep from * to **, join. (156(162:170)sts)
Round 2: 3 ch, (tr2tog) twice, tr to 5sts from marker, (tr2tog) twice, 1 tr, *slip marker, 1 tr, (tr2tog) twice, tr to 5sts from marker, (tr2tog) twice, 1 tr, rep from * to end of round. (140(146:154)sts)
Round 3: 3 ch, tr2tog, tr to 3sts from marker, tr2tog, 1 tr, *slip marker, 1 tr, tr2tog, tr to 3sts from marker, tr2tog, 1 tr, rep from * to end of round. (132(138:146)sts)
Rep last two rounds twice. (84(90:98)sts)
Rep round three, two (two:three) times. (68(74:74)sts)
Next round: 1 ch, 1 dc in each st to end.
Rep last round until dc rounds measure 3cm (1¼in).
Fasten off.

FINISHING
Seam together the underarm sts using ss on the inside of the garment.
Weave in all ends.

CHILD'S HOODIE

This cosy hooded jacket for the small person in your life
is worked straight and then seamed. The edging in crab stitch gives
a neat detail for a practical jacket.

Level of difficulty

TECHNIQUES USED Chain stitch **p.26**, Slip stitch **p.28**, Double crochet **p.34**, Treble crochet **p.44**, Shaping **p.50–52**, Button loops **p.87**

SIZE
To fit a child, aged 3–4 (4–5:6–7) years

YARN
Rowan Pure Wool 4-ply – 50g/160m/
175yds (100% wool; any 4-ply yarn
with a high wool content will produce
a similar effect)

A x 7 (7:8)   **B** x 1 (1:2)

HOOK
3mm hook

NOTIONS
Yarn needle
Five toggles, 3cm (1¼in) long

TENSION
21sts x 17 rows per 10cm (4in) square

SPECIAL ABBREVIATIONS
1 ch worked at the start of a row counts
   as a dc stitch.
3 ch worked at the start of a row counts
   as a tr stitch.
Crab stitch: See p.146

PATTERN
The garment is given in three sizes
with the smallest size first. The larger
sizes are shown in brackets.

BACK
With yarn B, work 68 (72:76) ch.
Foundation row: Starting in the second ch
from hook, work 1 dc into each st to end.
Break off yarn B and join yarn A. (67(71:75)sts)
Row 1: Work 3 ch (for the first tr), work 1 tr
into each st to end.
Row 2: Work 1 ch, work 1 dc into each st
to end.
These two rows form the pattern.
Repeat these rows until the piece measures
20 (24:28)cm/8 (9½:11)in from beginning,
ending with a row two.

SHAPE FOR ARMHOLES
Keep pattern correct throughout.
Next row: 1 ch, work 1 ss into each of the
first 4(5:6)st of the row. 3 ch (for first tr),
work 1 tr into each stitch to the last 3(4:5)sts,
turn. (61(63:65)sts)
Keeping pattern correct, work straight
until the piece measures 13.5 (15:16.5)cm/
5½ (6:6½)in from armhole.

SHAPE SHOULDERS AND NECK
Next row: 1 ch, work 1 ss into each of
the next 9(9:8)sts, work 1 dc into each
of the next 9sts, work 1 ss into each of
the next 25(27:31)sts, work 1 dc into each
of the next 9sts, work 1 ss into each of
the last 9(9:8)sts.
Fasten off yarn.

LEFT FRONT
With yarn B, work 34 (36:38) ch.
Foundation row: Starting in the second ch
from hook, work 1 dc into each st to end.
(33(35:37)sts)
Break off yarn B and join yarn A.

Neat wooden toggles look appropriate for
this hoodie and finish it off with a lovely
detail. They are easier for small hands to
do up, although buttons can be substituted
if preferred.

Row 1: Work 3 ch (for the first tr),
work 1 tr into each st to end.
Row 2: 1 ch, 1 dc into each st to end.
Repeat these rows until the piece measures
20 (24:28)cm/8 (9½/11)in from beginning,
ending with a row two.

SHAPE FOR ARMHOLES
Keep pattern correct throughout.
Next row right side (RS): 1 ch, work 1 ss
into each of the first 4(5:6)st of the row,
3 ch (for first tr), work 1 tr into each stitch
to end. (30(31:32)sts)
Keeping pattern correct, work straight until
the piece is six rows shorter than the back
(not including the shoulder shaping row)
ending on a wrong side (WS) row.

SHAPE NECK

Next row: 3 ch (for first tr), work 1 tr into each st until 9(9:11)sts to end, turn. (21(22:21)sts)
Next row: 3 ch (for first tr), tr2tog, work 1 tr into each st to end. (20(21:20)sts)
Next row: 3 ch (for first tr), work 1 tr into each st to the last 2sts, tr2tog. (19(20:19)sts)
Next row: 3 ch (for first tr), tr2tog, work 1 tr into each st to end. (18(19:18)sts)
Work two rows straight.

SHAPE SHOULDER

Next row (RS): 1 ch, work 1 ss into each of the next 8(9:8)sts, work 1 dc into each st to end. Fasten off yarn.

RIGHT FRONT

Make as per left front, but reverse the shaping.

SLEEVES (MAKE 2)

With yarn B, work 30 (32:35) ch.
Foundation row: Starting in the second ch from hook, work 1 dc into each st to end. (29(31:34)sts)
Break off yarn B and join yarn A.
Row 1: Work 3 ch (for the first tr), work 1 tr into each st to end.
Row 2: Work 1 ch, work 1 dc into each st to end.
Row 3: Work 3 ch (for the first tr), work 2 tr into next st, work 1 tr into each st to last 2sts, work 2 tr into next st, 1 tr into the last st. (31(33:36)sts)
Row 4: Work 1 ch, work 1 dc into each st to end.
Row 5: Work 3 ch (for the first tr), work 1 tr into each st to end.
Row 6: Work 1 ch, work 2 dc into next st, 1 dc into each st to last 2sts, work 2 dc into next st, work 1 dc into last st. (33(35:38)sts)
Continue in this way, increasing every third row, until there are 53(61:66)sts.
Work straight until the sleeve measures 26 (30:34)cm/10¼ (12:13½)in.
Fasten off yarn.

POCKETS (MAKE 2)

With yarn A, work 19 (23:25) ch.
Foundation row: Starting in the second ch from hook, work 1 dc into each st to end. (18(22:24)sts)
Working in patt as for back, work 13 rows.
Row 14: 1 ch, work 1 ss into each of the next 3sts, work 1 dc into each st to end. (15(19:21)sts)
Row 15: 3 ch (for first tr), work 1 tr into each st to end.
Row 16–20: Work in patt, decreasing 1st at the shaped edge (by working 2sts together) on each row. (10(14:16)sts)
Work two rows straight.
Fasten off yarn.
Block all pieces.

BUTTONHOLE BAND

Row 1: Join yarn A to the top of the left front and work 1 ch. Work in dc along the front edge, working 2sts into each tr row end and 1 dc into each dc row end. Do not work into the contrast colour at the base of the front.
Row 2: Work 1 ch, work 1 dc into each st to end.
Repeat row 2 once more.
Row 3: As row 2 but placing five buttonholes evenly along the row. Buttonholes are created by working 2 ch and missing 2sts.
Repeat row 2 twice more.
Fasten off yarn.

BUTTON BAND

Starting at the base of the right front, work as for the buttonhole band, replacing row 3 with another row 2 repetition.
Join the shoulder seams.

HOOD

With yarn A, starting at the top of the right front button band, work dc around the neck as follows: five across the button band, 17(18:20)sts around the right neck, 25(27:31)sts across the back neck, 17(18:20)sts around the left neck, five across the buttonhole band. (69(73:81)sts)
Work in patt as for back until the hood measures 24 (26:28)cm/9½ (10:11)in.
Fasten off yarn. Sew top of hood.

EDGINGS
Sleeves

Join yarn B to cuff and work in crab stitch along base.
Fasten off yarn.

The contrasting pale-coloured edging around the hem, hood, and sleeves gives this hoodie a professional and neat finish. Turn to pp.50–53 when working the increase and decrease stitches to shape the garment, and pp.85–87 for further details about edgings and finishings on crocheted items.

Pockets

Row 1: Join yarn B and work 1 ch. Work 15 dc evenly across the shaped edge.
Row 2: 1 ch, work in crab stitch back across the edging.
Fasten off yarn.

Body of jacket

Row 1: Join yarn B to the base of the buttonhole band, where it joins the main jacket, and work in dc as follows: base of buttonhole band 5sts, body and hood, 2sts into each tr row end and 1st into each dc row end, base of button band 5sts.
Row 2: 1 ch, work in crab stitch back across the edging.
Fasten off yarn.
Join sleeves to fronts and back of jacket.
Sew sleeve and side seams; sew pockets to front of jacket; sew toggles to button band.
Weave in all ends.

SUMMER TUNIC DRESS

Level of difficulty ✱✱✱

This sweet, summer tunic dress is worked in two pieces for the front and back, which are then seamed together. The skirt is worked in the round from the top down, using increases and decreases to create a chevron effect.

TECHNIQUES USED Chain stitch **p.26**, Slip stitch **p.28**, Half treble crochet **p.38**, Treble crochet **p.44**, Shaping **p.50–52**, Double crochet edging **p.86**

SIZE
To fit a child, aged 1–2 (2–3:4–5) years

YARN
Debbie Bliss Eco Baby – 50g/125m/137yds
   (100% cotton; you can use any
   DK weight cotton yarn to achieve
   a similar effect)

A x 2 (2:3)   **B** x 1   **C** x 1   **D** x 1

E x 1   **F** x 1

HOOK
3.5mm hook

NOTIONS
Yarn needle
2 x 2cm (¾in) buttons

TENSION
17sts x 12 rows per 10cm (4in)

PATTERN
The garment is given in three sizes with the smallest size first. The larger sizes are shown in brackets.
Turn to p.233 for how to work htr2tog.

With yarn A, work 51 (55:59) ch.
Row 1: 1 htr in second ch from hook, 1 htr in each ch to end, turn. (49(53:57)sts)
Row 2: 2 ch, 1 htr in each st to end, turn.
Row 3: 2 ch, 2 (4:2) htr, *1 ch, miss 1st, 3 htr, rep from * to last 3sts, 1 ch, miss 1st, 2 (4:2) htr.
Row 4: 2 ch, 1 htr in each st and ch sp as you come to them, turn.
Rep row 2, one (two:three) times.

SHAPE UNDERARM
Row 1: Ss into next 3sts, 3 ch, 43 (47:51) htr, turn. (43(47:51)sts)
Row 2: 2 ch, 1 htr, htr2tog, htr to 3sts from end of row, htr2tog, 1 htr, turn. (41(45:49)sts)
Rep row 2, five times. (31(35:39)sts)

Row 8: 2 ch, 1 htr in each st to end.
Rep row 8 until piece measures 6 (6:7)cm/ 2¼ (2¼:2¾)in from underarm shaping.

SHAPE NECKLINE
Left side
Row 1: 2 ch, 9 (10:11) htr, turn.
Row 2: 2 ch, miss next st, 1 htr in each st to end, turn. (8(9:10)sts)
Row 3: 2 ch, htr in each st to end, turn.
Rep last two rows a further 2 (3:4) times. (6sts)
Fasten off.

Right side
Row 1: Join yarn with ss to 13 (15:17)th st from edge of left side shaping, 2 ch, 1 htr in each st across, turn. (9(10:11)sts)
Row 2: 2 ch, 1 htr in each st to last 2sts, miss next st, 1 htr. (8(9:10)sts)
Row 3: 2 ch, 1 htr in each st to end, turn.
Rep last two rows a further two (three:four) times. (6sts)
Fasten off.

Crocheting a chevron design is really simple, but you must remember to count all the stitches up one side and then count them down the other side for an even M-shape across your fabric.

BACK

Work as front to end of first row 2.

Row 3: 2 ch, 1 htr, *1 ch, miss 1 st, 3 htr, rep from * to end.

Continue as front from first row 4 to row 8 of underarm shaping.

Rep row 8 until piece measures 11 (12:14)cm /4½ (5:5½)in from underarm shaping.

SHAPE NECKLINE

Right side

Row 1: 2 ch, 6 htr, turn.

Rep row 1 a further three times.

Row 5: 2 ch, 2 htr, htr2tog, 2 htr, turn. (5sts)

Row 6 (Buttonhole): 2 ch, 2 htr, 1 ch, miss next st, 2 htr, turn.

Row 7: 2 ch, 2 htr, htr in ch sp, 2 htr, turn.

Row 8: 1 ch, 1 htr in each st to end, turn.

Rep row 8 once.

Fasten off.

Left side

Join yarn with ss to 19 (23:27)th st from edge of right shaping.

Work as right side.

JOIN FRONT AND BACK PANELS

With right sides (RS) facing, using ss, seam tog side seams under arm holes on both sides.

SKIRT

With RS facing, join yarn A at the right side seam.

Round 1: 2 ch, 2 htr in next st, 1 htr in each st to left seam, 2 htr in next st, 1 htr in each st to end of round. (96(104:112)sts)

Round 2: With yarn B, 3 ch (counts as a st), 1 tr in same st as ch 3, *1 tr, (tr2tog) twice, 1 tr, (2 tr in next st)** twice, rep from * to end of round, ending last rep at **, join to top of first st with ss.

Rep round 2.

With yarn A, rep round 2.

Round 5: With yarn C, 3 ch, 2 tr in same st as ch 3, *1 tr, (tr2tog) twice, 1 tr, (3 tr in next st)** twice, rep from * to end of round, ending last rep at **, join. (120(130:140)sts)

Round 6: 3 ch, 1 tr in same st as ch 3, *2 tr, (tr2tog) twice, 2 tr, (2 tr in next st)** twice, rep from * to end, ending last rep at **, join.

Round 7: With yarn A, rep round 6.

Rounds 8–9: With yarn D, rep round 6.

Round 10: With yarn A, rep round 6.

Rounds 11–12: With yarn E, rep round 6.

Round 13: With yarn A, 3 ch, 2 tr in same st as ch 3, *2 tr, (tr2tog) twice, 2 tr, (3 tr in next st)** twice, rep from * to end of round, ending last rep at **, join. (144(156:168)sts)

Round 14: With yarn F, 3 ch, 1 tr in same st as ch-3, *3 tr, (tr2tog) twice, 3 tr, (2 tr in next st)** twice, rep from * to end of round, ending last rep at **, join.

Round 15: Rep round 14.

Round 16: With yarn A, rep round 14.

Round 17: With yarn B, rep round 14.

Sizes 2–3 and 4–5 years only

Round 18: Rep round 14.

Size 4–5 years only

Round 19: With yarn A, rep round 14.

Rounds 20–21: With yarn C, rep round 14.

All sizes

Fasten off.

FINISHING

With yarn E, join to right underarm side seam, 1 ch, evenly work a round of dc all the way around the edge of the top, front, and back, join. Fasten off.

TIE

With yarn F, work 150 ch, fasten off, weave in ends. Thread tie through eyelets in row 3 of bodice and fasten with a bow at the front. Weave in ends. Sew buttons in place. Block lightly.

The shoulder straps on this tunic dress are secured with tiny buttons. Choose a decorative button to make a pretty feature, or crochet your own buttons (see p.87).

This simple tie in a contrasting colour is made in chain stitch and threaded through the bodice of the dress to provide a pretty bow detail at the front.

CROPPED SWEATER

This pretty top is a great addition to a summer wardrobe. Lacy, with three-quarter length sleeves, it's perfect for layering on cold days. Worked flat in four pieces, the sweater is seamed together at the end.

TECHNIQUES USED Double crochet **p.34**, Treble crochet **p.44**, Shaping **p.50–52**, Blocking and seams **p.68–70**, Clusters **p.77**, Double crochet edging **p.86**

SIZE
To fit an adult woman, S (M:L)

YARN
Louisa Harding Orielle DK – 50g/110m/ 120yds (97% alpaca and 3% polyester; you can use any DK weight alpaca or wool yarn here. This has a slight sparkle, which you could recreate with Lurex®)

x 10 (12:12)

HOOK
6mm hook

NOTIONS
Safety pins
Yarn needle

TENSION
Seven 2tr-cl sts x 7.5 rows per 10cm (4in) in upturned V st

SPECIAL ABBREVIATIONS
2TR-CL: 2 treble crochet cluster (2tr-cl). Yrh, insert in ch sp below, yrh, draw through, yrh, draw through two loops, yrh, insert in next ch sp, yrh, draw through, yrh, draw through two loops, yrh, draw through remaining three loops.

Upturned V stitch: Row 1: (working into row of dc) 3 ch, *2tr-cl (see above) (work first tr into first dc, miss 1 dc, work second tr in next dc), 1 ch, rep from * to end, 1 tr in last st.
Row 2: 3 ch, *2tr-cl , 1 ch, rep from * to end, 1 tr in last st. Rep row 2 for pattern.

PATTERN
The pattern will fit three bust sizes: small: 81cm (32in), medium: 91cm (36in), and large: 101cm (40in).

FRONT
Work 77 (85:92) ch.
Row 1: 1 dc in second ch from hook, 1 dc in each ch to end, turn. (76(84:91)sts)
Row 2: 1 ch, 1 dc in each st to end, turn. Rep row 2 a further seven times.

Small and large sizes only
Row 10: 1 ch, 4 (1) dc, *2 dc in next st, 2 dc, rep from * to end. (100(121)sts)

Medium size only
Row 10: 1 ch, 4 (6:1) dc, *2 dc in next st, 2 (2:2) dc **, 2dc in next st, 2 (1:2) dc, rep from * to end, ending last rep of size M at **. (100(115:121)sts)

All sizes
Row 11: Work row 1 of Upturned V stitch pattern. (33 (38:40) 2tr-cl)
Row 12: Work row 2 of Upturned V stitch pattern.
Rep row 12 until piece measures 31 (32:33)cm/12¼ (12½:13)in.

SHAPE THE ARMHOLES
Row 1: *ss into next 2tr-cl, ss in ch-1 sp, rep from * once, 3 ch, work row 2 of Upturned V stitch pattern across to third from last ch sp (leaving two 2tr-cl unworked). (29 (34:36) 2tr-cl)
Row 2: Work row 2 of Upturned V stitch pattern.
Rep row 2 until armhole measures 14 (15:16)cm/5½ (6:6¼)in from armhole shaping, ending on wrong side (WS) row.

The main body of the sweater is made up of a simple-to-follow lace repeat, with double crochet worked into the edges. Turn to pp.106–107 for more information about simple lace techniques, and pp.108–110 for lace and filet patterns.

SHAPE THE NECK
Left side
Row 1 right side (RS): 3 ch, *2tr-cl, 1 ch, rep from * eight (10:10) times, 1 tr in same ch sp as last st, turn. (nine (11:11) 2tr-cl)
Row 2 (WS): 3 ch, miss first ch sp, *2tr-cl, 1 ch, rep from * across, turn. (eight (10:10) 2tr-cl)
Row 3 (RS): 3 ch, *2tr-cl, 1 ch, rep from * seven (nine:nine) times, 1 tr in same ch sp as last st, turn. (eight (10:10) 2tr-cl)
Row 4 (WS): 3 ch, miss first ch sp, *2tr-cl, 1 ch, rep from * across, turn. (seven (nine:nine) 2tr-cl)

Row 5 (RS): 3 ch, *2tr-cl, 1 ch, rep from *
six (eight:eight) times, 1 tr in same ch sp
as last st, turn. (seven (nine:nine) 2tr-cl)
Row 6 (WS): 3 ch, miss first ch sp, *2tr-cl, 1 ch,
rep from * across, turn. (six (eight:eight) 2tr-cl)
Fasten off.

Right side
Row 1 (RS): Join yarn to 11th (12:14)-ch sp
after row end for left side shaping, 3 ch,
*2tr-cl, 1 ch, rep from * to end, 1 tr, turn.
(nine (11:11) 2tr-cl)
Row 2 (RS): 3 ch, *2tr-cl, 1 ch, rep from *
seven (nine:nine) times, 1 tr into turning ch.
(eight (10:10) 2tr-cl)
Row 3: Work row 2 of Upturned V stitch
pattern.
Row 4: 3 ch, *2 tr-cl, 1 ch, rep from *
six (eight:eight) times, 1 htr into turning ch,
turn. (seven (nine:nine) 2tr-cl)
Row 5: Rep row 3.
Row 6: 3 ch, *2tr-cl, 1 ch, rep from *
five (seven:seven) times, 1 htr into
turning ch, turn. (six (eight:eight) 2tr-cl)
Fasten off.

BACK
Work as front to row 2 of Shape
the armholes.
Rep row 2 until piece measures
19.5 (20.5:21.5)cm/7½ (8:8½)in from
armhole shaping ending on a WS row.

SHAPE THE NECK
Right side
Row 1 (RS): 3 ch, *2tr-cl, 1 ch, rep from *
six (eight:eight) times, 1 tr in same ch sp
as last st, turn. (seven (nine:nine) 2tr-cl)
Row 2 (WS): 3 ch, miss first ch sp, *2tr-cl,
1 ch, rep from * across row, turn.
(six (eight:eight) 2tr-cl)
Fasten off.

Left side
Row 1 (RS): Join yarn to 15 (16:18)th 1-ch sp
after end of left side shaping, 3 ch, *2tr-cl, 1 ch,
rep from * to end, 1 tr, turn.
(seven (nine:nine) 2tr-cl)
Row 2 (WS): 3 ch, *2tr-cl, 1 ch, rep from *
five (seven:seven) times, 1 tr into
turning ch. (six (eight:eight) 2tr-cl)
Fasten off.

SLEEVES (MAKE 2)
Work 68 (72:74) ch.
Row 1: 1 dc in second ch from hook, 1 dc
in each ch to end, turn. (67(71:73)sts)
Row 2: 1 ch, 1 dc in each st to end, turn.
Rep row two a further seven times.
Row 10: 1 ch, 1 dc, *2 dc in next st, 1 dc,
rep from * to end, turn. (100(106:109)sts)

Refer to pp.68–69 for information about
blocking and seaming your finished crochet
garment. When blocking a textured fabric
such as this treble cluster stitch design, it
is best to wet block it.

Row 11: Work row 1 of Upturned V stitch
pattern. (33 (35:36) 2tr-cl)
Row 12: Work row 2 of Upturned V stitch
pattern.
Rep row 12 until piece measures 37 (38:39)cm/
14½ (15:15½)in.
Fasten off.

FINISHING
Block all pieces to size.
With Front and Back body pieces RS
together, seam together along the
shoulder seams, using a ss.

NECKLINE
Round 1: Turn work back so RS is facing,
join yarn at shoulder seam, 1 ch, work dc
evenly around the neckline, front, and back,
working into sides of rows where necessary,
join with a ss, turn.

Round 2: 1 ch, 1 dc in each st around, join
with a ss, turn.
Rep round 2 a further two times.
Fasten off.

ATTACHING SLEEVES
With RS together, using safety pins, pin
sleeves into place on body armholes, seam
together using a ss.

SEAM SIDES
Using a ss, seam together the sides
and sleeves. Weave in all ends.

Double crochet edging makes the garment
tighter around the cuffs and waist for a better
fit. Make sure that you keep an eye on the
tension so that the cuffs still contain
a level of natural elasticity from the yarn.

WOMEN'S LACY CARDIGAN

Level of difficulty

A lightweight, three-quarter-length cardigan in a fine lace pattern, the main body of this pretty garment is worked in one piece. Adjust the length to your size by simply increasing the rows of crochet before shaping.

TECHNIQUES USED Chain stitch **p.26**, Treble crochet **p.44**, Treble crochet increases **p.50**, Shaping **p.50–53**, Blocking and seams **p.68–70**, Double crochet edging **p.86**

WHAT TO WEAR

SIZE
To fit an adult woman S (M:L)

YARN
Rowan Kidsilk Haze Glamour – 25g/162m/177yds (70% mohair and 30% silk with sequins; you can use any 4-ply fine weight yarn to achieve a similar effect)

x 8 (8:9)

HOOK
3.5mm hook

NOTIONS
Yarn needle
2cm (¾in) diameter button

TENSION
32sts x 14 rows per 14cm (5½in)

SPECIAL ABBREVIATIONS
TR2TOGCL: work 2 tr tog over 3sts. (Yrh and insert hook in next st, yrh and draw a loop through, yrh, draw through first two loops on hook) miss next st, (yrh and insert hook in next st, yrh and draw a loop through, yrh draw through first two loops on hook), yrh, and draw through all three loops on hook – 2st decreased.

TR4TOGCL: work 4 tr tog over the next 5sts. Yrh, insert hook in next st, yrh and draw a loop through, yrh and draw through first two loops on hook) twice, miss next st, (yrh, insert hook into the following st, yrh and draw a loop through, yrh and draw through first two loops on hook) twice, yrh, draw through all five loops – 4sts decreased.

➤ PATTERN
The sizes S(M:L) will fit bust 81 (91:102)cm/32 (36:40)in.

BODY
Work 196 (228:260) ch.
Foundation row: Tr2tog (see p.53), working into fifth ch from hook for first st, (1 ch, miss next ch, tr) twice, 1 ch, miss next ch, (2 tr, 1 ch, 2 tr) into the next ch, (1 ch, miss next ch, tr) twice, *1 ch, miss next ch, tr4togcl (see special abbreviations), (1 ch, miss next ch, tr) twice, 1 ch, miss next ch, (2 tr, 1 ch, 2 tr) into next ch, (1 ch, miss next ch, tr) twice, repeat from * to last 4sts, 1 ch, miss next ch, tr3tog (see p.313).
Row 1: 3 ch (counts as a st), tr2tog, (1 ch, miss next st, tr) twice, 1 ch, miss next st, (2 tr, 1 ch, 2 tr) into the next ch, (1 ch, miss next st, tr) twice, *1 ch, miss next st, tr4togcl, (1 ch, miss next st, tr) twice, 1 ch, miss next st (2 tr, 1 ch, 2 tr) into the next ch, (1 ch, miss next st, tr) twice, repeat from * to last 4sts, 1 ch miss next st, tr3tog.
Rows 2–33: Repeat row 1.

DIVIDE FOR ARMS AND NECK SHAPING
Small and large sizes only: Right Front
Row 1: 3 ch (does not count as st), tr2tog, *(1 ch, miss next st, tr) twice, 1 ch, miss next st, (2 tr, 1 ch, 2 tr) into next ch, (1 ch, miss next st, tr) twice, 1 ch, miss next st**, tr4togcl, repeat from * one (two) more times, then from * to ** once, tr3tog, turn. (49(65)sts)
Leave rem sts unworked. Place a stitch marker into base of last st in tr3tog, (these sts will be worked later for Back and Left Front).

Row 2: 3 ch, tr2tog, *(1 ch, miss next st, tr) twice, 1 ch, miss next st, (2 tr, 1 ch, 2 tr) into next ch, (1 ch, miss next st, tr) twice**, 1 ch, miss next st, tr4togcl, repeat from * one (two) more times, then from * to ** once, 1 ch, miss next st, tr2togcl (see special abbreviations).
Row 3: 3 ch, miss next st, tr2tog, *(1 ch, tr, miss next st) twice, 1 ch, (2 tr, 1 ch, 2 tr) into next ch, (1 ch, miss next st, tr) twice, 1 ch**, miss next st, tr4togcl, miss next st, repeat from * one (two) more times, then from * to ** once, tr3tog.
Row 4: 3 ch, tr2tog, *(1 ch, miss the next st, tr) twice, 1 ch, miss next st (2 tr, 1 ch, 2 tr) into next ch, (1 ch, miss next st, tr) twice**, 1 ch, miss next st, tr4togcl, repeat from * one (two) more times, then from * to ** once, miss next st, tr3tog. (48(64)sts)
Row 5: 3 ch, miss next st, tr2tog, 1 ch, miss next st, 1 tr, 1 ch, miss next st, *(2 tr, 1 ch, 2 tr) into next ch, (1 ch, miss next st, tr) twice, 1 ch, miss next st**, tr4togcl, (1 ch, miss next st, 1 tr) twice, 1 ch, repeat from * one (two) times, then from * to ** once, tr3tog. (47(63)sts).
Row 6: 3 ch, tr2tog, *(1 ch, miss next st, tr into the next st) twice, 1 ch, miss next st (2 tr, 1 ch, 2 tr) into the next ch**, (1 ch, miss next st, tr) twice, 1 ch, miss next st, tr4togcl, repeat from * one (two) more times, then from * to ** once, 1 ch, miss next st, tr, miss next st, tr3tog. (46(62)sts)
Row 7: 3 ch, miss next st, tr2tog, 1 ch, * miss next st (2 tr, 1 ch, 2 tr) into next ch, (1 ch, miss next st, tr) twice, 1 ch, miss next st**, tr4togcl, (1 ch, miss next st, 1 tr) twice, 1 ch, repeat from * one (two) times, then from * to ** once, tr3tog. (45(61)sts)
Row 8: 3 ch, tr2tog, *(1 ch, miss next st, tr) twice, 1 ch, miss next st (2 tr, 1 ch, 2 tr) into next ch**, (1 ch, miss next st, tr) twice, 1 ch, miss next st, tr4togcl, repeat from * one (two) more times, then from * to ** once, 1 ch, miss next st, tr3tog.

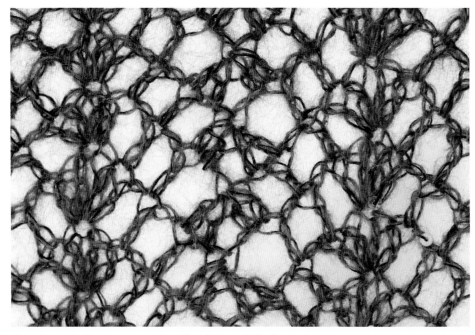

The tr2tog stitches create a series of lacy holes within the crochet, which helps the cardigan fabric to grow quite quickly. Refer to p.313 to decipher the crochet terms used in this pattern.

Row 9: 3 ch, tr2tog, 1 ch, * miss next st (2 tr, 1 ch, 2 tr) into next ch, (1 ch, miss next st, tr) twice, 1 ch, miss next st**, tr4togcl, (1 ch, miss next st, 1 tr) twice, 1 ch, repeat from * one (two) times, then from * to ** once, tr3tog.

Row 10: Repeat row 8.

Row 11: Repeat row 9.

Row 12: Repeat row 8.

Row 13: 3 ch, miss next st, tr2tog, 1 ch, 2 tr into the next ch, *(1 ch, miss next st, tr) twice, 1 ch, miss next st**, tr4togcl, (1 ch, miss next st, 1 tr) twice, 1 ch, miss next st, (2 tr, 1 ch, 2 tr) into the next st, repeat from * one (two) times, then from * to ** tr3tog. (42(58)sts)

Row 14: 3 ch, tr2tog, *(1 ch, miss next st, tr) twice, 1 ch, miss next st (2 tr, 1 ch, 2 tr) into next ch, (1 ch, miss next st, tr) twice, 1 ch, miss next st, tr4togcl, repeat from * one (two) more times, (1 ch, miss next st, tr) twice, miss next st, tr2tog. (38(54)sts)

Row 15: 3 ch, tr2tog, 1 ch, *tr4togcl, (1 ch, miss next st, 1 tr) twice, 1 ch, miss next st, (2 tr, 1 ch, 2 tr) into the next ch, (1 ch, miss next st, 1 tr) twice, 1 ch, miss next st, repeat from * one (two) times, tr3tog. (35(51)sts)

Row 16: 3 ch, tr2tog, *(1 ch, miss next st, tr) twice, 1 ch, miss next st (2 tr, 1 ch, 2 tr) into next ch, (1 ch, miss next st, tr) twice, 1 ch, miss next st, tr4togcl, repeat from * one (two) more times. (33(49)sts)

Row 17: 3 ch, tr2tog, *(1 ch, miss next st, 1 tr) twice, 1 ch, miss next st, (2 tr, 1 ch, 2 tr) into next st, (1 ch, miss next st, 1 tr) twice, 1 ch, miss next st**, tr4togcl, repeat from * to **, tr3tog.

Row 18: 3 ch, tr2tog, *(1 ch, miss next st, tr) twice, 1 ch, miss next st, (2 tr, 1 ch, 2 tr) into next ch, (1 ch, miss next st, tr) twice, 1 ch, miss next st**, tr4togcl, repeat from * zero (one) times, then from * to ** once, tr3tog.

Large size only

Row 19: Repeat row 17.

Row 20: Repeat row 18.

Medium size only: Right Front

Row 1: 3 ch, tr2tog, *(1 ch, miss next st, tr) twice, 1 ch, miss next st** (2 tr, 1 ch, 2 tr) into the next ch, (1 ch, miss next st, tr) twice, 1 ch, miss next st, tr4togcl, repeat from * twice, then from * to ** once, 3 tr into the next ch. (57sts)
Leave rem sts unworked. Place a stitch marker into base of third tr, these stitches will be worked later for Back and Left Front.

Row 2: 3 ch (counts as a st), 2 tr into base st, *(1 ch, miss next st, tr) twice, 1 ch, miss next st**, tr4togcl, (1 ch, miss next st, tr) twice, 1 ch, miss next st, (2 tr, 1 ch, 2 tr) into next ch, repeat from * twice, then from * to ** once, tr2togcl.

Row 3: 3 ch, miss next st, tr2tog, *(1 ch, tr, miss next st) twice, 1 ch, miss next st**,

(2 tr, 1 ch, 2 tr) into next ch, (1 ch, miss next st, tr) twice, 1 ch, miss next st, tr4togcl, repeat from * twice, then from * to ** once, 3 tr into last st.

Row 4: 3 ch, 2 tr into base st, *(1 ch, miss next st, tr) twice**, 1 ch, miss next st, tr4togcl, (1 ch, miss next st, tr) twice, 1 ch, miss next st (2 tr, 1 ch, 2 tr) into next ch, repeat from * twice, then from * to ** once, tr3tog.

Row 5: 3 ch, miss next st, tr2tog, 1 ch, miss next st, 1 tr, 1 ch, miss next st *(2 tr, 1 ch, 2 tr) into next ch, (1 ch, miss next st, tr) twice, 1 ch, miss next st, tr4togcl, (1 ch, miss next st, 1 tr) twice, 1 ch, repeat from * twice, 3 tr into last st.

Row 6: 3 ch, 2 tr into base st, *(1 ch, miss next st, tr) twice, 1 ch, miss next st, tr4togcl, (1 ch, miss next st, tr) twice, 1 ch, miss next st, (2 tr, 1 ch, 2 tr) into next ch, repeat from * twice, 1 ch, miss next st, tr, miss next st, tr3tog.

Row 7: 3 ch, miss next st, tr2tog, 1 ch, * miss next st, (2 tr, 1 ch, 2 tr) into next ch, (1 ch, miss next st, tr) twice, 1 ch, miss next st, tr4togcl, (1 ch, miss next st, 1 tr) twice, 1 ch, repeat from * twice, 3 tr into last st.

Row 8: 3 ch, 2 tr into base st, *(1 ch, miss next st, tr) twice, 1 ch, miss next st, tr4togcl, (1 ch, miss next st, tr) twice, 1 ch, miss next st (2 tr, 1 ch, 2 tr) into next ch, repeat from * twice, 1 ch, miss next st, tr3tog.

Row 9: 3 ch, tr2tog, 1 ch, * miss next st (2 tr, 1 ch, 2 tr) into next ch, (1 ch, miss next st, tr) twice, 1 ch, miss next st, tr4togcl, (1 ch, miss next st, 1 tr) twice, 1 ch, repeat from * twice, 3 tr into last st.

Row 10: Repeat row 8.

Row 11: Repeat row 9.

Row 12: Repeat row 8.

Row 13: 3 ch, miss next st, tr2tog, 1 ch, 2 tr into next ch, *(1 ch, miss next st, tr) twice, 1 ch, miss next st, tr4togcl, (1 ch, miss next st, 1 tr) twice, 1 ch, miss next st**, (2 tr, 1 ch, 2 tr) into next ch, repeat from * once, then from * to ** once, 3 tr into last st.

Row 14: 3 ch, 2 tr into base st, *(1 ch, miss next st, tr) twice, 1 ch, miss next st, tr4togcl**, (1 ch, miss next st, tr) twice, 1 ch, miss next st (2 tr, 1 ch, 2 tr) into the next ch, repeat from * once, then from * to ** once, (1 ch, miss next st, tr) twice, miss next st, tr2tog.

Row 15: 3 ch, tr2tog, 1 ch, *tr4togcl, (1 ch, miss next st, 1 tr) twice, 1 ch, miss next st**, (2 tr, 1 ch, 2 tr) into the next ch, (1 ch, miss next st, 1 tr) twice, 1 ch, miss next st, repeat from * once, then from * to ** once, 3 tr into the last st.

Row 16: 3 ch, 2 tr into base st, *(1 ch, miss next st, tr) twice, 1 ch, miss next st, tr4togcl**, (1 ch, miss next st, tr) twice, 1 ch, miss next st, (2 tr, 1 ch, 2 tr) into next ch, repeat from * once, then from * to ** once.

Row 17: 3 ch, tr2tog, *(1 ch, miss next st, 1 tr) twice, 1 ch, miss next st**, (2 tr, 1 ch, 2 tr) into the next ch, (1 ch, miss next st, 1 tr) twice, 1 ch, miss next st, tr4togcl, repeat from * once, then from * to ** once, 3 tr into the last st.

Row 18: 3 ch, 2 tr into base st, *(1 ch, miss next st, tr) twice, 1 ch, miss next st**, tr4togcl, (1 ch, miss next st, tr) twice, 1 ch, miss next st (2 tr, 1 ch, 2 tr) into the next ch, repeat from * once, then from * to ** once, tr3tog.

Row 19: Repeat row 17.

Row 20: Repeat row 18.

BACK

With right sides facing, rejoin yarn to main Body at stitch marker and work as follows:

Small and large sizes only

Row 1: 3 ch (counts as st), tr2tog, *(1 ch, miss next st, tr) twice, 1 ch, miss next st, (2 tr, 1 ch, 2 tr) into next st, (1 ch, miss next st, tr) twice, 1 ch, miss next st**, tr4togcl, repeat from * four (six) times, then from * to ** once, tr3tog.

Medium size only

Row 1: 3 ch (counts as st), 2 tr into the base of 3 ch, *(1 ch, miss next st, tr) twice, 1 ch miss next st, tr4togcl, (1 ch, miss next st, tr) twice, 1 ch, miss next st**, (2 tr, 1 ch, 2 tr), repeat from * five times, then from * to ** once, 3 tr into the next st.

All sizes

Place marker at the base of last st. Repeat row 1 until back measures the same as the front. (18 (20:20) rows)

Left Front

Rejoin yarn to point at stitch marker and work as for Right Front, reversing all shaping.

SLEEVES

Work 84 (100:100) ch.

Foundation row: Tr2tog, working into fifth ch from hook for the first st, *(1 ch, miss next ch, tr) twice, 1 ch, miss next ch, (2 tr, 1 ch, 2 tr) into the next ch, (1 ch, miss next ch, tr) twice, 1 ch, miss next ch**, tr4togcl, repeat from * four (five:five) times, then from * to ** once, tr3tog.

Row 1: 3 ch, tr2tog, *(1 ch, miss next st, tr) twice, 1 ch, miss next st, (2 tr, 1 ch, 2 tr) into next st, (1 ch, miss next st, tr) twice*, 1 ch, miss next st**, tr4togcl, repeat from * four (five:five) times, then from * to ** once, tr3tog.

Repeat row 1, 36 (38:40) more times.

EDGING

For edging starting at the highest ripple point: *1 ch, miss next st, 1 dc, 1 ch, miss next st, 1 htr, 1 ch, miss next 3 sts, (2 tr, 1 ch, 2 tr) into the next st, 1 ch, miss next 3sts, 1 htr, 1 ch, miss next st, 1 dc, 1 ch, miss next st, ss into the next st (highest point of ripple), repeat from * to end.

For edging starting at the lowest ripple point: 3 ch, 2 tr into base of ch, 1 ch, miss next 3sts, 1 htr, 1 ch, miss next st, 1 dc, 1 ch, miss next st, ss into next st (highest point of ripple), then repeat as for edging starting at highest ripple point to end.

FINISHING

Work edging along top shoulders and back to even stitches before sewing shoulder seams. Set in sleeves. Work edging along the cuffs. With wrong side facing, dc evenly along left front edge, neckline, and down right front edge, 1 ch, turn, dc along whole row again. Repeat the last row, working one buttonhole on right front edge of row 34 as follows: dc to buttonhole point, 2 ch, miss next 2 dc, dc. Continue in dc to the end of the row, 1 ch, work 1 further row. Edge bottom of cardigan.

Fasten off, weave in all ends, and sew on button.

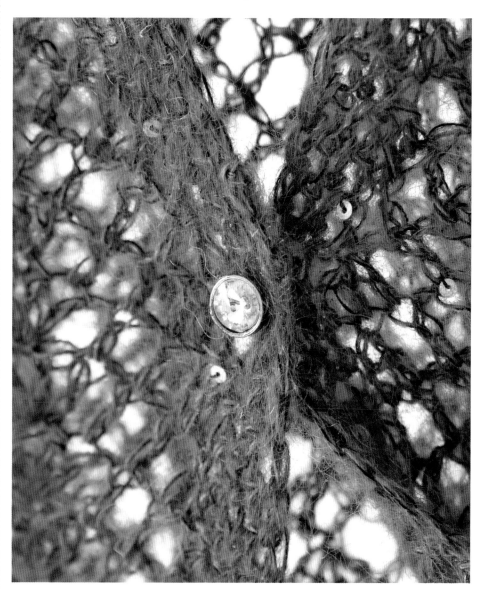

This classic-style cardigan has just one button fastening. Choose a mother-of-pearl wood button that will co-ordinate with the colour of your yarn. Attach it firmly with a strand of 4-ply yarn or matching thread.

TOYS

From the super-cuteness of amigurumi animals to other irresistibly cuddly creatures, little ones (and many grown-ups, too) will be delighted with these adorable toys.

ANIMAL RATTLES

These bright and colourful rattles will delight any young baby. The double crochet stitch makes the toy robust and durable for lots of cheerful play. Change the character of each rattle by choosing a different animal's face.

Level of difficulty

TECHNIQUES USED Double crochet **p.34**, Shaping **p.50–52**, Working in the round **p.56**, Making a simple adjustable ring **p.57**, Toy techniques **p.132–33**

SIZE
12cm (5in)

YARN
Rico Design Essential Cotton DK – 50g/ 130m/142yds (100% mercerized cotton; you can use any DK weight cotton yarn for a similar effect)

A x 1   B x 1   C x 1   D x 1   E x 1

HOOK
3mm hook

NOTIONS
Stitch marker
Yarn needle
Black and pink embroidery thread and needle
Toy stuffing
Soft toy bell (to place inside the rattle)

TENSION
Exact tension is not essential

SPECIAL ABBREVIATIONS
Adjustable ring: Wind the yarn twice around your finger. Insert the hook and wrap the yarn around it. Pull the hook back through and work a chain. Work the first round of sts into the "ring", then pull the tail of yarn gently to close it, before joining the sts into a round using a ss.

PATTERN: DOG RATTLE

Note: Work in continuous spirals unless pattern states otherwise. Mark the end of the round with a st marker, and move it up as you work.

Round 1: With yarn A, make an adjustable ring with 6 dc. (6sts)
Round 2: 2 dc into each st. (12sts)
Round 3: *1 dc, work 2 dc into next st; rep from * around. (18sts)
Round 4: *2 dc, work 2 dc into next st; rep from * around. (24sts)
Round 5: *3 dc, work 2 dc into next st; rep from * around. (30sts)
Rounds 6–9: Dc around. (30sts)
Round 10: *3 dc, dc2tog; rep from * around. (24sts)
Round 11: *2 dc, dc2tog; rep from * around. (18sts)
Rounds 12–14: With yarn B, dc around. (18sts)
Rounds 15–17: With yarn C, dc around. (18sts)
Rounds 18–20: With yarn B, dc around. (18sts)
Rounds 21–23: With yarn C, dc around. (18sts)
Rounds 24–26: With yarn B, dc around. (18sts)

Round 27: With yarn A, *2 dc, work 2 dc into next st; rep from * around. (24sts)
Round 28: *3 dc, work 2 dc into next st; rep from * around. (30sts)
Rounds 29–32: Dc around. (30sts)
Round 33: *3 dc, dc2tog; rep from * around. (24sts)
Place a small bell in the base of the rattle and stuff the rattle firmly before continuing with the crochet.
Round 34: *2 dc, dc2tog; rep from * around. (18sts)
Round 35: *1 dc, dc2tog; rep from * around. (12sts)
Round 36: *dc2tog; rep from * around. (6sts)
Using a yarn needle gather the last 6sts together. Fasten off, weave in ends.

EARS (MAKE 2)
Round 1: With yarn A, make an adjustable ring with 4 dc. (4sts)
Round 2: 2 dc into each st. (8sts)
Rounds 3–4: Dc around. (8sts)
Round 5: *2 dc, dc2tog; rep from * around. (6sts)
Rounds 6–7: Dc around. (6sts)
Ss to join. Fasten off, weave in ends.

FINISHING
Sew ears firmly to either side of rattle head. Embroider nose and eyes with black thread.

The mouse's ears are made from two different-coloured pieces of crocheted fabric. Once both are complete, place the shapes wrong sides together and work a series of double crochet stitches in the head colour around them both to create the edging.

Keep your tension even when working each round. This will ensure a firm, close-knit fabric. To stuff each rattle, push the toy stuffing gently with your index finger to the base of the animal, then complete the design by crocheting its head and ears.

Each animal's eyes, nose, and mouth are sewn with six strands of black and pink embroidery thread. Bend the earflap of the dog downwards and secure it with a small stitch from underneath the ear to the side of the dog's head.

PATTERN: CAT RATTLE

Repeat main pattern for rattle, replacing the colours with C, D, and B in that sequence.

EARS (MAKE 2)
Round 1: With yarn C, make an adjustable ring with 4 dc. (4sts)
Round 2: * 1 dc, 2 dc into next st; rep from * around. (6sts)
Round 3: * 2 dc, 2 dc into next st; rep from * around. (8sts)
Ss to join and fasten off. Weave in ends.

FINISHING
Sew ears firmly to either side of rattle head. Embroider nose, whiskers, and eyes with black yarn.

PATTERN: MOUSE RATTLE

Repeat main pattern for rattle, replacing the colours with D, E, and A in that sequence.

EAR FRONT (MAKE 2)
Round 1: With yarn A, make an adjustable ring with 8 dc. (8sts)
Round 2: Work 2 dc into each st. (16sts)
Round 3: * 1 dc, 2 dc into next st; rep from * around. (24sts)
Ss to join and fasten off. Weave in ends.

EAR BACK (MAKE 2)
Round 1: With yarn D, make an adjustable ring with 8 dc. (8sts)
Round 2: Work 2 dc into each st. (16sts)
Round 3: * 1 dc, 2 dc into next st; rep from * around. (24sts)
Ss to join and fasten off. Weave in ends.

FINISHING
Take one ear front and ear back and place wrong sides together, using yarn D and with the ear front facing, dc both sides of the ear together. Ss to join and fasten off, weave in ends. Sew ears firmly to either side of rattle head. Embroider nose with pink thread and whiskers and eyes with black thread.

GIANT PLAY BALL

This cute toddler's ball is made up of hexagons and pentagons stitched together three dimensionally. If filling the ball with toy stuffing, first place the stuffing in a white pillowcase or lining so that it doesn't poke through.

TECHNIQUES USED Treble crochet **p.44**, Working in the round **p.56,** Overcast stitch (or whip stitch) seam **p.68**, Working into a chain space **p.75**, Clusters **p.77**

SIZE
Large ball: 74cm (29in) in circumference;
   Small ball: 35cm (13¾in) in
   circumference

YARN
Rico Design Baby Cotton Soft DK – 50g/
   125m/137yds (50% acrylic and 50%
   cotton; you can use any DK weight,
   machine-washable yarn)

A x 1   **B** x 1   **C** x 1   **D** x 1

HOOK
4mm hook

NOTIONS
Yarn needle
Toy stuffing or foam football

TENSION
Exact tension is not essential

SPECIAL ABBREVIATIONS
Cluster: See p.77
Puff: See p.144

PATTERN

HEXAGON (MAKE 20 FOR LARGE BALL)
Note: Work all hexagons in stripes of random colour and all pentagons in solid colours.

Work 4 ch, ss in first ch to form a ring.
Round 1: 3 ch, (cluster into ring, 2 ch) six times. 6cl. Change colour, attaching new colour to any 2-ch sp.
Round 2: 2 ch, (1 puff, 2 ch, 1 puff) into each 2-ch sp, join round with a ss into top of first ch.Change colour, attaching new colour to any 2-ch sp.
Round 3: 3 ch, 2 tr into 2-ch sp, *3 tr into sp between next 2 puffs, (3 tr, 3 ch, 3 tr) into next 2-ch sp; rep from * ending with (3 tr, 3 ch) back into first 2-ch sp, join round with a ss to top of third ch.
Fasten off yarn.

PENTAGON (MAKE 12)
Work 4 ch, ss in first ch to form a ring.
Round 1: 3 ch, (cl into ring, 2ch) five times. (five clusters)
Round 2: 2 ch, (1 puff, 2 ch, 1 puff) into each 2-ch sp, join round with a ss into top of first ch.
Round 3: 3 ch, 2 tr into 2-ch sp, *3 tr into sp between next 2 puffs, (3 tr, 3 ch, 3 tr) into next 2-ch sp; rep from * ending with (3 tr, 3 ch) back into first 2-ch sp, join round with a ss to top of third ch.
Fasten off yarn.

FINISHING
Block pieces lightly. If making a large ball, sew all pieces together three dimensionally, using whip stitch (see p.66), with five hexagons around each pentagon; the ball will take shape organically, pulling into a sphere. When there are only a few shapes left to attach, stuff the ball and join remaining pieces. For a small ball, sew only 12 pentagons together in the same way as the large ball, making two sets of five pentagons around a central pentagon. Sew together to form a sphere.

MOTHER ELEPHANT AND BABY

Level of difficulty ✱✱✱

These mother and baby elephants are worked simply in the round, the head and body in one piece and the legs, ears, and tail worked and attached separately. Turn to pp.132–133 for information about assembling crocheted toys.

TECHNIQUES USED Slip stitch **p.28**, Double crochet **p.34**, Shaping **p.50–52**, Making a simple adjustable ring **p.57**, Toy techniques **p.132–33**

TOYS

SIZE
Mother: approx 13 x 8.5cm (5¼ x 3¼in);
 Baby: approx 10 x 7cm (4 x 2¾in)

YARN
Wendy Merino Pure Ultra Soft DK – 50g/
 116m/127yds (100% super soft merino
 wool; any DK weight yarn will
 substitute here. Wool and acrylic fibres
 will work well)

A x 1   **B** x 1

HOOK
4mm hook

NOTIONS
Black safety toy eyes, buttons, or black
 embroidery thread and needle
Toy stuffing
Yarn needle

TENSION
Exact tension is not essential

SPECIAL ABBREVIATIONS
Adjustable ring: Wind the yarn twice
 around your finger. Insert the hook
 and wrap the yarn around it. Pull the
 hook back through and work a chain.
 Work the first round of sts into the
 "ring", then pull the tail of yarn gently
 to close it, before joining the sts into
 a round using a ss.

❯ PATTERN: MOTHER ELEPHANT
Work the stitches fairly tightly to create
a firm-textured fabric and conceal
the stuffing.

HEAD AND BODY
Round 1: Work 6 dc in an adjustable ring.
Round 2: 2 dc in each st around. (12sts)
Round 3: *2 dc in next st, dc in next st,
repeat from * to end. (18sts)
Round 4: *2 dc in next st, dc in next 2sts,
repeat from * to end. (24sts)
Rounds 5–15: Dc in each st around.
Round 16: 2 dc in each of the next 6sts,
dc in last 18sts. (30sts)
Round 17: *2 dc in next st, dc in next st,
repeat from * five times, dc in last 18sts.
(36sts)
Round 18: *2 dc in next st, dc in next 2sts,
repeat from * five times, dc in last 18sts.
(42sts)
Round 19: Dc in each st around.
Round 20: Dc in next 24sts, *dc2tog, dc in
next 4sts, repeat from * to end. (39sts)
Round 21: Dc in next 24sts, *dc2tog, dc in
next 3sts, repeat from * to end. (36sts)
Round 22: Dc in next 24sts, *dc2tog, dc in
next 2sts, repeat from * to end. (33sts)
Round 23: Dc in next 24sts, *dc2tog, dc in
next st, repeat from * to end. (30sts)
Round 24: Dc in next 24sts, *dc2tog, repeat
from * to end. (27sts)
Round 25: *dc2tog, dc in next 2sts, repeat
from * five times, 2 dc in each of next
3sts. (24sts)
Round 26: *dc2tog, dc in next st, repeat
from * five times, dc in last 6sts. (18sts)
Begin to stuff the body firmly and attach
the safety eyes, if you are using them. If
using buttons or embroidering eyes, this is
done on completion of the toy. Continue to

stuff as your work progresses. The trunk is
quite small, so add stuffing little and often,
and pull decreasing stitches (dc2tog) quite
tight to avoid gaps.
Round 27: *dc2tog, repeat from * five times,
dc in last 6sts. (12sts)
Round 28: *dc2tog, dc in next 2sts, repeat
from * to end. (9sts)
Rounds 29–36: Dc in each st around.
Round 37: Dc2tog, dc in last 7sts. (8sts)
Round 38: Dc2tog, dc in last 6sts. (7sts)
Round 39: Dc2tog, dc in last 5sts. (6sts)
Fasten off.

EARS (MAKE 2)
Work rounds 1–4 of the Head and body.
(24sts)
Round 5: *2 dc in next st, dc in next 3sts,
repeat from * to end. (30sts)
Fasten off.

FRONT LEGS (MAKE 2)
Work rounds 1 and 2 of Head and body,
as above. (12sts)
Round 3: Dc TBL of each st around.
Rounds 4–12: dc in each st around.
Fasten off.

BACK LEGS (MAKE 2)
Work rounds 1–3 of Front legs, as above.
(12sts)
Rounds 4–10: Dc in each st around.
Fasten off.

TAIL
Work 9 ch.
Row 1: Ss in fourth chain from hook, ch 3,
ss in same chain, ch 3, ss in same chain.
Fasten off.
Sew legs, ears, and tail to body with a yarn
needle, and weave in ends.

The cute ears are folded and sewn closed along the turning edges, and then stitched to the baby elephant's head.

PATTERN: BABY ELEPHANT

As with the mother elephant, work the stitches tightly to create a firm-textured fabric and conceal the stuffing.

HEAD AND BODY

Round 1: Work 6 dc in an adjustable ring.
Round 2: 2 dc in each st around. (12sts)
Round 3: *2 dc in next st, dc in next st, repeat from * to end. (18sts)
Rounds 4–10: Dc in each st around.
Round 11 2 dc in next 4sts, dc in last 14sts. (22sts)
Round 12: *2 dc in next st, dc in next st, repeat from * three times, dc in last 14sts. (26sts)
Round 13: *2 dc in next st, dc in next 2sts, repeat from * three times, dc in last 14sts. (30sts)
Round 14: *2 dc in next st, dc in next 3sts, repeat from * three times, dc in last 14sts. (34sts)
Round 15: Dc in each st around.
Round 16: Dc in next 19sts, *dc2tog, dc in next 3sts, repeat from * to end. (31sts)
Round 17: Dc in next 19sts, *dc2tog, dc in next 2sts, repeat from * to end. (28sts)
Round 18: Dc in next 19sts, *dc2tog, dc in next st, repeat from * to end. (25sts)
Round 19: Dc in next 19sts, *dc2tog, repeat from * to end. (22sts)
Round 20: *dc2tog , dc in next 4sts, repeat from * two times, dc in last 4sts. (19sts)
Round 21: *dc2tog, dc in next 3sts, repeat from * two times, dc in last 4sts. (16sts)
Begin to stuff the body firmly and attach the safety eyes, if you are using them. If using buttons or embroidering eyes this is done on completion of the toy. Continue to stuff as your work progresses; as with the mother elephant, the trunk is quite small so add stuffing little and often, and pull decreasing stitches (dc2tog) quite tight to avoid gaps.
Round 22: *dc2tog , dc in next 2sts, repeat from * two times, dc in last 4sts. (13sts)
Round 23: *dc2tog, dc in next st, repeat from * two times, dc in last 4sts. (10sts)
Round 24: *dc2tog, dc in next 3sts, repeat from * to end. (8sts)
Rounds 25–27: Dc in each st around.
Round 28: Dc2tog, dc in last 6sts. (7sts)
Fasten off.

EARS (MAKE 2)

Round 1: Work 6 dc in an adjustable ring, turn, ch 1.
Round 2: 2 dc in each st, turn, ch 1. (12sts)
Round 3: 2 dc in each st. (24sts)
Fasten off.
Fold ear in half and join along turning edges, attach to head.

LEGS (MAKE 4)

Round 1: Work 6 dc in an adjustable ring.
Round 2: *2 dc in next st, dc in next 2sts, repeat from * to end. (8sts)
Rounds 3–7: Dc in each st around.
Fasten off.

FINISHING

Sew legs to the body firmly with a yarn needle, secure yarn, and weave in all ends.

TAIL

To make tail, after sewing on a back leg, take the end of the yarn through the elephant's bottom, make a knot about 1.5cm (½in) from the body and cut the wool after this, leaving about 1cm (¼in) to fluff out the fibres.

The elephant mum's tail is a chain with slip stitches to form a tuft. Her baby's tail is simply a knotted length of yarn.

RAG DOLL

This crocheted version of the traditional rag doll will soon become your child's best friend. Strands of yarn are used to make her hair, while her stockings, pretty dress, and matching shoes are all integral parts of the toy.

TECHNIQUES USED Double crochet **p.34**, Shaping **p.50–52**, Working in the round **p.56**, Making a simple adjustable ring **p.57**, Toy techniques **p.132–33**

SIZE
30 x 12cm (12 x 5in)

YARN
Sirdar Double Crêpe DK – 50g/135m/
  148yds (55% acrylic and 45% nylon;
  you can use any DK weight yarn)

A x 2 **B** x 1 **C** x 1 **D** x 1 **E** x 1

HOOK
3.5mm hook

NOTIONS
Two stitch markers
Yarn needle
15mm (½in) black safety toy eyes
Black and red embroidery thread
  and needle
Blue ribbon
Toy stuffing

TENSION
Exact tension is not essential

SPECIAL ABBREVIATIONS
Adjustable ring: See p.134
Bobble stitch: Yrh, insert hook in stitch,
  yrh, draw loop through, yrh, draw
  through two loops on the hook, *yrh,
  insert hook in same space, yrh, draw
  loop through, yrh, draw through two loops
  on hook; repeat from * four times, yrh,
  draw through all six loops on hook.

PATTERN
The head and body are worked together
in one piece.

HEAD AND BODY
With yarn A, make an adjustable ring and
work 6 dc into the ring. (6sts)
Round 1: 2 dc into each st to the end. (12sts)
Round 2: *1 dc, 2 dc in next st; repeat
from * to end. (18sts)
Round 3: *2 dc, 2 dc in next st; repeat
from * to end. (24sts)
Round 4: *3 dc, 2 dc in next st; repeat
from * to end. (30sts)
Round 5: *9 dc, 2 dc in next st; repeat
from * to end. (33sts)
Round 6: *10 dc, 2 dc in next st; repeat
from * to end. (36sts)
Round 7: *11 dc, 2 dc in next st; repeat
from * to end. (39sts)
Round 8: *12 dc, 2 dc in next st; repeat
from * to end. (42sts)
Round 9: *13 dc, 2 dc in next st; repeat
from * to end. (45sts)
Round 10: *14 dc, 2 dc in next st; repeat
from * to end. (48sts)
Round 11: *15 dc, 2 dc in next st; repeat
from * to end. (51sts)
Round 12: *16 dc, 2 dc in next st; repeat
from * to end. (54sts)
Place two stitch markers on the next row,
12sts apart, to mark where you will put
the toy eyes.
Rounds 13–14: Dc in each st to the end.
Round 15: *dc2tog, 7 dc; repeat from *
to end. (48sts)
Round 16: *dc2tog, 6 dc; repeat from *
to end. (42sts)
Round 17: *dc2tog, 5 dc ; repeat from *
to end. (36sts)
Round 18: *dc2tog, 4 dc; repeat from *
to end. (30sts)
Round 19: *dc2tog; repeat from *
to end. (15sts)

Put your working loop on a stitch holder
and attach the toy eyes to your head in the
places you marked on round 13. Stuff the
head with toy stuffing. Put your working
loop back on the hook and continue.
Round 20: *4 dc, 2 dc in next st; repeat
from * to end. (18sts)
Round 21: Dc in each st to end.
Round 22: *5 dc, 2 dc in next st; repeat
from * to end. (21sts)
Round 23: Dc in each st to end.
Round 24: *6 dc, 2 dc in next st; repeat
from * to end. (24sts)
Round 25: Dc in each st to end.
Round 26: *7 dc, 2 dc in next st; repeat
from * to end. (27sts)
Round 27: Dc in each st to end.
Round 28: *8 dc, 2 dc in next st; repeat
from * to end. (30sts)
Round 29: Dc in each st to end.
Round 30: *9 dc, 2 dc in next st; repeat
from * to end. (33sts)
Round 31: Dc in each st to end.
Round 32: *10 dc, 2 dc in next st; repeat
from * to end. (36sts)
Round 33: Dc in each st to end.
Change to yarn D at the end of this round.
Round 34: *dc2tog, 10 dc; repeat from *
to end. (33sts)
Round 35: *dc2tog, 9 dc; repeat from *
to end. (30sts)
Round 36: *dc2tog, 3 dc; repeat from *
to end. (24sts)
Round 37: *dc2tog, 2 dc; repeat from *
to end. (18sts)
Round 38: *dc2tog, 1 dc; repeat from *
to end. (12sts)
Round 39: *dc2tog; repeat from * to
end. (6sts)
Cut the yarn, leaving a long tail, and pull
through loop to secure.
Do not stuff the body of the doll yet.

ARMS (MAKE 2)

Note: Stuff the arms as you go along.
With yarn A, make an adjustable ring
and work 6 dc into the ring. (6sts)
Round 1: 2 dc into each st to end. (12sts)
Round 2: *1 dc, 2 dc in next st; repeat
from * to end. (18sts)
Round 3: *5 dc, 2 dc in next st; repeat
from * to end. (21sts)
Round 4: Dc in each st to end. (21sts)
Round 5: *dc2tog, 5 dc; repeat from *
to end. (18sts)
Round 6: Bobble stitch in first st, dc in
each st to end.
Round 7: *dc2tog, 4 dc; repeat from *
to end. (15sts)
Round 8: *dc2tog, 3 dc; repeat from *
to end. (12sts)
Rounds 9–18: Dc in each st to end.
Round 19: Dc2tog, dc in each st to
end. (11sts)
Rounds 20–24: Dc in each st to end.
Round 25: Dc2tog, dc in each st to
end. (10sts)
Rounds 26–30: Dc in each st to the
end. (10sts)
Cut the yarn, leaving a long tail, and
pull through loop to secure.
Finish stuffing the arm firmly.
Thread the cut yarn onto a yarn needle
and weave through the last 10sts, pull
the yarn to close the hole at the top
of the arm, weave in yarn to secure.

LEGS (MAKE 2)

Note: Stuff the legs as you go along.
With yarn B, make an adjustable ring
and work 6 dc into the ring. (6sts)
Round 1: 2 dc into each st to the end. (12sts)
Round 2: 2 dc, 2 dc in the next st, 2 dc,
3 htr in the next st, 2 htr, 3 htr in the next
st, 2 dc, 2 dc in the last st. (18sts)
Round 3: 3 dc, 2 dc in the next st, 2 dc,
1 htr, 2 htr in the next st, 4 htr, 2 htr in the
next st, 1 htr, 1 dc, 2 dc in the next st, dc
in the last 2sts. (22sts)
Round 4: 2 dc in the first st, 8 dc, 3 htr in
the next st, 5 htr, 3 htr in the next st, dc
in the last 6sts. (27sts)
Round 5: Dc in each st to the end.
Round 6: 1 dc, dc2tog, 8 dc, dc2tog, 6 dc,
dc2tog, dc in the last 6sts. (24sts)
Round 7: 11 dc, htr3tog, 3 htr, htr3tog, dc
in the last 4sts. (20sts)
Round 8: 3 dc, dc2tog, 4 dc, dc2tog, 1 dc,
dc2tog, 1 dc, dc2tog, dc in the last 3sts. (16sts)
Round 9: 8 dc, dc2tog, 1 dc, dc2tog, dc in
the last 3sts. (14sts)
Round 10: Dc in each st to the end.
Round 11: Dc2tog, dc in each st to
end. (13sts)

Change to yarn D at the end of the row and
start stripe pattern. Work two rounds D
and two rounds C; repeat to round 33 then
work one round (34) in D.
Rounds 12–16: Dc in each st to the end.
Round 17: Dc2tog, dc in each st to the
end. (12sts)
Rounds 18–22: Dc in each st to the end.
Round 23: Dc2tog, dc in each st to the
end. (11sts)
Rounds 24–28: Dc in each st to the end.
Round 29: Dc2tog, dc in each st to the
end. (10sts)
Rounds 30–34: Dc in each st to the end.
Cut the yarn, leaving a long tail, and pull
through loop to secure.
Finish stuffing the leg firmly.
Thread the cut yarn onto a yarn needle and
weave through the last 10sts, pull the yarn
to close the hole at the top of the leg. Leave
the tail of yarn in place to sew onto the
body later.

DRESS

With yarn B, ch 21, ss into start of chain to
form a loop. (21sts)
Round 1: *6 dc, 2 dc in next st; repeat from *
to end. (24sts)
Round 2: Dc in each st to end.
Round 3: *7 dc, 2 dc in next st; repeat from *
to end. (27sts)
Round 4: Dc in each st to end.
Round 5: *8 dc, 2 dc in next st; repeat
from * to end. (30sts)
Round 6: Dc in each st to end.
Round 7: *9 dc, 2 dc in next st; repeat
from * to end. (33sts)

Thread the ribbon through the eyelet spaces
created in the crochet fabric that forms the
doll's skirt. A satin ribbon will give a pretty
sheen, while a matt ribbon will be more
muted. Tie a double bow if your doll is being
made for a child under 36 months.

Rounds 8–9: Dc in each st to end.
Round 10: *10 dc, 2 dc in next st; repeat
from * to end. (36sts)
Round 11: Dc in each st to end.
The next two rounds create the holes
for the ribbon to go through.
Round 12: *ch 2, miss 1st, dc in next st;
repeat from * to end.
Round 13: *dc in the ch sp, dc in next st;
repeat from * to end.
Round 14: *5 dc, 2 dc in next st; repeat
from * to end. (42sts)
Round 15: *6 dc, 2 dc in next st; repeat
from * to end. (48sts)
Round 16: *3 dc, 2 dc in next st; repeat
from * to end. (60sts)
Cut the yarn, leaving a long tail, and pull
through loop to secure.
Place the dress over the body of the doll
so that the top of it sits on the third round
at the top of the body.
Stuff the body of the doll now.
Thread the cut yarn from the body of the
doll onto a yarn needle and weave through
the last six stitches at the base, pull the
yarn to close the hole. Weave in yarn to
secure and cut off any loose ends.

DRESS SLEEVES (MAKE 2)

With yarn B, make an adjustable ring and
work 6 dc into the ring. (6sts)
Round 1: *1 dc, 2 dc in next st; repeat from *
to end. (9sts)
Round 2: *2 dc, 2 dc in next st; repeat from *
to end. (12sts)
Rounds 3–6: Dc in each st to end.
Cut the yarn, leaving a long tail, and pull
through loop to secure.
Place over the top of the arms, sew in place.
Then sew the arms to the body using the
photo as a guide. Weave in yarn to secure
and cut off any loose ends.

BOOT CUFF (MAKE 2)

With yarn B, ch 16.
Row 1: Dc in the second ch from hook, dc
in each st to the end. (15sts)
Cut the yarn, leaving a long tail, and pull
through loop to secure.
Sew in place around the top of the boots.
Then sew the legs onto the base of the
body. Weave in yarn to secure and cut
off any loose ends.

See below to work the two cuffs on the doll's booties. The main part of each shoe is crocheted as one piece by joining the pink shoe yarn (B) with the blue yarn (D) and continuing in double crochet.

EMBROIDERING THE FACIAL DETAILS

With yarn A, embroider nose by working four or five long stitches in the middle of the round where you placed the eyes. Use black embroidery thread to sew on eyebrows and red embroidery thread to create a V stitch a couple of rounds under the nose to form the mouth. Catch any loose ends to the back of the head (where they won't show), weave in to secure, and cut off.

CREATING THE HAIR

Use an A4-sized piece of card and wrap yarn F around it widthways several times. Cut the strands of yarn in half down the middle of the card. This will give you plenty of pieces of yarn the same length.
To attach to the head, start at the crown, put your crochet hook through one of the stitches on the doll's head, fold a piece of yarn in half, and pick up the loop end of the folded yarn with your hook, and pull part way through your stitch. Thread the cut ends of yarn through the loop you have just created and pull the cut ends to close the knot and attach to the head.
Repeat this process, going round in circles until you have a good covering of hair. Finish off by threading a blue ribbon through the loops on the bottom of the dress and tie with a bow.

The doll's hair is created by first cutting same-sized lengths of yarn and attaching them to her crocheted head (see left). Use yarn A for her nose and give her a jolly smile. Safety toy eyes are available from craft stores or online shops.

AMIGURUMI PENGUIN

Level of difficulty

This super-cute penguin is crocheted in the Japanese amigurumi style. It makes a fun project for any level of crocheter, even a beginner. Soon you'll have a menagerie of adorable crocheted creatures.

TECHNIQUES USED Double crochet **p.34**, Shaping **p.50–52**, Working in the round **p.56**, Making a simple adjustable ring **p.57**, Toy techniques **p.132–33**

TOYS

SIZE
9 x 12cm (3.5 x 4¾in)

YARN
Stylecraft Special DK – 100g/285m/322yds
(100% acrylic; you only need small amounts (approx. 25g) of the yarns B, C, and D)

A x 1   **B** x 1   **C** x 1   **D** x 1

HOOK
3.5mm hook

NOTIONS
Tapestry needle
Stitch marker
Polyester stuffing
2 x 8mm (⅓in) black safety eyes

TENSION
Exact tension is not essential

PATTERN
Note: Work in continuous spirals unless otherwise stated but use a marker in the first stitch to ensure you keep track of each round. All parts of the penguin, start with an adjustable "magic" ring.

EYES (MAKE 2)
Round 1: With yarn C, make an adjustable ring with 6dc. (6sts)
Round 2: 2 dc in each st. (12sts)
Fasten off and weave in ends.

BODY AND HEAD
Round 1: With yarn A, make an adjustable ring with 6dc. (6sts)
Round 2: 2 dc in each st. (12sts)
Round 3: *1dc, 2 dc in next st; repeat from * to end. (18sts)

Round 4: *2dc, 2 dc in next st; repeat from * to end. (24sts)
Round 5: *3dc, 2 dc in next st; repeat from * to end. (30sts)
Round 6: *4dc, 2 dc in next st; repeat from * to end. (36sts)
Round 7: *5dc, 2 dc in next st; repeat from * to end. (42sts)
Round 8: Dc in each st tbl to end.
Rounds 9–19: Dc in each st to end. Change to yarn B.
Round 20: Dc in each st tbl to end.
Rounds 21–25: Dc in each st to end.
Round 26: *dc2tog, 5 dc; repeat from * to end. (36sts)
Round 27: *dc2tog, 4 dc; repeat from * to end. (30sts)
Round 28: *dc2tog, 3 dc; repeat from * to end. (24sts)

Spiralling up Working in spirals is a quick and easy way of working in the round but you can quite easily lose count of where you are due to the small size of the double crochet stitches. Try placing a lockable stitch marker at the beginning of every round and moving it up each round to keep track of your place.

Flappy wings Flatten each wing and hold closed while sewing to the body, to create a flat, flap-like shape. You could slightly curve the top line of the wing when sewing on to create the streamlined shape you'd see on a waddling penguin.

Happy feet Keep the yarn ends on the feet pieces quite long. Use one to sew the feet to the body and stuff the other inside the feet before you sew on to ensure they keep a three-dimensional shape.

Cheeky beak Where the beak is positioned creates this little creature's personality, so sew it on with care. Try curving the edges slightly for a cheeky smile. Keep the yarn ends long; use one to sew the beak onto the face and the other can be stuffed inside.

Round 29: *dc2tog, 2 dc; repeat from * to end. (18sts)
Put your working loop on a stitch holder and attach the white crochet eyes and black safety eyes to the head – use the photograph as a guide. Stuff the body and the head with toy stuffing. Put your working loop back on the hook and continue.
Round 30: *dc2tog, 1 dc; repeat from * to end. (12sts)
Round 31: *dc2tog; repeat from * to end. (6sts)
Fasten off leaving a long tail of yarn. Weave the tail of yarn through the remaining sts to gather the top of the head. Weave in ends.

WINGS (MAKE 2)
Round 1: With yarn A, make an adjustable ring with 4dc. (4sts)
Round 2: 2 dc in each st. (8sts)
Round 3: *1dc, 2 dc in next st; repeat from * to end. (12sts)
Round 4: *2dc, 2 dc in next st; repeat from * to end. (16sts)
Rounds 5-9: Dc in each st to end.
Fasten off and leave a tail of yarn.
Fold each wing in half.

BEAK AND FEET
Make 2 in yarn B for the feet and 1 in yarn D for the beak.
Round 1: Make an adjustable ring with 6dc. (6sts)
Round 2: *1dc, 2 dc in next st; repeat from * to end. (9sts)

Round 3: Dc in each st to end.
Fasten off and leave a tail of yarn.
Fold in half.

FINISHING
Sew each wing firmly to the body at the neck edge. Sew the feet firmly at the bottom edge of the body. Sew the beak to the head, using the photograph as a guide.

Eyes up close Position the eyes quite wide apart and low down on the penguin's head to make it even cuter. Use the long yarn ends from the white eyes to sew them to the face. Insert the safety eyes both through the centre of the eye circle and then through the head.

FLOPPY-EARED BUNNY

Level of difficulty ✱✱✱

This fun little rabbit will be at home sitting in a pram or nursery, or being cuddled by a toddler. It is a great project for practising your colour changes since you have them on the bunny's body, legs, and arms.

TECHNIQUES USED Chain stitch **p.26**, Double crochet **p.34**, Simple stripes **p.39**, Shaping **p.50–52**, Working in the round **p.56**, Toy techniques **p.132–33**

SIZE
Approx 22 x 10cm (8¾ x 4in)

YARN
DMC Natura Just Cotton – 50g/155m/ 170yds (100% cotton; you can use any DK weight yarn for this project; cotton or acrylic are best for toys)

A x 1   **B** x 1   **C** x 1

HOOK
3.5mm hook

NOTIONS
Stitch markers
Yarn needle
12mm (½in) black safety toy eyes
Black and yellow embroidery thread and needle
White felt
Toy stuffing

TENSION
Exact tension is not essential

SPECIAL ABBREVIATIONS
Adjustable ring: Wind the yarn twice around your finger. Insert the hook and wrap the yarn around it. Pull the hook back through and work a chain. Work the first round of sts into the "ring", then pull the tail of yarn gently to close it, before joining the sts into a round using a ss.

PATTERN
Stripes are worked on the body, arms and legs. Begin with yarn B and work as follows:
Two rows blue (B)
Two rows white (C)
Two rows yellow (A)
Keep colour changes at the back of your work.

BODY AND HEAD
The head and body are worked together in one piece.
With yarn A, make an adjustable ring and work 6 dc into the ring. (6sts)
Round 1: 2 dc into each st to the end. (12sts)
Round 2: *1 dc, 2 dc in next st; repeat from * to end. (18sts)
Round 3: *2 dc, 2 dc in next st; repeat from * to end. (24sts)
Round 4: *3 dc, 2 dc in next st; repeat from * to end. (30sts)
Round 5: *9 dc, 2 dc in next st; repeat from * to end. (33sts)
Round 6: *10 dc, 2 dc in next st; repeat from * to end. (36sts)
Round 7: *11 dc, 2 dc in next st; repeat from * to end. (39sts)
Round 8: *12 dc, 2 dc in next st; repeat from * to end. (42sts)
Round 9: *13 dc, 2 dc in next st; repeat from * to end. (45sts)
Round 10: *14 dc, 2 dc in next st; repeat from * to end. (48sts)
Round 11: *15 dc, 2 dc in next st; repeat from * to end. (51sts)
Round 12: *16 dc, 2 dc in next st; repeat from * to end. (54sts)
Place two stitch markers on the next row, 12sts apart, to mark where you will put the toy eyes.
Rounds 13–14: Dc in each st to the end.
Round 15: *dc2tog, 7 dc; repeat from * to end. (48sts)
Round 16: *dc2tog, 6 dc; repeat from * to end. (42sts)

Round 17: *dc2tog, 5 dc; repeat from * to end. (36sts)
Round 18: *dc2tog, 4 dc; repeat from * to end. (30sts)
Round 19: *dc2tog; repeat from * to end. (15sts)
Put your working loop on a stitch holder and attach the toy eyes to the head in the places you marked on round 13.
Stuff the head with toy stuffing.
Put your working loop back on your hook and continue.
Starting with yarn B, begin stripe pattern:
Round 20: *4 dc, 2 dc in the next st; repeat from * to end. (18sts)
Round 21: Dc in each st to end.
Round 22: *5 dc, 2 dc in next st; repeat from * to end. (21sts)
Round 23: Dc in each st to end.
Round 24: *6 dc, 2 dc in next st; repeat from * to end. (24sts)
Round 25: Dc in each st to end.
Round 26: *7 dc, 2 dc in next st; repeat from * to end. (27sts)
Round 27: Dc in each st to end.
Round 28: *8 dc, 2 dc in next st; repeat from * to end. (30sts)
Round 29: Dc in each st to end.
Round 30: *9 dc, 2 dc in next st; repeat from * to end. (33sts)
Round 31: Dc in each st to end.
Round 32: *10 dc, 2 dc in next st; repeat from * to end. (36sts)
Round 33: Dc in each st to end.
Round 34: *dc2tog, 10 dc; repeat from * to end. (33sts)
Round 35: *dc2tog, 9 dc; repeat from * to end. (30sts)
Round 36: *dc2tog, 3 dc; repeat from * to end. (24sts)
Round 37: *dc2tog, 2 dc; repeat from * to end. (18sts)
Round 38: *dc2tog, 1 dc; repeat from * to end. (12sts)

Round 39: *dc2tog; repeat from * to end. (6sts)
Cut the yarn, leaving a long tail, and pull through loop to secure.
Stuff the body firmly. Thread the cut yarn onto a yarn needle and weave through the last six stitches, pull the yarn to close the hole at the base of the body, weave in yarn to secure, and cut off any loose ends.

ARMS (MAKE 2)
Note: Stuff the arms as you go along.
With yarn A, make an adjustable ring and work 6 dc into the ring. (6sts)
Round 1: 2 dc into each st to end. (12sts)
Round 2: *1 dc, 2 dc in next st; repeat from * to end. (18sts)
Round 3: *2 dc, 2 dc in next st; repeat from * to end. (24sts)
Rounds 4–6: Dc in each st to end.
Round 7: *dc2tog, 2 dc; repeat from * to end. (18sts)
Round 8: *dc2tog, 4 dc; repeat from * to end. (15sts)
Round 9: *dc2tog, 3 dc; repeat from * to end. (12sts)
Starting with yarn B, begin stripe pattern:
Rounds 10–19: Dc in each st to end.
Round 20: Dc2tog, dc in each st to end. (11sts)
Rounds 21–25: Dc in each st to end.
Round 26: Dc2tog, dc in each st to end. (10sts)
Rounds 27–31: Dc in each st to end.
Cut the yarn, leaving a long tail, and pull through loop to secure.
Finish stuffing the arm firmly.
Thread the cut yarn onto a yarn needle and weave through the last 10sts, pull the yarn to close the hole at the top of the arm, weave in yarn to secure.

LEGS (MAKE 2)
With yarn A, make an adjustable ring and work 6 dc into the ring. (6sts)
Round 1: 2 dc into each st to end. (12sts)
Round 2: 2 dc, 2 dc in next st, 2 dc, 3 htr in next st, 2 htr, 3 htr in next st, 2 dc, 2 dc in last st. (18sts)
Round 3: 3 dc, 2 dc in next st, 2 dc, 1 htr, 2 htr in next st, 4 htr, 2 htr in next st, 1 htr, 1 dc, 2 dc in next st, dc in last 2sts. (22sts)
Round 4: 2 dc in first st, 8 dc, 3 htr in next st, 5 htr, 3 htr in next st, dc in the last 6sts. (27sts)
Round 5: Dc in each st to end.
Round 6: 1 dc, dc2tog, 8 dc, dc2tog, 6 dc, dc2tog, dc in the last 6sts. (24sts)
Round 7: 11 dc, htr3tog, 3 htr, htr3tog, dc in the last 4sts. (20sts)

Round 8: 3 dc, dc2tog, 4 dc, dc2tog, 1 dc, dc2tog, 1 dc, dc2tog, dc in last 3sts. (16sts)
Round 9: 8 dc, dc2tog, 1 dc, dc2tog, dc in last 3sts. (14sts)
Starting with yarn B, begin stripe pattern:
Round 10: Dc in each st to end.
Round 11: Dc2tog, dc in each st to end. (13sts)
Rounds 12–16: Dc in each st to end.
Round 17: Dc2tog, dc in each st to end. (12sts)
Rounds 18–22: Dc in each st to end.
Round 23: Dc2tog, dc in each st to end. (11sts)
Rounds 24–28: Dc in each st to end.
Round 29: Dc2tog, dc in each st to end. (10sts)
Rounds 30–33: Dc in each st to the end.
Cut the yarn, leaving a long tail, and pull through loop to secure.
Finish stuffing the leg firmly.
Thread the cut yarn onto a yarn needle and weave through the last 10sts, pull the yarn to close the hole at the top of the leg, weave in yarn to secure.

BUNNY EARS (MAKE 2)
With yarn A, make an adjustable ring and work 6 dc into the ring. (6sts)
Round 1: 2 dc into each st to end. (12sts)
Round 2: *1 dc, 2 dc in next st; repeat from * to end. (18sts)
Round 3: Dc in each st to end.
Round 4: *2 dc, 2 dc in next st; repeat from * to end. (24sts)
Round 5: Dc in each st to end.
Round 6: *3 dc, 2 dc in next st; repeat from * to end. (30sts)
Rounds 7–8: Dc in each st to end.
Round 9: Dc2tog, dc in each st to end. (29sts)
Round 10: Dc in each st to end.
Rounds 11–45: Repeat the last two rounds 17 times. (12sts at the end of round 45)
Cut the yarn, leaving a long tail, and pull through loop to secure. Press flat and sew the opening at the top of the ear closed.
Cut felt to fit inside ear and sew in place with yellow embroidery thread.

TAIL
With yarn B, make an adjustable ring and work 6 dc into the ring. (6sts)
Round 1: 2 dc into each st to end. (12sts)
Round 2: Dc in each st to end.
Round 3: Dc in each st to end.
Round 4: Dc2tog six times. (6sts)
Cut the yarn, leaving a long tail, and pull through loop to secure.
Stuff firmly with toy stuffing.
Thread the cut yarn onto a yarn needle and weave through the last 6sts, pull the yarn to close the hole, weave in yarn to secure but do not cut the yarn off.

Give your bunny a friendly smile using six strands of embroidery thread or a length of black yarn. Sew the nose by making a series of increasingly smaller stitches to form a triangle, and use backstitches for the mouth.

For a neat rabbit's foot, make an adjustable ring using six double crochet stitches. It is described on p.134. This will create a neat circle underneath his paddy paw from which the crochet stitches will circulate out.

FINISHING
Sew the arms, legs, ears, and tail in place with matching yarn. Weave in any loose ends and cut off. Embroider face detail using black embroidery thread.

Cut two pieces of white felt, approximately 1cm (½in) smaller all round than the finished crocheted ears. Attach them using small running stitches, cross-stitches, or blanket stitch (see p.85). Place your stitches close to the edge of the felt and secure with a knot at the end.

POLAR BEAR COMFORTER

Level of difficulty

Who could resist cuddling up to this little bear? Crocheting in the round creates a wonderfully open-textured blanket with cute amigurumi-style head and arms, and crocheted pompoms to boot.

TECHNIQUES USED Shaping **p.50–52**, Making a simple adjustable ring **p.57**, Working into the back loop of a double crochet **p.75**, Working into a chain space **p.75**

SIZE
Approx. 30 x 30cm (11 x 11in) when flat

YARN
Paintbox Yarns Cotton DK – 50g/125m/137yds (100% cotton; you only need small amounts (approx. 25g) of the yarns B, C, D, and E. You can use any similar weight yarn for this project.)

A x 1 **B** x 1 **C** x 1 **D** x 1 **E** x 1

HOOKS
3mm hook
3.75mm hook

NOTIONS
Toy stuffing
Tapestry needle

TENSION
Exact tension is not essential, keep stitches close together for the head and arms

PATTERN

HEAD
Using yarn A and 3mm hook, make an adjustable ring.
Round 1: Work 6 dc into ring, pull ring tight. (6sts)
Round 2: 2 dc in each st. (12sts)
Round 3: (1 dc, 2 dc in next st) six times. (18sts)
Round 4: (2 dc, 2 dc in next st) six times. (24sts)
Round 5: (3 dc, 2 dc in next st) six times. (30sts)
Round 6: (4 dc, 2 dc in next st) six times. (36sts)
Round 7: (5 dc, 2 dc in next st) six times. (42sts)
Round 8: (6 dc, 2 dc in next st) six times. (48sts)
Rounds 9-13: 1 dc in each st.
Round 14: 2 dc in each of next 6st, 42 dc. (54sts)
Rounds 15–18: 1dc in each st.
Round 19: (dc2tog, 7 dc) six times. (48sts)
Round 20: (dc2tog. 6 dc) six times. (42sts)
Round 21: (dc2tog. 5 dc) six times. (36sts)
Round 22: (dc2tog. 4 dc) six times. (30sts)
Round 23: (dc2tog, 3 dc) six times. (24sts)
Round 24: Working in back loops, 1 dc in each st.
Round 25: (dc2tog, 2 dc) six times. (18sts)
Add toy stuffing.
Round 26: dc2tog nine times. (9sts)
Fasten off, with a tapestry needle pick up all front loops and pull tight to close.

BLANKET
Using yarn A and 3.75mm crochet hook, attach yarn to the remaining front loops from round 24 of the head.
Round 1: Attach yarn to the remaining front loops, ch 2 (doesn't count as st throughout), 24 tr, ss in first st to join. (24sts)

Round 2: Ss to next space between stitches, ch 2, (1 tr in first space, 2 tr in next space), (1 tr in next space, 2 tr in next space) to end, ss in first st to join. (36sts)
Round 3: Ss to next space between sts, ch 2, 2 tr in space between each cluster, of 1 or 2 tr, ss in first st to join. (48sts – 24 2-tr clusters)
Round 4: Ss to last space between sts, ch 2, (2 tr, ch 1) between each cluster, ss in first st to join. (48sts + 24ch-sp)

Open texture Working treble clusters – in this case, in clusters of two trebles – creates an attractive texture to the skirt of the comforter.

Denser fabric Working with half trebles and trebles as the skirt is squared off creates this contrasting texture for added interest.

From above You can see how the use of different heights of stitches turns the circular shape of the skirt into a neat square.

Fast asleep Take time embroidering these features, using the rounds of double crochet as a guide, to create a symmetrical face that looks calm and peacefully asleep.

Round 5: Ss to last space between sts, ch 2, (4 tr in first space, 2 tr in next space), (4 tr in next space, 2 tr in next space) to end, ss in first st to join. (72sts – 12 4-tr clusters, 12 2-tr clusters)

Rounds 6–8: Ss in last space between sts, ch 2, (2 tr in-between each 2 tr) around, ss in first st to join. (72sts - 36 2tr clusters)

Round 9: Ss in last space between sts, ch 2, (4 tr in next space, 2 tr in next space) around, ss in first st to join. (108sts – 18 4-tr clusters, 18 2-tr clusters)

Round 10: SS in last space between sts, ch 2, (2 tr in-between each 2 tr) around, ss in first st to join. (108sts – 54 2-tr cluster)

Round 11: Ch 1, [5 dc, 5 htr, 3 tr, (2 tr, ch2, 2 tr) in next st to make corner, 3 tr, 5 htr, 5 dc] repeat four times, ss in first st to join. (120sts + 4 ch-sp)

Round 12: Ch 2, [10 htr, 5 tr, (2 tr, ch 2, 2 tr) in corner ch-sp, 5 tr, 10 htr] repeat four times, ss in first st to join. [136sts + 4 ch-sp]

Round 13: Ch 2, [10 htr, 7 tr, (2 tr, ch 2, 2 tr) in corner ch-sp, 7 tr, 10 htr] four times, ss in first st to join. (152sts + 4 ch-sp)

Round 14: Ch 2, [1 tr in each st to corner, (2 tr, ch 2, 2 tr) in corner ch-sp] four times, 1 tr in each st to end, ss in first st to join. (168sts + 4 ch-sp)

Round 15: Ch 2, [1 tr in each st to corner, (2 tr, ch2, 2 tr) in corner ch-sp] four times, 1 tr in each st to end, ss in first st to join. (184sts + 4 ch-sp)
Fasten off and weave in the ends.

ARMS
Using yarn A and 3mm hook make an adjustable ring.
Round 1: Work 6 dc into ring, pull ring tight. (6sts)
Round 2: 2 dc in each st. (12sts)
Round 3: (2 dc in next 3st, 3 dc) twice. (18sts)
Rounds 4–48: 1 dc in each st. (45 rounds total)
Add toy stuffing.
Round 49: (dc2tog three times, 3 dc) twice. (12sts)
Round 50: dc2tog six times. (6sts)
Fasten off, place around the back of the head, and sew in place.

EARS (MAKE 2)
Using yarn A and 3mm hook make an adjustable ring.
Round 1: Work 6 dc into ring, pull ring tight. (6sts)
Round 2: 2 dc in each st. (12sts)
Round 3: (1 dc, 2 dc in next st) six times. (18sts)
Round 4: (2 dc, 2 dc in next st) six times. (24sts)
Rounds 5-7: 1 dc in each st.
Fasten off, sew to the back of the head.

COLOURFUL POMPOMS (MAKE 4)
Make one in each of yarns B, C, D and E.
Using 3mm hook make an adjustable ring.
Round 1: Work 6 dc into ring, pull ring tight. (6sts)
Round 2: 2 dc in each st. (12sts)
Round 3: (1 dc, 2 dc in next st) six times. (18sts)
Rounds 4–6: 1 dc in each st.
Round 7: (1 dc, dc2tog) six times. (12sts)
Add toy stuffing.
Round 8: dc2tog six times. (6sts)
Fasten off, securely sew the pompoms to the corners of the blanket.

FINISHING
Embroider sleepy eyes onto the head in yarn B. Next embroider the nose in yarn E and add some claw lines to the paws in yarn B to finish.

JUNGLE FINGER PUPPETS

Give your child hours of fun making up stories of animals living in the wild. These little puppets are suited to a reasonably experienced crocheter.

Level of difficulty

TECHNIQUES USED Chain stitch **p.26**, Double crochet **p.34**, Working in the round **p.56**, Double crochet increases **p.50**, Double crochet decreases **p.52**

SIZE
Approx 8 x 4cm (3 x 1½in)

YARN
DMC Natura Just Cotton 4-ply – 50g/155m/179yds (100% cotton; you can use any 4-ply yarn for this project)

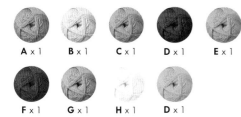

A x 1   B x 1   C x 1   D x 1   E x 1

F x 1   G x 1   H x 1   D x 1

HOOK
3.5mm hook

NOTIONS
Yarn needle
Toy stuffing
Black embroidery thread and needle
Pipe cleaner
White felt
Fabric glue

TENSION
Exact tension is not essential

SPECIAL ABBREVIATIONS
Adjustable ring: Wind the yarn twice around your finger. Insert the hook and wrap the yarn around it. Pull the hook back through and work a chain. Work the first round of sts into the "ring", then pull the tail of yarn gently to close it, before joining the sts into a round using a ss.

Loop stitch: Wrap the yarn from front to back over the index finger of your yarn hand. Insert the hook in the next stitch, grab the strand of yarn from behind your index finger and draw the yarn through the stitch. The yarn on your finger becomes the loop. With the yarn loop still on your index finger, yarn over the hook and draw the yarn through the two loops on your hook.

PATTERN
The "basic" pattern relates to all puppets. Refer to individual patterns for specific details.

BASIC BODY
Make an adjustable ring and work 6 dc into the ring. (6sts)
Round 1: *1 dc, 2 dc in next st; repeat from * to end. (9sts)
Round 2: *2 dc, 2 dc in next st; repeat from * to end. (12sts)
Rounds 3–10: Dc in each st to end. (12sts) Cut the yarn and pull through loop to secure. Sew in loose end and cut off.

BASIC HEAD
Make an adjustable ring and work 6 dc into the ring. (6sts)
Round 1: 2 dc into each st to end. (12sts)
Round 2: *dc, 2 dc in next st; repeat from * to end. (18sts)
Round 3: *2 dc, 2 dc in next st; repeat from * to end. (24sts)
Rounds 4–6: Dc in each st to end. (24sts)
Round 7: *dc2tog, 2 dc; repeat from * to end. (18sts)
Round 8: *dc2tog, dc; repeat from * to end. (12sts)
Round 9: *dc2tog; repeat from * to end. (6sts). Cut yarn, leaving a long tail, and pull through to secure. Stuff firmly. Weave the yarn through the last 6sts, pull to close at the base of head. Sew onto body and weave in loose end.

BASIC ARM
Make an adjustable ring and work 4 dc into the ring. (4sts)
Rounds 1–3: Dc in each st to the end. (4sts) Cut and secure the yarn leaving a long tail. Stuff the arms, then weave the yarn end through the last 4sts. Pull to close at top of arm. Sew in place and weave in loose ends.

TOYS

For the lion's mane, refer to the Special stitches panel on p.287 to form the loop stitches. Make even loops by wrapping the yarn around your fingers.

PATTERN: LION

Make one Basic body, one Basic head, and two Basic arms in yarn A.

MANE

With yarn B, ch 26, ss to join and form a loop. (26sts)
Rounds 1–2: Loop stitch in each stitch. (26sts)
Cut yarn, leaving long tail, and secure. Sew in place on head. Weave in loose ends.

TAIL

With yarn A, ch 12, ss in second ch from hook, ss along ch. (11sts)
Cut yarn and secure. Sew in place and weave in loose ends. Cut two strands of yarn B, fold in half and sew to end of tail to form tassel.

FINISHING

With black embroidery thread, add the facial details. Make two French knots for the eyes, a small triangle for the nose, and lines to form the mouth. Weave in loose ends.

The elephant's trunk is made from a "tube" of eight chain stitches with a pipe cleaner inserted inside to make it stick out.

PATTERN: ELEPHANT

Make one Basic body, one Basic head, and two Basic arms in yarn C.

EARS (MAKE 2)

This is not worked in a spiral. Turn your work at the end of each row to form a semi circle.
With yarn C, make an adjustable ring and work 4 dc into the ring. (4sts)
Row 1: *dc, 2 dc in next st; repeat from * to end, ch 1, turn. (6sts)
Row 2: 2 dc, 2 dc in next st, 1 dc, 1 htr, 2 htr in last st. (8sts)
Cut yarn, leaving a long tail, and secure. Sew in place and weave in loose ends.

TRUNK

With yarn C, make an adjustable ring and work 4 dc into the ring. (4sts)
Rounds 1–8: Dc in each st to the end. (4sts)
Cut yarn, leaving a long tail, and secure. Cut a pipe cleaner to the length of the trunk and place inside. Weave yarn end through last 4sts; pull to close at base of trunk. Sew in place and weave in loose ends.

TAIL

With yarn C, ch 8, ss in second ch from hook, ss along ch. (7sts)
Cut yarn and secure. Sew in place and weave in loose ends.
With black embroidery thread, add the facial details. Make two French knots for the eyes.

To work the French knot eyes, wrap black embroidery thread around your needle once or twice before inserting the needle back through the stitching.

PATTERN: MONKEY

Make one Basic body, one Basic head, and two Basic arms in yarn D.

MUZZLE

With yarn E, make an adjustable ring and work 6 dc into the ring. (6sts)
Round 1: Dc in each st to the end. (6sts)
Cut yarn, leaving a long tail, and secure. Weave yarn through last 6sts and pull to close at base of body. Sew onto head and weave in loose ends.

EARS (MAKE 2)

With yarn D, make an adjustable ring and work 8 dc into the ring, ss to join ring. (8sts)
Cut yarn and pull through to secure. Sew in place and weave in loose ends.

EYE PATCHES

With yarn E, make an adjustable ring and work 8 dc into the ring, ss to join ring. (8sts)
Cut yarn and pull through to secure. Sew in place and weave in loose ends.

TAIL

With yarn D, ch 12, ss in second ch from hook, ss along ch. (11sts)
Cut yarn and secure. Sew in place and weave in yarn and cut off any loose ends. With black embroidery thread, add the facial details. Make two French knots in the centre of the eye patches for the eyes.

Use bright colours, such as blue, red, and yellow as shown above, for the parrot, or a tropical bird. Alternatively, try green, orange, and yellow, or blue, green, and yellow.

PATTERN: PARROT
Make one Basic body using yarn F.
Make head pattern up to round 8 using yarn F.
Cut yarn, leaving a long tail, and secure. Stuff the head firmly and sew onto body. Weave in loose ends.

LOWER BEAK
With yarn B, make an adjustable ring and work 4 dc into the ring. (4sts)
Round 1: Dc in each st to the end. (4sts)
Cut yarn, leaving a long tail, and secure. Stuff.

TOP BEAK
With yarn B, make an adjustable ring and work 6 dc into the ring. (6sts)
Rounds 1–2: Dc in each st to the end. (6sts)
Cut yarn, leaving a long tail, and secure. Stuff and sew the top and lower beak in place. Weave in loose ends.

WINGS
With yarn F, make an adjustable ring, and work 6 dc into the ring. (6sts)
Round 1: 2 dc into each st to the end. (12sts)
Round 2: *3 dc, 2 dc in the next st; repeat from * to end. (15sts)
Round 3: Dc in each st to the end.
Round 4: *dc2tog, 3 dc; repeat from * to end. Change to yarn G at end of this row. (12sts)
Round 5: Working through the back loop of the stitch only, dc in each st to end.
Round 6: *dc2tog, 4 dc; repeat from * to end. (10sts)
Round 7: Working through the back loop of the stitch only, dc in each st to end.
Round 8: *dc2tog, 3 dc; repeat from * to end. (8sts)

Round 9: Dc in each st to end.
Round 10: *dc2tog, 2 dc; repeat from * to end. (6sts)
Round 11: Dc in each st to end.
Round 12: Dc in the first stitch, ch 4, dc in the next st, ch 4, dc to end.
Cut yarn, leaving a long tail, and secure. Sew closed the hole at the base of the wing. Rejoin yarn F to first round of loops left by back loop only rounds and work as follows:
Round 1: *ss in first loop, dc in next, tr in next; repeat from * to end.
Rejoin yarn G to second round of loops left by back loop only rounds and work as follows:
Round 2: *ss in first loop, dc in next, tr in next; repeat to last st, ss in last st.
Cut yarn and secure. Sew the wings onto the body. Weave in loose ends.

TAIL
This is not worked in a spiral. Turn your work at the end of each row.
With yarn G, ch 7.
Row 1: Starting in second ch from hook, 3 dc, 3 htr, 2 ch, turn. (6sts)
Row 2: Starting at first htr of prev row, 3 htr, 3 dc, 1 ch, turn. (6sts)
Row 3: Starting at the first dc of prev row, 3 dc, 3 htr. (6sts)
Cut yarn and pull through loop to secure.

TAIL TOP
This is not worked in a spiral. Turn your work at end of each row.
With yarn F, ch 4.
Row 1: Starting in second ch from hook, 2 dc, htr in last ch, ch 2, turn. (4sts)
Row 2: 1 htr into htr from prev row, 2 dc, ch 1, turn.
Row 3: 2 dc, htr in the last st.
Cut yarn and secure. Sew top of tail onto bottom, then sew in place on the body. Weave in loose ends.

EYE PATCHES
With yarn H, make an adjustable ring and work 8 dc into the ring, ss to join ring. (8sts)
Cut yarn and secure. Sew in place and weave in loose ends. Make two French knots in the centre of the eye patches for the eyes.

White felt makes a great set of teeth for this crocodile. Use one long piece or two pieces, as here, to create the right expression.

PATTERN: CROCODILE
Make one Basic body, one Basic head, and two Basic arms in yarn I.

MOUTH (MAKE 2)
With yarn I, make an adjustable ring and work 6 dc into the ring. (6sts)
Round 1: *1 dc, 2 dc in the next st; repeat from * to end. (9sts)
Round 2: 2 dc in first st, dc in each st to end. (10sts)
Round 3: Dc in each st to the end.
Round 4: 2 dc in first st, dc in each st to end. (11sts)
Round 5: Dc in each st to the end.
Round 6: 2 dc in first st, dc in each st to end. (12sts)
Round 7: Dc in each st to end.
Cut yarn and secure. Cut a felt zigzag and attach with fabric glue as teeth. Sew head in place and weave in loose ends.

EYES (MAKE 2)
With yarn H, make an adjustable ring and work 4 dc into the ring.
Round 1: Dc in each st to the end. (4sts)
Cut the yarn and weave it through the 4sts, pull to close the hole and form the eyeball. Weave in loose ends.

EYE SOCKETS (MAKE 2)
With yarn I, make an adjustable ring and work 5 dc into the ring.
Rounds 1–2: Dc in each st to the end. (5sts)
Cut yarn and secure. Place around the eyeball. It should be a tight fit. Sew in place and weave in loose ends. Make two French knots in the centre of the eye patches for the eyes. With yarn I, work two French knots at the end of the top of the mouth for the nostrils.

BAGS

Quick to make and eco-friendly, crocheted bags can be as simple or as complex as you like. And you can take your project out with you, be it a shopper, a vibrant motif bag, or an elegant clutch.

GRANNY SQUARE BAG

Level of difficulty

A stylish twist on a classic crochet motif, this simple granny square shoulder bag relies on bright colour combinations to give it the "wow" factor. Turn to p.100 for more information about creating a granny square.

TECHNIQUES USED Double crochet **p.34**, Treble crochet **p.44**, Working in the round **p.56**, Joining on a new colour **p.57**, A basic granny square **p.100**

BAGS

SIZE
32cm (12½in) square

YARN
Artesano Superwash Merino DK – 50g/
112m/122yds (100% merino wool; you
can substitute any DK weight, wool-
blend yarn for this project)

A x 3   **B** x 1   **C** x 1   **D** x 1

HOOK
3.75mm hook

NOTIONS
Yarn needle
Cotton material for lining, measuring
62 x 31cm (24½ x 12¼in), plus
seam allowance
Sewing needle and matching thread

TENSION
Rounds 1–3 measure 8cm (3in)

PATTERN (MAKE 2)
With yarn A, work 4 ch, ss in first ch to
form a ring.
Round 1: 4 ch (counts as 1 tr and 1 ch),
*3 tr into ring, 1 ch, rep from * twice,
2 tr into ring, join with a ss to third of 4 ch.
Fasten off A.
Round 2: Join B into any ch sp, 3 ch (counts
as first tr), (2 tr, 2 ch, 3 tr) in same ch sp, 1 ch,
*(3 tr, 2 ch, 3 tr) in next ch sp, 1 ch, rep from *
twice, join with a ss in top of initial 3 ch.
Fasten off B.
Round 3: Join C into any corner 2 ch sp, 3 ch
(counts as first tr), (2 tr, 2 ch, 3 tr) in same
ch sp, 1 ch, 3 tr in next ch sp, 1 ch, *(3 tr, 2 ch,
3 tr) in next ch sp, 1 ch, 3 tr in next ch sp,
1 ch rep from * twice, join with a ss in top
of initial 3 ch.
Fasten off C.
Round 4: Join A into any corner ch sp, 3 ch
(counts as first tr), (2 tr, 2 ch, 3 tr) in same
ch sp, 1 ch, 3 tr in next ch sp, 1 ch, 3 tr in next
ch sp, 1 ch, *(3 tr, 2 ch, 3 tr) in next ch sp, 1 ch,
3 tr in next ch sp, 1 ch, 3 tr in next ch sp,
1 ch, rep from * twice, join with a ss in
top of initial 3 ch.
Fasten off A.
Continue working each round in colour
sequence as follows, working as round 4.
Each round will have one extra 3 tr in ch sp
and 1 ch, worked on each side of the square;
corners remain the same.
Round 5: Yarn D.
Round 6: Yarn B.
Round 7: Yarn A.
Round 8: Yarn B.
Round 9: Yarn C.
Round 10: Yarn A.
Round 11: Yarn D.
Round 12: Yarn A.

MAKING THE STRAP
Work 121 ch.
Row 1: 1 dc into second ch from hook,
1 dc in each ch to end, turn. (120sts)
Row 2: 1 dc in each dc, turn.
Repeat row 2 four more times. Fasten
off yarn.

FINISHING
Press the front and back pieces according
to ballband instructions.
Place front and back with wrong sides
together, rejoin yarn A to top left corner
space and working through front and back
join on three sides as follows, 1 dc in ch sp,
*1 dc in top of each of next 3 tr, 1 dc in ch sp,
rep from * to corner, 3 dc in corner ch sp, rep
from * to next corner sp, 3 dc in corner ch sp,
rep from * to top right-hand corner, leaving
top of bag open. Work one row of dc evenly
along top edges of front and back.
Sew shoulder strap to sides of bag.
Weave in all ends.
Fold lining material in half with right sides
together, sew around three sides. Place lining
in bag and fold over top edge. Stitch top
seam of lining to crochet bag.

STRAW BEACH BAG

The base of this eye-catching yet practical bag is worked in rows, and then the rest of the bag is worked in the round to the desired height.

TECHNIQUES USED Chain stitch **p.26**, Double crochet **p.34**, Half treble crochet **p.38**, Working in the round **p.56**

SIZE
32 x 56cm (12½ x 22in)

YARN
Expressions hand-coloured hemp, 4-ply – 50g/85m/93yds (100% hemp; any 4-ply weight, durable yarn (held double) such as cotton, linen, or string will work)

A x 7   **B** x 6

HOOK
5mm hook

NOTIONS
Yarn needle
2cm (¾in) button

TENSION
Exact tension is not essential

❯ PATTERN

Note: 2 ch at the beginning of each htr row or round is classed as the first st worked in the first st of previous row.
1 ch at the beginning of each dc row or round is classed as the first st worked in the first st of previous row. Hold yarn double for extra strength.

Foundation row: With yarn A, work 47 ch.
Row 1: Htr in third ch from hook and in each ch across, turn. (46sts)
Row 2: 2 ch, htr in each stitch across, turn. (46sts)
Rows 3–11: Repeat row 2.
Now working in rounds.
Round 1: 1 ch, dc in each st to end of row, 2 dc in each row end, 1 dc in back of each foundation ch, 2 dc in each row end, join with a ss. (136sts)
Round 2: 2 ch, htr in each st around, join with a ss.
Rounds 3–16: Repeat round 2.
Rounds 17–28: With yarn B, repeat round 2.

HANDLES
Round 29: 2 ch, htr in next 12sts, 60 ch, miss next 20sts, htr in next 48sts, 60 ch, miss next 20sts, htr in next 35sts, join with a ss.
Round 30: Htr in each stitch and ch around, join with a ss.
Rounds 31–32: Htr in each stitch around. Fasten off.

FASTENING FLAP
With yarn B, work 11 ch.
Row 1: Dc in second ch from hook and in each ch across, turn. (10sts)

This bag has a very sturdy base, achieved by working in straight rows. The hemp yarn used here makes for a summery feel, but try using raffia for a slightly more rigid bag.

Row 2: 1 ch, dc in each st across, turn. (10sts)
Rows 3–4: Repeat row 2.
Row 5: 1 ch, dc in first 4sts, 2 ch, miss next 2sts, dc in last 4sts, turn.
Row 6: 1 ch, dc in first 4sts, dc in each of the 2 chs, dc in last 4sts, turn.
Rows 7–20: Repeat row 2.
Dc evenly around entire flap to neaten. Fasten off. Sew flap and button onto bag.

SUPER-STRETCHY SHOPPER

Level of difficulty ✳✳✳

This handy bag is made in the round with a solid base and a mesh body. Worked in double crochet, the fabric is strong and flexible, and so the bag will expand to fit lots of shopping inside.

TECHNIQUES USED Chain stitch **p.26**, Double crochet **p.34**, Working in the round **p.56**

SIZE
Approx 25.5 x 33cm (10 x 13in),
   with 48.5cm (19in) handles

YARN
Rowan Softknit Cotton – 50g/105m/115yds
   (92% cotton and 8% nylon/polyamide;
   you can use any DK cotton or cotton
   mix yarn here to get a similar effect)

x 5

HOOK
4.5mm hook

NOTIONS
Stitch marker
Yarn needle

TENSION
Exact tension is not essential

⟩ PATTERN

Note: Mark the first stitch of each round.

Work 2 ch.
Round 1: 8 dc in second chain from hook.
Round 2: 2 dc in first st, and in each st around. (16 dc). Do not join with a ss. Continue to work in a spiral, remembering to mark the first st of each round.
Round 3: *2 dc in next st, 1 dc in next st, rep from * around. (24sts)
Round 4: *2 dc in next st, 1 dc in next 2sts, rep from * around. (32sts)
Round 5: *2 dc in next st, 1 dc in next 3sts, rep from * around. (40sts)

Round 6: *2 dc in next st, 1 dc in next 4sts, rep from * around. (48sts)
Round 7: *2 dc in next st, 1 dc in next 5sts, rep from * around. (56sts)
Round 8: *2 dc in next st, 1 dc in next 6sts, rep from * around. (64sts)
Round 9: *2 dc in next st, 1 dc in next 7sts, rep from * around. (72sts)
Round 10: *2 dc in next st, 1 dc in next 8sts, rep from * around. (80sts)
Round 11: *2 dc in next st, 1 dc in next 9sts, rep from * around. (88sts)
Round 12: *2 dc in next st, 1 dc in next 10sts, rep from * around. (96sts)
Round 13: *2 dc in next st, 1 dc in next 11sts, rep from * around. (104sts)
Round 14: *2 dc in next st, 1 dc in next 12sts, rep from * around. (112sts)
Round 15: *2 dc in next st, 1 dc in next 13sts, rep from * around. (120sts)
Round 16: *2 dc in next st, 1 dc in next 14sts, rep from * around. (128sts)
Round 17: *2 dc in next st, 1 dc in next 15sts, rep from * around. (136sts)
Round 18: *2 dc in next st, 1 dc in next 16sts, rep from * around. (144sts)
Round 19: Dc in each st around.
Rounds 20–23: Repeat round 19.

MESH ROUNDS
Now mark the first 4-ch sp (see p.74) at the beginning of each round.
Round 24: *4 ch, miss 2 sts, dc in next st, rep from * around, ending with a 4 ch.
Round 25: Dc in first 4-ch sp, *4 ch, dc in next 4-ch sp, rep from * around, ending with a 4 ch.
Rounds 26–65: Repeat round 25.
Round 66: Dc in next dc (mark this stitch), *2 dc in next 4-ch sp, dc in next st, rep from * around.
Round 67: Dc in first st (mark this stitch), and in each st around.
Rounds 68–70: Repeat round 67.
Fasten off.

HANDLES (MAKE 2)
Work 13 ch.
Row 1: Dc in second chain from hook and in each ch across, turn. (12sts)
Row 2: 1 ch, dc in each st across, turn. (12sts)
Rows 3–46: (or work to length required).
Repeat row 2.
Fasten off.
Sew the handles on the bag and weave in ends.

Crocheting in the round is easy to achieve and allows you to be more versatile with your stitching. Turn to p.129 if you want to try something new, such as making this bag from string.

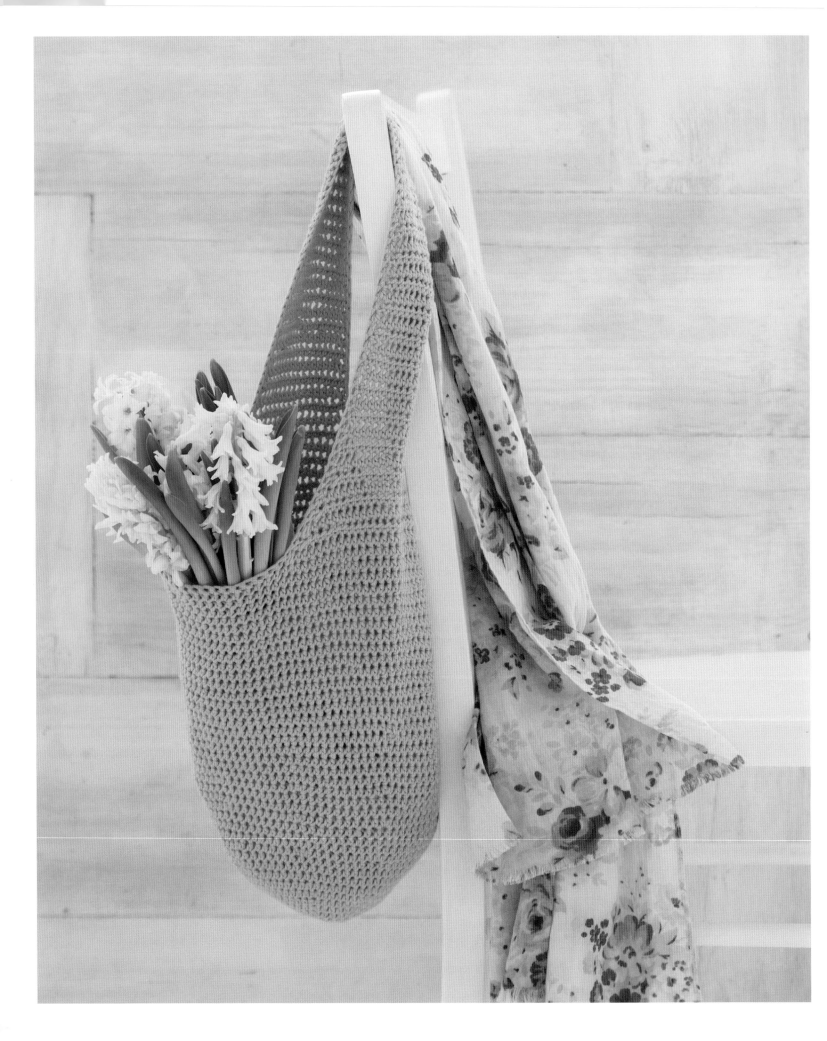

EVERYDAY BAG

Level of difficulty

This useful everyday bag is worked in the round, increasing until you reach the desired width, then working straight to the desired height. The bag is then divided for the handles, which are broad, making them comfortable to hold.

TECHNIQUES USED Using slip stitch to form a foundation ring **p.28**, Double crochet **p.34**, Half treble crochet **p.38**, Shaping **p.50–52**, Working in the round **p.56**

SIZE
Approx 30 x 25cm (12 x 9¾in) with 24cm
(9½in) straps

YARN
Debbie Bliss Eco Baby – 50g/125m/137yds
(100% cotton; you can use any 100% cotton
4-ply weight yarn for this project)

x 3

HOOK
3.5mm hook

NOTIONS
Yarn needle

TENSION
18 htr x 16 rows per 10cm (4in)

SPECIAL ABBREVIATIONS
BEG HTR: begin half treble stitch. 2 ch, insert hook in second ch from hook, yrh, pull up a loop, insert hook in next stitch, yrh, pull up a loop, yrh and draw hook through all three loops.

HTR2TOG: work 2 half treble stitches together. (Yrh and insert hook in next st, yrh and draw a loop through) twice, yrh and draw through all five loops on hook – 1st decreased.

PATTERN
Work 4 ch, ss in first chain to form a ring.
Round 1: 2 ch, insert hook in second chain from hook, yrh, pull up a loop, insert hook into loop, yrh, pull up a loop, yrh, draw hook through all three loops on hook (beg htr made), work 7 htr into loop, join with a ss to beg htr. (8sts)
Round 2: Work beg htr, work another htr in same st, *2 htr in next st, repeat from * to end, join with a ss to beg htr. (16sts)
Round 3: Work beg htr, work another htr in same st, * htr in next st, 2 htr in next st, repeat from * to end, join with a ss to beg htr. (24sts)
Round 4: Work beg htr, work another htr in same st, *htr in next 2sts, 2 htr in next st, repeat from * to end, join with a ss to beg htr. (32sts)
Round 5: Work beg htr, work another htr in same st, *htr in next 3sts, 2 htr in next st, repeat from * to end, join with a ss to beg htr. (40sts)
Round 6: Work beg htr, work another htr in same st, *htr in next 4sts, 2 htr in next st, repeat from * to end, join with a ss to beg htr. (48sts)
Round 7: Work beg htr, work another htr in same st, *htr in next 5sts, 2 htr in next st, repeat from * to end, join with a ss to beg htr. (56sts)
Round 8: Work beg htr, work another htr in same st, *htr in next 6sts, 2 htr in next st, repeat from * to end, join with a ss to beg htr. (64sts)
Round 9: Beg htr in next st, htr in each st to end, join with a ss to beg htr. (64sts)
Rounds 10–12: Repeat round 9.
Round 13: Work beg htr, htr in same st, *htr in next 7sts, 2 htr in next st, repeat from * to end, join with a ss to beg htr. (72sts)
Rounds 14–16: Repeat round 9.
Round 17: Work beg htr, htr in same st, *htr in next 8sts, 2 htr in next st, repeat from * to end, join with a ss to beg htr. (80sts)
Rounds 18–20: Repeat round 9.
Round 21: Work beg htr, htr in same st, *htr in next 9sts, 2 htr in next st, repeat from * to end, join with a ss to beg htr. (88sts)

Rounds 22–24: Repeat round 9.
Round 25: Work beg htr, htr in same st, *htr in next 10sts, 2 htr in next st, repeat from * to end, join with a ss to beg htr. (96sts)
Rounds 26–42: Repeat round 9. At the end of round 42, do not fasten off. (96sts)

HANDLES (WORKING IN ROWS)
Row 1: Beg htr, htr in next 10sts, htr2tog, htr in next 24sts, htr2tog, turn, leaving remaining 58sts unworked.
Row 2: 2 ch, htr2tog, htr in next 22sts, htr2tog, turn.
Row 3: 2 ch, htr2tog, htr in next 20sts, htr2tog, turn.
Row 4: 2 ch, htr2tog, htr in next 18sts, htr2tog, turn.
Row 5: 2 ch, htr2tog, htr in next 16sts, htr2tog, turn.
Row 6: 2 ch, htr2tog, htr in next 14sts, htr2tog, turn.
Row 7: Beg htr in first st, htr in next 15sts, turn.
Rows 8–36: Repeat row 7. At the end of row 36 fasten off.
Join yarn with a ss in beg htr of row 1, and work as follows:
Htr in next 10 sts, htr2tog, htr in next 24sts, htr2tog, turn leaving remaining 20sts unworked.
Repeat rows 2–36. At the end of row 36, do not fasten off.
With wrong sides of handles held together, htr ends of handles together to join. Fasten off.

EDGING FOR HANDLES
Join yarn with a dc in row end where handles are joined, dc in each row end of handle, dc in next 20sts of bag, and dc in each row end of other side of handle; join with a ss to first dc.
Repeat for other side of handles.
Fasten off, weave in ends.

DIAMOND GRANNY BAG

Textured granny squares crocheted together ensure this fully lined bag will be a joy both to crochet and to use. This bright and cheerful project has an attractive, striped strap and button closure.

TECHNIQUES USED Treble crochet **p.44**, Working into the back loop of a double crochet **p.75**, Double crochet edging **p.86**, A basic granny square **p.100**

SIZE
32 x 30cm (12½ x 12in); the strap
measures 70cm (27½in) long

YARN
King Cole Cotton Bamboo DK – 100g/
230m/252yds (50% cotton, 50% bamboo;
any DK weight yarn will be suitable)

A x 2   B x 1   C x 1   D x 1   E x 1

HOOK
4mm hook

NOTIONS
Stitch marker
Yarn needle
Two bag rings, 3.5cm (1½in) wide
Button, 2cm (¾in) diameter
Cotton material for lining, measuring
60 x 32cm (23¾ x 12½in), plus seam
allowance

TENSION
Exact tension is not essential

SPECIAL ABBREVIATIONS
DCFLO: Double crochet in front loop only:
work a dc in front loop only of next st.
DCBLO: Double crochet in back loop only:
work a dc in back loop only of next st.

PATTERN
Note: You'll need to work into the
back bump of a chain, see p.26 to see
which bump to work into.
Each completed granny square should
measure approx. 12 x 12cm (5 x 5in).

GRANNY SQUARE
With yarn B work 4 ch. Join with ss in last
ch from hook to form loop.
Round 1: 3 ch (always counts as 1 tr), (2 tr,
2 ch) into the ring, *(3 tr, 2 ch) into the ring,
repeat from * twice, ending with a ss into
the third ch at the beginning of the round,
changing to yarn C to work the ss, turn
work. Fasten off yarn B.
Round 2: (3 ch, 2 tr, 2 ch, 3 tr) into the 2-ch
sp, *1 ch, (3 tr, 2 ch, 3 tr), into the corner
2-ch sp, repeat from * twice, 1 ch, ss into
the third ch at beginning of round,
changing to yarn D to work the ss, turn
work. Fasten off yarn C.
Round 3: (3 ch, 2 tr, 1 ch), into the 1-ch sp, *
(3 tr, 2 ch, 3 tr) into the corner 2-ch sp, (1 ch,
3 tr, 1 ch) into the following 1-ch sp, repeat
from * twice, (3 tr, 2 ch, 3 tr) into the 2-ch
sp, 1 ch, ss into the third ch at beginning of
round, changing to yarn E to work the ss,
turn work. Fasten off yarn D.

Round 4: (3 ch, 2 tr, 1 ch), into the ch sp,
*(3 tr, 2 ch, 3 tr) into the corner 2-ch sp,
([1 ch, 3 tr] into the following 1-ch sp)
twice, 1 ch, repeat from * twice, (3 tr, 2 ch,
3 tr) into the corner 2-ch sp, (1 ch, 3 tr, 1 ch)
into the following ch sp, ending with a ss
into the third ch at beginning of round,
changing to yarn A to work the ss, turn
work. Fasten off yarn E.
Round 5: (3 ch, 2 tr, 1 ch) into the ch sp,
(3 tr, 1 ch) into next 1-ch sp *(3tr, 2 ch, 3 tr)
into the corner 2-ch sp, ([1 ch, 3 tr] into
the following 1-ch sp) 3 times, 1 ch, repeat
from * twice, (3 tr, 2 ch, 3 tr) into the corner
2-ch sp, (1 ch, 3 tr, 1 ch) into the following
1-ch sp, ss into the third ch at beginning of
round. Fasten off yarn A.
Work 12 more squares using the same
colour sequence.

JOINING SQUARES
Follow the chart given for placement of
each square, see p.302.
To join the squares, place two squares
wrong sides together, and with yarn A, join
with a ss at the corner, into one loop from
each square, 1 ch, dc along the edges into
two loops only, one from each square (thus
creating a ridge on the right side of work).

Joining the squares Use a
double crochet seam to join
the motifs together – this
creates a strong ridge for
durability and added texture.

BAG LOOPS

With yarn A, work 16 ch.
Row 1: Dc into the second ch from the hook and dc to end. (15sts)
Row 2: 1 ch, dc in each st to end of row.
Repeat row 2 for eight rows. Fasten off, leaving a long end for weaving in.

STRAP

With yarn A, work 112 ch, fasten off, leaving a long end for weaving in.
Row 1: Starting back at the first ch, join yarn B into the first ch with a ss, working into the back bump of the chain only, 1 dc in each ch to end, fasten off.
Row 2: Do not turn, join yarn C into the first st of row with a ss, 1 ch, 1 dcblo in each st to end of row, fasten off.
Repeat row 2 for three more rows, changing colour for each row to D, E, C.
Next row: With yarn A, ss along edge of last row, in back loop only. Fasten off.

EDGING FOR BAG OPENING

With yarn A and RS of the back of bag facing, join with a ss at the point on the right-hand side of the flap square where it joins the next square, 1 ch, dc evenly around whole of the top of bag opening.

FLAP EDGING

Row 1 (RS): Work 39 dc along the edge of flap, place a marker, turn work.
Row 2 (WS): Join in yarn B with a ss, work 39 dcblo to end of flap, fasten off. Do not turn.

Row 3: Beginning at marker, join in yarn C with a ss, work 39 dcblo to end of flap, fasten off. Do not turn.
Row 4: Beginning at marker, join in yarn D with a ss, work 39 dcblo to end of flap, fasten off. Do not turn.
Row 5: Beginning at marker, join in yarn E with a ss, work 39 dcblo to end of flap, fasten off. Do not turn.
Row 6: Beginning at marker, join in yarn A with a ss, 1 ch, work 19 dc along edge of flap, ch 6 to make buttonhole, miss next st, dc to end, working up the side edge of flap to neaten, turn work.
Row 7: 1 ch, dc in each st to 6-ch loop, work 10 dc into the 6-ch loop, dc in each st to end of flap, ending with a ss into last st.

FINISHING

Fold bag loop in half, lengthways, insert plastic loop and sew onto top-most granny square. Repeat for other side.
Neaten strap edges and sew onto bag loops. Weave in all ends.
Cut the cotton lining material to shape using the bag as a template. Make a small hem and sew the lining inside the bag. Sew on a button.

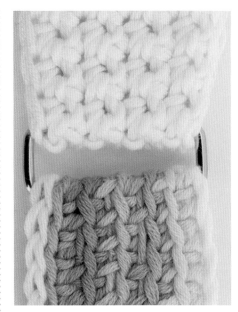

O-rings and D-rings make it easy to attach straps to a handmade bag. They are available in metal, plastic, and wood, and come in a variety of sizes. We've chosen metal to co-ordinate with the yarn. Fold the edges of your crocheted straps around the bars of each ring and sew in place to secure.

FRONT

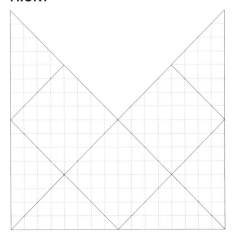

BACK

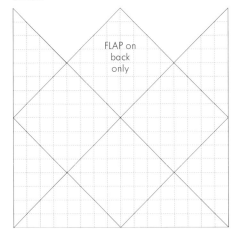

FLAP on back only

Bag construction chart After you've crocheted the 13 granny squares, it's a case of joining them together in the right way to create the basis of the bag. Once joined, you can add on the flap edging and straps to complete the item.

CLUTCH BAG

This bag is worked in rows, with two different stitches on different parts of the bag. It is then folded and sewn to turn it into a clutch bag. Refer to pp.106–107 for more information about lacework.

TECHNIQUES USED Chain stitch **p.26**, Double crochet **p.34**, Treble crochet **p.44**, Simple lace techniques **p.106**

SIZE
21 x 11.5cm (8¼ x 4½in)

YARN
Sirdar Ella Summer Luxe Cotton Blend DK – 50g/126m/138yds (49% cotton, 48% acrylic, and 3% polyester; you can use any cotton or cotton-blend DK yarn; try adding Lurex® to get a similar effect)

x 2

HOOK
4mm hook

NOTIONS
Yarn needle
1cm (½in) pearl button

TENSION
Exact tension is not essential

> **PATTERN**
Work 38 ch.
Row 1: Dc in second chain from hook and in each chain across, turn. (37sts)
Row 2: 1 ch, dc in each st across, turn. (37sts)
Repeat row 2: Until piece measures approx. 24cm (9½in) from beginning.
Next row: 4 ch (counts as first tr and 1 ch), miss dc directly below 4 ch, and the next dc, (tr, 1 ch, tr) all in next dc, 1 ch, * miss next dc, (tr, 1 ch, tr) all in next dc, 1 ch, rep from * across to last 2 dc, miss next dc and tr in last st, turn.

Next row: 1 ch, dc in first tr, and in each 1-ch sp across to last st, dc in third of ch 4 of previous row, turn.
Repeat last two rows until lacy section measures approx 6cm (2¾in) from the start of trebles row, ending with a dc row.

FINISHING
Fold bottom of bag up 12cm (4¾in) and sew side seams. Line up top of bag to sew on button, using photo as a guide. Weave in all ends.

The yarn used for this evening pochette has a silver thread running through it for a party finish. Alternatively, crochet your bag in a dark, matte yarn and apply one or two small rhinestones.

CHILD'S TURTLE BACKPACK

Level of difficulty

This animal-themed bag is a great, fun way for children to carry around their bits and bobs. The turtle's tummy is made with double crochet stitch worked in the round, while its shell is formed from seven granny hexagons.

TECHNIQUES USED Chain stitch **p.26**, Slip stitch **p.28**, Bobbles **p.77**, A basic granny square **p.100**, Joining motifs **p.101**

SIZE
Approx. 39 x 36cm (15¼ x 14¼in)

YARN
Rowan Handknit Cotton – 50g/85m/93yds
  (100% cotton; you can use any DK yarn
  for this project)

A x 2   **B** x 1   **C** x 1   **D** x 1   **E** x 1

HOOKS
3.5mm hook
4mm hook

NOTIONS
Stitch marker
Yarn needle
2 x 4.5cm (1¾in) buckles
12mm (½in) black safety toy eyes
30cm (12in) zip
Fabric for lining: two circles 33cm (13in)
  in diameter
Strong cotton tape for straps, optional

TENSION
19sts x 14 rows per 10cm (4in)

SPECIAL ABBREVIATIONS
Adjustable ring: See p.134
Beginning bobble st: 2 ch, yrh, insert hook
  in stitch, yrh, draw loop through, yrh,
  draw through two loops on the hook,
  yrh, insert hook in same space, yrh,
  draw loop through, yrh, draw through
  two loops on hook, yrh, draw through
  all three loops on hook.

Bobble stitch: Yrh, insert hook in stitch, yrh,
  draw loop through, yrh, draw through
  two loops on the hook, *yrh, insert hook
  in same space, yrh, draw loop through,
  yrh, draw through two loops on hook;
  repeat from * twice, yrh, draw through
  all four loops on hook.
HDTR: half double treble stitch. This is
  a simple variation on the double treble
  stitch (see p.48). Yrh twice, insert hook
  in next stitch and draw up a loop (four
  loops on hook), yrh and draw through
  two loops (three loops on hook), yrh
  and draw through all three loops (one
  loop on hook).

PATTERN
BAG FRONT
Hexagon motifs pattern:
With first yarn (colour 1) and 3.5mm
hook, make an adjustable ring and work
6 dc into the ring, ss to join ring. (6sts)
Round 1: Work beginning bobble st in
first st, (2 ch, bobble st) in remaining 5sts,
ss into top of first bobble to join round.
(six bobbles, 6-ch sp)
Cut yarn, leaving a long tail, and pull through.
Join second yarn (colour 2) at any ch sp.
Round 2: Work beginning bobble st in ch sp,
2 ch, bobble st in same ch sp, 2 ch, (bobble st,
2 ch, bobble st, 2 ch) in remaining 5-ch sp.
Ss into top of first bobble to join round.
12 bobbles, 12-ch sp)
Cut yarn, leaving a long tail, and pull through.
Join third yarn (colour 3) at any ch sp.
Round 3: (2 ch, 2 tr, 2 ch, 3 tr) in first ch sp,
3 tr in next ch sp, *(3 tr, 2 ch, 3 tr) in next
ch sp, 3 tr in next ch sp; rep from * to end,
ss to join the round. (54 tr, 6-ch sp)

Hexagon motifs
Motif 1: Colour 1 A, colour 2 E,
colour 3 D.
Motifs 2, 3, and 4: Colour 1 A,
colour 2 E, colour 3 B.
Motifs 5, 6, and 7: Colour 1 D,
colour 2 E, colour 3 C.

JOINING MOTIFS
Use yarn E to join motifs together. Put
motifs 1 and 2 together with the wrong
sides facing. Work stitches over both
of the motifs to join together. Join yarn at
a ch sp, dc in ch sp, dc along next 9sts, dc in
ch space. Motif 2 is now attached. Next
attach motif 5 to the next side of motif 1 in
the same way. Then working anticlockwise
around all the sides of motif 1, add the next
four motifs as shown in the diagram below.
Complete by joining the sides of the motifs
together in the same way.
Join yarn E to the ch sp marked by the
arrow in the Hexagon motifs diagram
below. Work in rounds around the edges
of the joined-up hexagons.

Hexagon motifs diagram

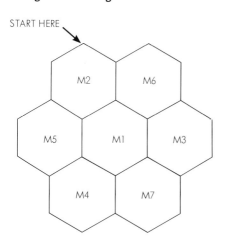

BAGS

Round 1: Dc in every st and every outer ch sp around. (174sts)
Change to yarn A and use a stitch marker to mark the first stitch of each new round.
Round 2: *10 dc, 2 htr, 2 tr, 2 hdtr, 5 dtr, 2 hdtr, 2 tr, 2 htr, 2 dc; rep from * to end.
Round 3: Dc in each st to end.
Round 4: *27 dc, dc2tog; rep from * to end. (168sts)
Round 5: Dc in each st to end.
Round 6: *26 dc, dc2tog; rep from * to end. (162sts)
Round 7: Dc in each st to end.
Round 8: *25 dc, dc2tog; rep from * to end. (156sts)
Round 9: Dc in each st to end.
Cut the yarn, leaving a long tail, and secure.

BAG BACK
With yarn A and 3.5mm hook, make an adjustable ring and work 6 dc into ring. (6sts)
Round 1: 2 dc into each st to end, place marker. (12sts)
Round 2: *1 dc, 2 dc in next st; rep from * to end. (18sts)
Round 3: *2 dc, 2 dc in next st; rep from * to end. (24sts)
Round 4: *3 dc, 2 dc in next st; rep from * to end. (30sts)
Round 5: *4 dc, 2 dc in next st; rep from * to end. (36sts)
Round 6: *5 dc, 2 dc in next st; rep from * to end. (42sts)
Round 7: *6 dc, 2 dc in next st; rep from * to end. (48sts)
Round 8: *7 dc, 2 dc in next st; rep from * to end. (54sts)
Round 9: *8 dc, 2 dc in next st; rep from * to end. (60sts)
Round 10: *9 dc, 2 dc in next st; rep from * to end. (66sts)
Round 11: *10 dc, 2 dc in next st; rep from * to end. (72sts)
Round 12: *11 dc, 2 dc in next st; rep from * to end. (78sts)
Round 13: *12 dc, 2 dc in next st; rep from * to end. (84sts)
Round 14: *13 dc, 2 dc in next st; rep from * to end. (90sts)
Round 15: *14 dc, 2 dc in next st; rep from * to end. (96sts)
Round 16: *15 dc, 2 dc in next st; rep from * to end. (102sts)
Round 17: *16 dc, 2 dc in next st; rep from * to end. (108sts)
Round 18: *17 dc, 2 dc in next st; rep from * to end. (114sts)
Round 19: *18 dc, 2 dc in next st; rep from * to end. (120sts)
Round 20: *19 dc, 2 dc in next st; rep from * to end. (126sts)

Give your turtle a happy smile using two large backstitches. Use safety eyes to prevent little fingers from pulling them out and attach them when stated in the pattern.

Round 21: *20 dc, 2 dc in next st; rep from * to end. (132sts)
Round 22: *21 dc, 2 dc in next st; rep from * to end. (138sts)
Round 23: *22 dc, 2 dc in next st; rep from * to end. (144sts)
Round 24: *23 dc, 2 dc in next st; rep from * to end. (150sts)
Round 25: *24 dc, 2 dc in next st; rep from * to end. (156sts)
Rounds 26–29: Dc in each st to end. Cut the yarn, leaving a long tail, and secure. Sew the front and back together leaving a 30cm (12in) gap at one end. Cut two pieces of lining fabric slightly

larger than the entire bag. Sew the pieces together, leaving a 30cm (12in) gap at one end. Turn right sides out and pin in place inside the bag. Pin a 30cm (12in) zip into the opening. Sew zip and lining in place.

TURTLE HEAD
With yarn A and 3.5mm hook, make an adjustable ring and work 6 dc into ring. (6sts)
Round 1: 2 dc into each st to end, place marker. (12sts)
Round 2: *1 dc, 2 dc in next st; rep from * to end. (18sts)

Round 3: *2 dc, 2 dc in next st; rep from * to end. (24sts)

Round 4: *3 dc, 2 dc in next st; rep from * to end. (30sts)

Round 5: *9 dc, 2 dc in next st; rep from * to end. (33sts)

Round 6: *10 dc, 2 dc in next st; rep from * to end. (36sts)

Round 7: *11 dc, 2 dc in next st; rep from * to end. (39sts) Mark this round with a stitch marker.

Round 8: *12 dc, 2 dc in next st; rep from * to end. (42sts)

Rounds 9–12: Dc in each st to end.

Round 13 *12 dc, dc2tog; rep from * to end. (39sts)

Round 14: *11 dc, dc2tog; rep from * to end. (36sts)

Rounds 15–16: Dc in each st to end.

Round 17: *dc2tog , 4 dc; rep from * to end. (30sts)

Round 18: *dc2tog, 3 dc; rep from * to end. (24sts)

Cut the yarn and secure. Put eyes on the marked round 12sts apart.
Stuff the head.

LEGS (MAKE 4)

With yarn A and 3.5mm hook, make an adjustable ring and work 6 dc into ring. (6sts)

Round 1: 2 dc into each st to the end, place marker. (12sts)

Round 2: *1 dc, 2 dc in next st; rep from * to end. (18sts)

Round 3: *2 dc, 2 dc in next st; rep from * to end. (24sts)

Rounds 4–6: Dc in each st to end.

Round 7: *dc2tog, 6 dc; rep from * to end. (21sts)

Rounds 8–9: Dc in each st to end.

Round 10: *dc2tog, 5 dc; rep from * to end. (18sts)

Rounds 11–12: Dc in each st to the end.
Cut the yarn, leaving a long tail, and secure. Stuff.

TAIL

With yarn A and 3.5mm hook, make an adjustable ring and work 4 dc into ring. (4sts)

Round 1: *1 dc, 2 dc in next st; rep from * to end, place marker. (6sts)

Round 2: *2 dc, 2 dc in next st; rep from * to end. (8sts)

Round 3: *3 dc, 2 dc in next st; rep from * to end. (10sts)

Round 4: *4 dc, 2 dc in next st; rep from * to end. (12sts)

Rounds 5–6: Dc in each st to end.
Cut the yarn, leaving a long tail, and secure. Stuff the tail. Sew the head, legs, and tail onto the body of the backpack. Weave in loose ends.

STRAPS (MAKE 4)

These are worked straight. Turn your work at the end of each row.
With yarn A and 4mm hook, ch 7.

Row 1: Starting in second ch from hook, dc in each st, ch 1, turn.

Row 2: Dc in each st, ch 1, turn.
Repeat the last row until the strap is 35cm (14in) long. Cut the yarn and secure. Strengthen the straps with strong cotton tape, if desired. Sew the end of two straps onto the middle bar of the buckles. Sew the straps in place on the bag. Thread the other end of the straps through the buckle to finish.

A white zip and lining fabric work well for this project, but as they will not be visible for most of the time, you can use whichever colour you prefer. Attach the zip using a long strand of matching yarn or sewing cotton.

An adjustable buckle is really useful as it will allow the straps to be as long or short as you like. Buckles are available at most haberdashery stores. Choose a contrasting colour to stand out or a co-ordinating shade of green to blend in.

COIN PURSES

These tiny projects are ideal for getting children into crochet. They are both worked in the round, in two different ways, to create small pouches for change.

TECHNIQUES USED Chain stitch **p.26**, Slip stitch **p.28**, Double crochet **p.34**, Simple stripes **p.39**, Shaping **p.50–52**, Working in the round **p.56**

SIZE

Round purse: approx. 10cm (4in) in
  diameter
Rectangular purses: approx. 9 x 7cm
  (3½ x 2¾in)

YARN

DMC Petra Crochet Cotton Perle No. 3 –
  100g/280m/306yds (100% cotton; any
  fine crochet thread will work)

A x 3   **B** x 1   **C** x 1   **D** x 1   **E** x 3

HOOK

2.5mm hook

NOTIONS

Stitch marker
Yarn needle
9cm (3½in) zip for each purse
Bead (optional)

TENSION

Exact tension is not essential

PATTERN: ROUND PURSE

Note: Purses are worked in spirals. Do not join rounds, but place a marker at first stitch of the round, moving it each round to mark the beginning of the next round.

Make 2 ch and work 6 dc into second ch from hook, join round with a ss to first st.
Round 1: 1 ch, work 2 dc in each dc around, do not join round, place marker. (12sts)
Round 2: (2 dc in next dc, 1 dc in next 1 dc) around. (18sts)
Round 3: (2 dc in next dc, 1 dc in next 2 dc) around. (24sts)
Round 4: (2 dc in next dc, 1 dc in next 3 dc) around. (30sts)
Round 5: (2 dc in next dc, 1 dc in next 4 dc) around. (36sts)
Round 6: (2 dc in next dc, 1 dc in next 5 dc) around. (42sts)
Continue in this way, working one extra st between increases in each round until you have worked nine rounds and have 60sts.
Work straight on these 60sts for seven rounds.
Round 17: (dc2tog, 1 dc in next 8 dc) around. (54sts)
Work 2 rounds straight.
Round 20: (dc2tog, 1 dc in next 7 dc) around. (48sts)
Work one round straight.
Round 22: (dc2tog, 1 dc in next 6 dc) around. (42sts)
Work two rounds straight.
Fasten off yarn and weave in ends.

PATTERN: RECTANGULAR PURSE

Work 31 ch
Round 1: 3 dc into second ch from hook, 1 dc in each ch to last ch, 3 dc in last ch, turn work 180 degrees and work along other side of ch, working 1 dc into the bottom of each ch, do not join round.

When choosing a bead to attach to your zip pull, make sure that its central hole is large enough to thread the strands of DMC cotton through. Tie a knot right up close to the bead to secure.

Round 2: 1 dc into each dc around.
Rep last round for desired height of purse, sample shown is 7cm (2¾in), changing colours for striping where desired.
Fasten off yarn and weave in ends.

FINISHING

Sew zip into top of each purse. Make a tassel (see p.71) and attach it by inserting the strands through the zip hole, securing as normal and adding a bead, if desired.

GLOSSARY

adjustable ring: A method of beginning crochet in the round that allows you to pull the ring tightly closed after the first round, thus eliminating the unsightly central hole (see p.57).

Afghan stitch: See **Tunisian stitch**. Afghan stitches are shaped like small squares with two horizontal strands of yarn and a vertical bar on top.

Afghan square: An alternative name for the granny square.

amigurumi: A Japanese style of crocheting, or knitting, small animals and other objects, often with anthropomorphic features.

back and front posts: Vertical segments of a crochet stitch.

ballband: The wrapper around a ball of yarn, which usually details fibre content, weight, length, hook size, tension, and washing instructions.

ball-winder: A device for winding hanks of yarn into balls; also used to wind two or more strands together to make a double-stranded yarn. Often used in conjunction with a swift.

blocking: Manipulating the finished piece into the correct shape by wetting and pinning it out, or pinning it out and steam pressing it.

broomstick crochet: A lacy stitch made using both a crochet hook and a knitting needle.

button loop: An alternative to a buttonhole, a chain loop is crocheted into the last two rows, or edging, on a piece of crocheted fabric (see p.87).

chain loop, chain space: A length of chain stitches worked between basic stitches to create a space in the fabric.

colourwork: Any method of incorporating colour into crochet, including stripes, tapestry, and intarsia.

corner to corner crochet: A type of colourwork in which increases are made at the beginning of each row until the maximum desired diagonal width is reached. Then the work is decreased back down.

darning in ends: The process of completing a piece of crochet by weaving in the yarn ends using a blunt-ended yarn needle to disguise them.

decrease: Removing a stitch or stitches in order to reduce the number of working stitches and shape the fabric.

double crochet join: An invisible way of joining in new yarn, using double crochet stitches, when at the end of the current row or round.

dye lot: A record taken during the dyeing of yarn to identify it. Use yarn from one dye lot for each project and do not mix the dye batches or your crochet fabric may change in tone.

fabric yarn: A unique, super bulky yarn produced from stretchy jersey fabric as a by-product of garment manufacturing. This type of yarn is becoming popular in crochet for making sturdy items (see p.167). Because the material is recycled, every colourway is a limited edition.

fibres: Yarn is made up of fibres, such as the hair from an animal, synthetic fibres, or fibres derived from a plant. The fibres are processed and spun into a yarn.

filet crochet: A form of openwork crochet created by working a combination of squares or rectangles of open mesh and solid blocks.

foundation chain: The base of chain stitches that the first row of crochet is worked onto.

front and back loop only: A crochet instruction to indicate that the hook should be inserted into either the front or the back loop only of a stitch.

gauge: Another term for tension.

hank: A twisted ring of yarn, which needs to be wound into one or more balls before it can be used.

increase: Adding a stitch or stitches to increase the number of working stitches and shape the fabric.

intarsia: A technique in which a colour appears only in a section of a row and is not needed across the whole row. Unlike tapestry crochet, more than two colours may be worked in a row. A separate ball or length of yarn is used for each area of colour and carried vertically up to the next row when it is needed again.

Möbius strip: Also called a twisted cylinder, this shape is a loop with a half-twist in it. Often used as a shape for crocheted cowls.

motif: A flat shaped piece of crochet worked from the centre outwards.

notions: Items of haberdashery, other than fabric, needed to complete a project, such as a button, zip, or elastic. Notions are normally listed in the pattern.

openwork crochet: A lace-like effect created by working chain spaces and/or loops between the basic stitches.

plying: This is a process used to create a strong, balanced yarn. All yarns are made from more than one strand of spun fibre, so 4-ply is four strands plied together. Plying prevents the yarn from twisting.

raised stitches: Three-dimensional crochet stitches, such as bobbles and puffs, which create texture. Great for hats and blankets.

right side (RS): The front of a piece of fabric, the side that will normally be in view when the piece is made up.

round: A row worked in a circle, with the last stitch of a row being joined to the first to complete the circle.

roving: A long and narrow bundle of unspun fibre, produced during the process of making spun yarn from wool fleeces. Rovings are used mainly for spinning, but can also be used for making many kinds of felted items and other specialist textiles.

row: Working back and forth in rows to create a piece of crocheted fabric. Turn the work at the end of each row, making a turning chain, and start back across the next row.

seam: The join formed when two pieces of fabric are sewn or crocheted together.

slip knot: A knot that is formed when placing the first loop on a crochet hook.

slip stitch: The shortest of all the crochet stitches. Although slip stitches can be worked in rows, the resulting fabric is very dense and suitable only for bag handles. Slip stitches are frequently used to join new yarn, to work invisibly along the top of a row to move to a new position, and to join rounds.

skein: Yarn wound into an oblong shape, which is ready to crochet.

stitch marker: A device used to mark locations on a work in progress (see p.20). Often used in circular crochet to mark the start and end of a round.

swift: An umbrella-like tool used to hold a hank of yarn while it is being wound off into a ball.

tapestry crochet: A type of colourwork crochet worked in double crochet stitch, with no more than two colours in each row, in which the colour not in use is carried across the top of the row below and covered with the stitches of the other colour so that it is hidden from view. This results in a thicker-than-normal fabric, so it is best worked in a fine yarn.

tension: The number of stitches and rows over a given area, usually 10cm (4in) square. Also, the relative tightness used by the crocheter. Changing hook size can help achieve correct tension.

Tunisian crochet: Also known as Afghan crochet, a style of crochet that takes elements from both knitting and crochet, creating a fusion of techniques. A Tunisian hook looks similar to a knitting needle but either has a hook at both ends, or a hook

at one end and a stopper at the other. The resulting fabric is slightly less elastic than normal crochet.

turning chain: A length of stitches worked at the start of a row in order to bring the hook up to the necessary height to work the first stitch of that row (see p.66).

Velcro™: Two-part fabric fastening consisting of two layers, a "hook" side and a "loop" side; when pressed together the two pieces cling together.

wool: A natural animal fibre, available in a range of weights, weaves, and textures. It is warm, comfortable to wear, and crease-resistant.

wrong side (WS): The reverse of a piece of fabric, the side that will normally be hidden from view when the piece is made up.

yarn: Fibres that have been spun into a long strand. Yarns may be made of natural fibres, synthetic fibres, a blend of the two, or even non-standard materials.

yarn bobbin: Small plastic shape for holding yarn when doing intarsia work, where there are many yarns in different colours (see p.20).

CROCHET TERMINOLOGY

The following terms are commonly used in crochet patterns. Many crochet terms are the same in the UK and the US, but where they differ, the US equivalent is given in parentheses. Turn to the pages indicated for how to work the various increases, decreases, or stitch techniques listed.

bobble: A cluster stitch generally made up of trebles, where several half-finished stitches are worked into the same stitch from the row below and then joined at the top (see p.77).

cluster: A group of stitches worked into the same stitch, but only equating to one stitch in total. They are usually decreased in some way, or left half-finished, and then finished all at once to produce one stitch (see p.77).

crab stitch: A reverse single crochet stitch. Instead of working from right to left, it is worked from left to right, creating a twisted edge.

dc2tog (work 2 dc together): See p.52. (US sc2tog)

dc3tog (work 3 dc together): (Insert hook in next st, yrh and draw a loop through) three times, yrh and drawthrough all four loops on hook – 2sts decreased. (US sc3tog)

fasten off: Cut the yarn and draw it through the remaining loop on the hook to secure (see p.27).
foundation row: The first row of a piece of crochet (the row worked onto the foundation chain) is sometimes called the foundation row.

htr2tog (work 2 htr together): (Yrh and insert hook in next st, yrh and draw a loop through) twice, yrh and draw through all five loops on hook – 1st decreased. (US hdc2tog)

htr3tog (work 3 htr together): (Yrh and insert hook in next st, yrh and draw a loop through) three times, yrh and draw through all seven loops on hook – 2sts decreased. (US hdc3tog)

miss a stitch: Do not work into the stitch, but go on to the next stitch. (US "skip" a stitch)

popcorn: A bobble made with complete stitches, generally trebles, then drawn together at the top (see p.77).

puff stitch: A bobble made with half trebles; also called a pineapple stitch.

shell: Several stitches worked into the same stitch in the previous row or into the same chain space (see p.76).

tr2tog (work 2 tr together): See p.53. (US dc2tog)

tr3tog (work 3 tr together: (Yrh and insert hook in next st, yrh and draw a loop through, yrh and draw through first two loops on hook) three times, yrh and draw through all four loops on hook – 2sts decreased. (US dc3tog)

INDEX

ACKNOWLEDGMENTS

SECOND EDITION

Dorling Kindersley UK would like to thank: the following crochet designers for the new projects commissioned for this edition:
Claire Montgomerie: Octopus mobile p.176, Nordic fingerless mitts p.216; **Rosina Northcott:** Crafter's wrap p.122; **Irene Strange:** Polar bear comforter p.282; **Emma Varnam:** Glasses case p.42, Amigurumi penguin p.274; the crochet technicians and crocheters for their invaluable work to the projects remade for this book:
Ali Campbell: Diamond granny bag p.300; **Tessa Dennison:** Striped beret p.198; **Shannon Reed:** Book cover p.184, Child's wristwarmers p.210, Women's wristwarmers p.214; **Claire Montgomerie** for a review of the book and for providing expert assistance at the photo shoot; **Carol Ibbetson** for pattern checking; **Ruth Jenkinson** for photography; **XAB Design** for photography art direction; and **Millie Andrew** for photography assistance.

Dorling Kindersley Delhi would like to thank: Purvi Gadia for editorial assistance.

All images © Dorling Kindersley Limited. For further information see www.dkimages.com

FIRST EDITION

Dorling Kindersley would like to thank the following crochet designers for their hard work and contributions towards *Crochet*:

Lesley Arnold-Hopkins: Child's hat with earflaps p.196, Tweed stitch cowl p.204, Child's hoodie p.240; **Vicki Brown:** Men's beanie hat p.194, Men's chunky scarf p.206, Ladies' ankle socks p.224, Men's chunky socks p.226, Stripy sweater p.236, Cropped sweater p.250, Summer tunic dress p.246; **Ali Campbell:** Baby blanket p.148, Fish and starfish garland p.180; **May Corfield:** Desktop storage pots p.162, Cat basket p.174; **Simone Francis:** Intarsia cushion p.122, Ladies' textural cardigan p.254; Diamond granny bag p.296; **Melanie Galloway:** Straw beach bag p.290, Super-stretchy shopper p.292, Everyday bag p.294, Clutch bag p.300; **Shelley Gould:** Fabric cushions p.98; **Helen Jordan:** Broomstick shawl p.202; **Claire Montgomerie:** Beaded necklace p.28, Chunky bracelet p.30, Mobile phone covers p.36, Pretty headbands p.46, Party bunting p.54, Circular cushion p.64, Flower garland p.80, Crochet-edged cushions p.98, Flower blanket p.142, Lap blanket p.144, Colourful granny blanket p.146, Chevron cushion p.152, Structured baskets p.164, Fruit bowl p.176, Filigree bookmarks p.178, Flower pin cushion p.184, Baby bonnet p.190, Child's hat with ears p.192, Lacy scarf p.200, Ladies' wrist warmers p.214, Giant play ball p.264, Coin purses p.306; **Margaret O'Mara:** Owl cushion p.156, Child's crossover cardigan p.230, Child's poncho p.234; **Wendy Rainthorpe:** Shell mesh scarf p.116, Mother elephant and baby p.266, Tablet sleeve p.308; **Irene Strange:** Baby girl's booties p.216, Baby boy's booties p. 218; **Tracey Todhunter:** Striped washcloths p.34, Self-fringing scarf p.40, Textured cushion p.44, Coaster set p.58, Pot holders p60, Granny cushion p.154, Hanging toy basket p.166, Round stool cover p.168, Rustic pouffes p.170, Chunky rug p.186, Child's wrist warmers p.210, Child's mittens with string p.212, Child's edged slippers p.220, Ladies' soft pumps p.222, Granny square bag p.288; **Emma Varnam:** Woman's beret p.198, Baby rattles p.260; **Liz Ward:** Teddy Bear p.132, Rag doll p.270, Polar bear with scarf p.274, Floppy-eared bunny p.278, Jungle finger puppets p.282, Turtle backpack p.302.

Pattern checker Carol Ibbetson; **proofreader** Angela Baynham; **indexer** Marie Lorimer; **design assistance** Elaine Hewson, Hannah Moore, and Navidita Thapa; **editorial assistance** Christine Stroyan; **photography assistant** Julie Stewart; **props** Backgrounds Prop Hire; **location for photography** 1st Option; **models** Estelle Abberley, Georgia Abberley, Celia Arn, Liz Boyd, Joshua Caulfield, Maria Clancy, Claire Cross, Maria Elston, Marco Elston, Lucas Goldstein, Saskia Janssen, Martha Jenkinson, Bodhi Nair, Tulsi Nair, Clara Proctor, Martha Rhodes, Julie Stewart, Eden White, Mia White, and Oscar the cat; **yarn manufacturers and distributors who supplied yarn for projects:** Artesano Ltd, Coats Craft UK, Designer Yarns Ltd, DMC Creative World, King Cole Ltd, Rico Design, Sirdar Spinning Ltd, Texere Yarns Ltd, Thomas B. Ramsden & Co.

Senior Editor May Corfield
Senior Art Editor Glenda Fisher
Editor Katharine Goddard
Managing Editor Penny Smith
Managing Art Editor Marianne Markham
Jacket Designer Rosie Levine
Producer, Pre-production Sarah Isle
Producer Che Creasey
Creative Technical Support Sonia Charbonnier
Photography Ruth Jenkinson
Art Director/Stylist for Photography Isabel de Cordova
Art Director Jane Bull
Publisher Mary Ling

ABOUT THE CONSULTANT

Claire Montgomerie is a textiles designer who specializes in crochet and knitting, constructing fabrics, garments, creatures, and accessories that are fun, quirky, and modern. Her main aim is to reinvent the products of ancient and traditional needlecraft processes, while retaining all their intricacies and comforting charm. Claire has written many crochet and knitting books and also edits the UK craft magazine *Inside Crochet*.

SECOND EDITION
Senior Editors Nikki Sims, Dawn Titmus
Senior Designer Glenda Fisher
Project Editor Amy Slack
Editorial Assistant Millie Andrew
Designer Anne Fisher
Senior Jacket Designer Nicola Powling
Jackets Co-ordinator Lucy Philpott
Pre-production Producer David Almond
Senior Producer Stephanie McConnell
Managing Editors Stephanie Farrow, Ruth O'Rourke
Managing Art Editor Christine Keilty
Art Director Maxine Pedliham
Publishing Director Mary-Clare Jerram

DK DELHI
Senior Editor Arani Sinha
Assistant Editor Ankita Gupta
Managing Editor Soma B. Chowdhury
Senior DTP Designer Tarun Sharma
DTP Designers Satish Gaur, Umesh Singh Rawat,
Anurag Trivedi
Pre-production Manager Sunil Sharma

This edition published in 2020
First published in Great Britain in 2014 by
Dorling Kindersley Limited
DK, One Embassy Gardens, 8 Viaduct Gardens, London, SW11 7BW

Copyright © 2014, 2020 Dorling Kindersley Limited
A Penguin Random House Company
10 9 8 7 6 5 4 3 2
003–318363–Aug/2020

A CIP catalogue record for this book
is available from the British Library.
ISBN: 978-0-2414-3584-7

Printed and bound in China

For the curious

www.dk.com